GW00771216

THE BOOK

Honda CB600F Hornet
Service and Repair Manual

by Phil Mather

Models covered

CB600F. 599cc. 1998 to 2002
CB600FS. 599cc. 2000 to 2002

(3915-256-12AB1)

ABCDE
FGHIJ
KLMNO
PQR

© Haynes Publishing 2003

 A book in the **Haynes Service and Repair Manual Series**

All rights reserved. No part of this book may be reproduced or transmitted
in any form or by any means, electronic or mechanical, including photo-
copying, recording or by any information storage or retrieval system,
without permission in writing from the copyright holder.

ISBN 1 85960 915 5

British Library Cataloguing in Publication Data
A catalogue record for this book is available from the British Library

Printed in the USA

Haynes Publishing
Sparkford, Yeovil, Somerset BA22 7JJ, England

Haynes North America, Inc
861 Lawrence Drive, Newbury Park, California 91320, USA

Editions Haynes
4, Rue de l'Abreuvoir
92415 COURBEVOIE CEDEX, France

Haynes Publishing Nordiska AB
Box 1504, 751 45 UPPSALA, Sweden

Contents

Contents

REPAIRS AND OVERHAUL

REFERENCE

The Birth of a Dream

by Julian Ryder

There is no better example of the Japanese post-war industrial miracle than Honda. Like other companies which have become household names, it started with one man's vision. In this case the man was the 40-year old Soichiro Honda who had sold his piston-ring manufacturing business to Toyota in 1945 and was happily spending the proceeds on prolonged parties for his friends.

However, the difficulties of getting around in the chaos of post-war Japan irked Honda, so when he came across a job lot of generator engines he realised that here was a way of getting people mobile again at low cost.

A 12 by 18-foot shack in Hamamatsu became his first bike factory, fitting the generator motors into pushbikes. Before long he'd used up all 500 generator motors and

started manufacturing his own engine, known as the 'chimney', either because of the elongated cylinder head or the smoky exhaust or perhaps both. The chimney made all of half a horsepower from its 50 cc engine but it was a major success and became the Honda A-type.

Less than two years after he'd set up in Hamamatsu, Soichiro Honda founded the Honda Motor Company in September 1948. By then, the A-type had been developed into the 90 cc B-type engine, which Mr Honda decided deserved its own chassis not a bicycle frame. Honda was about to become Japan's first post-war manufacturer of complete motorcycles. In August 1949 the first prototype was ready. With an output of three horsepower, the 98 cc D-type was still a simple two-stroke but it had a two-speed transmission and most importantly a pressed steel frame with telescopic forks and hard tail rear end. The frame was almost triangular in profile with the top rail going in a straight line from the massively braced steering head to the rear axle. Legend has it that after the D-type's first tests the entire workforce went for a drink to celebrate and try and think of a name for the bike. One man broke one of those silences you get when people are thinking, exclaiming 'This is like a dream!' 'That's it!' shouted Honda, and so the Honda Dream was christened.

'This is like a dream!' 'That's it' shouted Honda

Mr Honda was a brilliant, intuitive engineer and designer but he did not bother himself with the marketing side of his business. With hindsight, it is possible to see that employing Takeo Fujisawa who would both sort out the home market and plan the eventual expansion into overseas markets was a masterstroke. He arrived in October 1949 and in 1950 was made Sales Director. Another vital new name was Kiyoshi Kawashima, who along with Honda himself, designed the company's first four-stroke after Kawashima had told them that the four-stroke opposition to Honda's two-strokes sounded nicer and therefore sold better. The result of that statement was the overhead-valve 148 cc E-type which first ran in July 1951 just two months after the first drawings were made. Kawashima was made a director of the Honda Company at 34 years old.

The E-type was a massive success, over 32,000 were made in 1953 alone, a feat of mass-production that was astounding by the

Honda C70 and C90 OHV-engined models

standards of the day given the relative complexity of the machine. But Honda's lifelong pursuit of technical innovation sometimes distracted him from commercial reality. Fujisawa pointed out that they were in danger of ignoring their core business, the motorised bicycles that still formed Japan's main means of transport. In May 1952 the F-type Cub appeared, another two-stroke despite the top men's reservations. You could buy a complete machine or just the motor to attach to your own bicycle. The result was certainly distinctive, a white fuel tank with a circular profile went just below and behind the saddle on the left of the bike, and the motor with its horizontal cylinder and bright red cover just below the rear axle on the same side of the bike. This was the machine that turned Honda into the biggest bike maker in Japan with 70% of the market for bolt-on bicycle motors, the F-type was also the first Honda to be exported. Next came the machine that would turn Honda into the biggest motorcycle manufacturer in the world.

The C100 Super Cub was a typically audacious piece of Honda engineering and marketing. For the first time, but not the last, Honda invented a completely new type of motorcycle, although the term 'scooterette' was coined to describe the new bike which had many of the characteristics of a scooter but the large wheels, and therefore stability, of a motorcycle. The first one was sold in August 1958, fifteen years later over nine-million of them were on the roads of the world. If ever a machine can be said to have brought mobility to the masses it is the Super Cub. If you add

The CB250N Super Dream became a favorite with UK learner riders of the late seventies and early eighties

in the electric starter that was added for the C102 model of 1961, the design of the Super Cub has remained substantially unchanged ever since, testament to how right Honda got it first time. The Super Cub made Honda the world's biggest manufacturer after just two years of production.

Honda's export drive started in earnest in 1957 when Britain and Holland got their first bikes, America got just two bikes the next year. By 1962 Honda had half the American market with 65,000 sales. But Soichiro Honda had already travelled abroad to Europe and the USA, making a special

The GL1000 introduced in 1975, was the first in Honda's line of GoldWings

Carl Fogarty in action at the Suzuka 8 Hour on the RC45

An early CB750 Four

point of going to the Isle of Man TT, then the most important race in the GP calendar. He realised that no matter how advanced his products were, only racing success would convince overseas markets for whom 'Made in Japan' still meant cheap and nasty. It took five years from Soichiro Honda's first visit to the Island before his bikes were ready for the TT. In 1959 the factory entered five riders in the 125 class. They did not have a massive impact on the event being benevolently regarded as a curiosity, but sixth, seventh and eighth were good enough for the team prize. The bikes were off the pace but they were well engineered and very reliable.

The TT was the only time the West saw the Hondas in '59, but they came back for more the following year with the first of a generation of bikes which shaped the future of motorcycling – the double-overhead-cam four-cylinder 250. It was fast and reliable – it revved to 14,000 rpm – but didn't handle anywhere near as well as the opposition. However, Honda had now signed up non-Japanese riders to lead their challenge. The first win didn't come until 1962 (Aussie Tom Phillis in the Spanish 125 GP) and was followed up with a world-shaking performance at the TT. Twenty-one year old Mike Hailwood won both 125 and 250 cc TTs and Hondas filled the top five positions in both races. Soichiro Honda's master plan was starting to come to fruition, Hailwood and Honda won the 1961 250 cc World Championship. Next year Honda won three titles. The other Japanese factories fought back and inspired Honda to produce some of the most fascinating racers ever seen: the awesome six-cylinder 250, the five-cylinder 125, and the 500 four with which the immortal Hailwood battled Agostini and the MV Agusta.

When Honda pulled out of racing in '67 they had won sixteen rider's titles, eighteen manufacturer's titles, and 137 GPs, including 18 TTs, and introduced the concept of the modern works team to motorcycle racing. Sales success followed racing victory as Soichiro Honda had predicted, but only because the products advanced as rapidly as the racing machinery. The Hondas that came to Britain in the early '60s were incredibly sophisticated. They had overhead cams where the British bikes had pushrods, they had electric starters when the Brits relied on the kickstart, they had 12V electrics when even the biggest British bike used a 6V system. There seemed no end to the technical wizardry. It wasn't that the technology itself was so amazing but just like that first E-type, it was the fact that Honda could mass-produce it more reliably than the lower-tech competition that was so astonishing.

When in 1968 the first four-cylinder CB750 road bike arrived the world of motorcycling changed for ever, they even had to invent a new word for it, 'Superbike'. Honda raced again with the CB750 at Daytona and won the

World Endurance title with a prototype DOHC version that became the CB900 roadster. There was the six-cylinder CBX, the CX500T – the world's first turbocharged production bike, they invented the full-dress tourer with the GoldWing, and came back to GPs with the revolutionary oval-pistoned NR500 four-stroke, a much-misunderstood bike that was more a rolling experimental laboratory than a racer. Just to show their versatility Honda also came up with the weird CX500 shaft-drive V-twin, a rugged workhorse that powered a new industry, the courier companies that oiled the wheels of commerce in London and other big cities.

It was true, though, that Mr Honda was not keen on two-strokes – early motocross engines had to be explained away to him as lawnmower motors! However, in 1982 Honda raced the NS500, an agile three-cylinder lightweight against the big four-cylinder opposition in 500 GPs. The bike won in its first year and in '83 took the world title for Freddie Spencer. In four-stroke racing the V4 layout took over from the straight four, dominating TT, F1 and Endurance championships with the RVF750, the nearest thing ever built to a Formula 1 car on wheels. And when Superbike arrived Honda were ready with the RC30. On the roads the VFR V4 became an instant classic while the CBR600 invented another new class of bike on its way to becoming a best-seller. The V4 road bikes had problems to start with but the VFR750 sold world-wide over its lifetime while the VFR400 became a massive commercial success and cult bike in Japan. The original RC30 won the first two World Superbike Championships is 1988 and '89, but Honda had to wait until 1997 to win it again with the RC45, the last of the V4 roadsters. In Grands Prix, the NSR500 V4 two-stroke superseded the NS triple and became the benchmark racing machine of the '90s. Mick Doohan secured his place in history by winning five World Championships in consecutive years on it.

In yet another example of Honda inventing a new class of motorcycle, they came up with the astounding CBR900RR FireBlade, a bike with the punch of a 1000 cc motor in a package the size and weight of a 750. It became a cult bike as well as a best seller, and with judicious redesigns continues to give much more recent designs a run for their money.

When it became apparent that the high-tech V4 motor of the RC45 was too expensive to produce, Honda looked to a V-twin engine to power its flagship for the first time. Typically, the VTR1000 FireStorm was a much more rideable machine than its opposition and once accepted by the market formed the basis of the next generation of Superbike racer, the VTR-SP-1.

One of Mr Honda's mottos was that technology would solve the customers' problems, and no company has embraced

The CX500 – Honda's first V-Twin and a favorite choice of dispatch riders

cutting-edge technology more firmly than Honda. In fact Honda often developed new technology, especially in the fields of materials science and metallurgy. The embodiment of that was the NR750, a bike that was misunderstood nearly as much as the original NR500 racer. This limited-edition technological tour-de-force embodied many of Soichiro Honda's ideals. It used the latest techniques and materials in every component, from the oval piston, 32-valve V4 motor to the titanium coating on the windscreen, it was – as Mr Honda would have wanted – the best it could possibly be. A fitting memorial to the man who has shaped the motorcycle industry and motorcyles as we know them today.

Fun for All

Honda had a pretty good reason for building the Hornet: fun. Specifically, they reckoned it would be good fun and, just as importantly, manageable fun for newly qualified riders. The recipe was pleasingly simple (and no doubt economic), a slightly detuned CBR600 motor in a backbone chassis as used on the SLR650 with suspension from the 250 Hornet that

The VFR400R was a cult bike in Japan and a popular grey import in the UK

The naked CB600F Hornet

The faired CB600FS Hornet

appeared on the Japanese home market in 1997.

This formula of a middleweight motor in a budget chassis had been a massive success for Suzuki and their Bandits of various capacities and in 1998 both the Honda Hornet and the Yamaha Fazer appeared. Price was a major factor in the Bandits' success so it is obvious why Honda had to have a good look in the parts bin when assembling the Hornet. For instance, the lack of a Pro-Link rising rate linkage shows a desire to cut costs. Nevertheless, the wheels and tyres raised a few eyebrows; both the unfashionably small 16-inch front and the unfeasibly large 180/55 rear came straight off the FireBlade! Believe it or not, the 250 used the same sizes. Overtyred? Hmmm… Honda actually claimed that the tyres 'suit this type of bike'. Obviously nothing to do with looks then. Similarly, the lack of initial bite from the brakes was deliberately dialled in to protect newly qualified riders, and the born-agains who would be attracted to this type of bike, from the consequences of an over-anxious handful. As the brake calipers were straight off the CBR600, a change of pads was an easy route to sharper braking.

The motor came from the CBR600F3 but with some significant modifications. The cylinder bank is slightly more upright than on the CBR, carb bore is down from 36 to 34 mm and the exhaust is longer. The inlet and exhaust mods help flatten the power curve and beef-up the mid-range, all in search of the easy riding fun the factory promises. There was only one blot on the first model's escutcheon, the tank capacity. Honda claim 16 litres but it's almost impossible to persuade that volume into the container and the result is that the Hornet struggles to cover 100 miles before needing a top-up.

But did the Hornet deliver its target objective of providing fun for newly qualified riders? Yes it did, and what's more you didn't have to be a newbie to enjoy the bike. Sure the motor produced progressive, user-friendly power up to a point – and then it went joyfully crazy with the sort of top-end rush you expect from a sporting 600. It was fast, it was frenetic and it most certainly was fun.

But two short years into its life the Hornet became the Hornet-S and went , well, not staid by any means, but ever so slightly more sensible. The prime change to the original concept was the change to a 17-inch front wheel which necessitated chassis changes to cope, notably a 5 mm increase in both wheelbase and fork offset, the later producing more trail and the whole lot producing a notably more stable bike. Modified brake hoses did away with complaints about weedy brakes but the new-found stopping power unfortunately exposed the front forks as too softly sprung and lacking in damping as well. Still, there are plenty of specialist firms who can uprate the standard equipment and the 17-inch wheel meant a much larger range of replacement tyres were now available to owners.

The other obvious change was the addition of a half-fairing to produce the Hornet-S, although an unfaired option remained in the range. Some thought the changes might reduce the fun factor, but all the fairing did was make long journeys less of a pain in the neck (literally). And strangely, the new, bigger front wheel and chassis geometry changes helped achieve one of the primary objectives of the first model, it made the bike more suitable for newly-qualified and born-again bikers; inexperienced riders could have been caught out by the original model's twitchy handling and spongy brakes. More experienced riders will be grateful for the fairing's effect on fuel economy which put tank range up around the 110-mile mark, but both newcomers and veteran riders will agree on one thing: the Hornet is fun.

Acknowledgements

Our thanks are due to Bransons Motorcycles of Yeovil who supplied the machines featured in the illustrations throughout this manual. We would also like to thank NGK Spark Plugs (UK) Ltd for supplying the colour spark plug condition photographs, the Avon Rubber Company for supplying information on tyre fitting and Draper Tools Ltd for some of the workshop tools shown.

Thanks are also due to Julian Ryder who wrote the introduction 'The Birth of a Dream' and to Honda (UK) Ltd who supplied some of the model photographs.

About this Manual

The aim of this manual is to help you get the best value from your motorcycle. It can do so in several ways. It can help you decide what work must be done, even if you choose to have it done by a dealer; it provides information and procedures for routine maintenance and servicing; and it offers diagnostic and repair procedures to follow when trouble occurs.

We hope you use the manual to tackle the work yourself. For many simpler jobs, doing it yourself may be quicker than arranging an appointment to get the motorcycle into a dealer and making the trips to leave it and pick it up. More importantly, a lot of money can be saved by avoiding the expense the shop must pass on to you to cover its labour and overhead costs. An added benefit is the sense of satisfaction and accomplishment that you feel after doing the job yourself.

References to the left or right side of the motorcycle assume you are sitting on the seat, facing forward.

We take great pride in the accuracy of information given in this manual, but motorcycle manufacturers make alterations and design changes during the production run of a particular motorcycle of which they do not inform us. No liability can be accepted by the authors or publishers for loss, damage or injury caused by any errors in, or omissions from, the information given.

Frame and engine numbers

The frame serial number is stamped into the right-hand side of the steering head. The engine number is stamped into the top of the crankcase on the right-hand side. These numbers should be recorded and kept in a safe place so they can be furnished to law enforcement officials in the event of a theft. There is also a carburettor identification number on the intake side of each carburettor body, and a colour code label on the top of the frame under the seat.

The frame serial number, engine serial number, carburettor identification number and colour code should be recorded and kept in a handy place (such as with your driver's licence) so that they are always available when purchasing or ordering parts for your machine.

The procedures in this manual identify the bikes by year and model (e.g. 1999 CB600F).

The model codes for all years and models covered are listed below, together with initial engine and frame numbers. Note that the engine, frame and carburettor ID details relate specifically to the UK market.

Buying spare parts

Once you have found all the identification numbers, record them for reference when buying parts. Since the manufacturers change specifications, parts and vendors (companies that manufacture various components on the machine), providing the ID numbers is the only way to be reasonably sure that you are buying the correct parts.

Whenever possible, take the worn part to the dealer so direct comparison with the new component can be made. Along the trail from the manufacturer to the parts shelf, there are numerous places that the part can end up with the wrong number or be listed incorrectly.

The two places to purchase new parts for your motorcycle – the accessory store and the franchised dealer – differ in the type of parts they carry. While dealers can obtain virtually every part for your motorcycle, the accessory dealer is usually limited to normal high wear items such as shock absorbers, tune-up parts, various engine gaskets, cables, chains, brake parts, etc. Rarely will an accessory outlet have major suspension components, cylinders, transmission gears, or cases.

Used parts can be obtained for roughly half the price of new ones, but you can't always be sure of what you're getting. Once again, take your worn part to the breaker's yard for direct comparison.

Whether buying new, used or rebuilt parts, the best course is to deal directly with someone who specialises in parts for your particular make.

The colour code label is stuck to the frame

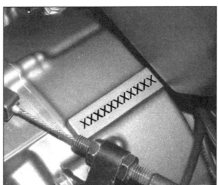
The engine number location

The frame number location

UK/Europe models	Year	Code	Initial engine no.	Initial frame no.	Carb ID no.
CB600F	1998	W	PC25E-6500001	JH21PC34A-WM000001	VP49E
CB600F	1999	X	PC25E-65550001	JH2PC34A-XM11000001	VP49E
CB600F	2000	Y	PC25E-6570001	JH2PC34A-YM200001	VP49F
CB600FS	2000	Y	PC25E-7000001	JH2PC34E-YM200001	VP49F
CB600F	2001	1	PC25E-6600001	JH2PC34A-1M300001	VP49F
CB600FS	2001	1	PC25E-7010001	JH2PC34E-1M300001	VP49F
CB600F	2002	2	Not available		
CB600FS	2002	2	Not available		

Model development

CB600F-W (1998 model year)

The first CB600F was the CB600F-W model introduced in 1998. It combined a detuned version of the CBR600F3 engine with a new mono-backbone chassis that utilised the engine as a stressed member.

The engine is a 16-valve four-cylinder, liquid cooled unit with chain driven double overhead camshafts. The exhaust system is a four-into-one unit with a high level silencer mounted on the right-hand side of the machine.

The clutch is a conventional cable-operated, wet, multi-plate unit and the gearbox is six speed. Final drive is by chain to the rear wheel.

The frame is of steel construction with an alloy swingarm. Rear suspension is by a single gas-damped unit. Front suspension is by non-adjustable, oil damped telescopic forks. Braking is by twin discs at the front and a single disc at the rear.

The CB600F-W was available in candy red, candy blue and silver metallic.

CB600F-X (1999 model year)

The CB600F-X was introduced in November 1998. There were no significant changes from the W model. The CB600F-X was available in candy blue, pearl yellow and Italian red.

CB600F-Y and CB600FS-Y (2000 model year)

The CB600F-Y was introduced in November 1999. Changes from the F-X model consisted of a 17 inch front wheel to replace the previous 16 inch item and the front brake hose between the left and right-hand calipers was changed to a steel item.

This was the first year for the CB600FS model. It differed from the CB600F-Y in addition to having a half-fairing and new headlight and instrument cluster. The speedometer was driven electronically as opposed to the cable driven instrument used on the CB600F.

The CB600F-Y and CB600FS-Y were available in candy blue, pearl yellow and black.

CB600F-1 and CB600FS-1 (2001 model year)

The CB600F-1 and CB600FS-1 were introduced in November 2000. There were no significant changes from the Y models. Colours were candy blue, pearl yellow and black.

CB600F-2 and CB600FS-2 (2002 model year)

The CB600F-2 and CB600FS-2 were unchanged from the year 2001 models. Colours were pearl yellow, candy blue and black metalic for the F-2, and silver metallic, candy blue and black metallic for the FS-2 model.

Bike spec

Weight and dimensions

Overall length . . . . .2055 mm	Seat height . . . . .795 mm
Overall width . . . . .745 mm	Ground clearance . . . . .135 mm
Overall height	Dry weight (no fuel or oil)
CB600F . . . . .1070 mm	CB600F . . . . .176 kg
CB600FS . . . . .1190 mm	CB600FS . . . . .178 kg
Wheelbase	Max load (combined weight of rider, passenger, accessories
CB600F-W and X models . . . . .1420 mm	and luggage) . . . . .188 kg
CB600F-Y and 1 models and CB600FS models . . . . .1425 mm	

Engine

Type	Liquid cooled, 16 valve in-line four cylinder
Capacity	599 cc
Weight	61.9 kg
Bore and stroke	65 x 45.2 mm
Compression ratio	12 : 1
Camshafts	DOHC, chain driven
Carburettors	4 x 34 mm Keihin VP 49A
Ignition system	Transistorised, electronic advance
Clutch	Wet, multi-plate, cable-operated
Gearbox	6-speed constant mesh
Final drive chain	RK525R or DID525M2 (110 links)

Chassis

Type	Single spar backbone, box-section steel construction
Rake	25° 40'
Trail	98 mm
Front suspension	
Type	Oil damped 41 mm telescopic forks
Travel	108 mm
Rear suspension	
Type	Swingarm
Travel	127 mm
Adjustment	7 position spring preload
Tyres	
Front	
CB600F-W and F-X models	130/70-ZR16 (61W)
CB600F-Y models onward and all CB600FS models	120/70-ZR17 (61W)
Rear	180/55-ZR17 (73W)
Brakes	
Front	Nissin twin 296 mm discs with 2-piston calipers
Rear	Nissin single 220 mm disc with single piston caliper

Performance data

Maximum power . . . . .86 bhp (64 kW) @ 11,600 rpm

Maximum torque . . . . .44 lbf ft (60 Nm) @ 9500 rpm

Power to weight ratio . . . . . .530 bhp per tonne (0.39 kW per kg)

Top speed
CB600F . . . . .131.8 mph (212 km)
CB600FS . . . . .135 mph (217 km)

Acceleration
CB600F
  Time taken to cover a ¼ mile from a standing start . . .12.8 seconds
  Terminal speed after ¼ mile . . . . .114 mph (183 km)
CB600FS
  Time taken to cover a ¼ mile from a standing start . . .12.4 seconds
  Terminal speed after ¼ mile . . . . .116 mph (187 km)

Average fuel consumption
Miles per Imp gal, miles per litre,
  litres per 100 km . . . . .35 mpg, 7.7 mpl, 8.1 l/100 km

Fuel tank range
Based on average fuel consumption rate
CB600F . . . . .120 miles (193 km)
CB600FS . . . . .123 miles (198 km)

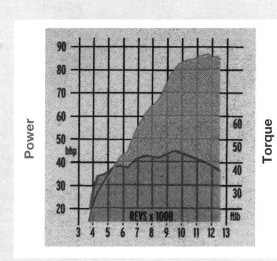

Performance data sourced from Motor Cycle News road test features. See the MCN website for up-to-date biking news.

MCN www.motorcyclenews.com

Professional mechanics are trained in safe working procedures. However enthusiastic you may be about getting on with the job at hand, take the time to ensure that your safety is not put at risk. A moment's lack of attention can result in an accident, as can failure to observe simple precautions.

There will always be new ways of having accidents, and the following is not a comprehensive list of all dangers; it is intended rather to make you aware of the risks and to encourage a safe approach to all work you carry out on your bike.

Asbestos

● Certain friction, insulating, sealing and other products - such as brake pads, clutch linings, gaskets, etc. - contain asbestos. Extreme care must be taken to avoid inhalation of dust from such products since it is hazardous to health. If in doubt, assume that they do contain asbestos.

Fire

● Remember at all times that petrol is highly flammable. Never smoke or have any kind of naked flame around, when working on the vehicle. But the risk does not end there - a spark caused by an electrical short-circuit, by two metal surfaces contacting each other, by careless use of tools, or even by static electricity built up in your body under certain conditions, can ignite petrol vapour, which in a confined space is highly explosive. Never use petrol as a cleaning solvent. Use an approved safety solvent.

● Always disconnect the battery earth terminal before working on any part of the fuel or electrical system, and never risk spilling fuel on to a hot engine or exhaust.
● It is recommended that a fire extinguisher of a type suitable for fuel and electrical fires is kept handy in the garage or workplace at all times. Never try to extinguish a fuel or electrical fire with water.

Fumes

● Certain fumes are highly toxic and can quickly cause unconsciousness and even death if inhaled to any extent. Petrol vapour comes into this category, as do the vapours from certain solvents such as trichloro-ethylene. Any draining or pouring of such volatile fluids should be done in a well ventilated area.
● When using cleaning fluids and solvents, read the instructions carefully. Never use materials from unmarked containers - they may give off poisonous vapours.
● Never run the engine of a motor vehicle in an enclosed space such as a garage. Exhaust fumes contain carbon monoxide which is extremely poisonous; if you need to run the engine, always do so in the open air or at least have the rear of the vehicle outside the workplace.

The battery

● Never cause a spark, or allow a naked light near the vehicle's battery. It will normally be giving off a certain amount of hydrogen gas, which is highly explosive.

● Always disconnect the battery ground (earth) terminal before working on the fuel or electrical systems (except where noted).
● If possible, loosen the filler plugs or cover when charging the battery from an external source. Do not charge at an excessive rate or the battery may burst.
● Take care when topping up, cleaning or carrying the battery. The acid electrolyte, evenwhen diluted, is very corrosive and should not be allowed to contact the eyes or skin. Always wear rubber gloves and goggles or a face shield. If you ever need to prepare electrolyte yourself, always add the acid slowly to the water; never add the water to the acid.

Electricity

● When using an electric power tool, inspection light etc., always ensure that the appliance is correctly connected to its plug and that, where necessary, it is properly grounded (earthed). Do not use such appliances in damp conditions and, again, beware of creating a spark or applying excessive heat in the vicinity of fuel or fuel vapour. Also ensure that the appliances meet national safety standards.
● A severe electric shock can result from touching certain parts of the electrical system, such as the spark plug wires (HT leads), when the engine is running or being cranked, particularly if components are damp or the insulation is defective. Where an electronic ignition system is used, the secondary (HT) voltage is much higher and could prove fatal.

Remember...

✗ **Don't** start the engine without first ascertaining that the transmission is in neutral.
✗ **Don't** suddenly remove the pressure cap from a hot cooling system - cover it with a cloth and release the pressure gradually first, or you may get scalded by escaping coolant.
✗ **Don't** attempt to drain oil until you are sure it has cooled sufficiently to avoid scalding you.
✗ **Don't** grasp any part of the engine or exhaust system without first ascertaining that it is cool enough not to burn you.
✗ **Don't** allow brake fluid or antifreeze to contact the machine's paintwork or plastic components.
✗ **Don't** siphon toxic liquids such as fuel, hydraulic fluid or antifreeze by mouth, or allow them to remain on your skin.
✗ **Don't** inhale dust - it may be injurious to health (see Asbestos heading).
✗ **Don't** allow any spilled oil or grease to remain on the floor - wipe it up right away, before someone slips on it.
✗ **Don't** use ill-fitting spanners or other tools which may slip and cause injury.
✗ **Don't** lift a heavy component which may be beyond your capability - get assistance.

✗ **Don't** rush to finish a job or take unverified short cuts.
✗ **Don't** allow children or animals in or around an unattended vehicle.
✗ **Don't** inflate a tyre above the recommended pressure. Apart from over-stressing the carcass, in extreme cases the tyre may blow off forcibly.
✔ **Do** ensure that the machine is supported securely at all times. This is especially important when the machine is blocked up to aid wheel or fork removal.
✔ **Do** take care when attempting to loosen a stubborn nut or bolt. It is generally better to pull on a spanner, rather than push, so that if you slip, you fall away from the machine rather than onto it.
✔ **Do** wear eye protection when using power tools such as drill, sander, bench grinder etc.
✔ **Do** use a barrier cream on your hands prior to undertaking dirty jobs - it will protect your skin from infection as well as making the dirt easier to remove afterwards; but make sure your hands aren't left slippery. Note that long-term contact with used engine oil can be a health hazard.
✔ **Do** keep loose clothing (cuffs, ties etc. and long hair) well out of the way of moving mechanical parts.

✔ **Do** remove rings, wristwatch etc., before working on the vehicle - especially the electrical system.
✔ **Do** keep your work area tidy - it is only too easy to fall over articles left lying around.
✔ **Do** exercise caution when compressing springs for removal or installation. Ensure that the tension is applied and released in a controlled manner, using suitable tools which preclude the possibility of the spring escaping violently.
✔ **Do** ensure that any lifting tackle used has a safe working load rating adequate for the job.
✔ **Do** get someone to check periodically that all is well, when working alone on the vehicle.
✔ **Do** carry out work in a logical sequence and check that everything is correctly assembled and tightened afterwards.
✔ **Do** remember that your vehicle's safety affects that of yourself and others. If in doubt on any point, get professional advice.
● If in spite of following these precautions, you are unfortunate enough to injure yourself, seek medical attention as soon as possible.

Note: *The daily (pre-ride) checks outlined in the owner's manual covers those items which should be inspected on a daily basis.*

Engine/transmission oil level check

The correct oil
● Modern, high-revving engines place great demands on their oil. It is very important that the correct oil for your bike is used.
● Always top up with a good quality oil of the specified type and viscosity and do not overfill the engine.

Oil type	API grade SE, SF or SG
Oil viscosity	SAE 10W40*

Refer to the viscosity table to select the oil best suited to your conditions.

Before you start:
✔ Start the engine and let it idle for several minutes to allow it to reach normal operating temperature.
✔ Stop the engine and support the motorcycle in an upright position, using an auxiliary stand if required. Make sure it is on level ground.
Caution: Do not run the engine in an enclosed space such as a garage or workshop.
✔ Leave the motorcycle undisturbed for a few minutes to allow the oil level to stabilise.

Bike care:
● If you have to add oil frequently, you should check whether you have any oil leaks. If there is no sign of oil leakage from the joints and gaskets the engine could be burning oil (see *Fault Finding*).

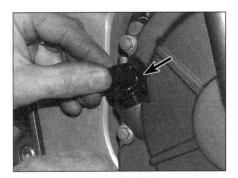

1 Remove the oil filler cap (arrowed) from the right-hand side of the engine. The dipstick is integral with the cap and is used to check the engine oil level.

2 Using a clean rag or paper towel, wipe all the oil off the dipstick. Insert the clean dipstick in the filler cap hole, but **do not** screw it in.

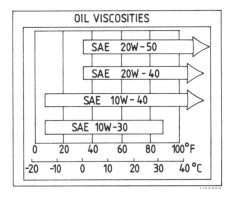

OIL VISCOSITIES

SAE 20W-50	→
SAE 20W-40	→
SAE 10W-40	→
SAE 10W-30	

```
0    20   40   60   80   100°F
-20  -10   0   10   20   30   40°C
```

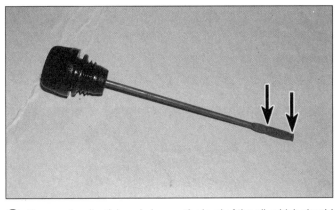

3 Remove the dipstick and observe the level of the oil, which should be somewhere in between the upper and lower level lines (arrowed).

4 If the level is below the lower line, add the recommended grade and type of oil to bring the level up to the upper line on the dipstick. Do not overfill. Install the filler cap.

Suspension, steering and drive chain checks

Suspension and steering:
● Check that the front and rear suspension operates smoothly without binding.
● Check that the suspension is adjusted as required.
● Check that the steering moves smoothly from lock-to-lock.

Drive chain:
● Check that the drive chain slack isn't excessive, and adjust it if necessary (see Chapter 1).
● If the chain looks dry, lubricate it (see Chapter 1).

Brake fluid level checks

> ⚠️ **Warning:** *Brake hydraulic fluid can harm your eyes and damage painted surfaces, so use extreme caution when handling and pouring it and cover surrounding surfaces with rag. Do not use fluid that has been standing open for some time, as it absorbs moisture from the air which can cause a dangerous loss of braking effectiveness.*

Before you start:

✔ Support the motorcycle in an upright position, using an auxiliary stand if required. Turn the handlebars until the top of the front master cylinder is as level as possible. The rear master cylinder reservoir is located behind the right-hand side cover.

✔ Make sure you have the correct hydraulic fluid. DOT 4 is recommended.

✔ Wrap a rag around the reservoir being worked on to ensure that any spillage does not come into contact with painted surfaces.

Bike care:

● The fluid in the front and rear brake master cylinder reservoirs will drop slightly as the brake pads wear down.

● If any fluid reservoir requires repeated topping-up this is an indication of a hydraulic leak somewhere in the system, which should be investigated immediately.

● Check for signs of fluid leakage from the hydraulic hoses and brake system components – if found, rectify immediately (see Chapter 7).

● Check the operation of both brakes before taking the machine on the road; if there is evidence of air in the system (spongy feel to lever or pedal), it must be bled as described in Chapter 7.

Front brake fluid level

1 The front brake fluid level is visible through the sightglass in the reservoir body – it must be above the LOWER level line.

2 If the level is below the LOWER level line, undo the reservoir cap screws and remove the cap, the diaphragm plate and the diaphragm.

3 Top up with new, clean DOT 4 hydraulic fluid, until the level is just below the UPPER level line cast on the inside of the reservoir (arrowed). Take care to avoid spills (see **Warning** above) and do not overfill.

4 Ensure that the diaphragm is correctly seated before installing the plate and cap, then tighten the screws securely.

Rear brake fluid level

5 Remove the seat (see Chapter 8). The rear brake fluid level is visible through the reservoir body – it must be between the UPPER and LOWER level lines.

6 If the level is below the LOWER level line, unscrew the cap and remove the diaphragm plate and the diaphragm. Top up with new, clean DOT 4 hydraulic fluid. Take care to avoid spills (see **Warning** above) and do not overfill. Ensure that the diaphragm is correctly seated before installing the plate and cap. Install the seat.

Coolant level check

 Warning: DO NOT remove the radiator pressure cap to add coolant. Topping up is done via the coolant reservoir tank filler. DO NOT leave open containers of coolant about, as it is poisonous.

Before you start:
✔ Make sure you have a supply of coolant available – a mixture of 50% distilled water and 50% corrosion inhibited ethylene glycol anti-freeze is needed.
✔ Check the coolant level when the engine is at operating temperature and idling.
✔ Support the motorcycle in an upright position, using an auxiliary stand if required. Make sure it is on level ground.

Bike care:
● Use only the specified coolant mixture. It is important that anti-freeze is used in the system all year round, and not just in the winter. Do not top the system up using only water, as the system will become too diluted.
● Do not overfill the reservoir. If the coolant is significantly above the FULL level line at any time, the surplus should be siphoned or drained off to prevent the possibility of it being expelled out of the overflow hose.
● If the coolant level falls steadily, check the system for leaks (see Chapter 1). If no leaks are found and the level continues to fall, it is recommended that the machine be taken to a Honda dealer for a pressure test.

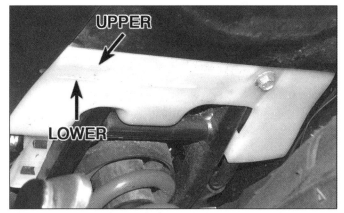

1 The coolant reservoir is mounted beneath the frame top section, behind the rear shock absorber. The coolant UPPER and LOWER level lines (arrowed) are marked on the reservoir and are visible from below.

2 If the coolant level does not lie between the FULL and LOW level lines, remove the seat (see Chapter 8), then remove the reservoir filler cap and top the coolant level up with the recommended coolant mixture. Fit the cap securely and install the seat.

Legal and safety checks

Lighting and signalling:
● Take a minute to check that the headlight, tail light, brake light, instrument lights and turn signals all work correctly.
● Check that the horn sounds when the switch is operated.
● A working speedometer graduated in mph is a statutory requirement in the UK.

Safety:
● Check that the throttle grip rotates smoothly and snaps shut when released, in all steering positions. Also check for the correct amount of freeplay (see Chapter 1).

● Check that the engine shuts off when the kill switch is operated.
● Check that sidestand return spring holds the stand up securely when it is retracted.

Fuel:
● This may seem obvious, but check that you have enough fuel to complete your journey. If you notice signs of fuel leakage – rectify the cause immediately.
● Ensure you use the correct grade fuel – see Chapter 4 Specifications.

Tyre checks

The correct pressures:

● The tyres must be checked when **cold**, not immediately after riding. Note that low tyre pressures may cause the tyre to slip on the rim or come off. High tyre pressures will cause abnormal tread wear and unsafe handling.

● Use an accurate pressure gauge. Many garage forecourt gauges are wildly inaccurate. If you buy your own, spend as much as you can justify on a quality gauge.

● Correct air pressure will increase tyre life and provide maximum stability, handling capability and ride comfort.

Tyre care:

● Check the tyres carefully for cuts, tears, embedded nails or other sharp objects and excessive wear. Operation of the motorcycle with excessively worn tyres is extremely hazardous, as traction and handling are directly affected.

● Check the condition of the tyre valve and ensure the dust cap is in place.

● Pick out any stones or nails which may have become embedded in the tyre tread. If left, they will eventually penetrate through the casing and cause a puncture.

● If tyre damage is apparent, or unexplained loss of pressure is experienced, seek the advice of a tyre fitting specialist without delay.

Tyre tread depth:

● At the time of writing UK law requires that tread depth must be at least 1 mm over the entire tread breadth all the way around the tyre, with no bald patches. Many riders, however, consider 2 mm tread depth minimum to be a safer limit. Honda recommend a minimum of 1.5 mm for the front tyre and 2 mm for the rear tyre.

● Many tyres now incorporate wear indicators in the tread. Identify the triangular pointer or TWI mark on the tyre sidewall to locate the indicator bar and renew the tyre if the tread has worn down to the bar.

Front 36 psi (2.50 Bar)	**Rear** 42 psi (2.90 Bar)

1 Check the tyre pressures when the tyres are **cold** and keep them properly inflated.

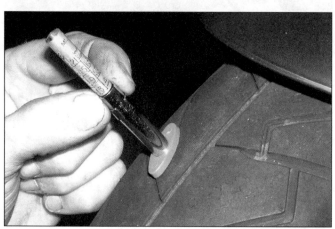

2 Measure tread depth at the centre of the tyre using a tread depth gauge.

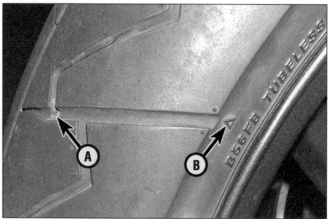

3 Tyre tread wear indicator bar (A) and its location marking (B) - usually either an arrow, a triangle or the letters TWI - on the sidewall.

4 Look for the tyre information label on the chainguard

Chapter 1
Routine maintenance and servicing

Contents

Degrees of difficulty

| Easy, suitable for novice with little experience | Fairly easy, suitable for beginner with some experience | Fairly difficult, suitable for competent DIY mechanic | Difficult, suitable for experienced DIY mechanic | Very difficult, suitable for expert DIY or professional |

Engine

Cylinder identification	1 to 4 from left to right
Spark plugs	
Type	NGK CR9EH-9 or ND U27FER9
Electrode gap	0.8 to 0.9 mm
Engine idle speed	1300 ± 100 rpm
Carburettor synchronisation – max. difference from No. 3 cylinder	30 mm Hg
Valve clearances (COLD engine)	
Intake valves	0.16 ± 0.03 mm
Exhaust valves	0.22 ± 0.03 mm
Cylinder compression	185 to 191 psi (12.8 to 13.2 bar)
Engine oil pressure (at 80°C)	71 psi (4.9 bar) @ 6000 rpm

Cycle parts

Drive chain slack	30 to 40 mm
Throttle cable freeplay	2 to 6 mm
Clutch lever freeplay	10 to 20 mm
Tyre pressures (cold)	see *Daily (pre-ride) checks*

Recommended lubricants and fluids

Engine/transmission oil type	see *Daily (pre-ride) checks*
Engine/transmission oil capacity	
Oil change	3.5 litres
Oil and filter change	3.8 litres
Following engine overhaul – dry engine, new filter	4.2 litres
Coolant type	50% distilled water, 50% ethylene glycol anti-freeze with corrosion inhibitors for aluminium engines.
Coolant capacity	
Radiator	2.0 litres
Reservoir	0.2 litres
Brake fluid	DOT 4
Drive chain	SAE 80 or 90W gear oil or chain lubricant suitable for O-ring chains
Steering head bearings	Lithium-based multi-purpose grease
Swingarm pivot and bearings	Lithium-based multi-purpose grease
Shock absorber lower bearing	Lithium-based multi-purpose grease
Bearing seals	Lithium-based multi-purpose grease
Gearchange lever, clutch lever, front brake lever, rear brake pedal, sidestand pivots	Lithium-based multi-purpose grease
Cables	10W30 motor oil or cable lubricant
Throttle twistgrip	Multi-purpose grease or dry film lubricant

Torque wrench settings

Drive chain slider bolts	9 Nm
Fork clamp bolt (top yoke)	23 Nm
Handlebar clamp bolts	26 Nm
Oil drain bolt	29 Nm
Oil filter	10 Nm
Rear axle nut	88 Nm
Spark plugs	12 Nm
Steering stem bearing adjuster nut	25 Nm
Steering stem nut	103 Nm
Timing cover inspection cap	18 Nm
Water pump drain bolt	12 Nm

Note: *The Daily (pre-ride) checks outlined in the owner's manual covers those items which should be inspected on a daily basis. Always perform the pre-ride inspection at every maintenance interval (in addition to the procedures listed). The intervals listed below are the intervals recommended by the manufacturer for each particular operation during the model years covered in this manual. Your owner's manual may have different intervals for your model.*

Daily (pre-ride)
- [ ] See *Daily (pre-ride) checks* at the beginning of this manual.

After the initial 600 miles (1000 km)
Note: *This check is usually performed by a Honda dealer after the first 600 miles (1000 km) from new. Thereafter, maintenance is carried out according to the following intervals of the schedule.*

Every 600 miles (1000 km)
- [ ] Check, adjust, clean and lubricate the drive chain (Section 1)

Every 4000 miles (6000 km) or 6 months (whichever comes sooner)
- [ ] Check and adjust the idle speed (Section 2)
- [ ] Check the brake pads (Section 3)
- [ ] Lubricate the throttle/choke cables and clutch/gearchange/brake lever/brake pedal and sidestand pivots (see Section 4)

Every 8000 miles (12,000 km) or 12 months (whichever comes sooner)
- [ ] Change the engine/transmission oil and filter (Section 5)
- [ ] Check and adjust the throttle and choke cables (Section 6)
- [ ] Check and adjust the spark plugs (Section 7)
- [ ] Check/adjust the carburettor synchronisation (Section 8)
- [ ] Check the fuel hose (Section 9)
- [ ] Check the cooling system (Section 10)
- [ ] Check the condition of the PAIR system hoses (Section 11)
- [ ] Check the brake system (Section 12)
- [ ] Check and adjust the headlight aim (Section 13)
- [ ] Check and adjust the clutch and clutch cable (Section 14)

Every 8000 miles (12,000 km) or 12 months (whichever comes sooner) (continued)
- [ ] Check the sidestand and sidestand switch (Section 15)
- [ ] Check the condition of the drive chain slider (Section 16)
- [ ] Check the suspension (Section 17)
- [ ] Check the condition of the tyres and wheels (Section 18)
- [ ] Check and adjust the steering head bearings (Section 19)
- [ ] Check the tightness of all nuts, bolts and fasteners (Section 20)

Every 12,000 miles (18,000 km) or 18 months (whichever comes sooner)
- [ ] Renew the air filter element (see Section 21)
- [ ] Change the brake fluid (Section 22)

Every 16,000 miles (24,000 km) or every two years (whichever comes sooner)
- [ ] Renew the spark plugs (see Section 23)
- [ ] Check and adjust the valve clearances (Section 24)

Every 24,000 miles (36,000 km) or every two years (whichever comes sooner)
- [ ] Change the coolant (Section 25)

Non-scheduled maintenance
- [ ] Check the battery (Section 26)
- [ ] Renew the brake master cylinder and caliper seals (Section 27)
- [ ] Renew the brake hoses (Section 28)
- [ ] Check the cylinder compression (Section 29)
- [ ] Check the engine oil pressure (Section 30)
- [ ] Change the front fork oil (Section 31)

1

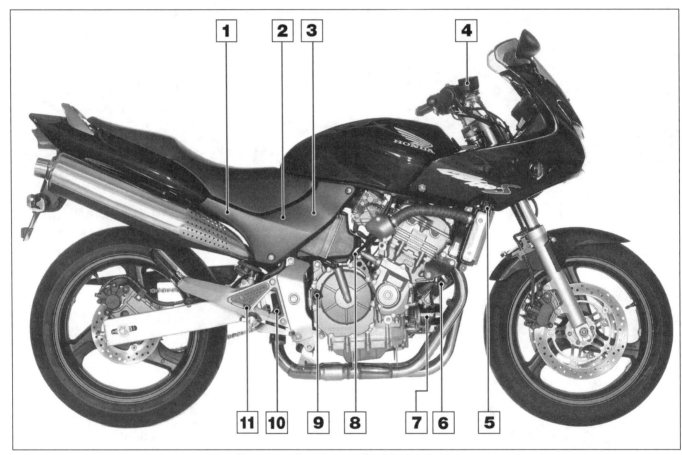

Component locations on the right-hand side

1 Rear brake fluid reservoir
2 Battery
3 Sub-air cleaner
4 Front brake fluid reservoir

5 Radiator pressure cap
6 Pulse secondary air valve
   (PAIR)

7 Engine/transmission oil filter
8 Clutch cable lower adjuster
9 Engine/transmission oil filler
   cap/dipstick

10 Rear brake light switch
11 Rear brake pedal height
   adjuster

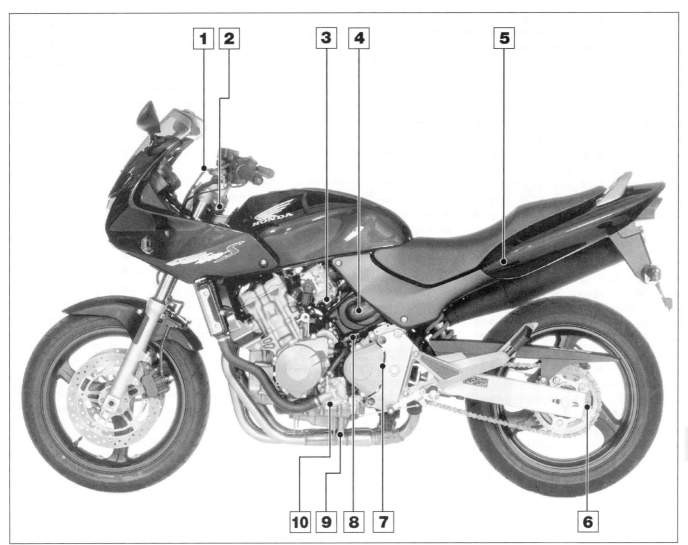

Component locations on the left-hand side

1 Clutch cable upper adjuster
2 Steering head bearing
   adjuster
3 Idle speed adjuster
4 Air filter
5 Coolant reservoir
6 Drive chain adjuster
7 Drive chain slider
8 Air filter housing drain valve
9 Engine/transmission oil drain
   plug
10 Coolant drain plug

1

1 This Chapter is designed to help the home mechanic maintain his/her motorcycle for safety, economy, long life and peak performance.
2 Deciding where to start or plug into the routine maintenance schedule depends on several factors. If the warranty period on your motorcycle has just expired, and if it has been maintained according to the warranty standards, you may want to pick up routine maintenance as it coincides with the next mileage or calendar interval. If you have owned the machine for some time but have never performed any maintenance on it, then you may want to start at the beginning and

include all frequent procedures to ensure that nothing important is overlooked. If you have just had a major engine overhaul, then you should start the engine maintenance routines from the beginning. If you have a used machine and have no knowledge of its history or maintenance record, you should combine all the checks into one large initial service and then settle into the maintenance schedule prescribed.
3 Before beginning any maintenance or repair, the machine should be cleaned thoroughly, especially around the oil filter, spark plugs, valve cover, carburettors, etc. Cleaning will help ensure that dirt does not

contaminate the engine and will allow you to detect wear and damage that could otherwise easily go unnoticed.
4 Certain maintenance information is sometimes printed on decals attached to the motorcycle. If any information on the decals differs from that included here, use the information on the decal.

> **HAYNES HiNT** Read the *Safety first!* section of this manual carefully before starting work.

Every 600 miles (1000 km)

1 Drive chain and sprockets – check, adjustment and lubrication

Check

1 As the chain stretches with wear, adjustment will periodically be necessary. A neglected drive chain won't last long and can quickly damage the sprockets. Routine chain adjustment and lubrication isn't difficult and will ensure maximum chain and sprocket life.
2 To check the chain tension, support the

1.3 Push up on the chain and measure the slack

motorcycle on its sidestand with the transmission in neutral.
3 Push up on the bottom run of the chain and measure the slack midway between the two sprockets **(see illustration)**, then compare your measurement to that listed in this Chapter's Specifications. Since the chain will rarely wear evenly, rotate the rear wheel so that another section of chain can be checked; do this several times to check the entire length of the chain. Any adjustment should be based upon the measurement taken at the tightest point.
Caution: If the machine is ridden with more than 50 mm of slack in the drive chain, the chain will contact the frame and swingarm, causing severe damage.
4 Check the position of the lower index mark on the left-hand chain adjuster plate against the chain wear indicator label **(see illustration)**. If the index mark has reached the red area on the indicator the chain has stretched beyond its service limit and should be replaced with a new one (see Chapter 6).
5 In some cases where lubrication has been neglected, corrosion and galling may cause the links to bind and kink, which effectively shortens the chain's length. Any such links should be thoroughly cleaned and worked free. If the chain is tight between the

sprockets, rusty or kinked, it is time to replace it with a new one. If you find a tight area, mark it with felt pen or paint, and repeat the measurement after the bike has been ridden. If the chain is still tight in the same area, it may be damaged or worn. Because a tight or kinked chain can damage the transmission output shaft bearing, it is a good idea to replace it with a new one (see Chapter 6).
6 Check the entire length of the chain for damaged or missing rollers, loose links and pins, and missing O-rings and replace with a new one it if damage is found. **Note:** *Never install a new chain on old sprockets, and never use the old chain if you install new sprockets – renew the chain and sprockets as a set.*
7 Remove the front sprocket cover (see Chapter 6). Check the teeth on the engine sprocket and the rear wheel sprocket for wear **(see illustration)**.

Adjustment

8 Rotate the rear wheel until the chain is positioned with the tightest point at the centre of its bottom run. Support the motorcycle on its sidestand with the transmission in neutral.
9 Loosen the axle nut **(see illustration)**.
10 Loosen the adjuster locknut on each side of the swingarm, then turn the adjusters evenly, a small amount at a time, until the

1.4 Check the amount of stretch shown by the chain wear indicator (arrowed)

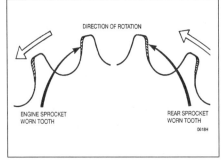

DIRECTION OF ROTATION

ENGINE SPROCKET WORN TOOTH

REAR SPROCKET WORN TOOTH

1.7 Check the sprockets in the areas indicated to see if they are worn excessively

1.9 Loosen the rear axle nut

1.10 Loosen the adjuster locknut (A) and turn the adjuster (B)

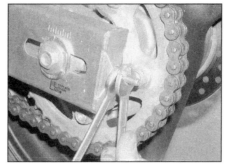

1.12 Tighten the locknut securely

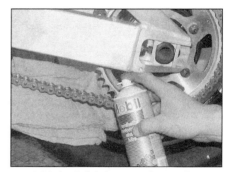

1.14 Apply lubricant to the overlap between the chain sideplates

specified chain tension is obtained **(see illustration)**. Following chain adjustment, check that the upper index marks on both chain adjuster plates are aligned with the same marks on each side of the swingarm; if not, the rear wheel will be out of alignment with the front.

 Refer to Chapter 7 for information on checking wheel alignment.

11 If there is a discrepancy in the position of the marks, correct it with the adjusters and then check the chain tension as described above. Also check that there is no clearance between the adjuster plates and the ends of the swingarm – push the wheel forwards to eliminate any clearance.
12 Tighten the axle nut to the torque setting

specified at the beginning of this Chapter, then tighten the adjuster locknuts securely **(see illustration)**. Recheck the adjustment.

Lubrication

13 If required, wash the chain in paraffin (kerosene), then wipe it off and allow it to dry, using compressed air if available. If the chain is excessively dirty, remove the rear wheel (see Chapter 7) and clean the chain as described in Chapter 6.
Caution: Don't use petrol (gasoline), solvent or other cleaning fluids which might damage the internal sealing properties of the chain. Don't use high-pressure water. The entire process shouldn't take longer than five – six minutes – if it does, the O-rings in the chain rollers could be damaged.
14 For routine lubrication, the best time to lubricate the chain is after the motorcycle has

been ridden. When the chain is warm, the lubricant will penetrate the joints between the side plates better than when cold. **Note:** *Honda specifies SAE 80 or SAE 90 gear oil or chain lube that is specifically for O-ring chains; do not use chain lube that is not specifically for O-ring chains, as it may contain solvents that could damage the O-rings.* Apply the lubricant to the area where the side plates overlap – not the middle of the rollers and protect the tyre from overspray with a rag **(see illustration)**.

 Apply the lubricant to the top of the lower chain run, so centrifugal force will work it into the chain when the bike is moving. After applying the lubricant, let it soak in a few minutes before wiping off any excess.

Every 4000 miles (6000 km) or 6 months (whichever comes sooner)

1

2 Idle speed – check and adjustment

1 The idle speed should be checked and adjusted after the carburettors are synchronised (balanced), and when it is obviously too high or too low. Before adjusting the idle speed, make sure that all other engine maintenance procedures have been carried out. Also, turn the handlebars back-and-forth and see if the idle speed changes as this is done. If it does, the throttle cables may not be adjusted or routed correctly, or may be worn out. This is a dangerous condition that can cause loss of control of the bike. Be sure to correct this problem before proceeding.
2 The engine should be at normal operating temperature, which is usually reached after 10 to 15 minutes of stop-and-go riding. Make sure the transmission is in neutral, and place the motorcycle on its stand.

 Warning: Take great care not to burn your hand on the hot engine unit. Do not allow exhaust gases to build up in the work area; either perform the check outside or use an exhaust gas extraction system.
3 The idle speed is adjusted by turning the adjuster located between Nos. 2 and 3 carburettors **(see illustration)**. With the

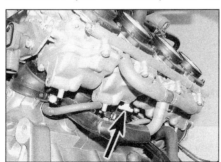

2.3 Turn the adjuster (arrowed) clockwise to increase idle speed, anticlockwise to decrease it

engine idling, turn the adjuster until the speed listed in this Chapter's Specifications is obtained. Turn the adjuster clockwise to increase idle speed, and anti-clockwise to decrease it.
4 Snap the throttle open and shut a few times, then recheck the idle speed. If necessary, repeat the adjustment procedure.
5 If a smooth, steady idle cannot be achieved, the fuel/air mixture may be incorrect (check the pilot screw settings – see Chapter 4) or the carburettors may need synchronising (see Section 8). Also check the intake manifold rubbers for cracks which will cause an air leak, resulting in a weak mixture.

3 Brake pads – wear check

 Warning: The dust created by the brake system may contain asbestos, which is harmful to

3.2 Check brake pad wear from underside of caliper

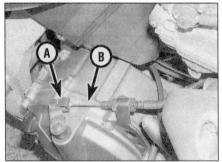

4.2 Lubricate pivot points (A) and exposed cables (B)

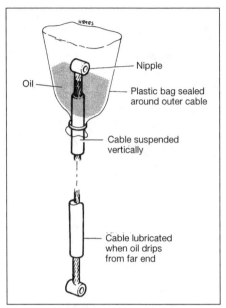

4.3 Lubricating a cable with a makeshift funnel and motor oil

your health. Never blow it out with compressed air and don't inhale any of it. An approved filtering mask should be worn when working on the brakes.

1 Each brake pad is marked with wear indicator cut-outs that can be viewed without removing the pads from the caliper.

2 The wear indicators are visible by looking at the pads from the underside of the caliper **(see illustration)**.

3 Renew the pads when they are worn level with the indicators.

Note: *Some after-market pads may use different indicators.*

4 If the pads are dirty or if you are in doubt as to the amount of friction material remaining, remove them for inspection (see Chapter 7).

Note: *It is not possible to degrease the friction material; if the pads are contaminated in any way they must be renewed.*

5 Refer to Chapter 7 for details of pad renewal.

4 Cables, lever and stand pivots – lubrication

1 Since the controls, cables and various other components of a motorcycle are exposed to the elements, they should be lubricated periodically to ensure safe and trouble-free operation.

2 The footrest pivots, clutch and brake levers, brake pedal and gearchange lever pivots and linkage and sidestand pivot should be lubricated frequently. In order that the lubricant is applied where it will do the most good, the component should be disassembled. However, lubricant applied to the pivot joints will usually work its way into the areas where friction occurs **(see illustration)**. If motor oil or light grease is being used, apply it sparingly as it may attract dirt (which could cause the controls to bind or

wear at an accelerated rate). **Note:** *One of the best lubricants for the control lever pivots is a dry-film lubricant (available from many sources by different names).*

3 To lubricate the throttle and choke cables, disconnect the relevant cable at its upper end, then lubricate the cable with a pressure adapter or, if one is not available, using the set-up shown **(see illustration)**. See Chapter 4 for the throttle and choke cable removal procedures, and Chapter 2 for the clutch cable.

Every 8000 miles (12,000 km) or 12 months (whichever comes sooner)

5 Engine/transmission – oil and filter change

Carry out all the items under the 4000 mile (6000 km) check, plus the following:

 Warning: Be careful when draining the oil, as the exhaust pipes, the engine, and the oil itself can cause severe burns.

1 Regular oil and filter changes are the single most important maintenance procedure you can perform on a motorcycle. The oil not only lubricates the internal parts of the engine, transmission and clutch, but it also acts as a coolant, a cleaner, a sealant, and a protector. Because of these demands, the oil takes a terrific amount of abuse and should be drained and the engine/transmission refilled with new oil of the recommended grade and

type. Saving a little money on the difference in cost between a good oil and a cheap oil won't pay off if the engine is damaged.

2 Before changing the oil and filter, warm up the engine so the oil will drain easily.

3 Unscrew and remove the oil filler cap from the clutch cover to vent the engine unit and to

act as a reminder that there is no oil in the engine **(see illustration)**.

4 Position a clean drain tray below the engine, then unscrew the oil drain plug from the underside of the engine sump and allow the oil to flow into the drain tray **(see illustration)**. Check the condition of the sealing washer on

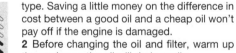

5.3 Unscrew the oil filler cap to vent the crankcase

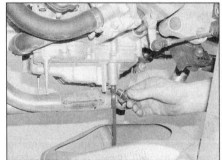

5.4 Remove the drain plug and allow the oil to drain completely

5.5 Unscrew the oil filter using a suitable tool

5.6 Smear the filter seal with clean engine oil before fitting

the drain plug and discard it if it is damaged or worn. It is always advisable to use a new washer even if the old one looks all right.

5 Now place the drain tray below the oil filter, which is on the front of the engine unit. Clean the crankcase around the filter, then unscrew the oil filter using a filter socket (one can be obtained as a kit with the new filter from Honda dealers), a filter removing strap or a chain-wrench, and tip any residual oil into the drain tray **(see illustration)**. The filter socket is preferable because it allows a means of tightening the new filter to the correct torque.

6 Clean the sealing surface on the crankcase with a suitable solvent, then smear clean engine oil onto the rubber seal on the new filter, and screw the filter onto the engine until the seal just seats **(see illustration)**. If a suitable filter adapter tool is available, tighten the filter to the torque setting specified at the beginning of this Chapter. Otherwise, tighten the filter as tight as possible by hand, or by the number of turns specified on the filter or its packaging. **Note:** *Do not use a strap or chain wrench to tighten the filter as you may damage it.*

7 When the oil has completely drained, fit the plug with its washer into the sump and tighten it to the torque setting specified at the beginning of this Chapter **(see illustration)**. Avoid overtightening, as you will damage the sump.

8 Refill the engine to the proper level using the recommended type and amount of oil (see *Daily (pre-ride) checks*). With the motorcycle vertical on level ground, the oil level should lie between the maximum and minimum level lines on the dipstick (see *Daily (pre-ride) checks*). Install the filler cap **(see illustration 5.3)**. Start the engine and let it run for two or three minutes. Stop the engine, wait a few minutes, then check the oil level. If necessary, add more oil to bring the level up to the maximum level line on the dipstick. Check that there are no leaks around the drain plug.

9 The old oil drained from the engine cannot be re-used and should be disposed of properly. Check with your local refuse disposal company, disposal facility or

environmental agency to see whether they will accept the used oil for recycling. Don't pour used oil into drains or onto the ground. The old filter should be taken to the oil disposal facility rather than disposed of with the household rubbish.

> **HAYNES HINT**
> *Check the old oil carefully – if it is very metallic coloured, then the engine is experiencing wear from break-in (new engine) or from insufficient lubrication. If there are flakes or chips of metal in the oil, then something is drastically wrong internally and the engine will have to be disassembled for inspection and repair. If there are pieces of fibre-like material in the oil, the clutch is experiencing excessive wear and should be checked.*

OIL CARE
FOLLOW THE CODE
OIL BANK LINE
0800 66 33 66
www.oilbankline.org.uk

Note: It is antisocial and illegal to dump oil down the drain. To find the location of your local oil recycling bank in the UK, call this number free. In the USA, note that any oil supplier must accept used oil for recycling.

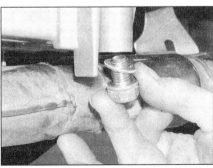

5.7 Replace the sealing washer with a new one if necessary

6 Throttle and choke cables – check and adjustment

Throttle cables

1 Make sure the throttle twistgrip rotates easily from fully closed to fully open with the front wheel turned at various angles. The twistgrip should return automatically from fully open to fully closed when released.

2 If the throttle sticks, this is probably due to a cable fault. Remove the cables (see Chapter 4) and lubricate them (see Section 4). If the inner cables still do not run smoothly in the outer cables, renew the cables.

3 With the cables removed, check that the twistgrip turns smoothly around the handlebar – dirt combined with a lack of lubrication can cause the action to be stiff. Clean and lightly grease the twistgrip pulley and the inside of the twistgrip housing. Install the lubricated or new cables, making sure they are correctly routed (see Chapter 4). If this fails to improve the operation of the throttle, the fault could lie in the carburettors. Remove them and check the action of the throttle linkage and butterflies (see Chapter 4).

4 With the throttle operating smoothly, check for a small amount of freeplay in the cables, measured in terms of the amount of twistgrip rotation before the throttle opens, and compare the amount to that listed in this Chapter's Specifications **(see illustration)**. If it is incorrect, adjust the cables.

1

6.4 Throttle cable freeplay is measured in terms of twistgrip rotation

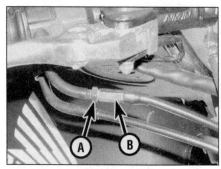

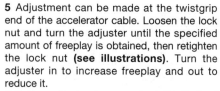

6.5a Loosen locknut (A) and turn adjuster (B)

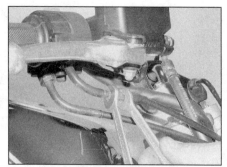

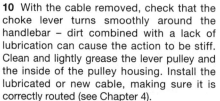

6.5b Tighten locknut against the adjuster when freeplay is satisfactory

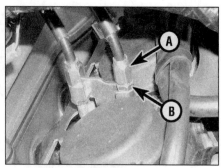

6.7 Throttle cable adjuster (A) and locknut (B) at the carburettor end

5 Adjustment can be made at the twistgrip end of the accelerator cable. Loosen the lock nut and turn the adjuster until the specified amount of freeplay is obtained, then retighten the lock nut (see illustrations). Turn the adjuster in to increase freeplay and out to reduce it.

6 If the adjuster has reached its limit of adjustment, reset it so that the freeplay is at a maximum, then adjust the cable at the carburettor end as follows. Remove the fuel tank (see Chapter 4).

7 Loosen the lock nut on the accelerator cable adjuster and turn the adjuster nut until the specified amount of freeplay is obtained, then tighten the lock nut (see illustration). Further adjustments can now be made at the twistgrip (see Step 5). If the cable cannot be adjusted as specified, renew the cable (see Chapter 4).

 Warning: Turn the handlebars all the way through their travel with the engine idling. Idle speed should not change. If it does, the cables may be routed incorrectly. Correct this condition before riding the motorcycle.

8 Check that the throttle twistgrip operates smoothly and snaps shut quickly when released.

Choke cable

9 If the choke does not operate smoothly this is probably due to a cable fault. Remove the cable (see Chapter 4) and lubricate it (see Section 4). If the inner cable still does not run smoothly in the outer cable, renew the cable.

10 With the cable removed, check that the choke lever turns smoothly around the handlebar – dirt combined with a lack of lubrication can cause the action to be stiff. Clean and lightly grease the lever pulley and the inside of the pulley housing. Install the lubricated or new cable, making sure it is correctly routed (see Chapter 4).

11 If this fails to improve the operation of the choke, the fault could lie in the carburettors, necessitating their removal and inspection of the choke plungers (see Chapter 4).

12 Make sure there is a small amount of freeplay in the cable before the plungers move. If there isn't, check that the cable is correctly installed at both ends.

13 Remove the fuel tank (see Chapter 4) to access the carburettor end of the cable.

7 Spark plugs – check and adjustment

1 Make sure your spark plug socket is the correct size (16 mm) before attempting to remove the plugs – a special plug spanner is supplied in the motorcycle's tool kit which is stored under the seat. Remove the fuel tank (see Chapter 4).

2 Disconnect the spark plug caps from the spark plugs. Note the plug leads are numbered to aid reassembly. If the numbers are not visible, mark the leads to ensure they are connected to the correct plugs on reassembly. Using compressed air if

available, clean the area around the base of the spark plugs to prevent any dirt falling into the engine when the plugs are removed.

3 Unscrew the plugs from the cylinder head with either a plug spanner or a deep socket type wrench (see illustration). Lay each plug out in relation to its cylinder so that, if any plug shows up a problem, it will be easy to identify the troublesome cylinder.

4 Inspect the electrodes for wear. Both the centre and side electrodes should have square edges and the side electrodes should be of uniform thickness. Look for excessive deposits and evidence of a cracked or chipped insulator around the centre electrode. Compare your spark plugs to the colour spark plug reading chart at the end of this manual. Check the threads, the washer and the ceramic insulator body for cracks and other damage.

5 If the electrodes are not excessively worn, and if the deposits can be easily removed with a wire brush, and there are no cracks or chips visible in the insulator, the plugs can be re-gapped and re-used. If in doubt concerning the condition of the plugs, replace them with new ones, as the expense is minimal. Note that the spark plugs should be renewed every 16,000 miles (24,000 km).

6 Cleaning spark plugs by sandblasting is permitted, provided you clean the plugs with a high flash-point solvent afterwards.

7 Before installing the plugs, make sure they are the correct type and heat range and check the gap between the electrodes (see illustrations). Compare the gap to that

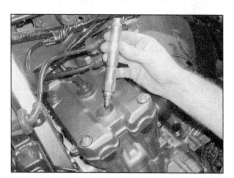

7.3 Removing the spark plug using the Honda socket

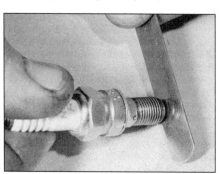

7.7a Using a feeler gauge to measure the spark plug electrode gap

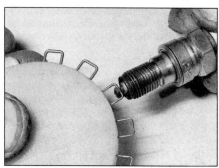

7.7b Using a wire gauge to measure the spark plug electrode gap

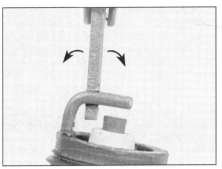

7.7c Using a feeler gauge to measure the spark plug electrode gap

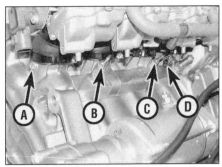

8.4 Intake manifold blanking plug (A), fuel tap hose connection (B), PAIR hose connection (C) and blanking cap (D)

8.8 Carburettor synchronising screw (arrowed)

specified and adjust as necessary. If the gap must be adjusted, bend the side electrodes only and be very careful not to chip or crack the insulator nose (see illustration). Make sure the sealing washer is in place on the plug before installing it.

8 Since the cylinder head is made of aluminium, which is soft and easily damaged, thread the plugs into the head and turn the tool by hand. Once the plugs are finger-tight, the job can be finished with a spanner on the tool supplied or a socket drive. If a torque wrench is available, tighten the spark plugs to the torque setting specified at the beginning of this Chapter. Otherwise tighten them by 1/4 to 1/2 turn after they have been fully hand tightened and have seated. Do not over-tighten them.

 HAYNES HINT *As the plugs are quite recessed, you can slip a short length of hose over the end of the plug to use as a tool to thread it into place. The hose will grip the plug well enough to turn it, but will start to slip if the plug begins to cross-thread in the hole – this will prevent damaged threads.*

9 Install the spark plug caps then install the remaining components in the reverse order of removal.

 HAYNES HINT *Stripped plug threads in the cylinder head can be repaired with a thread insert – see Section 2 of 'Tools and Workshop Tips' in the Reference section.*

8 Carburettors – synchronisation

> ⚠ Warning: Petrol (gasoline) is extremely flammable, so take extra precautions when you work on any part of the fuel

system. Don't smoke or allow open flames or bare light bulbs near the work area, and don't work in a garage where a natural gas-type appliance is present. If you spill any fuel on your skin, rinse it off immediately with soap and water. When you perform any kind of work on the fuel system, wear safety glasses and have a fire extinguisher suitable for a Class B type fire (flammable liquids) on hand.

> ⚠ Warning: Take great care not to burn your hand on the hot engine unit when accessing the gauge take-off points on the intake manifolds. Do not allow exhaust gases to build up in the work area; either perform the check outside or use an exhaust gas extraction system.

1 Carburettor synchronisation is simply the process of adjusting the carburettors so that they pass the same amount of fuel/air mixture to each cylinder. This is done by measuring the vacuum produced in each cylinder. Carburettors that are out of synchronisation will result in decreased fuel mileage, increased engine temperature, less than ideal throttle response and higher vibration levels. Before synchronising the carburettors, make sure that the idle speed is correctly adjusted.

2 To synchronise the carburettors you will need a set of vacuum gauges or a manometer (see Tools and Workshop Tips in the Reference section). These instruments measure engine vacuum, and can be obtained from motorcycle dealers or mail order parts suppliers. The equipment used should be suitable for a four cylinder engine and come complete with the necessary adapters and hoses to fit the take-off points. Note: Because of the nature of the synchronisation procedure and the need for special instruments, most owners leave the task to a Honda dealer.

3 Start the engine and let it run until it reaches normal operating temperature, then shut it off. Remove the fuel tank (see Chapter 4).

4 Remove the blanking plug and washer from the No. 1 intake manifold. Disconnect the fuel tap vacuum hose from the No. 2 intake manifold and the PAIR control valve vacuum hose from the No. 3 intake manifold. Remove the blanking cap from the No. 4 intake manifold (see illustration).

5 Install the intake manifold adapters and connect the appropriate vacuum gauge or manometer hoses. Make sure the No. 1 gauge is attached to the No. 1 (left-hand) intake manifold, and so on. Arrange a temporary fuel supply using an auxiliary tank and some hosing.

6 Start the engine and let it idle; if necessary, adjust the idle speed (see Section 2). If the gauges are fitted with damping adjustment, set this so that the needle flutter is just eliminated but so that they can still respond to small changes in pressure.

7 The vacuum readings for all cylinders should be the same, using the No. 3 carburettor as the base carburettor (see the Specifications at the beginning of this Chapter). If the vacuum readings differ, proceed as follows.

8 The carburettors are adjusted by turning the synchronising screws situated in between each carburettor in the throttle linkage (see illustration). Note: Do not press on the screws whilst adjusting them, otherwise a false reading will be obtained. Adjust each carburettor in turn so that its vacuum reading matches the reading of the No. 3 cylinder. Note: There is no adjusting screw for the No. 3 carburettor.

9 When all the carburettors are synchronised, open and close the throttle quickly to settle the linkage, and recheck the gauge readings, readjusting if necessary.

10 When the adjustment is complete, check the idle speed (see Section 2), and check the throttle cable freeplay (see Section 6). Remove the gauges and the manifold adapters and refit the vacuum hoses and the hose clips and the blanking plugs (see Step 4). Detach the temporary fuel supply and install the fuel tank (see Chapter 4).

9 Fuel hose – check and renewal

> ⚠ Warning: Petrol (gasoline) is extremely flammable, so take extra precautions when you work on any part of the fuel

 1

9.1 Check the joints between the fuel hose and the carburettors (arrowed)

9.6 Ensure the clip (arrowed) is properly installed when fitting a fuel hose

system. Don't smoke or allow open flames or bare light bulbs near the work area, and don't work in a garage where a natural gas-type appliance is present. If you spill any fuel on your skin, rinse it off immediately with soap and water. When you perform any kind of work on the fuel system, wear safety glasses and have a fire extinguisher suitable for a Class B type fire (flammable liquids) on hand.

1 Remove the fuel tank (see Chapter 4) and check the tank, the fuel tap, the fuel hose and the fuel tap vacuum hose for signs of leakage, deterioration or damage. In particular check that there is no leakage from the fuel hose where it is connected to the carburettors **(see illustration)**. Renew any hoses that are cracked or deteriorated (see Step 5).

2 If the fuel tap to tank joint is leaking, tightening the retaining nut may help. Hold the tap to prevent it twisting while tightening the nut. If leakage persists, remove the tap and renew the O-ring (see Chapter 4).

3 If the tap appears blocked, first check the operation of the tap diaphragm and then the fuel strainer (see Chapter 4).

4 If the carburettor gaskets are leaking, the carburettors should be disassembled and rebuilt using new gaskets and seals (see Chapter 4).

5 To renew the hoses, disconnect the fuel hose from the fuel tap and from the carburettor joint pipe and the vacuum hose from the tap and the no.2 cylinder intake manifold, noting the routing of each hose (see Chapter 4 if required). If necessary, make a

sketch of the hoses before removing them, to ensure they are correctly installed.

6 Secure each new hose to its unions using new clips **(see illustration)**. Run the engine and check the operation of the vacuum tap and that there are no fuel leaks before taking the machine out on the road.

10 Cooling system – check

⚠ *Warning: The engine must be cool before beginning this procedure.*

1 Check the coolant level (see *Daily (pre-ride) checks*).

2 The entire cooling system should be checked for evidence of leakage. Remove the fuel tank (see Chapter 4) and examine each coolant hose along its entire length. Look for splits, abrasions and other signs of deterioration. Squeeze each hose at various points. They should feel firm, yet pliable, and return to their original shape when released. If they are cracked or hard, replace them with new ones.

3 Check for evidence of leaks at each cooling system joint. If necessary, tighten the hose clips carefully to prevent future leaks.

4 Examine the hoses to the oil cooler and the coolant reservoir for damage and signs of deterioration. Ensure that the hose clips are secure and that there are no signs of leakage at the oil cooler to crankcase joint.

5 To prevent leakage of water from the cooling system to the lubrication system a mechanical seal is fitted on the water pump shaft inside the pump body. If the seal fails, a drain hole in the underside of the pump body allows the coolant to escape **(see illustration)**. Look for telltale signs of leakage around the drain hole.

6 If the mechanical seal has failed the water pump will have to be replaced with a new one (see Chapter 3).

7 Check the radiator for leaks and other damage. Leaks in the radiator leave tell-tale scale deposits or coolant stains on the outside of the core below the leak. If leaks are noted, remove the radiator (see Chapter 3) and have it repaired by a specialist.
Caution: Do not use a liquid leak stopping compound to try to repair leaks.

8 Check the radiator fins for mud, dirt and insects, which may impede the flow of air through the radiator. If the fins are dirty, remove the radiator (see Chapter 3) and clean it, using water or low pressure compressed air directed through the fins from the back. If the fins are bent or distorted, straighten them carefully with a screwdriver. Bent or damaged fins will restrict the air flow and impair the efficiency of the radiator causing the engine to overheat. Where there is substantial damage to the radiator's surface area, renew the radiator.

9 Remove the locking screw from the radiator pressure cap, then cover the pressure cap with a heavy cloth and remove the cap by turning it slowly anti-clockwise **(see illustration)**. If you hear a hissing sound (indicating that there is still pressure in the system), wait until it stops, then continue turning the cap until it can be removed.

10 Check the condition of the coolant in the system. If it is rust-coloured or if accumulations of scale are visible, drain, flush and refill the system with new coolant (see Section 25). Check the cap seal for cracks and other damage. If in doubt about the pressure cap's condition, have it tested by a Honda dealer or replace it with a new one.

11 Check the antifreeze content of the coolant with an antifreeze hydrometer. Sometimes coolant looks like it's in good condition, but might be too weak to offer adequate protection. If the hydrometer indicates a weak mixture, drain, flush and refill the system (see Section 25). A mixture with less than 40% antifreeze (40/60 antifreeze to distilled water) will not provide proper corrosion protection. A higher than specified concentration of antifreeze decreases the performance of the cooling system and should only be used when additional protection against freezing is needed.

12 Install the cap by aligning the tabs on the cap with the slots in the filler neck and turning

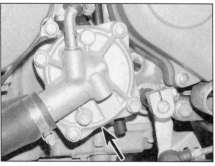

10.5 Check for signs of coolant leakage underneath the water pump

10.9 Radiator cap is retained by a locking screw

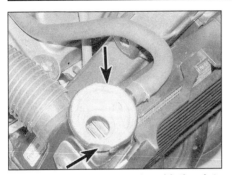

10.12 Align radiator cap tabs with the slots (arrowed)

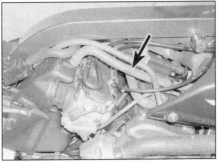

11.2a Check the condition of the PAIR hose (arrowed) from the air filter housing . . .

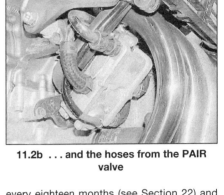

11.2b . . . and the hoses from the PAIR valve

the cap clockwise until it will turn no further **(see illustration)**. Install the locking screw.

13 Install the fuel tank and start the engine and let it reach normal operating temperature, then check for leaks again. As the coolant temperature increases beyond normal, the fan should come on automatically and the temperature should begin to drop. If it does not, refer to Chapter 3 and check the fan switch, fan motor and fan circuit carefully.

14 If the coolant level is consistently low, and no evidence of leaks can be found, have the entire system pressure-checked by a Honda dealer.

11 Pulse secondary air system (PAIR) hoses – check

1 If the valves clearances are all correct and the carburettors have been synchronised and have no other faults, but the idle speed cannot be set properly, it is possible that the pulse secondary air injection (PAIR) system is faulty. Information on the function of the system is in Chapter 4.

2 Remove the fuel tank (see Chapter 4). Check the air supply hose from the air filter housing to the PAIR valve at the front of the engine unit **(see illustration)**, and also the small diameter vacuum hose from the intake manifold to the PAIR valve. Check the hoses and metal pipes from the PAIR valve to the exhaust ports for signs of deterioration or damage **(see illustration)**. Check that the

hoses are all securely connected and clamped at each end. Renew any hoses which are cracked or deteriorated (see Chapter 4).

3 Check that the metal pipes are securely fixed to the exhaust ports and that there is no sign of gas leakage around the pipe flanges. Renew the pipe flange gaskets if necessary (see Chapter 4).

4 Check the PAIR valve assembly at the front of the engine for signs of physical damage and replace it with a new one if necessary (see Chapter 4).

12 Brake system – check

1 A routine general check of the brake system will ensure that any problems are discovered and remedied before the rider's safety is jeopardised.

2 Check the brake lever and pedal for looseness, improper or rough action, excessive play, bends, and other damage. Replace any damaged parts with new ones (see Chapter 7). Clean and lubricate the lever and pedal pivots if their action is stiff or rough (see Section 4).

3 Make sure all brake fasteners are tight. Check the brake pads for wear (see Section 3) and make sure the fluid level in the reservoirs is correct (see *Daily (pre-ride) checks*). Look for leaks at the hose connections and check for cracks in the hoses themselves. If the lever or pedal is spongy, bleed the brakes (see Chapter 7). The brake fluid should be changed

every eighteen months (see Section 22) and the hoses renewed if they deteriorate, or every four years irrespective of their condition (see Chapter 7). The master cylinder and caliper seals should be renewed every four years, or if leakage from them is evident (see Chapter 7).

4 Make sure the brake light operates when the front brake lever is pulled in. The front brake light switch, mounted on the underside of the master cylinder, is not adjustable. If it fails to operate properly, check it (see Chapter 9).

5 Make sure the brake light is activated just before the rear brake takes effect. If adjustment is necessary, hold the switch and turn the adjuster sleeve on the switch body until the brake light is activated when required **(see illustration)**. If the brake light comes on too late, turn the sleeve clockwise. If the brake light comes on too soon or is permanently on, turn the sleeve anti-clockwise. If the switch doesn't operate the brake light, check the switch and the electrical system (see Chapter 9).

6 The front brake lever has a span adjuster which alters the distance of the lever from the handlebar. Turn the adjuster forwards to increase the distance and backwards to reduce the distance **(see illustration)**. Ensure the index mark on the adjuster is aligned with the arrow on the lever when adjustment is complete.

7 Check the position of the brake pedal (brake pedal height). To adjust the pedal height, first disconnect the pedal from the master cylinder pushrod (see Chapter 7, Section 9). Loosen the locknut on the master cylinder pushrod clevis, then turn the clevis until the pedal is at the desired height **(see illustration)**. On

1

12.5 Rear brake light switch adjuster sleeve (arrowed)

12.6 Front brake lever span adjuster (arrowed)

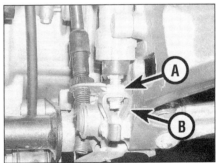

12.7 Rear brake master cylinder pushrod locknut (A) and clevis (B)

13.2 Alignment marks on the headlight shell (A) and bracket (B)

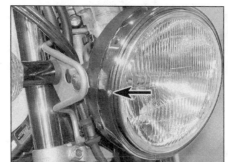

13.3 CB600F headlight adjuster screw (arrowed)

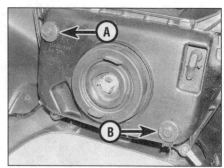

13.4 CB600FS vertical headlight adjuster screw (A) and horizontal headlight adjuster screw (B)

completion tighten the locknut securely. Check the operation of the rear brake light switch after adjusting the pedal height (see Step 5).

13 Headlight aim –
check and adjustment

Note: *An improperly adjusted headlight may cause problems for oncoming traffic or provide poor, unsafe illumination of the road ahead. Before adjusting the headlight aim, be sure to consult with local traffic laws and regulations – for UK models refer to MOT Test Checks in the Reference section.*

1 The headlight beam can be adjusted both horizontally and vertically. Before making any adjustment, check that the tyre pressures are correct and the suspension is adjusted as required. Make any adjustments to the headlight aim with the motorcycle on level ground, with the fuel tank half full and with an assistant sitting on the seat. If the bike is usually ridden with a passenger on the back, have a second assistant to do this. Always check the operation of the headlight after making adjustments.

CB600F models

2 Vertical adjustment is made by slackening the headlight mounting bolts and tilting the headlight shell up or down as required. A midway setting is achieved by aligning the

index marks on the headlight brackets with the lines moulded in the headlight shell **(see illustration)**. Tighten the bolts securely after the adjustment has been made.

3 Horizontal adjustment is made by turning the adjuster screw on the left-hand side of the headlight rim **(see illustration)**. Turn the screw clockwise to move the beam to the right, and anti-clockwise to move it to the left.

CB600FS models

4 Vertical adjustment is made by turning the adjuster screw on the upper left-hand side of the headlight unit **(see illustration)**. Turn it clockwise to move the beam up, and anti-clockwise to move it down.

5 Horizontal adjustment is made by turning the adjuster screw on the lower right-hand side of the headlight unit **(see illustration 13.4)**. Turn it clockwise to move the beam to the right, and anti-clockwise to move it to the left.

14 Clutch –
check and adjustment

1 Check that the clutch lever operates smoothly and easily.

2 If the lever action is heavy or stiff, remove the cable (see Chapter 2) and lubricate it (see Section 4). If the inner cable still does not run smoothly in the outer cable, replace the cable

with a new one. Install the lubricated or new cable (see Chapter 2).

3 If the lever itself is stiff, remove the lever from its bracket (see Chapter 6) and check for damage or distortion, or any other cause, and remedy as necessary. Clean and lubricate the pivot and contact areas (see Section 4).

4 If the lever and cable are good, refer to Chapter 2 and check the release mechanism in the clutch cover and the clutch itself.

5 With the clutch operating smoothly, check that the clutch lever is correctly adjusted. Periodic adjustment is necessary to compensate for wear in the clutch plates and stretch of the cable. Check that the amount of freeplay at the clutch lever end is within the specifications listed at the beginning of this Chapter **(see illustration)**.

6 If adjustment is required, loosen he lockring and turn the adjuster in or out until the required amount of freeplay is obtained **(see illustration)**. To increase freeplay, turn the adjuster clockwise (into the lever bracket). To reduce freeplay, turn the adjuster anti-clockwise (out of the lever bracket). Tighten the locking ring securely.

7 If all the adjustment has been taken up at the lever, reset the adjuster to give the maximum amount of freeplay, then set the correct amount of freeplay using the adjuster on the lower end of the cable in the bracket on the right-hand side of the engine unit.

8 Loosen the locknut, then turn the adjuster nut as required to obtain the correct freeplay **(see illustration)**. When the correct amount of

14.5 Measuring clutch lever freeplay

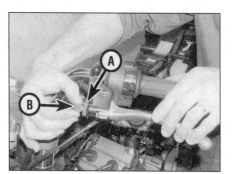

14.6 Loosen the lockring (A) and turn the adjuster (B) as required

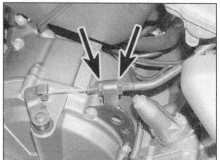

14.8 Clutch cable adjuster and locknuts (arrowed)

freeplay has been achieved, hold the adjuster nut and tighten the locknut.

9 Subsequent adjustments can now be made using the clutch lever adjuster.

15 Sidestand and sidestand switch – check

1 The stand return spring must be capable of retracting the stand fully and holding it retracted when the motorcycle is in use. If a spring has sagged or broken, it must be replaced with a new one.

2 Lubricate the stand pivot regularly (see Section 4).

3 The sidestand switch prevents the motorcycle being started if the transmission is in gear and the stand is down, and cuts the engine if the stand is put down while the engine is running and in gear.

4 Check the operation of the switch by shifting the transmission into neutral, retracting the stand and starting the engine. Pull in the clutch lever and select a gear. Extend the sidestand. The engine should stop as the sidestand is extended. If the sidestand switch does not operate as described, check its circuit (see Chapter 9).

16 Drive chain slider – check and renewal

Check

1 Remove the front sprocket cover (see Chapter 6). Inspect the drive chain slider above and below the swingarm for wear and damage. Clean the slider to check the wear at the wear indicator arrow **(see illustration)**.

Renewal

2 Remove front sprocket (see Chapter 6).

3 Undo the bolts and collars securing the slider to the swingarm, then prise the pegs on the slider out of the locating holes in the swingarm. Pull the slider forward and remove it from the machine. Note how the slider locates on the peg on the forward edge of the swingarm.

4 Installation is the reverse of removal, tightening the bolts to the specified torque (see Specifications).

17 Suspension – check

1 The suspension components must be maintained in top operating condition to ensure rider safety. Loose, worn or damaged suspension parts decrease the motorcycle's stability and control.

Front suspension

2 While standing alongside the motorcycle, apply the front brake and push on the handlebars to compress the forks several times. See if they move up and down smoothly without binding. If binding is felt, the forks should be disassembled and inspected (see Chapter 6).

3 Inspect the fork tubes for signs of scratches, corrosion and pitting, and oil leakage. Carefully lever up the dust seals using a flat-bladed screwdriver and inspect the area around the fork seals (see Chapter 6). Any scratches, corrosion and pitting will cause premature seal failure. If the damage is excessive, new tubes should be installed (see Chapter 6). If oil leakage is evident, new seals must be fitted (see Chapter 6).

4 Check the tightness of all suspension nuts and bolts to be sure none have worked loose, referring to the torque settings specified at the beginning of Chapter 6.

Rear suspension

5 Inspect the rear shock for fluid leakage and tightness of its mountings. If leakage is found,

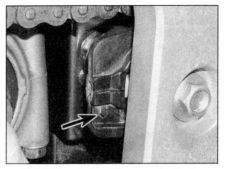

16.1 Drive chain slider wear indicator (arrowed)

a new shock should be installed (see Chapter 6).

6 With the aid of an assistant to support the bike, compress the rear suspension several times. It should move up and down freely without binding. If any binding is felt, the worn or faulty component must be identified and renewed. The problem could be due to either the shock absorber or the swingarm components.

7 Support the motorcycle using an auxiliary stand so that the rear wheel is off the ground. Grasp the swingarm and rock it from side to side – there should be no discernible movement at the rear **(see illustration)**. If there is a little movement or a slight clicking can be heard, inspect the tightness of all the rear suspension mounting bolts and nuts, referring to the torque settings specified at the beginning of Chapter 6, and re-check for movement.

8 Next, grasp the top of the rear wheel and pull it upwards – there should be no discernible freeplay before the shock absorber begins to compress **(see illustration)**. Any freeplay felt in either check indicates worn bearings in the swingarm or shock absorber mountings. The worn components must be renewed (see Chapter 6).

9 To make an accurate assessment of the swingarm bearings it is necessary to remove

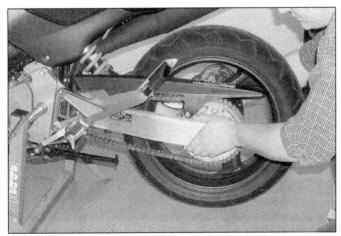

17.7 Checking for play in the swingarm bearings

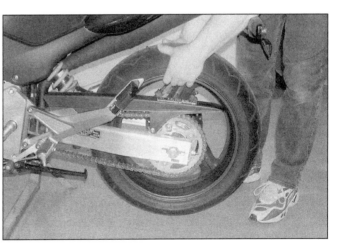

17.8 Checking for play in the shock absorber mounts

17.10 Rear shock absorber spring seat location (arrowed)

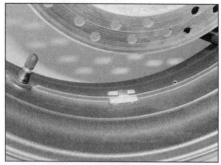

18.2 Check that any wheel balance weights are firmly attached

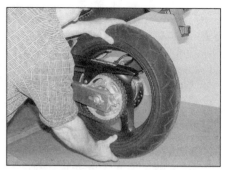

18.5 Checking for play in the wheel bearings

the rear wheel (see Chapter 7) and the bolt securing the shock absorber to the swingarm (see Chapter 6). Grasp the rear of the swingarm with one hand and place your other hand at the junction of the swingarm and the frame. Try to move the rear of the swingarm from side to side. Any wear (play) in the bearings should be felt as movement between the swingarm and the frame at the front. If there is any play, the swingarm will be felt to move forward and backward at the front (not from side-to-side). Next, move the swingarm up and down through its full travel. It should move freely, without any binding or rough spots. If any play in the swingarm is noted or if the swingarm does not move freely, the bearings must be removed for inspection or renewal (see Chapter 6).

10 The rear shock is adjustable for spring pre-load. Ensure that the spring seat is correctly located on the adjustment stopper **(see illustration)**. See Chapter 6 for shock adjustment.

18 Tyres and wheels –
general check

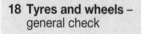

Tyres

1 Check the tyre condition and tread depth thoroughly – see *Daily (pre-ride) checks*.
2 Check the valve rubber for signs of damage or deterioration and have it renewed if necessary. Also, make sure the valve cap is in place and tight. Check that any wheel balance weights are fixed firmly to the wheel rim **(see illustration)**. If the weights have fallen off, have the wheel rebalanced by a motorcycle tyre specialist.

Wheels

3 Cast wheels are virtually maintenance free, but they should be kept clean and checked periodically for cracks and other damage. Also check the wheel runout and alignment (see Chapter 7). Never attempt to repair damaged cast wheels; they must be replaced with new ones.

4 Wheel bearings will wear over a period of time and result in handling problems.
5 Support the motorcycle upright using an auxiliary stand. Check for any play in the bearings by pushing and pulling the wheel against the hub **(see illustration)**. Also rotate the wheel and check that it turns smoothly.
6 If any play is detected in the hub, or if the wheel does not rotate smoothly (and this is not due to brake or transmission drag), the wheel bearings must be removed and inspected for wear or damage (see Chapter 7).

19 Steering head bearings –
check and adjustment

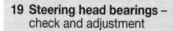

1 This motorcycle is equipped with caged ball steering head bearings which can become dented, rough or loose during normal use of the machine. In extreme cases, worn or loose steering head bearings can cause steering wobble – a condition that is potentially dangerous.

Check

2 Support the motorcycle in an upright position using an auxiliary stand with all the weight of the motorcycle off the front forks.
3 Point the front wheel straight ahead, and slowly turn the handlebars from side to side. Any dents or roughness in the bearing races

19.4 Checking for play in the steering head bearings

will be felt and if the bearings are too tight the bars will not move smoothly and freely. If the bearings are damaged or the action is rough, they should be renewed (see Chapter 6). If the bearings are too tight they should be adjusted as described below.
4 Next, grasp the fork sliders and try to pull and push them forwards and backwards **(see illustration)**. Any looseness in the steering head bearings will be felt as front-to-rear movement of the forks. If play is felt in the bearings, adjust them as follows.

> **HAYNES HINT**
> *Freeplay in the fork due to worn fork bushes can be misinterpreted as steering head bearing play – do not confuse the two.*

Adjustment

5 Position the motorcycle in an upright position using an auxiliary stand with all the weight of the motorcycle off the front forks. Remove the fuel tank (see Chapter 4) and, on CB600FS models, the fairing (see Chapter 8). **Note:** *Although it is not strictly necessary to remove the fuel tank and fairing, doing so will prevent the possibility of damage, should a tool slip.*
6 Displace the handlebars (see Chapter 6) and loosen the fork clamp bolts in the top yoke **(see illustration)**.
7 Unscrew the steering stem nut and remove

19.6 Loosen the top yoke fork clamp bolts

19.7a Remove the steering stem nut . . .

19.7b . . . and washer . . .

19.7c . . . then remove the top yoke

it along with its washer **(see illustrations)**, then ease the top yoke off the fork tubes and position it clear of the steering head **(see illustration)**. If necessary, use a rag to protect other components. **Note:** *On CB600F models the instrument assembly is attached to the top yoke. Ensure no strain is placed on the instrument wiring.*

8 Prise the lockwasher tabs out of the notches in the locknut, unscrew the locknut using either a C-spanner or a suitable drift located in one of the notches, and remove the lockwasher. Discard the lockwasher as a new one must be fitted on reassembly.

9 To adjust the bearings as specified by Honda, a special service tool (Pt. No. 07916-3710101) and a torque wrench are required. If the tool is available, first slacken the adjuster nut slightly to take pressure off the bearing, then tighten the nut to the torque setting

specified at the beginning of this Chapter. Turn the steering from lock to lock five times to settle the bearings, then recheck the torque setting. The object is to set the adjuster nut so that the bearings are under a very light loading, just enough to remove any freeplay.

10 If the Honda tool is not available, using either a C-spanner, pin spanner or a drift located in one of the notches, slacken the adjuster nut slightly to take pressure off the bearing then tighten the nut until all freeplay is removed **(see illustration)**. Now tighten the nut a little more to pre-load the bearings. Now slacken the nut and retighten it, setting it so that all freeplay is just removed from the bearings, yet the steering is able to move freely from side to side. Tighten the nut only a little at a time and after each adjustment repeat the checks outlined in Steps 3 and 4.

Caution: Take great care not to apply excessive pressure because this will cause premature failure of the bearings.
Note: Bearing preload can be checked using a spring scale (spring balance). Attach the spring scale to one fork leg and position the forks straight ahead. Ensure that the cables and wiring will not interfere with the forks turning, then pull the balance to turn the forks. The forks should start to move when a loading of 0.10 to 0.15 kg registers on the scale.

11 When the bearings are correctly adjusted, install the lockwasher onto the adjuster nut and bend two of the washer tabs down into the slots in the adjuster nut **(see illustrations)**.

12 Install the locknut and tighten it finger-tight, then tighten it further (to a maximum of 90°) to align the slots in the locknut with the remaining tabs on the lockwasher **(see illustration)**. Hold the adjuster nut to prevent it from moving if necessary. Bend the remaining lockwasher tabs up to secure the locknut **(see illustration)**.

13 Fit the top yoke onto the steering stem and the fork legs. On CB600F models, ensure that the headlamp bracket is correctly located in the underside of the top yoke. Install the washer and steering stem nut and tighten it and the fork clamp bolts to the torque settings specified at the beginning of this Chapter.

14 Install the handlebars (see Chapter 6).

15 Check the bearing adjustment as described above and re-adjust if necessary.

19.10 Tighten the adjuster nut carefully to remove freeplay

19.11a Fit the lockwasher . . .

19.11b . . . with two tabs in the slots on the adjuster nut (arrowed)

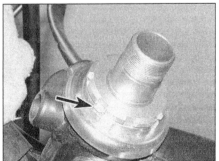

19.12a Align the locknut with the lockwasher tabs (arrowed) . . .

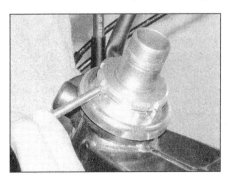

19.12b . . . and bend the tabs to secure the locknut

1

20 Nuts and bolts – tightness check

1 Since vibration of the machine tends to loosen fasteners, all nuts, bolts, screws, etc. should be periodically checked for proper tightness.

2 Pay particular attention to the following:
Spark plugs
Engine oil drain plug
Gearchange lever, brake and clutch lever, and brake pedal mounting bolts
Footrest and stand bolts
Engine mounting bolts
Shock absorber and swingarm pivot bolts
Handlebar clamp bolts
Front axle nut and axle clamp bolts
Front fork clamp bolts (top and bottom yoke)
Rear axle nut
Brake caliper mounting bolts
Brake hose banjo bolts and caliper bleed valves
Brake disc bolts
Exhaust system bolts/nuts

3 If a torque wrench is available, use it along with the torque specifications at the beginning of this and other Chapters.

Every 12,000 miles (18,000 km) or 18 months (whichever comes sooner)

Carry out all the items under the 4000 mile (6000 km) check, plus the following:

21 Air filter – renewal

Air filter

Note: If the machine is continually ridden in dusty conditions, the filter should be cleaned more frequently than specified.

1 Remove the left-hand side cover (see Chapter 8).

2 Remove the screws securing the air filter housing cover, then remove the cover and withdraw the filter element **(see illustrations)**. The element cannot be cleaned and must be replaced with a new one.

3 Inspect the inside of the filter housing and clean out any dust or dirt particles. Check the air intake passage in the housing cover and the housing drain tube for obstructions. Check the secondary air intake port for carbon deposits (see Section 11).

4 Install the new filter element, then install the cover and tighten the cover screws carefully to avoid damaging the screw threads.

5 Inspect the drain valve on the lower left-hand side of the air filter housing **(see illustration)**. Pinch the sides of the valve between your fingers to release any trapped moisture. If required, release the clip securing the valve to the housing and remove the valve for cleaning.

Sub-air cleaner

Note: *There is no specific interval for cleaning the filter, but it should be inspected periodically to ensure the carburettor air vent system is clear.*

6 Remove the fuel tank (see Chapter 4). Release the clip securing the sub-air cleaner hose to the right-hand rear face of the air filter housing and detach the clips securing the two halves of the sub-air cleaner **(see illustrations)**. Remove the sub-air cleaner element from its housing and wash the element in warm, soapy water. Rinse the element in clean water and dry before refitting. If the element is damaged or shows signs of deterioration, fit a new one.

7 Install the fuel tank (see Chapter 4).

22 Brakes – fluid change

1 The brake fluid should be changed at the prescribed interval or whenever a master cylinder or caliper overhaul is carried out. Refer to the brake bleeding section in Chapter 7. Ensure that all old fluid is pumped from the hydraulic system and that the level in the fluid reservoir is checked and the brakes tested before riding the motorcycle.

> **HAYNES HiNT**
> *Old brake fluid is invariably much darker in colour than new fluid, making it easy to see when all old fluid has been expelled from the system.*

21.2a Undo the air filter housing cover screws (arrowed) . . .

21.2b . . . and withdraw the filter element

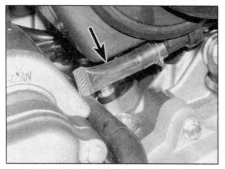

21.5 Air filter housing drain valve (arrowed)

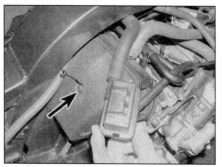

21.6a Release the sub-air cleaner housing from its clip (arrowed)

21.6b Open the housing to inspect the element

Every 16,000 miles (24,000 km) or two years (whichever comes sooner)

Carry out all the items under the 4000 mile (6000 km) and 8000 mile (12,000 km) checks, plus the following:

23 Spark plugs – renewal

1 Renew the spark plugs irrespective of their apparent condition (see Section 7).

24 Valve clearances – check and adjustment

1 The engine must be completely cool for this maintenance procedure, so let the machine sit overnight before beginning.
2 Remove the fuel tank (see Chapter 4).
3 Remove the valve cover (see Chapter 2). Each cylinder is referred to by a number. They are numbered 1 to 4 from left to right, viewed as normally seated on the bike.
4 Make a chart or sketch of all valve positions so that a note of each clearance can be made against the relevant valve.
5 Referring to Chapter 2, Section 8, remove the centre bolt and sealing washer from the end of the cam chain tensioner body **(see illustration)** and retract the tensioner plunger to release all tension on the cam chain **(see illustration)**. This procedure ensures that the valve clearances are measured with the oil clearance between the camshafts and their holders taken up.
6 Remove the centre cap from the ignition rotor cover on the right-hand side of the engine **(see illustration)**. To turn the engine in a clockwise direction only, use a spanner on the ignition rotor bolt. Alternatively, to turn the engine in either direction, place the motorcycle on an auxiliary stand so that the rear wheel is off the ground, select a high gear and rotate the rear wheel by hand.
7 Turn the engine clockwise until the 'T' mark

on the timing rotor aligns with the index mark on the rotor cover **(see illustration)**. The 'IN' timing mark on the intake camshaft sprocket and the 'EX' mark on the exhaust camshaft sprocket should align the cylinder head surface with each mark on the outside of its respective sprocket **(see illustration)**. If the timing marks are on the inside of their respective sprockets, turn the engine one full turn (360°) clockwise until the 'T' mark on the alternator rotor again aligns with the index mark. The marks on the camshaft sprockets should now align correctly with the cylinder head surface.
8 Check the clearances on the No. 1 and No. 3 cylinder *intake* valves. Insert a feeler gauge of the same thickness as the correct valve

clearance (see Specifications) between the camshaft lobe and follower of each valve and check that it is a firm sliding fit – you should feel a slight drag when the you pull the gauge out **(see illustration)**. If not, use the feeler gauges to obtain the exact clearance. Record the measured clearance on your chart.
9 Now turn the engine clockwise 180° (half a turn) so that the line on the timing rotor points straight up **(see illustration)**. Check the clearances on the No. 2 and No. 4 cylinder *exhaust* valves using a feeler gauge of the correct valve clearance (see Specifications). If the feeler gauge is not a firm, sliding fit, use the gauges to obtain the exact clearance. Record the measured clearance on your

24.5a Remove the cam chain tensioner centre bolt and washer (arrowed)

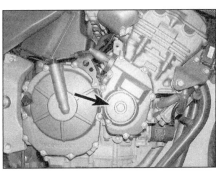

24.6 Unscrew the ignition rotor centre cap (arrowed)

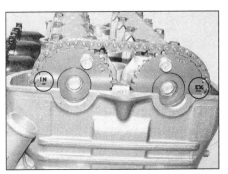

24.7b Ensure camshaft sprocket timing marks are aligned as shown

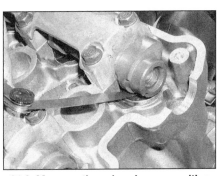

24.8 Measure the valve clearance with a feeler gauge

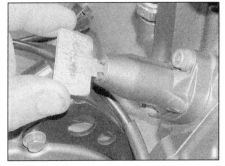

24.5b Retract the camchain tensioner plunger

24.7a Align 'T' mark on rotor with index mark on cover

24.9 The line on the rotor should point straight up

1

24.14a Remove the cam follower . . .

24.14b . . . and the shim

chart. **Note:** *The intake and exhaust valve clearances are different.*

10 Now turn the engine clockwise 180° (half a turn) so that the 'T' mark on the rotor aligns with the index mark on the rotor cover **(see illustration 24.7a)**. Check the clearance on the No. 2 and No. 4 cylinder *intake* valves, using the method described in Step 8. Record the measured clearance on your chart.

11 Now turn the engine clockwise 180° (half a turn) so that the line on the timing rotor points straight up **(see illustration 24.9)**. Check the clearance on the No. 1 and No. 3 cylinder *exhaust* valves, using the method described in Step 9. Record the measured clearance on your chart.

12 When all clearances have been measured and recorded, identify whether the clearance on any valve falls outside that specified. If it does, the shim between the cam follower and the valve must be replaced with one of a thickness which will restore the correct clearance.

13 Shim replacement requires removal of the camshafts (see Chapter 2). There is no need to remove both camshafts if shims from only one need replacing. Place rags over the spark plug holes and the cam chain tunnel to prevent a shim from dropping into the engine on removal.

14 With the camshaft removed, remove the cam follower of the valve in question, then retrieve the shim from inside the follower **(see illustrations)**. If it is not in the follower, pick it out of the top of the valve using either a magnet, a small screwdriver with a dab of grease on it (the shim will stick to the grease), or a screwdriver and a pair of pliers. Do not allow the shim to fall into the engine.

15 A size should be marked on the upper face of the shim – a shim marked 205 is 2.05 mm thick. If the mark is not visible, the shim thickness will have to be measured with a micrometer. It is recommended that the shim is measured anyway, to check that it has not worn (see *Tools and Workshop Tips* in the

Reference section). The new shim thickness required can then be calculated as follows. **Note:** *Always aim to get the clearance at the mid-point of the specified range.*

16 If the valve clearance is less than specified, subtract the measured clearance from the specified clearance then deduct the result from the original shim thickness. For example:

Sample calculation – inlet valve clearance too small

Measured clearance: 0.10 mm
Specified clearance:
  0.16 mm (0.13 to 0.19 mm)
Difference: 0.06 mm
Shim thickness fitted: 2.475 mm
Correct shim thickness required
  is 2.475 – 0.06 = 2.415 mm

17 If the valve clearance is greater than specified, subtract the specified clearance from the measured clearance, and add the result to the thickness of the original shim. For example:

Sample calculation – exhaust valve clearance too large

Measured clearance: 0.35 mm
Specified clearance:
  0.22 mm (0.19 to 0.25 mm)
Difference: 0.13 mm
Shim thickness fitted: 1.975 mm
Correct shim thickness required
  is 1.975 + 0.13 = 2.105 mm

18 Obtain the correct thickness shims from a Honda dealer. Shims are available in 0.025 mm increments from 1.200 mm to 2.800 mm. Where the required thickness is not equal to the available shim thickness, round off the measurement to the nearest available size. **Note:** *If the required replacement shim is greater than 2.800 mm (the largest available), the valve is probably not seating correctly due to a build-up of carbon deposits and should be checked and cleaned or resurfaced as required (see Chapter 2).*

19 When replacing a shim, lubricate it with molybdenum disulphide oil (a 50/50 mixture of molybdenum disulphide grease and engine oil) and fit it into its recess on the top of the valve, with the size marking facing up **(see illustration 24.14b)**. Check that the shim is correctly seated, then lubricate the follower with molybdenum disulphide oil and install it onto the valve. Repeat the process for any other valves until all the clearances are correct.

20 Install the camshafts (see Chapter 2). Rotate the engine several turns to seat the new shim(s), then check the clearances again. Remove the cam chain tensioner locking tool or install the tensioner (as applicable) as described in Chapter 2, Section 8. Note that the cam chain tensioner centre bolt sealing washer should be renewed. Check that the valve timing marks align correctly (see Step 7) before fitting the valve cover (Chapter 2, Section 7).

21 Install all disturbed components in a reverse of the removal sequence. Fit a new O-ring on the ignition rotor cover centre cap if necessary, and grease the plug threads and O-ring before fitting **(see illustration)**.

24.21 Grease the O-ring and plug threads before fitting

Every 24,000 miles (36,000 km) or two years (whichever comes sooner)

25 Cooling system – draining, flushing and refilling

⚠ **Warning: Allow the engine to cool completely before performing this maintenance operation. Also, don't allow antifreeze to come into contact with your skin or the painted surfaces of the motorcycle. Rinse off spills immediately with plenty of water. Antifreeze is highly toxic if ingested. Never leave antifreeze lying around in an open container or in puddles on the floor; children and pets are attracted by its sweet smell and may drink it. Check with local authorities (councils) about disposing of antifreeze. Many communities have collection centres where antifreeze can be disposed of safely. Antifreeze is also combustible, so don't store it near open flames.**

Draining

1 Secure the motorcycle upright on a level surface using an auxiliary stand. Remove the seat cowling (see Chapter 8)
2 Remove the locking screw from the radiator pressure cap, cover the cap with a heavy cloth, then turn it slowly anti-clockwise. If you hear a hissing sound (indicating there is still pressure in the system), wait until it stops, then continue turning the cap until it can be removed **(see illustration)**.
3 Position a suitable container beneath the drain plug on the water pump, remove the plug and allow the coolant to completely drain from the system **(see illustration)**. Retain the old sealing washer for use during flushing.
4 Unclip the fusebox and secure it away from the coolant reservoir **(see illustration)**. Remove the coolant reservoir cap. Place a suitable container underneath the reservoir, then release the clip securing the radiator

overflow hose to the base of the reservoir. Detach the hose and allow the coolant to drain into the container **(see illustration)**. Rinse the inside of the reservoir with clean water and refit the overflow hose.

Flushing

5 Flush the system with clean tap water by inserting a garden hose in the radiator filler neck. Allow the water to run through the system until it is clear when it flows out of the drain hole. If there is a lot of rust in the water, remove the radiator and have it cleaned at a radiator shop (see Chapter 3).
6 Install the drain plug using the old sealing washer, then fill the system via the radiator with clean water mixed with a flushing compound. Make sure the flushing compound is compatible with aluminium components, and follow the manufacturer's instructions carefully. Install the pressure cap. Fill the coolant reservoir to the UPPER mark with clean water.
7 Start the engine and allow it to reach normal operating temperature. Let it run for about ten minutes.
8 Stop the engine and let it cool for a while. Cover the pressure cap with a heavy rag then press it down and turn it slowly anti-

clockwise, releasing any pressure that may be present in the system (see Step 2). Once the hissing stops, remove the cap completely.
9 Drain the system once again (see Step 3).
10 Fill the system with clean water and repeat the procedure in Steps 7 to 9.
11 Drain the coolant reservoir (see Step 4). Ensure the overflow hose is properly fitted and secured with its clip, then install the fusebox.

Refilling

12 Fit a new sealing washer onto the drain plug and tighten it to the torque setting specified at the beginning of this Chapter.
13 Fill the system via the radiator with the proper coolant mixture (see this Chapter's Specifications) **(see illustration)**. **Note:** *Pour the coolant in slowly to minimise the amount of air entering the system.*
14 When the system is full (all the way up to the top of the radiator filler neck) fill the coolant reservoir to the UPPER mark and fit the reservoir cap (see *Daily (pre-ride) checks*).
15 Start the engine and allow it to run for several minutes. Flick the throttle open 3 or 4 times, so that the engine speed rises to

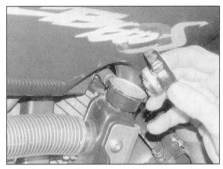
25.2 Carefully remove the radiator filler cap

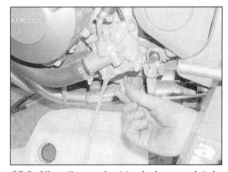
25.3 Allow the coolant to drain completely

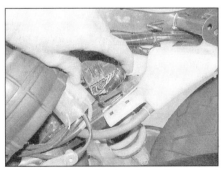
25.4a Detach the fusebox from the coolant reservoir . . .

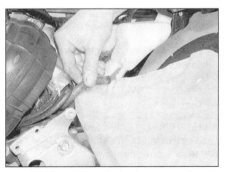
25.4b . . . then drain the reservoir

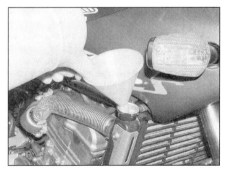
25.13 Fill the system with the specified coolant mixture

1

approximately 4000 – 5000 rpm, then stop the engine. Any air trapped in the system should bleed back to the top of the radiator.

16 Wait a few minutes for the coolant to settle, then check the coolant level in the coolant reservoir. If the level has fallen, add the specified mixture until it reaches the UPPER mark. Now install the radiator pressure cap.

17 Check the system for leaks and install the radiator pressure cap locking screw.

18 Do not dispose of the old coolant by pouring it down the drain. Instead pour it into a heavy plastic container, cap it tightly and take it into an authorised disposal site or service station – see **Warning** at the beginning of this Section.

19 Install the seat cowling (see Chapter 8).

Non-scheduled maintenance

26 Battery – check

1 All models are fitted with a sealed, maintenance-free battery. **Note:** *Do not attempt to open the battery as resulting damage will mean it will be unfit for further use.*

2 All that should be done is to check that the terminals are clean and tight and that the casing is not damaged or leaking. See Chapter 9 for further details.

Caution: Be extremely careful when handling or working around the battery. The electrolyte gel is very caustic and an explosive gas (hydrogen) is given off when the battery is charging.

3 If the machine is not in regular use, disconnect the battery and give it a refresher charge every month to six weeks (see Chapter 9).

27 Brake master cylinder and caliper seals – renewal

1 The seals will deteriorate over a period of time and lose their effectiveness, leading to sticky operation or fluid loss, or the ingress of air and dirt. Disassemble the master cylinders and calipers for seal renewal and to fit new cylinder kits (see Chapter 7).

28 Brake hoses – renewal

1 The hoses will deteriorate with age and should be replaced with new ones every four years regardless of their apparent condition (see Chapter 7).

2 Always replace the banjo union sealing washers with new ones and bleed the hydraulic system after fitting the new hoses.

29 Cylinder compression – check

1 Among other things, poor engine performance may be caused by leaking valves, incorrect valve clearances, a leaking head gasket, or worn pistons, rings and/or cylinder walls. A cylinder compression check will help pinpoint these conditions and can also indicate the presence of excessive carbon deposits in the cylinder heads.

2 The only tools required are a compression gauge and a spark plug wrench. A compression gauge with a threaded end for the spark plug hole is preferable to the type which requires hand pressure to maintain a tight seal. Depending on the outcome of the initial test, a squirt-type oil can may also be needed.

3 Make sure the valve clearances are correctly set (see Section 24) and that the cylinder head nuts are tightened to the correct torque setting (see Chapter 2).

4 Refer to *Fault Finding Equipment* in the *Reference* section for details of the compression test. Refer to the specifications at the beginning of this Chapter for compression figures.

30 Engine oil pressure – check

1 The oil pressure warning light should come on when the ignition (main) switch is turned ON – this serves as a check that the warning light bulb is sound. If the oil pressure warning light does not come on when the ignition is turned on, check the bulb, the fuse and the oil pressure switch (see Chapter 9). The light should extinguish a few seconds after the engine is started.

2 If the oil pressure warning light fails to extinguish, or comes on whilst the engine is running, low oil pressure is indicated – stop the engine immediately and carry out an oil level check (see *Daily (pre-ride) checks*). If the level is correct, test the oil pressure switch (see Chapter 9). If the switch is good, carry out an oil pressure check.

3 To check the oil pressure, a suitable pressure gauge (which screws into the crankcase) will be needed. Honda provide a gauge (part no. 07506 -3000000) and gauge adapter (part no. 07510 - 4220100) for this purpose.

4 Warm the engine up to normal operating temperature then turn it OFF.

5 Remove the oil pressure switch (see Chapter 9) and quickly screw the adapter into the crankcase threads. Connect the pressure gauge to the adapter.

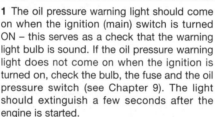

Warning: Take great care not to burn your hand on the hot engine unit, exhaust pipe or with engine oil when accessing the switch take-off point on the crankcase. Do not allow exhaust gases to build up in the work area; either perform the check outside or use an exhaust gas extraction system.

6 Start the engine and increase the engine speed to 6000 rpm whilst watching the pressure gauge reading. The oil pressure should be similar to that given in the Specifications at the start of this Chapter.

7 If the pressure is significantly lower than the standard, either the pressure relief valve is stuck open, the oil pump is faulty, the oil strainer or filter is blocked, or there is other engine damage. Begin diagnosis by checking the oil filter, strainer and relief valve, then the oil pump (see Chapter 2). If those items check out okay, chances are the engine bearing oil clearances are excessive and the engine needs to be overhauled.

8 If the pressure is too high, either an oil passage is clogged, the relief valve is stuck closed or the wrong grade of oil is being used.

9 Stop the engine and unscrew the gauge and adapter from the crankcase.

10 Install the oil pressure switch (see Chapter 9). Check the oil level (see *Daily (pre-ride) checks*).

11 Refer to Chapter 2 and rectify any problems before running the engine again.

31 Front forks – oil change

1 Fork oil degrades over a period of time and loses its damping qualities. Refer to the following sections of Chapter 6 for changing the oil. Note that the fork legs do not need to be completely disassembled.

2 Remove the fork legs from the yokes as described in Section 6. Follow the procedure in Section 7 (Steps 3 to 6) to remove the fork top bolt, spacer, spring seat and spring, then invert the fork leg over a suitable container and tip out the oil.

3 Refill the fork legs with new oil and reassemble them as described in steps 25 to 27 of the same section. Refit the fork legs as described in Section 6.

Chapter 2
Engine, clutch and transmission

Contents

Degrees of difficulty

Easy, suitable for novice with little experience	Fairly easy, suitable for beginner with some experience	Fairly difficult, suitable for competent DIY mechanic 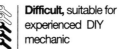	Difficult, suitable for experienced DIY mechanic	Very difficult, suitable for expert DIY or professional

Specifications

General

Capacity	599 cc
Bore	65.0 mm
Stroke	45.2 mm
Compression ratio	12.0 to 1
Engine unit weight	61.9 kg

Camshafts

Intake cam lobe height
    Standard . . . . 36.140 to 36.380 mm
    Service limit . . . . 36.11 mm
Exhaust cam lobe height
    Standard . . . . 35.300 to 35.540 mm
    Service limit . . . . 35.27 mm
Camshaft journal OD
    Standard . . . . 23.959 to 23.980 mm
    Service limit . . . . 23.955 mm
Camshaft bearing cap ID
    Standard . . . . 24.000 to 24.021 mm
    Service limit . . . . Not available
Camshaft bearing oil clearance
    Standard . . . . 0.020 to 0.062 mm
    Service limit . . . . 0.10 mm
Camshaft runout . . . . Less than 0.05 mm
Camshaft follower OD
    Standard . . . . 25.978 to 25.993 mm
    Service limit . . . . 25.968 mm
Camshaft follower bore ID
    Standard . . . . 26.010 to 26.026 mm
    Service limit . . . . 26.040 mm

Cylinder head

Maximum warpage . . . . 0.10 mm

Valves, guides and springs

Intake valve stem OD
    Standard . . . . 3.975 to 3.990 mm
    Service limit . . . . 3.965 mm
Exhaust valve stem OD
    Standard . . . . 3.965 to 3.980 mm
    Service limit . . . . 3.955 mm
Valve guide ID – intake and exhaust
    Standard . . . . 4.000 to 4.012 mm
    Service limit . . . . 4.040 mm
Intake valve stem-to-guide clearance
    Standard . . . . 0.010 to 0.037 mm
    Service limit . . . . 0.075 mm
Exhaust valve stem-to-guide clearance
    Standard . . . . 0.020 to 0.047 mm
    Service limit . . . . 0.085 mm
Intake valve guide projection above cylinder head . . . . 13.1 to 13.3 mm
Exhaust valve guide projection above cylinder head . . . . 11.3 to 11.5 mm
Valve seat width
    Standard . . . . 0.9 to 1.1 mm
    Service limit . . . . 1.5 mm
Valve spring free length
    Standard . . . . Not available
    Service limit . . . . 33.86 mm

Clutch

Friction plate thickness
    Standard . . . . 2.92 to 3.08 mm
    Service limit . . . . 2.60 mm
Plain plate maximum warpage . . . . 0.3 mm
Clutch spring free length
    Standard . . . . 49.7 mm
    Service limit . . . . 48.3 mm
Clutch housing bush OD
    Standard . . . . 34.975 to 34.991 mm
    Service limit . . . . 34.965 mm
Clutch housing bush ID
    Standard . . . . 21.994 to 22.007 mm
    Service limit . . . . 22.017 mm
Input shaft OD at bush contact point
    Standard . . . . 21.980 to 21.993 mm
    Service limit . . . . 21.95 mm

Lubrication system

Oil pressure	4.9 bars (71 psi) at 6000 rpm, 80°C (176°F)
Oil pump rotor tip-to-outer rotor clearance	
Standard	0.15 to 0.20 mm
Service limit	0.20 mm
Oil pump outer rotor-to-body clearance	
Standard	0.15 to 0.22 mm
Service limit	0.35 mm
Oil pump rotor endfloat	
Standard	0.02 to 0.07 mm
Service limit	0.10 mm
Oil pump drive sprocket ID	
Standard	35.025 to 35.075 mm
Service limit	35.10 mm
Oil pump drive sprocket collar OD	
Standard	34.050 to 34.075 mm
Service limit	34.03 mm

Starter clutch

Driven gear OD	
Standard	51.699 to 51.718 mm
Service limit	51.684 mm

Selector drum and forks

Selector fork end thickness	
Standard	5.93 to 6.00 mm
Service limit	5.90 mm
Selector fork bore ID	
Standard	12.000 to 12.021 mm
Service limit	12.030 mm
Selector fork shaft OD	
Standard	11.957 to 11.968 mm
Service limit	11.95 mm

Pistons

Piston OD (measured 11 mm up from base of skirt)	
Standard	64.970 to 64.990 mm
Service limit	64.90 mm
Piston oversizes	+0.25, +0.50, +0.75, +1.00 mm
Piston pin bore ID	
Standard	17.002 to 17.008 mm
Service limit	17.02 mm
Piston pin OD	
Standard	16.994 to 17.000 mm
Service limit	16.98 mm
Piston-to-piston pin clearance	
Standard	0.002 to 0.014 mm
Service limit	0.04 mm

Piston rings

Top ring-to-groove clearance	
Standard	0.025 to 0.060 mm
Service limit	0.08 mm
Second ring-to-groove clearance	
Standard	0.015 to 0.050 mm
Service limit	0.08 mm
Top ring end gap	
Standard	0.20 to 0.35 mm
Service limit	0.5 mm
Second ring end gap	
Standard	0.35 to 0.50 mm
Service limit	0.7 mm
Oil control ring side rail end gap	
Standard	0.2 to 0.7 mm
Service limit	1.0 mm

2

Cylinder block

Cylinder bore ID
   Standard . . . . 65.000 to 65.015 mm
   Service limit . . . . 65.10 mm
Maximum ovality (out-of-round) . . . . 0.10 mm
Maximum taper . . . . 0.10 mm
Cylinder-to-piston clearance
   Standard . . . . 0.010 to 0.045 mm
   Service limit . . . . 0.10 mm
Maximum gasket face warpage . . . . 0.10 mm

Connecting rods and bearings

Connecting rod side clearance
   Standard . . . . 0.10 to 0.25 mm
   Service limit . . . . 0.3 mm
Connecting rod piston pin bore ID
   Standard . . . . 17.016 to 17.034 mm
   Service limit . . . . 17.04 mm
Connecting rod crankpin bore ID
   Size code 1 . . . . 34.000 to 34.008 mm
   Size code 2 . . . . 34.008 to 34.016 mm
Crankshaft crankpin OD
   Size code A . . . . 31.492 to 31.500 mm
   Size code B . . . . 31.484 to 31.492 mm
Connecting rod bearing oil clearance
   Standard . . . . 0.028 to 0.052 mm
   Service limit . . . . 0.06 mm

Crankshaft and main bearings

Maximum crankshaft runout . . . . 0.05 mm
Crankcase main bearing bore ID
   Size code A . . . . 36.000 to 36.007 mm
   Size code B . . . . 36.007 to 36.014 mm
   Size code C . . . . 36.014 to 36.021 mm
Crankshaft journal OD
   Size code 1 . . . . 32.993 to 33.000 mm
   Size code 2 . . . . 32.986 to 32.993 mm
Main bearing oil clearance
   Standard . . . . 0.020 to 0.045 mm
   Service limit . . . . 0.05 mm

Transmission shafts

Ratios
   1st . . . . 2.9285 to 1 (41/14T)
   2nd . . . . 2.0625 to 1 (33/16T)
   3rd . . . . 1.6470 to 1 (28/17T)
   4th . . . . 1.3684 to 1 (26/19T)
   5th . . . . 1.2000 to 1 (24/20T)
   6th . . . . 1.0861 to 1 (25/23T)
Gear ID
   Input shaft 5th and 6th gears
      Standard . . . . 28.000 to 28.021 mm
      Service limit . . . . 28.04 mm
   Output shaft 2nd, 3rd and 4th gears
      Standard . . . . 31.000 to 31.025 mm
      Service limit . . . . 31.04 mm
Gear bushing OD
   Input shaft 5th and 6th gears
      Standard . . . . 27.959 to 27.980 mm
      Service limit . . . . 27.94 mm
   Output shaft 3rd and 4th gears
      Standard . . . . 30.950 to 30.975 mm
      Service limit . . . . 30.93 mm
   Output shaft 2nd gear
      Standard . . . . 30.959 to 30.980 mm
      Service limit . . . . 30.94 mm

Transmission shafts (continued)

Gear bushing ID
    Input shaft 5th gear
        Standard . . . . 24.985 to 25.006 mm
        Service limit . . . . 25.016 mm
    Output shaft 2nd gear
        Standard . . . . 27.985 to 28.006 mm
        Service limit . . . . 28.021 mm
Gear-to-bushing clearance
    Input shaft 5th and 6th gear . . . . 0.020 to 0.062 mm
    Output shaft 2nd, 3rd and 4th gears . . . . 0.020 to 0.070 mm
Input shaft OD at 5th gear bushing point
    Standard . . . . 24.967 to 24.980 mm
    Service limit . . . . 24.960 mm
Input shaft OD at clutch outer guide
    Standard . . . . 21.980 to 21.993 mm
    Service limit . . . . 21.95 mm
Output shaft OD at 2nd gear bushing point
    Standard . . . . 27.967 to 27.980 mm
    Service limit . . . . 27.96 mm
Shaft-to-bushing clearance
    Input shaft 5th gear . . . . 0.005 to 0.039 mm
    Output shaft 2nd gear . . . . 0.005 to 0.039 mm

Torque settings

Camchain tensioner bolts	10 Nm
Camchain tensioner cap bolt	10 Nm
Camchain tensioner slider nut	12 Nm
Camchain upper guide bolts	12 Nm
Camshaft holder bolts	12 Nm
Camshaft sprocket bolts	20 Nm
Clutch spring bolts	12 Nm
Clutch centre nut	108 Nm
Clutch cover bolts	12 Nm
Connecting rod bearing cap nuts	25 Nm
Crankcase bolts	
6 mm bolts	12 Nm
8 mm bolts	24 Nm
Main bearing journal 8 mm bolts	25 Nm
10 mm bolt	39 Nm
Cylinder head 6 mm bolts	10 Nm
Cylinder head 9 mm bolts	47 Nm
Engine mounting bolt nuts (front)	54 Nm
Engine mounting bolt nuts (rear)	54 Nm
Engine mounting bracket bolt nuts	22 Nm
Front sprocket bolt	54 Nm
Gearchange return spring pin	23 Nm
Gearchange stopper arm pivot bolt	12 Nm
Gearchange pedal pinch bolt	20 Nm
Oil pump sprocket bolt	15 Nm
Pulse generator rotor bolt	59 Nm
Selector drum cam bolt	23 Nm
Starter clutch bolts	16 Nm
Swingarm pivot bolt nut	88 Nm
Valve cover bolts	10 Nm
Valve cover breather separator plate bolts	12 Nm

1 General information

The engine/transmission unit is of water-cooled four-cylinder in-line design, fitted transversely across the frame. The sixteen valves are operated by double overhead camshafts, chain driven off the right end of the crankshaft. The engine/transmission unit is constructed in aluminium alloy with the crankcase being divided horizontally. The crankcase incorporates a wet sump, pressure fed lubrication system, and houses a chain driven dual rotor oil pump.

The alternator and flywheel are situated on the left end of the crankshaft with the starter clutch being built into the rear of the flywheel.

The water pump is mounted on the left side of the crankcase and is driven off the oil pump shaft.

The clutch is of the wet multi-plate type and is gear driven off the crankshaft. The transmission is of the six-speed constant mesh type. Final drive to the rear wheel is by chain and sprockets. The drive sprocket is mounted on the end of the transmission output shaft.

2

2 Operations possible with the engine in the frame

The components and assemblies listed below can be removed without having to remove the engine/transmission assembly from the frame. If however, a number of areas require attention at the same time, removal of the engine is recommended.

Valve cover
Camchain tensioner
Camshafts
Camchain, sprockets and guides
Cylinder head
Clutch assembly
Gearchange mechanism
Starter motor
Alternator
Oil sump, oil pump and relief valve
Oil cooler

3 Operations requiring engine removal

It is necessary to remove the engine/transmission assembly from the frame and separate the crankcase halves to gain access to the following components.

Crankshaft and bearings
Piston/connecting rod assemblies and bearings
Transmission shafts
Selector drum and forks (see Note in Section 30)

4 Major engine repair – general information

1 It is not always easy to determine when or if an engine should be completely overhauled, as a number of factors must be considered.
2 High mileage is not necessarily an indication that an overhaul is needed, while low mileage, on the other hand, does not preclude the need for an overhaul. Frequency of servicing is probably the single most important consideration. An engine that has regular and frequent oil and filter changes, as well as other required maintenance, will most likely give many miles of reliable service. Conversely, a neglected engine, or one which has not been run-in properly, may require an overhaul very early in its life.
3 Exhaust smoke and excessive oil consumption are both indications that piston rings and/or valve guides are in need of attention, although make sure that the fault is not due to oil leakage. Refer to *Fault Finding Equipment* in the *Reference* section and perform a cylinder compression check to determine for certain the nature and extent of the work required.
4 If the engine is making obvious knocking or rumbling noises, the connecting rod and/or main bearings are probably at fault.
5 Loss of power, rough running, excessive valve train noise and high fuel consumption rates may also point to the need for an overhaul, especially if they are all present at the same time. If a complete tune-up does not remedy the situation, major mechanical work is the only solution.
6 An engine overhaul generally involves restoring the internal parts to the specifications of a new engine. During an overhaul the piston rings are replaced and the cylinder walls are bored and/or honed. If a rebore is done, then new pistons will also be required. The main and connecting rod bearings are usually replaced during a major overhaul. Generally the valve seats are serviced as well, since they are usually in less than perfect condition at this point. While the engine is being overhauled, other components such as the carburettors and the starter motor can also be rebuilt. The end result should be a like new engine that will give as many trouble-free miles as the original.
7 Before beginning the engine overhaul, read through the related procedures to familiarise yourself with the scope and requirements of the job. Overhauling an engine is not all that difficult, but it is time consuming. Plan on the motorcycle being tied up for a minimum of two weeks. Check on the availability of parts and make sure that any necessary special tools, equipment and supplies are obtained in advance.
8 Most work can be done with typical shop hand tools, although a number of precision measuring tools are required for inspecting parts to determine if they must be replaced. Often a dealer service department or motorcycle repair shop will handle the inspection of parts and offer advice concerning reconditioning and replacement. As a general rule, time is the primary cost of an overhaul so it does not pay to install worn or substandard parts.
9 As a final note, to ensure maximum life and minimum trouble from a rebuilt engine, everything must be assembled with care in a spotlessly clean environment.

5 Engine – removal and installation

Caution: The engine is very heavy. Engine removal and installation should be carried out with the aid of an assistant. Personal injury or damage could occur if the engine falls or is dropped. A hydraulic or mechanical floor jack should be used to support and lower or raise the engine, if possible.

Removal

1 If the engine is dirty, particularly around its mountings, wash it thoroughly before starting any major dismantling work. This will make work much easier and rule out the possibility of dirt falling inside.
2 Support the motorcycle securely in an upright position using an auxiliary stand. Work can be made easier by raising the machine to a suitable working height on a hydraulic ramp or a suitable platform. Make sure the motorcycle is secure and will not topple over (see Section 1 of *Tools and Workshop Tips* in the *Reference* section). When disconnecting any wiring, cables and hoses, it is advisable to mark or tag them as a reminder of where they connect.
3 Remove the fuel tank (see Chapter 4) and, on CB600FS models, the fairing and left and right-hand fairing brackets (see Chapter 8).
4 Undo the battery retaining strap and pull the battery out of its holder. Disconnect the negative (–ve) lead from the battery, then disconnect the positive (+ve) lead and remove the battery (see Chapter 9).

 Warning: Always disconnect the battery negative lead first and reconnect it last.

5 Drain the engine oil (see Chapter 1).
6 Drain the coolant, disconnect the hoses between the radiator and the thermostat housing, coolant reservoir and water pump, and remove the radiator (see Chapter 3).
7 Remove the exhaust system (see Chapter 4).
8 Undo the clip and disconnect the small diameter hose from the No. 3 cylinder inlet manifold to the PAIR valve at the valve **(see illustration)**. Undo the clips securing the large diameter hose to the air filter housing and to the PAIR valve and detach the hose. Release both hoses from the clip on the right-hand front frame tube **(see illustration)**.

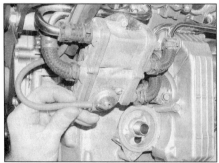
5.8a Detach the small hose from the PAIR valve

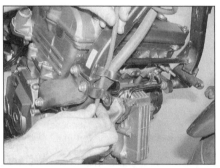
5.8b Release both PAIR valve hoses from the frame clip

5.11 Detach the clutch cable

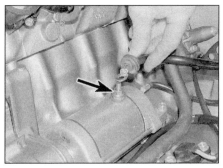

5.12 Disconnect the lead from the starter motor terminal (arrowed)

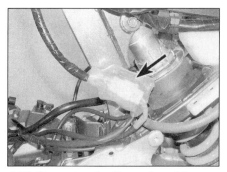

5.13 Connectors for the engine wiring are located inside the clear plastic boot (arrowed)

9 Drain any residual fuel from the carburettors and remove them (see Chapter 4). Plug the intake manifolds with clean rag.

10 Disconnect the spark plug caps from the plugs and remove the ignition coils (see Chapter 5).

11 Unscrew the rear nut on the lower clutch cable adjuster, disconnect the inner cable from the operating lever and remove the adjuster from the bracket **(see illustration)**. Replace the nut on the adjuster and secure the cable clear of the engine.

12 Peel back the boot on the starter motor terminal, then unscrew the starter motor terminal nut and detach the lead **(see illustration)**. Unscrew the starter motor mounting bolt retaining the earth (ground) lead and disconnect the lead.

13 Trace the wiring back from the alternator and disconnect it at the white, three-pin connector **(see illustration)**. Trace the wiring from the ignition pulse generator and disconnect it at the blue, two-pin connector. Trace the wires from the neutral switch, coolant temperature sender and oil pressure switch and disconnect them at the red, three-pin connector.

14 On CB600FS models, trace the wiring from the speed sensor and disconnect it at the black three-pin connector.

15 Release all relevant wiring from any retaining clips and ties so that it is free to be removed with the engine unit. Free any wiring from around the engine unit so that it will not interfere with unit removal.

16 On CB600F models, remove the screw retaining the speedometer cable in the speedometer gearbox and disconnect the cable **(see illustration)**. Secure the cable where it will not interfere with engine unit removal.

17 Make sure the transmission is in neutral. There should be a punch mark on the end of the gearchange shaft which aligns with the slot in the gearchange linkage lever; if not, make a mark to aid reassembly **(see illustration)**. Undo the pinch bolt and disconnect the linkage lever from the shaft.

18 Unscrew the two bolts securing the front sprocket cover to the engine unit, then remove the cover, the drive chain guide plate and, if they are loose, the two dowels **(see illustrations)**.

19 Remove the front sprocket and disengage the chain from the gearbox output shaft (see

Chapter 6). If you have to slacken the chain to remove the sprocket, note the position of the chain adjuster index marks for reassembly (see Chapter 1, Section 1).

20 At this point, position a jack under the engine with a block of wood between the jack head and the crankcase **(see illustration)**. Make sure the jack is centrally positioned so the engine will not topple in any direction when the last mounting bolt is removed and the engine is supported only by the jack. Take the weight of the engine on the jack. It is also advisable to place a block of wood between the rear wheel and the ground in case the motorcycle tilts back when the engine is removed.

21 Check around the engine and frame to make sure that all the necessary wiring, cables and hoses have been disconnected, and that any that remain connected to the

5.16 On CB600F models, disconnect the speedometer cable

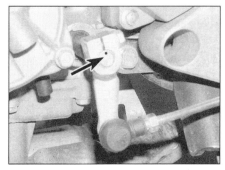

5.17 Note the punch mark (arrowed) then disconnect the gearchange linkage

2

5.18a Remove the sprocket cover . . .

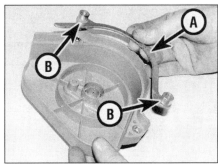

5.18b . . . with the chain guide plate (A) and dowels (B)

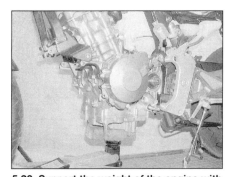

5.20 Support the weight of the engine with a jack

5.22a Remove the right-hand front engine bolt and spacer (arrowed)

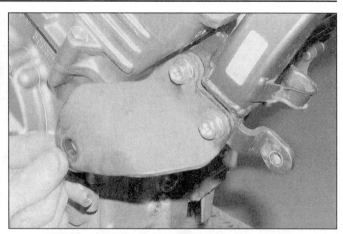

5.22b . . . and the right-hand front engine bracket

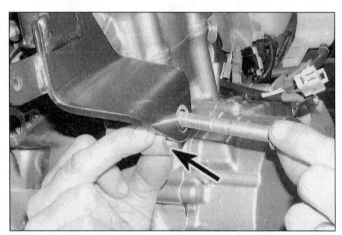

5.23 Remove the left-hand front engine bolt and spacer (arrowed)

5.25 Remove the left-hand pivot bracket mounting bolts (arrowed)

engine are not retained by any clips, guides or brackets on the frame.

22 Undo and remove the right-hand front engine mounting nut, bolt and spacer, then undo the right-hand front engine bracket bolts and remove the bracket **(see illustrations)**.

23 Undo and remove the left-hand front engine mounting nut, bolt and spacer **(see illustration)**.

24 Undo and remove the nut on the right-hand end of the swingarm pivot bolt. **Note:** *Do not remove the pivot bolt.*

25 Unscrew and remove the left-hand swingarm pivot bracket mounting bolts **(see**

illustration). Pull the bracket out slightly and turn it so that the lower rear engine mounting bolt can be removed.

26 Unscrew and remove the nuts on the upper and lower rear engine mounting bolts, but do not withdraw the bolts **(see illustrations)**. Make sure the engine is

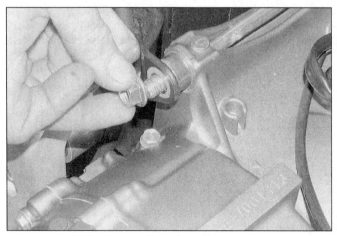

5.26a Remove the nuts on the upper . . .

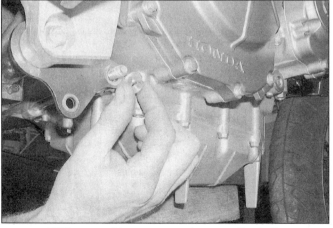

5.26b . . . and lower rear engine mounting bolts

5.26c Withdraw the lower mounting bolt . . .

5.26d . . . and spacer . . .

5.26e . . . then the upper mounting bolt and spacer (arrowed)

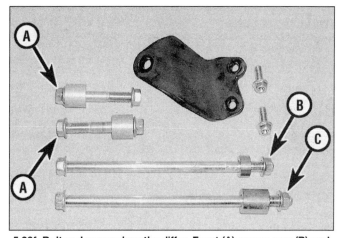

5.26f Bolt and spacer lengths differ. Front (A), upper rear (B) and lower rear (C)

properly supported on the jack, and have an assistant support it as well. Withdraw the lower mounting bolt and spacer first, and then upper mounting bolt and spacer **(see illustrations)**. Note the upper bolt is shorter than the lower bolt; keep each nut, bolt and spacer together to avoid mixing them up **(see illustration)**.

27 Carefully lower the engine, then manoeuvre it out of the frame from the right-hand side.

 Warning: The engine unit is heavy and may cause injury if it falls. Be sure it is securely supported. Have an assistant help you steady the engine as it is lowered out of position.

28 With the aid of an assistant, lift the engine unit off the jack and lower it carefully onto the work surface, taking care not to break the long fins cast onto the bottom of the oil pan. These fins are there specifically for the engine to stand on and keep it in an upright position.

Installation

29 With the aid of an assistant place the engine unit onto the jack and block of wood

and carefully raise it into position so that the mounting bolt holes align. Make sure no wires, cables or hoses become trapped between the engine and the frame.

30 First install the upper rear mounting bolt and then the lower rear mounting bolt from the left-hand side. Insert the spacers between the engine unit and the right-hand side of the frame, then fit the nuts, tightening them finger tight only **(see illustrations 5.26e, d, c, b and a)**.

31 Align the left-hand swingarm pivot bracket, install the mounting bolts and tighten them securely **(see illustrations)**.

32 Install the nut on the swingarm pivot bolt and tighten it to the specified torque setting.

33 Install the left-hand front engine mounting nut, bolt and spacer, tightening it finger tight only **(see illustration 5.23)**.

34 Install the right-hand front engine bracket and tighten the bolts to the specified torque

5.31a Align the pivot bracket and install the upper . . .

5.31b . . . and lower mounting bolts

setting, then install the right-hand front engine mounting nut, bolt and spacer **(see illustrations 5.22b and a)**.

35 In the following order, tighten the front engine mounting bolts, the lower rear mounting bolt and the upper rear mounting bolt to the specified torque settings.

36 The remainder of the installation is the reverse of removal, noting the following points:

● Tighten all nuts and bolts to the specified torque settings.

● Adjust the drive chain tension (see Chapter 1).

● On CB600F models, ensure the speedometer drive on the inside of the front sprocket cover engages properly on the head of the front sprocket bolt. To check, turn the rear wheel in the normal direction of rotation and observe that the spade drive in the gearbox rotates.

● Align the punch mark on the gearchange shaft with the slot in the linkage arm.

● Make sure all wires, cables and hoses are correctly routed and connected, and secured by any clips or ties.

● Check the throttle and clutch cable freeplay (see Chapter 4).

● Refill the engine with oil and coolant (see Chapter 1).

● Start the engine and check for any oil or coolant leaks before riding the motorcycle.

● Adjust the engine idle speed (see Chapter 1).

6 Engine disassembly and reassembly – general information

Note: *Refer to 'Tools and Workshop Tips' in the Reference section of this manual for further information.*

Disassembly

1 Before disassembling the engine, the external surfaces of the unit should be thoroughly cleaned and degreased. This will prevent contamination of the engine internals, and will also make working a lot easier and cleaner. A high flash-point solvent, such as kerosene (paraffin) can be used, or better still,

a proprietary engine degreaser such as Gunk. Use old paintbrushes and toothbrushes to work the solvent into the various recesses of the engine casings. Take care to exclude solvent or water from the electrical components and intake and exhaust ports.

> ⚠️ **Warning: The use of gasoline (petrol) as a cleaning agent should be avoided because of the risk of fire.**

2 When clean and dry, arrange the unit on the workbench, leaving suitable clear area for working. Gather a selection of small containers and plastic bags so that parts can be grouped together in an easily identifiable manner. Some paper and a pen should be on hand so that notes can be made and labels attached where necessary. A supply of clean rag is also required.

3 Before commencing work, read through the appropriate section so that some idea of the necessary procedure can be gained. When removing components it should be noted that, unless specified, great force is seldom required. In many cases, a component's reluctance to be removed is indicative of an incorrect approach or removal method. If in any doubt, re-check with the text.

4 When disassembling the engine, keep 'mated' parts together (e.g. valve assemblies, pistons and connecting rods, clutch plates etc. that have been in contact with each other during engine operation). These 'mated' parts must be reused or renewed as assemblies.

5 Engine/transmission disassembly should be done in the following general order with reference to the appropriate Sections (or Chapters where indicated).

Remove the valve cover
Remove the camshafts
Remove the cylinder head
Remove the camchain, tensioner blade and guides
Remove the clutch
Remove the oil pump
Remove the gearchange mechanism
Remove the starter motor (see Chapter 9)
Remove the alternator rotor (see Chapter 9)
Remove the water pump (see Chapter 3)
Remove the PAIR valve (see Chapter 4)
Remove the oil cooler
Remove the oil sump

Separate the crankcase halves
Remove the connecting rod/piston assemblies
Remove the crankshaft
Remove the transmission shafts/gears
Remove the selector drum and forks

Reassembly

6 Reassembly is accomplished by reversing the general disassembly sequence.

7 Valve cover – removal and installation

Note: *This procedure can be carried out with the engine in the frame. If the engine has been removed, ignore the steps that do not apply.*

Removal

1 Remove the fuel tank (see Chapter 4) and, on CB600FS models, the fairing if required (see Chapter 8).

2 Remove the ignition coils (see Chapter 5).

3 Release the retaining clip and disconnect the breather hose from the right-hand end of the valve cover **(see illustration)**.

4 Unscrew the bolts securing the valve cover and remove the bolts and their sealing washers **(see illustration)**. Lift the cover off the cylinder head; if the cover is stuck, break the gasket seal by tapping gently around the edge with a soft-faced hammer or block of wood. Do not lever the cover off as this will damage the sealing surface. Remove the gasket.

5 If required, undo the bolts retaining the breather baffle plate and remove the plate **(see illustration)**. Discard the gasket as a new one must be fitted on reassembly.

Installation

6 Examine the valve cover gasket for signs of damage or deterioration and renew it if necessary. Also check the cover bolt sealing washers for cracks, hardening and deterioration and renew them if necessary.

7 Clean the mating surfaces of the cylinder head and the valve cover with a suitable solvent. Remove all traces of sealant from the old gasket if re-using it.

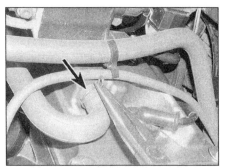

7.3 Disconnect the valve cover breather hose (arrowed)

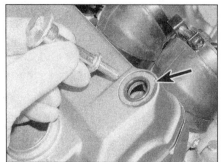

7.4 Remove the cover bolts and sealing washers (arrowed)

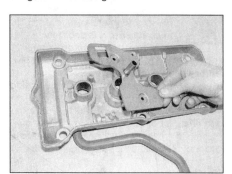

7.5 Remove the cover baffle plate

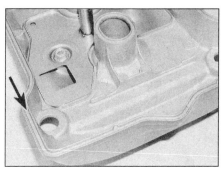

7.9 Ensure the groove in the cover (arrowed) is clean before fitting the gasket

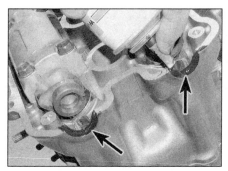

7.10 Apply sealant to the cut-outs in the cylinder head (arrowed)

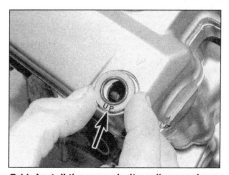

7.11 Install the cover bolt sealing washers with UP showing . . .

8 If removed, install the breather baffle plate with a new gasket. Apply a suitable locking compound to the retaining bolts and tighten them to the torque setting specified at the beginning of this Chapter.

9 Ensure the cover is clean and dry, then fit the gasket into the groove in the cover, making sure it is correctly located **(see illustration)**.

10 Apply a smear of suitable sealant into the cutouts in the cylinder head, then install the cover on the cylinder head taking great care not to dislodge the gasket **(see illustration)**.

11 Fit the sealing washers into the cover making sure the 'UP' mark on each one is facing upwards **(see illustration)**.

12 Install the cover bolts and tighten them to the specified torque setting **(see illustration)**.

13 Install the remaining components in the reverse order of removal.

7.12 . . . then install the cover bolts

2 Remove the valve cover as described in Section 7, then set the No. 1 piston at TDC compression as described in Steps 2 and 3 of Section 9.

3 If the Honda locking key or a home-made equivalent is available, insert it into the centre bolt hole so that it engages the slotted plunger. Turn the key fully clockwise to retract the tensioner plunger, then push it into the end of the tensioner body so that the key shoulders lock it in this position **(see illustrations)**. Unscrew the fixing bolts and withdraw the tensioner from the engine.

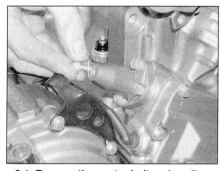

8.1 Remove the centre bolt and sealing washer

4 If the locking key is not available, use a small flat bladed screwdriver to turn the plunger. Hold the screwdriver in place while unscrewing the fixing bolts, then withdraw the tensioner from the engine. The plunger will spring back out once the tension on the screwdriver is released, but can be easily reset on installation.

5 Discard the camchain tensioner gasket and bolt sealing washers; new ones must be fitted on reassembly.

Note: *Do not dismantle the tensioner.*

Inspection

6 Apply hand pressure to the end of the tensioner plunger and wind it into the tensioner body by turning the screwdriver. Hold the plunger under pressure and remove the screwdriver, then slowly release the

8	Camchain tensioner – removal and installation

Note: *This procedure can be carried out with the engine in the frame. If the engine has been removed, ignore the steps that do not apply.*

Removal

1 Unscrew the camchain tensioner centre bolt and remove the sealing washer **(see illustration)**. Discard the washer as a new one must be fitted on reassembly.

 HAYNES HiNT *A cam chain tensioner spring key can be made from thin sheet steel as illustrated.*

2

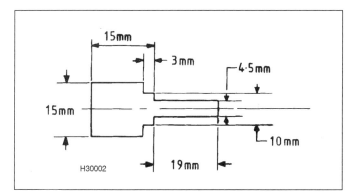

8.3a A copy of Honda's tensioner locking key can be made from a piece of 1 mm mild steel

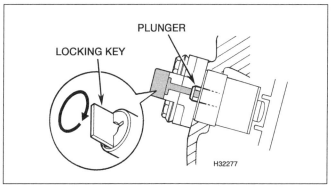

8.3b Locking key in position, tensioner plunger shown retracted

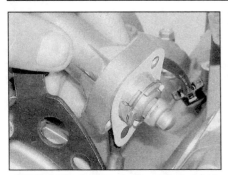

8.9 Hold the tensioner plunger retracted while the tensioner is installed

9.2a Unscrew the ignition rotor centre cap (arrowed)

9.2b Align 'T' mark on rotor with index mark on cover

plunger. Check that the plunger moves smoothly and springs out freely when released.

7 If the tensioner is worn or damaged, or if the plunger does not run smoothly in the body, the tensioner must be replaced with a new one – individual internal components are not available.

Installation

8 Ensure the tensioner and engine faces are clean and dry and fit a new gasket to the tensioner. Fit a new sealing washer to each fixing bolt.

9 If the locking key is available, insert it in the tensioner body and turn it fully clockwise to retract the plunger into the body, then engage the key shoulders to lock the plunger and install the tensioner on the engine **(see illustration)**. Tighten the fixing bolts to the torque setting specified at the beginning of this Chapter, then remove the key.

10 If the key is not available, turn the plunger fully clockwise with a flat-bladed screwdriver and hold it in this position while the tensioner is installed on the engine and the fixing bolts are tightened to the specified torque setting. Release the tension on the screwdriver and remove it.

11 Install the tensioner centre bolt with a new

sealing washer and tighten the bolt to the specified torque setting.

12 With the tensioner installed, check that the valve timing marks are correctly aligned as described in Steps 2 and 3 of Section 9. Install the valve cover and all other components as described in Section 7.

---

9 Camshafts and followers – removal, inspection and installation

Note: *This procedure can be carried out with the engine in the frame. If the engine has been removed, ignore the steps that do not apply.*

Removal

1 Remove the valve cover (see Section 7).

2 Remove the centre cap from the ignition rotor cover on the right-hand side of the engine **(see illustration)**. Turn the engine clockwise using a spanner on the ignition rotor bolt until the 'T' mark on the timing rotor aligns with the index mark on the rotor cover **(see illustration)**.

3 The 'IN' timing mark on the intake camshaft sprocket and the 'EX' mark on the exhaust camshaft sprocket should align with the

cylinder head surface with each mark on the outside of its respective sprocket **(see illustration)**. If the timing marks are on the inside of their respective sprockets, turn the engine one full turn (360°) clockwise until the 'T' mark on the alternator rotor again aligns with the index mark. The marks on the camshaft sprockets should now align correctly with the cylinder head surface.

4 Retract the camchain tensioner plunger and lock it using the special key; if the key is not available, remove the tensioner body (see Section 8).

5 Undo the bolts retaining the upper camchain guide and remove the guide **(see illustration)**.

6 Before removing the camshaft holders, make a note of how they fit. The intake camshaft holder is should be marked 'IN' and the exhaust camshaft holder should be marked 'EX' **(see illustration)**. Unscrew the camshaft holder bolts evenly and a little at a time in a criss-cross pattern, starting from the outside and working towards the centre. Loosen the bolts above any cam lobes that are pressing onto a valve last in the sequence so that the pressure from the open valves cannot cause the camshaft to bend. While loosening the bolts make sure that the camshaft holder is lifting squarely away from

9.3 Ensure camshaft sprocket timing marks are aligned as shown

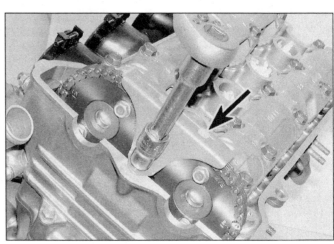

9.5 Remove the upper cam chain guide (arrowed)

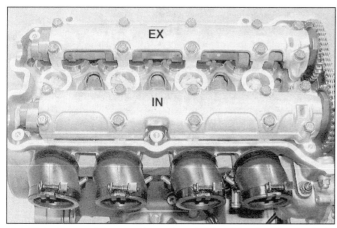

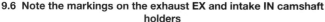

9.6 Note the markings on the exhaust EX and intake IN camshaft holders

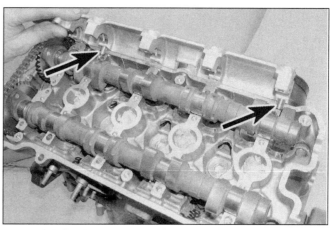

9.7 Retrieve the dowels (arrowed) for safekeeping

the cylinder head and is not sticking on the holder locating dowels.

Caution: If the bolts are loosened carelessly and the holder does not come away from the head squarely, the holder is likely to break. If this happens the complete cylinder head assembly must be renewed as the holder is matched to the cylinder head and cannot be renewed separately. Also, the camshaft could be damaged if the holder bolts are not slackened evenly and the pressure from a depressed valve causes a shaft to bend.

7 Remove the bolts, then lift off the camshaft holders. Retrieve the dowels from either the holders or the cylinder head, if they are loose **(see illustration)**.

8 The camshafts are not interchangeable; the intake camshaft is marked 'IN' and the exhaust camshaft is marked 'EX' **(see illustration)**. Disengage each camshaft sprocket from the cam chain and lift each camshaft out of the head **(see illustration)**. Secure the camchain with a length of wire to prevent it dropping into the crankcase and avoid rotating the crankshaft in case the chain jams between the timing sprocket and the case and damages them.

9 If the followers and shims are being removed from the cylinder head, obtain a container which is divided into sixteen compartments, and label each compartment

with the number of its corresponding valve in the cylinder head. If a container is not available, use labelled plastic bags (egg cartons also work very well). Remove the cam follower of the valve in question, then retrieve the shim from the inside of the follower (see Chapter 1, Section 24). If it is not in the follower, pick it out of the top of the valve using either a magnet, a small screwdriver with a dab of grease on it (the shim will stick to the grease), or a screwdriver and a pair of pliers **(see illustration)**. Do not allow the shim to fall into the engine. Store each shim with its respective follower.

10 If required, undo the bolts retaining the camshaft sprockets and remove the

sprockets, noting how they fit. **Note:** *Hold a non-bearing section of the camshaft in protected vice jaws to avoid damaging the camshaft when loosening the bolts* **(see illustration)**.

Inspection

11 Inspect the bearing surfaces in the cylinder head and camshaft holder and the corresponding journals on the camshaft **(see illustration)**. Look for score marks, deep scratches and evidence of spalling (a pitted appearance). Check that the oil ways in the camshaft holder are clear. If damage is noted or wear is excessive, the relevant parts must be replaced with new ones. The cylinder head

9.8a Note the markings on the exhaust EX and intake IN camshafts

9.8b Tilt the camshaft to disengage the chain from the camshaft sprocket

2

9.9 Ensure each shim (arrowed) is retrieved and stored correctly

9.10 Take care not to damage the camshaft lobes when removing the sprockets

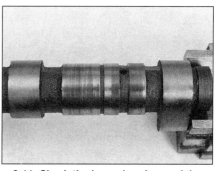

9.11 Check the journal surfaces of the camshaft for score marks or wear

9.14a Check the camshaft lobes for wear – here is an example of damage requiring repair or renewal

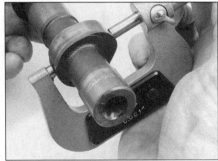

9.14b Measure the height of the camshaft lobes with a micrometer

9.19 Lay a strip of Plastigauge across each bearing journal, parallel with the camshaft axis

and holder must be replaced as a matched set – individual parts are not available.

12 Measure the camshaft journals with a micrometer (see *Tools and Workshop Tips* in the *Reference* section) and compare the results with the service limit specified at the beginning of this Chapter. If the journals are worn below the service limit the camshaft must be renewed.

13 Check camshaft runout by supporting each end of the shaft on V-blocks, and measuring any runout at the journals using a dial gauge (see *Tools and Workshop Tips* in the *Reference* section). If the runout exceeds the specified limit the camshaft must be renewed.

14 Check the camshaft lobes for heat discoloration (blue appearance), score marks, chipped areas, flat spots and spalling **(see illustration)**. Measure the height of each lobe with a micrometer **(see illustration)** and compare the results to the specified lobe height service limit. If damage is noted or wear is excessive, the camshaft must be renewed. Also check the condition of the cam followers.

 Refer to Tools and Workshop Tips (Section 3) in the Reference section for details of how to read a micrometer and dial gauge.

15 The camshaft journal oil clearance should now be checked. There are two possible ways of doing this, either by direct measurement

(see Steps 16 and 17) or by the use of a product known as Plastigauge (see Steps 18 to 21).

16 If the direct measurement method is to be used, make sure the camshaft holder dowels are in position then install the holders (see Step 6) and the holder bolts. Tighten the bolts to the specified torque settings in the numerical sequence marked on the top of each holder.

17 Make a chart or sketch of the cylinder head so that a note of each measurement can be made against the relevant bearing surface, then measure the inside diameter of each bearing surface with a telescoping gauge and record it on the chart. Calculate the oil clearance by subtracting the corresponding camshaft journal outside diameter from the recorded bearing surface internal diameter.

18 If the Plastigauge method is to be used, clean the camshafts, the bearing surfaces in the cylinder head and the camshaft holders with a clean, lint-free cloth, then lay the camshafts in place in the cylinder head (see Step 8).

19 Cut strips of Plastigauge and lay one piece on each camshaft journal, parallel with the camshaft centreline **(see illustration)**. Make sure the camshaft holder dowels are installed and fit the holders in their proper positions (see Step 6). Ensuring the camshafts are not rotated at all, tighten the camshaft holder bolts to the specified torque (see Step 35).

20 Now unscrew the bolts (see Step 6) and carefully lift off the camshaft holders, again making sure the camshafts are not rotated.

21 To determine the oil clearance, compare the crushed Plastigauge (at its widest point) on each journal to the scale printed on the Plastigauge container **(see illustration)**. Make a note of each measurement, then carefully clean away all traces of Plastigauge using a fingernail or other object that will not score the bearing surfaces.

22 Compare the results to this Chapter's Specifications. If any clearance is greater than specified, it is an indication of wear on the camshaft, the holder, or both.

23 First check to see if the camshaft journals are worn below the service limit (see Step 12). If they are, a new camshaft must be fitted. However, since it is likely that the holder is also worn, ensure that the specified journal diameter for a new camshaft will restore the oil clearance to within specification before buying a new camshaft.

24 If the camshaft journals are good, or if fitting a new camshaft will not restore the oil clearance to within specification, the holder and cylinder head will have to be replaced as a matched set.

 Before renewing the camshafts, cylinder head or holders because of damage, check with local machine shops specialising in motorcycle engine work. In the case of the camshafts, it may be possible for cam lobes to be welded, reground and hardened, at a cost far lower than that of a new camshaft. If the bearing surfaces in the cylinder head are damaged, it may be possible for them to be bored out to accept bearing inserts. Due to the cost of a new components it is recommended that all options are explored!

25 Inspect the outer surfaces of the cam followers for evidence of wear, scoring or other damage **(see illustration)**. If the side of a follower is in poor condition, it is probable that the bore in which it works is also damaged. Remove the valves (see Section 12) and measure the diameter of the cam followers and the internal diameters of the

9.21 Compare the width of the crushed Plastigauge with the scale supplied

9.25 Inspect the cam followers for wear

9.28 Note the correct position of the camshaft lobes (arrowed) before fitting the sprockets

9.32 Maintain tension in the chain when fitting it over the exhaust camshaft sprocket

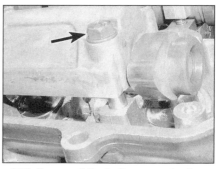

9.35 Ensure all the bolts are contacting the holders (arrowed) before starting the tightening sequence

follower bores in the cylinder head and compare the results with the service limits specified at the beginning of this Chapter. If the bores are seriously out-of-round, tapered or worn beyond the service limit, renew the cylinder head and followers.

26 Inspect the cam chain guides, tensioner blade and cam chain (see Section 13).

27 Inspect the camshaft sprockets; if they show signs of wear, chipped teeth or other damage, replace them, the crankshaft sprocket and the cam chain as a set.

28 The camshaft sprockets are retained by two bolts (see Step 10). Install the new sprockets on their respective camshafts with the marks facing out, apply a suitable non-permanent thread locking compound to the sprocket bolts, then tighten the bolts to the torque setting specified at this beginning of this Chapter.

 Warning: The camshaft sprockets are interchangeable. To avoid fitting them incorrectly, lay both the camshafts in position in the head with the lobes for the No.1 cylinder facing up (see illustration), then install the sprockets and align the appropriate timing mark with the cylinder head mating surface before installing the retaining bolts.

Installation

29 If removed, lubricate each valve shim and follower with molybdenum disulphide oil (a 50/50 mixture of molybdenum disulphide grease and engine oil). Fit each shim into its

9.37 Eliminate slack in the camchain before checking the timing marks

recess on the top of the valve, with the size marking on the shim facing up (see Chapter 1, Section 24). Make sure the shim is correctly seated, then install the follower, making sure it fits squarely in its bore. **Note:** *It is most important that the shims and followers are returned to their original valves, otherwise the valve clearances will be inaccurate.*

30 Ensure that the 'T' mark on the timing rotor still aligns with the index mark on the rotor cover (see Step 2).

31 Make sure the camshaft journals and the bearing surfaces in the cylinder head and camshaft holders are clean, then apply molybdenum disulphide oil to them and to the camshaft lobes.

32 Fit the exhaust camshaft (marked 'EX'), making sure the timing mark on the sprocket faces forward and aligns with the cylinder head mating surface, and hook the camchain over the sprocket. When fitting the chain, pull up on the front run to remove all slack but do not disturb the timing rotor alignment **(see illustration)** (see Step 30).

33 Now fit the inlet camshaft **(see illustration 9.8b)**, making sure the timing mark on the sprocket faces to the rear and aligns with the cylinder head mating surface, and hook the cam chain over the sprocket. When fitting the chain, pull it tight to make sure there is no slack between the two camshaft sprockets – any slack in the chain must lie in the rear run, so that it is taken up by the tensioner.

34 Make sure the locating dowels are in position and install the camshaft holders **(see illustration 9.7)**. **Note:** *Ensure the camshaft holders are fitted correctly, the intake holder is marked 'IN' and the exhaust holder 'EX'.*

35 Install the camshaft holder bolts by hand until all the bolts are contacting the holders **(see illustration)**. Working in the numerical sequence marked on the top of each holder, tighten the bolts by half a turn at a time to gradually draw the holders into position. Ensure the holders are being pulled squarely down onto the cylinder head and are not binding on the locating dowels, then tighten the bolts to the specified torque setting. *Caution: The camshaft holder is likely to break if it is not tightened down evenly*

and squarely and the camshaft is likely to bend if it is tightened down onto the closed valves before the open ones.

36 Undo the two camshaft holder bolts that retain the upper camchain guide, install the guide and its three fixing bolts and tighten the bolts to the specified torque **(see illustration 9.5)**.

37 Release the camchain tensioner plunger or, if the tensioner has been removed, use a dowel to press on the back of the tensioner blade via the tensioner bore in the crankcase to take up any slack in the cam chain. Check that all the timing marks are still in **exact** alignment as described in Step 2. If it is necessary to turn the engine slightly to align the marks with the engine mating surfaces, keep the dowel pressed onto the tensioner blade to prevent the chain slipping on the sprockets **(see illustration)**. Note that it is easy to be slightly out (by one tooth on a sprocket) without the marks appearing drastically out of alignment. If the marks aren't lined up, slacken the chain tension and disengage the sprocket(s) from the chain and adjust their position.

38 If removed, install the camchain tensioner (see Section 8).

39 Rotate the crankshaft a few times to settle all disturbed components, and check all valve clearances as described in Chapter 1.

40 Lubricate all bearing surfaces with clean engine oil and fit the valve cover (see Section 7).

41 Apply a smear of oil to the ignition rotor cover centre cap O-ring and tighten the cap to the specified torque setting.

10 Cylinder head – removal and installation

Caution: The engine must be completely cool before beginning this procedure or the cylinder head may become warped.
Note: *This procedure can be carried out with the engine in the frame. If the engine has been removed, ignore the steps that do not apply.*

Removal

1 Remove the camshafts and cam followers (see Section 9).

2

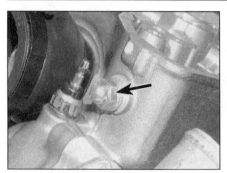

10.4a Unscrew the nut (arrowed) . . .

10.4b . . . and remove the washer . . .

10.4c . . . then lift out the tensioner blade

2 Remove the thermostat housing cover and thermostat and disconnect the coolant temperature sender wiring (see Chapter 3).

3 Remove the carburettors and the exhaust system and disconnect the PAIR secondary air tubes (see Chapter 4).

4 Unscrew the nut and sealing washer securing the camchain tensioner blade to the cylinder head and lift out the blade (see illustrations).

5 Release the clip and disconnect the cooling system bypass hose from the rear of the cylinder head (see illustration).

6 The cylinder head is secured by ten 9 mm bolts and two 6 mm bolts. Unscrew the two 6 mm bolts from the right-hand end of the cylinder head first (see illustration).

7 Working from the outside to the inside in a criss-cross pattern, loosen the 9 mm cylinder head bolts by half a turn at a time (see *Tools*

and Workshop Tips (Section 4) in the *Reference* section). Once all pressure is released from the bolts, unscrew them fully and remove along with their washers (see illustration). Discard the bolts and washers as new ones must be fitted on reassembly.

8 Lift the cylinder head up off the cylinder block. If it is stuck, tap around the joint faces of the head with a soft-faced hammer or block of wood to free it. Do not attempt to free the head by inserting a lever between it and the cylinder block – you will damage the sealing surfaces.

9 If they are loose, remove the dowels from the cylinder block and store them with the head for safe-keeping (see illustration). If they appear to be missing they are probably stuck in the underside of the cylinder head.

10 Check the head gasket and the mating surfaces on the cylinder head and block for signs of leakage from the cylinders, the oil or coolant

passages, which could indicate that the head is warped. Check the flatness of the head as described in Section 12. Discard the head gasket as a new one must be fitted on reassembly.

11 Secure the camchain with a piece of wire to prevent it falling down into the engine.

Installation

12 Clean all traces of old gasket material from the cylinder head and block with a suitable solvent. If you need to use a scraper, take care not to scratch or gouge the soft aluminium. Be careful not to let any of the gasket material fall into the crankcase, the cylinder bores or the oil or coolant passages.

> **HAYNES HiNT** *Refer to Tools and Workshop Tips (Section 7) in the Reference section for details of gasket removal methods.*

13 Ensure both cylinder head and block mating surfaces are clean and fit the locating dowels to the block (if removed). Apply a smear of engine oil to the surface of each cylinder bore.

14 Fit the new head gasket over the locating dowels, making sure all the holes are correctly aligned (see illustration).

15 Carefully fit the cylinder head onto the block, making sure it locates correctly onto the dowels, while feeding the camchain up through the head. Secure the chain to prevent it falling back into the engine.

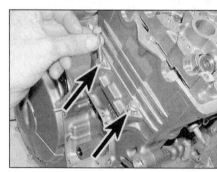

10.5 Disconnect the cooling system hose (arrowed)

10.6 Unscrew the two bolts (arrowed)

10.7 Remove the head bolts and washers

10.9 Remove the dowels (arrowed) for safe keeping

10.14 Ensure all the holes in the new gasket align correctly

10.16 Tighten the head bolts (arrowed) as described

12.3 Valve components

1 Follower	4 Spring retainer	7 Valve stem seal
2 Shim	5 Spring	8 Valve
3 Collets	6 Spring seat	

16 Lubricate the threads and seating surfaces of the 9 mm cylinder head bolts with clean engine oil. Install the bolts with their washers and tighten them finger-tight. Now tighten the bolts evenly and in two stages, working in a criss-cross pattern starting from the centre and moving outwards (see *Tools and Workshop Tips (Section 4)* in the *Reference* section), to the torque setting specified at the beginning of this Chapter (see illustration).

17 Install the two 6 mm bolts on the right-hand end of the cylinder head and tighten them to the specified torque setting (see illustration 10.6).

18 Install the remaining components in the reverse order of removal.

11 Valves/valve seats/valve guides – servicing

1 Because of the complex nature of this job and the special tools and equipment required, most owners leave servicing of the valves, valve seats and valve guides to a professional. However, you can make an initial assessment of whether the valves are seating, and therefore sealing, correctly by pouring a small amount of solvent into each of the valve ports. If the solvent leaks past any valve into the combustion chamber the valve is not seating and sealing correctly.

2 You can also remove the valves from the cylinder head, clean the components and check them for wear to assess the extent of the work needed. The head can then be reassembled.

3 The dealer service department will remove the valves and springs, renew the valves and guides, recut the valve seats, check and renew the valve springs, spring retainers and collets (as necessary), replace the valve stem seals with new ones and reassemble the valve components.

4 After the valve service has been performed, the head will be in like-new condition. When the head is returned, be sure to clean it again very thoroughly before installation on the engine, to remove any metal particles or abrasive grit that may still be present from the valve service operations. Use compressed air, if available, to blow out all the holes and passages.

12 Cylinder head and valves – disassembly, inspection and reassembly

1 As mentioned in the previous section, valve overhaul should be left to a Honda dealer. However, disassembly, cleaning and inspection of the valves and related components can be done by the home mechanic if the necessary special tools are available. This way, no expense is incurred if the inspection reveals that overhaul is not required at this time.

2 To disassemble the valve components without the risk of damaging them, a valve spring compressor is absolutely essential. Make sure it is suitable for motorcycle work.

12.5a If available, use a sleeve protector in the cam follower bore . . .

Disassembly

3 Before proceeding, arrange to label and store the valves along with their related components in such a way that they can be returned to their original locations without getting mixed up (see illustration). Either use the same container as the valve shims and followers are stored in (see Section 9), or obtain a separate container which is divided into sixteen compartments, and label each compartment with the identity of the valve which will be stored in it. Alternatively, labelled plastic bags will do just as well.

4 If not already done, clean all traces of old gasket material from the cylinder head with a suitable solvent (see Section 10).

5 Compress the valve spring on the first valve with a spring compressor, making sure it is correctly located onto each end of the valve assembly. Honda recommend the use of a protector sleeve to prevent damage to the cam follower bore. On the underside of the head, make sure the plate on the compressor only contacts the valve and not the soft aluminium of the head – if the plate is too big for the valve, use a spacer between them (see illustrations).

2

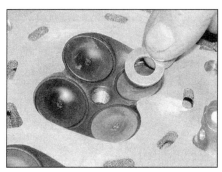

12.5b . . . and use washers to prevent the spring compressor binding on the cylinder head

12.5c Compress the valve spring . . .

12.6a . . . and remove the collets

12.6b Remove the spring retainer . . .

12.6c . . . the valve spring . . .

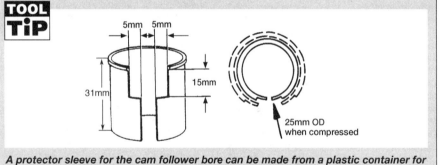

and the valve **(see illustrations)**. If the valve binds in the guide and won't pull through, push it back into the head and deburr the area around the collet groove with a very fine file or whetstone **(see illustration)**.

7 Pull the valve stem seal off the top of the valve guide with pliers and discard it (the old seals should never be reused) **(see illustration)**. Remove the spring seat, noting which way up it fits – using a magnet is the easiest way to lift the seat out of the head **(see illustration)**.

8 Repeat the procedure for the remaining valves. Remember to keep the parts for each valve together so they can be reinstalled in the same location.

9 Clean the cylinder head with solvent and dry it thoroughly. Compressed air will speed the drying process and ensure that all holes and recessed areas are clean. **Note:** *Do not use a wire brush mounted in a drill motor to clean the combustion chambers as the head material is soft and may be scratched or eroded away by the wire brush.*

10 Clean all the valve springs, collets, retainers and spring seats with solvent and dry them thoroughly. Do the parts from one valve at a time so that no mixing of parts between valves occurs.

11 Scrape off any deposits that may have formed on the valve, then use a motorised wire brush to remove deposits from the valve heads and stems. Again, make sure the valves do not get mixed up.

Inspection

12 Inspect the head very carefully for cracks and other damage. If cracks are found, a new

Do not compress the springs any more than is absolutely necessary.

Caution: Take great care not to mark the cam follower bore with the spring compressor.

6 Remove the collets, using either needle-

12.6d . . . and the valve. If the valve sticks . . .

nose pliers, tweezers, a magnet or a screwdriver with a dab of grease on it **(see illustration)** then carefully release the valve spring compressor and remove the spring retainer, noting which way up it fits, the spring

TOOL TiP

5mm 5mm

31mm

15mm

25mm OD when compressed

A protector sleeve for the cam follower bore can be made from a plastic container for a 35 mm film as shown.

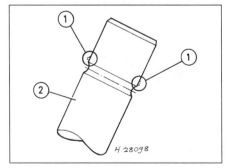

H 28098

12.6e . . . check the valve stem (2) above the collet groove (1) and remove any burrs

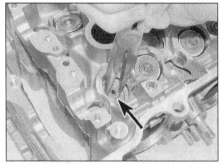

12.7a Discard the old valve stem seal (arrowed). . .

12.7b . . . and remove the spring seat

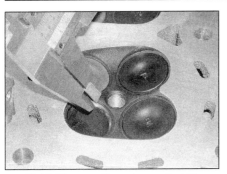

12.14 Measure the valve seat width

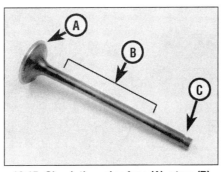

12.15 Check the valve face (A), stem (B) and collet groove (C) for signs of wear and damage

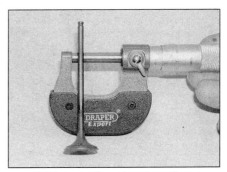

12.18 Measure the valve stem diameter

head will be required. Check the cam bearing surfaces for wear and evidence of seizure. Check the camshaft journals for wear as well (see Section 9).

13 Using a precision straight-edge and a feeler gauge, check the head gasket mating surface for warpage. Refer to *Tools and Workshop Tips (Section 3)* in the *Reference* section for details of how to use the straight-edge. If the head is warped beyond the limit specified at the beginning of this Chapter, consult your Honda dealer or take it to a specialist repair shop for rectification.

14 Examine the valve seats in the combustion chamber. If they are pitted, cracked or burned, the head will require work beyond the scope of the home mechanic. Measure the valve seat width and compare it to this Chapter's Specifications **(see illustration)**. If it exceeds the service limit, or if it varies around its circumference, consult your Honda dealer or take the head to a specialist repair shop for rectification.

15 Examine each valve face for cracks, pits and burned spots and replace the valve with a new one if necessary **(see illustration)**.

16 Inspect the valve stem and collet groove area for scuffing and cracks and check the end of the stem for pitting and wear **(see illustration 12.15)**. The presence of any of the above conditions indicates the need for fitting new valves.

17 Rotate the valve and check for any obvious indication that it is bent, using V-blocks and a dial gauge if available.

18 Measure the valve stem diameter **(see illustration)**. Clean the valve guide to remove any carbon build-up, then measure the inside diameter of the guide with a small hole gauge and micrometer (see *Tools and Workshop Tips (Section 3)* in the *Reference* section). Measure the guide at both ends and at the centre to determine if it is worn in a bell-mouth pattern (more wear at the ends). Subtract the valve stem outside diameter from the valve guide inside diameter to obtain the valve stem-to-guide clearance. If the stem-to-guide clearance is greater than listed in this Chapter's Specifications, renew whichever component is worn beyond its specified limits. If the valve guide is within specifications, but is worn unevenly, it should be renewed.

19 Check the end of each valve spring for wear. Measure the spring free length and compare it to that listed in the specifications **(see illustration)**. If any spring is shorter than specified it has sagged and must be replaced with a new one. Also place the spring upright on a flat surface and check it for bend by placing a set square against it **(see illustration)**. Note: *If a valve spring has worn beyond the service limit it is likely that the other springs will be worn to some extent and should be replaced at the same time.*

20 Check the spring retainers and collets for obvious wear and cracks. Any questionable parts should not be re-used, as extensive damage will occur in the event of failure during engine operation.

21 If the inspection indicates that no service

work is required, the valve components can be reinstalled in the head.

Reassembly

22 Working on one valve at a time, lay the spring seat in place in the cylinder head **(see illustration 12.7b)**. Fit a new valve stem seal onto the guide and use an appropriate size deep socket to press the seal over the end of the valve guide until it is felt to clip into place **(see illustrations)**. Don't twist or cock the seal, or it will not seal properly against the valve stem. Also, don't remove it again or it will be damaged.

23 Lubricate the valve stem with molybdenum disulphide oil, then install it into its guide, rotating it slowly to avoid damaging the seal. Check that the valve moves up and down freely in the guide. Next, install the spring with its closer-wound coils facing down into the cylinder head, followed by the spring retainer, with its shouldered side facing down

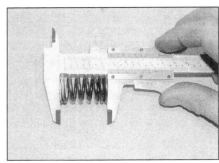

12.19a Measure valve spring free length

2

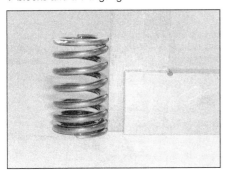

12.19b Check that the springs are not bent

12.22a Locate the seal on the guide with care . . .

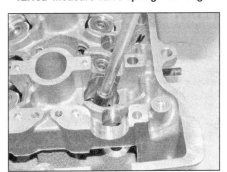

12.22b . . . then press the seal into position with a suitable socket

12.24 A small dab of grease will keep the collets in place on the valve during reassembly

so that it fits into the top of the spring **(see illustrations 12.6c and b)**.

24 Apply a small amount of grease to the inside of the collets – this will help to help hold them in place when fitting them on the valve stem **(see illustration)**. If available, fit the protector sleeve for the cam follower bore, then compress the spring with the valve spring compressor and install the collets **(see illustration 12.6a)**. When compressing the spring, do so only as far as is necessary to slip the collets into place. Make certain that the collets are securely located in the collet groove and release the spring compressor.

25 Repeat the procedure for the remaining valves. Remember to keep the parts for each valve together and separate from the other valves so they can be reinstalled in the correct location

26 Support the cylinder head on blocks so the valves can't contact the work surface,

13.3a Remove the dowels (arrowed)

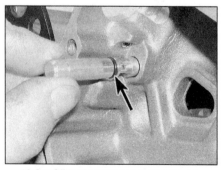

13.3c Oil jet is retained by the O-ring (arrowed)

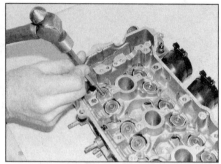

12.26 Tap the valve stem with a soft-faced punch to seat the collets

then very gently tap the end of each valve stem to seat the collets in their grooves **(see illustration)**.

> **HAYNES HiNT**
> *Check for proper valve sealing by pouring a small amount of solvent into each of the valve ports. If the solvent leaks past the valve(s) into the combustion chamber, disassemble the valve(s) and re-examine the components.*

13 Camchain, tensioner blade and guides – removal, inspection and installation

Note: *This procedure can be carried out with the engine in the frame. If the engine has*

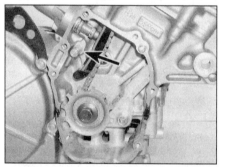

13.3b Note the position of the oil jet (arrowed)

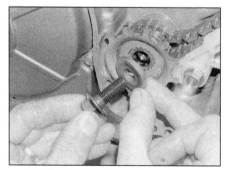

13.4a Remove the bolt, washer . . .

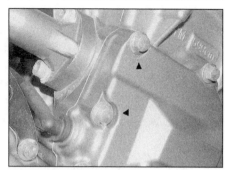

13.2 Note the cover bolts marked with an arrow

been removed, ignore the steps that do not apply.

Removal

1 Remove the camchain tensioner blade, upper camchain guide and camshafts (see Section 10, Step 4). Secure the upper end of the camchain to prevent it jamming around the sprocket on the crankshaft.

2 Unscrew the bolts retaining the ignition rotor cover and remove the cover. Note the bolts marked with an arrow on the cover **(see illustration)**. Be prepared to catch any residual oil when the cover is removed. If the cover is stuck, break the gasket seal by tapping gently around the edge with a soft-faced hammer or block of wood. Do not lever the cover off as this will damage the sealing surface. Secure the cover with a cable tie to avoid straining the pulse generator coil wiring.

3 Discard the gasket as a new one must be fitted on reassembly, and remove the cover locating dowels for safekeeping if they are loose **(see illustration)**. Note the position of the oil jet fitted in the crankcase and make sure it stays in position **(see illustration)**. **Note:** *The oil jet is secured in the crankcase with an O-ring. If the oil jet is loose or pulls out with the cover, replace the O-ring* **(see illustration)**.

4 Unscrew the bolt securing the ignition rotor. To prevent the crankshaft turning, either select a gear and apply the rear brake (if the engine is in the frame), or remove the alternator cover and use a rotor holding strap to counter-hold the crankshaft. Remove the bolt, washer and rotor, noting how it fits on the crankshaft splines **(see illustrations)**.

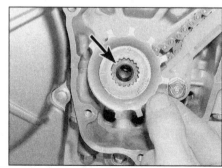

13.4b . . . and the ignition rotor. Note the alignment of the splines (arrowed)

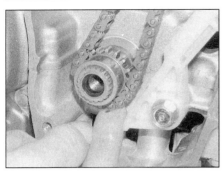

13.5 Remove the camchain and sprocket together

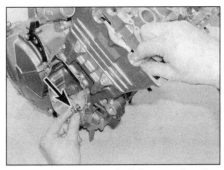

13.6a Unscrew the bolt (arrowed) and remove the front camchain guide

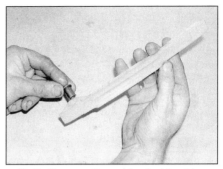

13.6b Remove the guide pivot bushing

5 Mark the outside edge of the camchain sprocket with paint or a suitable pen to ensure that it is reassembled the correct way round. Lower the camchain down into the engine and remove it together with the camchain sprocket (see illustration).
6 Unscrew the front camchain guide bolt and lift the guide upwards and out of the engine (see illustration). Remove the pivot bushing from the guide noting how it fits (see illustration).

Inspection

7 Check the tensioner blade and guides for deep grooves, cracking and other obvious damage, replacing them if necessary. A worn guide is an indication of a stretched camchain.
8 Check the camchain for binding and obvious damage and inspect the sprocket for damage such as chipped or missing teeth. If either of

these conditions are visible, or if the chain appears to be stretched, the camchain, camchain sprocket and camshaft sprockets should be replaced as a set. **Note:** *Except in cases of oil starvation, the camchain wears very little. If the camchain has stretched excessively, check the engine oil level and lubrication system.*

Installation

9 Installation is the reverse of removal, noting the following:
● Remove all traces of gasket from the crankcase and cover mating surfaces.
● Fit the bushing in the front camchain guide with the collar facing the engine.
● Make sure the camchain sprocket is fitted the correct way round.
● Install the ignition rotor with the timing marks facing out and align the splines on the rotor with those on the crankshaft. Lubricate

the threads of the rotor bolt with clean engine oil and tighten it to the torque setting specified at the beginning of this Chapter.
● Install the camshafts and camchain tensioner before fitting the ignition rotor cover.
● Make sure the oil jet is pushed fully into its location in the crankcase.
● If removed, install the ignition rotor cover locating dowels.
● Apply a smear of suitable sealant across the crankcase joint before fitting the new gasket. Also apply sealant to the pulse generator coil wiring grommet.
● Apply sealant to the threads of the bolts marked with an arrow on the ignition rotor cover (see illustration 13.2).
● Check the engine oil level before riding the motorcycle (see Daily (pre ride) checks).

14 Clutch cable – removal and installation

1 Remove the fuel tank (see Chapter 4).
2 Screw the adjuster at the handlebar end of the cable fully into the lever bracket and align the slot in the adjuster with that in the lever bracket. Pull the outer cable end from the socket in the adjuster and release the inner cable nipple from the lever (see illustrations).
3 Loosen the lower cable adjuster locknut and detach the inner cable from the clutch release arm (see illustration).
4 Free the outer cable from its mounting bracket (see illustration).

2

14.2a Screw the adjuster into the bracket . . .

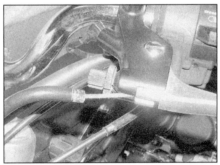

14.2b . . . then detach the outer cable . . .

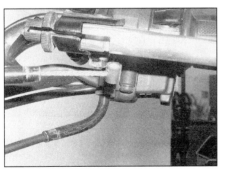

14.2c . . . and detach the inner cable

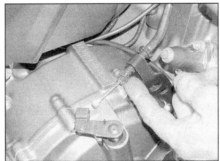

14.3 Detach the inner cable from the clutch release arm . . .

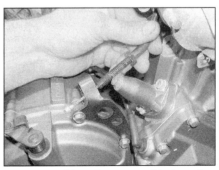

14.4 . . . and free the outer cable from the bracket

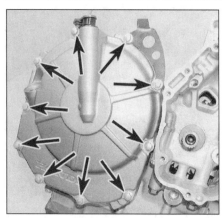

15.3 Unscrew the bolts (arrowed) and remove the cover

15.4 Remove the short pushrod for safekeeping

15.5 Remove the dowels (arrowed) if they are loose

5 Work back along the cable, freeing it from any relevant retaining clips while noting the correct routing and remove it from the bike.

> **HAYNES HiNT** *When fitting a new cable, tape the lower end of the new cable to the upper end of the old cable before removing it from the motorcycle. Slowly pull the lower end of the old cable out, guiding the new cable down into position. Using this method will ensure the cable is routed correctly.*

Installation

6 Installation is the reverse of removal. Apply grease to the cable ends and make sure the cable is correctly routed and clipped into place. With the cable installed, turn the adjuster on the lever bracket so that the slots are not aligned.

7 Adjust the cable as described in Chapter 1, then check the clutch release mechanism for smooth operation and any signs of wear or damage. Remove it for cleaning and re-greasing if required (see Section 15), then install the fuel tank (see Chapter 4).

15 Clutch – removal, inspection and installation

Note: *This procedure can be carried out with the engine in the frame. If the engine has been removed, ignore the steps that do not apply.*

Removal

1 Detach the clutch cable from the release mechanism arm (see Section 14) and secure the cable away from the clutch area.

2 Remove the oil filler cap to avoid damaging the dipstick.

3 Working in a criss-cross pattern, loosen the clutch cover retaining bolts and remove the bolts and the clutch cable bracket **(see illustration)**.

4 Remove the cover, being prepared to catch any residual oil. If the cover will not lift away easily, break the gasket seal by tapping gently around the edge with a soft-faced hammer or block of wood or operate the release arm. Take care not to lose the short pushrod from inside the cover **(see illustration)**.

5 Remove the gasket and discard it as a new one must be fitted on reassembly. Note the

two locating dowels fitted to the crankcase and remove them for safe-keeping if they are loose **(see illustration)**.

6 Working in a criss-cross pattern, gradually unscrew the clutch spring bolts until spring pressure is released. Remove the bolts, then remove the clutch lifting plate and pushrod and the clutch springs **(see illustrations)**. Note the bearing in the lifting plate.

7 The clutch nut is staked into a cutout in the

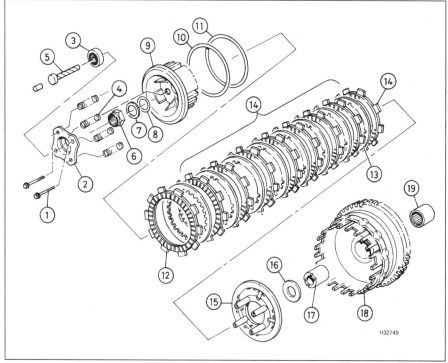

15.6a Clutch components

1 Bolt	8 Thrust washer	14 Friction plates - 8 off
2 Lifting plate	9 Clutch centre	15 Pressure plate
3 Bearing	10 Spring seat	16 Thrust washer
4 Spring	11 Anti-judder spring	17 Centre bush
5 Pushrod	12 Outermost friction	18 Clutch housing
6 Clutch nut	plate	19 Needle bearing
7 Belleville washer	13 Plain plates - 8 off	

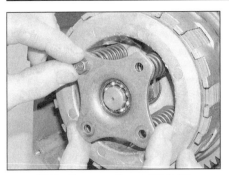

15.6b Unscrew the spring bolts gradually . . .

15.6c . . . then remove the lifting plate and pushrod . . .

15.6d . . . and the springs

transmission input shaft. Unstake the nut using a hammer and small chisel, taking care not to damage the input shaft **(see illustration)**.

8 To loosen the clutch nut the input shaft must be locked. This can be done in several ways:

● If the engine is in the frame, engage 1st gear and have an assistant hold the rear brake on hard with the rear tyre in firm contact with the ground.

● Use the Honda service tool, Part Number 07724-0050002.

● A home-made tool made from two strips of steel bent at the ends and bolted together in the middle, can be used to stop the

clutch centre from turning whilst the nut is slackened **(see illustration)**. Note that a proprietary clutch holding tool is also available.

9 Unscrew the clutch nut and discard it as a new one must be fitted on reassembly.

10 Remove the Belleville washer from the shaft, noting which way round it fits, then remove the thrust washer.

11 Screw two clutch spring bolts half way into the threads in the clutch pressure plate and use them to pull the clutch centre, the clutch plates and the pressure plate off the input shaft as an assembly **(see illustration)**. Unless the plates are being renewed, keep them in their original order **(see illustration)**.

Note that there are two types of friction plate – the outermost plate having a different internal diameter to fit over the anti-judder spring and spring seat. Take care not to mix them up.

12 Note the raised dot on the pressure plate which aligns with the raised dot on the clutch centre **(see illustration)**.

13 Remove the large thrust washer **(see illustration)**.

14 The primary driven gear on the back of the clutch housing is in two parts, spring loaded to eliminate backlash between the driven gear and the primary drive gear. To remove the clutch housing, first insert a 5 mm pin or other suitable tool such as the shank of a drill into

15.7 Unstake the clutch nut with a small chisel

15.8 Hold the clutch as described and unscrew the nut

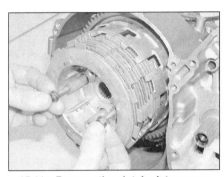

15.11a Remove the clutch plates as an assembly

2

15.11b The outer edges of the plates (arrowed) are marked so they can be kept in their original positions

15.12 Note the alignment dots on the pressure plate and clutch centre

15.13 Remove the thrust washer

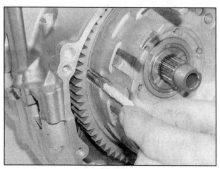

15.14 Insert a pin to keep the primary gear teeth aligned

15.15 Withdraw the bush

15.16a Withdraw the clutch housing between the crankcase projections (arrowed)

the hole in the gears to keep the teeth aligned **(see illustration)**.

15 Grip the lugs on the bush with two pairs of suitable pliers and pull the bush out while supporting the housing **(see illustration)**.

16 Align the two projections on the crankcase between the primary driven gear teeth and withdraw the clutch housing from the crankcase **(see illustration)**. Note how dogs on the oil pump drive sprocket locate in the back of the clutch housing. Ease the tension between the primary driven gear teeth and remove the 5 mm pin **(see illustration)**.

Inspection

17 After an extended period of service the clutch friction plates will wear and promote clutch slip. Measure the thickness of each friction plate using a vernier caliper **(see**

illustration). If any plate has worn to or beyond the service limit given in the Specifications at the beginning of this Chapter, the friction plates must be replaced as a set. Also, if any of the plates smell burnt or are glazed, they must be renewed as a set.

18 The plain plates should not show any signs of excess heating (bluing). Check for warpage using a flat surface and feeler gauges **(see illustration)**. If any plate exceeds the maximum permissible amount of warpage, or shows signs of bluing, all plain plates must be replaced as a set.

19 Inspect the clutch assembly for burrs and indentations on the edges of the protruding tangs of the friction plates and/or slots in the edge of the clutch housing with which they engage **(see illustration)**. Similarly check for wear between the inner tongues of the plain

plates and the slots in the clutch centre. Wear of this nature will cause clutch drag and slow disengagement during gear changes, since the plates will snag when the pressure plate is lifted. A small amount of wear can be corrected by dressing with a fine file, but if wear is excessive the components must be replaced.

20 Inspect the anti-judder spring and seat for signs of wear or distortion and replace if necessary.

21 Inspect the pressure plate for wear or damage and ensure the threads for the spring bolts are in good condition **(see illustration)**.

22 Inspect the bearing surfaces of the transmission input shaft and bush for signs of wear and damage and measure them **(see illustrations)**. If they are worn beyond their specified service limits they must be replaced.

15.16b Remove the locking pin

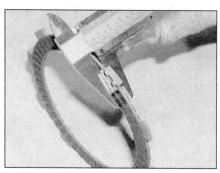

15.17 Measuring clutch friction plate thickness

15.18 Checking the plain plates for warpage

15.19 Check the slots in the clutch housing for wear and damage

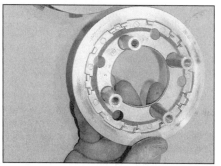

15.21 Check the condition of the pressure plate and the spring bolt threads

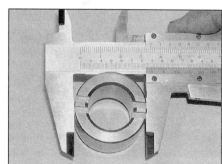

15.22a Measure the external . . .

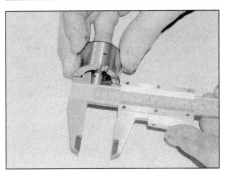

15.22b . . . and internal diameters of the bush

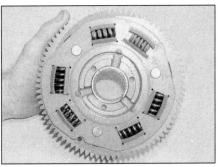

15.24 Check the condition of the cush-drive springs

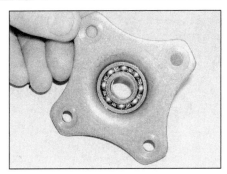

15.25 Inspect the clutch pushrod bearing

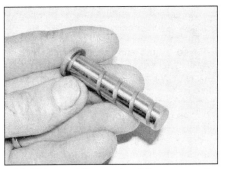

15.26 Inspect the pushrod for wear and score marks

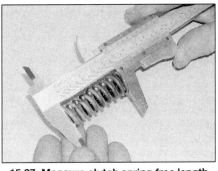

15.27 Measure clutch spring free length

15.28 Inspect the teeth of the primary driven gears

23 Inspect the clutch housing needle roller bearing for signs of wear or damage. If replacement is necessary, the task should be entrusted to a Honda dealer. The bearing is a press fit in the housing and an hydraulic press and suitable spacers will be required to remove the original bearing and install the new one.
24 The clutch housing incorporates a cush-drive mechanism; check that the springs are not loose or broken and that there is no backlash between the housing and the primary driven gear, otherwise renew the housing (see illustration).
25 Remove the clutch pushrod and check the clutch lifting plate bearing for wear (see

illustration). Ensure that the bearing is a tight fit in the plate, that the inner race of the bearing spins freely without any sign of notchiness and that there is no freeplay between the inner and outer races. If necessary, replace the bearing by driving the old bearing out of the plate and pressing the new bearing into position (see Tools and Workshop Tips in the Reference section).
26 Inspect the pushrod for wear and replace it if necessary (see illustration).
27 Measure the free length of each clutch spring (see illustration). If any spring is shorter than the specified service limit, the clutch springs must be replaced as a set.
28 Check the teeth of the primary driven

gears on the back of the clutch housing and the corresponding teeth of the primary drive gear on the crankshaft (see illustration). Renew the clutch housing if any teeth are worn or chipped. The primary drive gear is an integral part of the crankshaft; if the gear is damaged take the crankshaft to a Honda dealer or specialist engineer for assessment (see Section 27 for removal of the crankshaft).
29 Check that the clutch actuating shaft and short pushrod operate smoothly in the cover (see illustration). Check the condition of the spring and renew it if it has lost its tension (see illustration). Withdraw the pushrod from the cover and pull out the actuating shaft and return spring, noting how the spring fits.

2

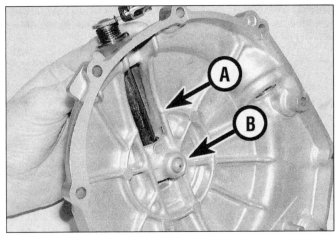

15.29a Check the action of the clutch shaft (A) and pushrod (B) . . .

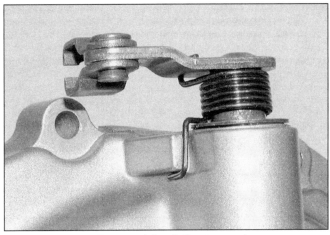

15.29b . . . and the shaft return spring

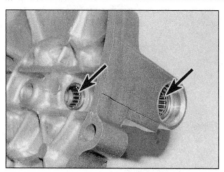

15.29c Inspect the bearings in the clutch cover . . .

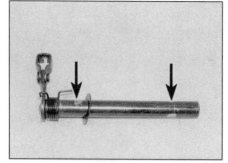

15.29d . . . and the bearing surfaces (arrowed) of the actuating shaft

15.29e Renew the oil seal if necessary

Inspect the condition of the oil seal and needle bearings fitted in the clutch cover and the condition of the actuating shaft **(see illustrations)**. **Note:** *The seal can be replaced but it is not possible to replace the bearings. If they are worn the complete cover must be replaced.*

30 Apply grease to the oil seal lip, needle bearings and actuating shaft. Assemble the spring on the shaft and carefully insert the shaft into the cover to avoid damaging the seal. Make sure the spring is correctly located, then fit the short pushrod. Check the operation of the clutch actuating shaft.

Installation

31 Remove all traces of old gasket from the crankcase and clutch cover surfaces.
32 Align the teeth of the two-part primary driven gear with a large screwdriver and insert a pin to keep the teeth aligned **(see illustration 15.16b)**. Lubricate the clutch housing needle roller bearing and the bush with molybdenum disulphide oil.

33 Manoeuvre the clutch housing into position on the transmission input shaft (see Step 16). Engage the primary driven gear with the crankshaft drive gear and locate the back of the clutch housing on the dogs on the oil pump drive sprocket. Rotate the oil pump sprocket to check the dogs are correctly engaged **(see illustration)**.

34 Slide the bush into position with the lugs on the outside, and install the large thrust washer **(see illustration)**.

35 Hold the assembly in position and remove the pin that is aligning the primary driven gear teeth. **Note:** *Make sure the clutch housing is*

still correctly engaged with the oil pump drive sprocket before proceeding.

36 Fit the spring seat onto the clutch centre, followed by the anti-judder spring, making sure its outer edge is raised off the spring seat – if it is touching the seat and the inner edge is raised, it is the wrong way round **(see illustrations)**.

37 Coat each clutch plate with clean engine oil, then build up the plates on the clutch centre, making sure the outermost friction plate is correctly identified and fitted first (see Step 11). Start with a friction plate, then a plain plate and alternate friction and plain plates until all are installed **(see illustrations)**. Align the tabs of the friction plates as they are fitted so that the assembly can be installed easily into the clutch housing.

38 Align the raised dot on the pressure plate

15.33 Turn the oil pump sprocket (arrowed) to check the drive is engaged

15.34 Install the bush

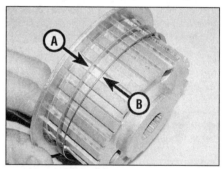

15.36a Fit the spring seat (A) and the spring (B) . . .

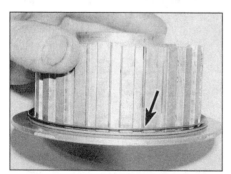

15.36b . . . so that the outer edge of the spring (arrowed) is off the seat

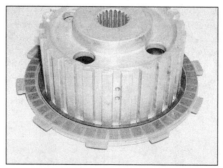

15.37a Fit the outermost friction plate first . . .

15.37b . . . then fit alternate plain and friction plates

15.38 Install the pressure plate

15.39 Outer friction plate tabs locate in short slots (arrowed)

15.40a Fit the thrust washer . . .

15.40b . . . and the Belleville washer

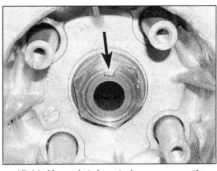

15.41 New clutch nut shown correctly staked

44 Make sure the short pushrod is in place in the clutch cover; its rounded end faces the clutch. Install the clutch cover.
45 Install the cover retaining bolts and the clutch cable bracket, and tighten the bolts finger-tight.
46 Ensure the clutch release mechanism arm is correctly positioned, then working in a criss-cross pattern, tighten the cover bolts to the specified torque setting **(see illustration 15.3)**.
47 If the engine is in the frame, fit the clutch cable through the bracket and into the release lever. Adjust the clutch cable (see Chapter 1).
48 Check the engine oil level before riding the motorcycle (see *Daily (pre ride) checks*).

16 Oil sump, oil strainer and pressure relief valve – removal, inspection and installation

Note: *This procedure can be carried out with the engine in the frame. If the engine has been removed, ignore the steps that do not apply.*

Removal

1 Remove the exhaust system (see Chapter 4) and drain the engine oil (see Chapter 1).
2 Unscrew the sump bolts, slackening them evenly in a criss-cross sequence to prevent distortion, and remove the sump **(see illustration)**.
3 Pull the oil strainer out of its socket in the crankcase, noting the position of the locating tab in the crankcase casting **(see illustration)**.

with the dot on the clutch centre (see Step 12) and install the pressure plate **(see illustration)**. Make sure the tabs on the pressure plate locate inside the innermost clutch plate.
39 Slide the assembly carefully into the clutch housing, making sure that the tabs on the outer friction plate align with the short slots in the housing **(see illustration)**. Align the clutch centre splines with the transmission input shaft.
40 Fit the thrust washer and the Belleville washer with the OUTSIDE mark facing out **(see illustrations)**.
41 Apply clean engine oil to the threads of the new clutch nut, then install the nut (with its shoulder facing outwards) and tighten it to the torque setting specified at the beginning of this Chapter while locking the input shaft using the method employed on removal (see

Step 8). Check that the clutch centre rotates freely after tightening, then stake the shoulder of the nut into the cutout in the end of the shaft using a suitable punch **(see illustration)**.
42 Install the clutch springs, lifting plate and pushrod and the clutch spring bolts. Tighten the bolts evenly, in a criss-cross pattern, to the specified torque setting. Ensure the pushrod is pressed fully into the lifting plate bearing **(see illustration)**.
43 Apply a smear of suitable sealant across the crankcase joint, make sure the locating dowels are in position and fit a new gasket to the crankcase **(see illustration 15.5)**.

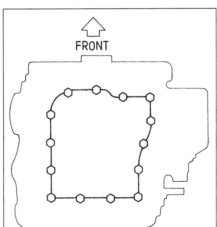

15.42 Ensure the pushrod is pushed fully into the bearing

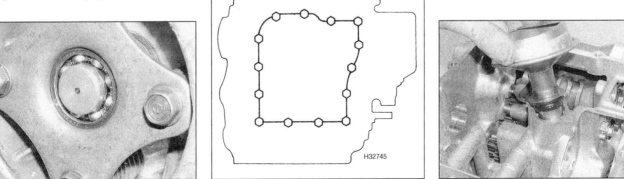

16.2 Sump bolts

16.3 Remove the oil strainer. . .

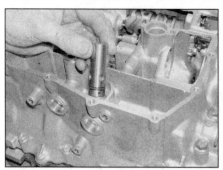

16.4 . . . and the pressure relief valve

16.6 Ensure the strainer mesh (arrowed) is clean

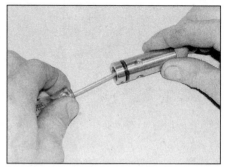

16.7a Check the operation of the valve as described

Remove the packing collar and discard it as a new one must be used.

4 Pull the pressure relief valve out of its socket in the crankcase. Discard the O-ring as a new one must be used **(see illustration)**.

Inspection

5 Remove all traces of sealant from the sump and crankcase mating surfaces. Clean the inside of the sump with solvent and inspect the sockets and sealing surfaces for the strainer and pressure relief valve in the underside of the crankcase.

6 Clean the oil strainer in solvent and remove any debris caught in the mesh. Inspect the strainer for any signs of damage and renew it if necessary **(see illustration)**.

7 Push the relief valve plunger into the valve body and check that it moves smoothly and

freely against the spring pressure **(see illustration)**. If the valve operation is rough or sticky, remove the circlip, noting that it is under spring pressure, and withdraw the washer, spring and piston. Clean all the parts in solvent and inspect the plunger and bore for wear and damage **(see illustrations)**. Apply clean engine oil to all parts and reassemble the valve. Check its operation again as above – if it is still rough or sticky it must be renewed – individual components are not available.

Installation

8 Fit a new O-ring onto the relief valve and smear it with clean engine oil, then push the valve into its socket in the crankcase **(see illustration 16.4)**.

9 Fit a new packing collar onto the oil strainer and smear it with clean engine oil, then align the tab on the strainer with the notch in the crankcase and push the strainer into its socket **(see illustrations)**.

10 Apply a coating of suitable sealant (Honda recommend Three Bond 1207B) to the sump mating surface, then fit the sump to the engine and install the bolts finger tight **(see illustrations)**.

11 Working in a criss-cross pattern, tighten the sump bolts securely.

12 Install the oil drain plug with a new sealing washer and refill the engine with oil (see Chapter 1).

13 Fit the exhaust system (see Chapter 4). Start the engine and check for leaks around the sump before riding the motorcycle.

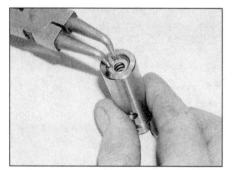

16.7b Remove the circlip to dismantle the valve

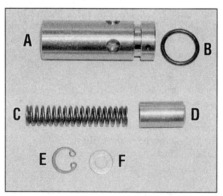

16.7c Valve body (A), O-ring (B), spring (C), plunger (D), circlip (E), washer (F)

16.9a Fit a new oil strainer packing collar

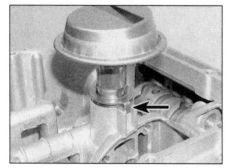

16.9b Align the tab on the strainer (arrowed) with the notch in the crankcase

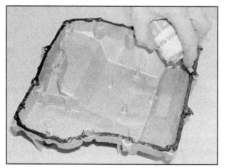

16.10a Apply a suitable sealant to the sump mating surface

16.10b Fit all the bolts finger-tight before tightening

17.2a Unscrew the pump sprocket bolt as described . . .

17.2b . . . and remove the bolt and washer

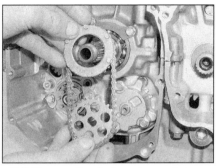

17.3 Remove the chain and sprockets as an assembly

17 Oil pump – removal, inspection and installation

Note: *This procedure can be carried out with the engine in the frame. If the engine has been removed, ignore the steps that do not apply. For details on how to check the oil pressure see Chapter 1.*

Removal

1 Remove the clutch as described in Section 15.

2 Hold the oil pump sprocket by passing a rod through the sprocket and locating it against the pump body, then unscrew the sprocket bolt and remove the bolt and washer **(see illustrations)**.

3 Note how the pump sprocket fits, then remove the drive sprocket, chain and pump sprocket as an assembly **(see illustration)**.

4 Remove the drive sprocket bushing from the transmission input shaft, noting how it fits **(see illustration)**.

5 Undo the three bolts securing the pump to the crankcase and withdraw the pump, noting how it fits **(see illustration)**.

Inspection

6 Remove the pump cover bolt then lift off the cover **(see illustrations)**.

7 Remove the thrust washer from the pump driveshaft **(see illustration)**.

8 Withdraw the driveshaft, noting which way around it is fitted. Remove the drive pin from

the shaft, noting how it locates in the pump inner rotor **(see illustration)**.

9 Remove the inner and outer rotors from the pump body and remove the cover locating dowel. **Note:** *The outer rotor is punch marked*

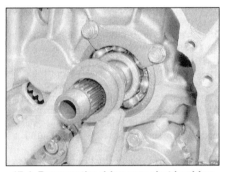

17.4 Remove the drive sprocket bushing

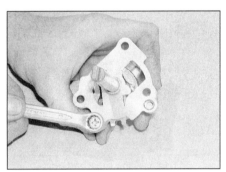

17.6a Undo the cover bolt . . .

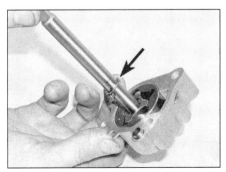

17.7 Remove the thrust washer (arrowed)

to show which way round it is fitted. Always install the rotor the same way as it was when it was removed so that mated surfaces continue to run together **(see illustration)**.

10 Clean all the components in solvent.

17.5 Unscrew the three bolts and remove the pump

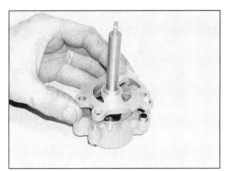

17.6b . . . and lift off the cover

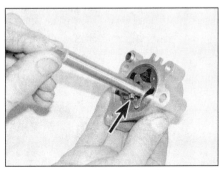

17.8 Note the position of the pin (arrowed) and withdraw the driveshaft

17.9 Note the punch mark (arrowed) on the outer rotor

2

17.11a Inspect the pump components . . .

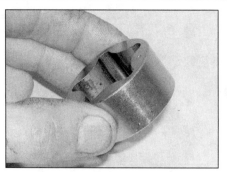

17.11b . . . for scoring and wear

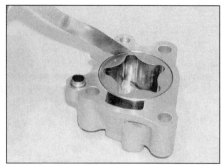

17.12 Measuring outer rotor-to-body clearance . . .

11 Inspect the pump body, cover and rotors for scoring and wear **(see illustrations)**. If any damage, scoring or uneven or excessive wear is evident, renew the pump (individual components are not available). If the engine is being rebuilt, it is advisable to fit a new oil pump as a matter of course.

12 Reassemble the pump components and measure the clearance between the outer rotor and the pump body with a feeler gauge and compare it to the maximum clearance listed in the specifications at the beginning of this Chapter **(see illustration)**. If the clearance is greater than the maximum listed, renew the pump.

13 Measure the clearance between the inner rotor tip and the outer rotor with a feeler gauge and compare it to the maximum clearance listed in the specifications at the beginning of this Chapter **(see illustration)**. If

the clearance is greater than the maximum listed, renew the pump.

14 Lay a straight-edge across the rotors and the pump body and, using a feeler gauge, measure the rotor end-float (the gap between the rotors and the straight-edge **(see illustration)**. If the clearance is greater than the maximum listed, renew the pump.

15 Check the pump drive chain and sprockets for wear or damage, and renew them as a set if necessary.

16 Inspect the bearing surfaces of the drive sprocket and the drive sprocket bushing and measure them. If either have worn more than the specified service limit they must be renewed.

17 If the pump is good, make sure all the components are clean and dry, then lubricate them with clean engine oil.

18 Install the cover locating dowel **(see illustration)**.

19 Install the outer rotor in the pump body with the punch mark facing the same way as noted on removal (see Step 9)

20 Install the inner rotor, then fit the drive pin into the driveshaft and install the shaft into the pump, thick-tabbed end first. Ensure the pin locates correctly in the inner rotor **(see illustration 17.8)**.

21 Slide the thrust washer onto the shaft and install the pump cover. Install the cover bolt and tighten it to the specified torque setting **(see illustrations 17.7 and 17.6b and a)**. Ensure that the pump driveshaft rotates freely.

Installation

22 Slide the pump into position, turning the driveshaft until it engages correctly with the water pump **(see illustration)**. Fit the pump mounting bolts and tighten them securely.

23 Slide the drive sprocket bushing onto the transmission input shaft, then install the drive sprocket, pump sprocket and chain as an assembly. **Note:** *The OUT mark on the pump sprocket must face away from the pump **(see illustration)**.*

24 Apply a suitable non permanent locking compound to the threads of the pump sprocket bolt, fit the washer and tighten the bolt to the specified torque setting. Prevent the sprocket from turning as on disassembly (see Step 2).

25 Install the clutch (see Section 15).

26 Check the engine oil level before riding the motorcycle (see *Daily (pre ride) checks*).

17.13 . . . inner rotor tip-to-outer rotor clearance . . .

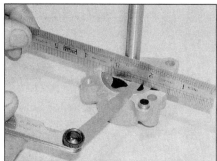

17.14 . . . and rotor end float

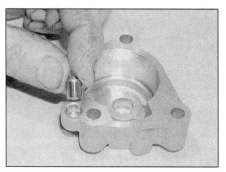

17.18 Install the cover locating dowel

17.22 Engage the flat (arrowed) on the driveshaft with the water pump

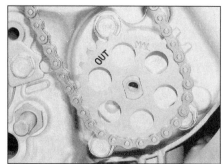

17.23 Fit sprocket with OUT mark facing away from pump

18.4a Remove the oil filter . . .

18.4b . . . from its location (arrowed) on the oil cooler housing

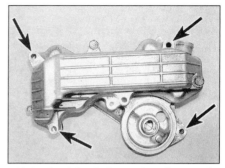

18.5a Retaining bolt locations (arrowed)

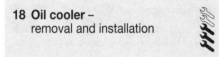

18 Oil cooler –
removal and installation

Note: *This procedure can be carried out with the engine in the frame. If the engine has been removed, ignore the steps that do not apply.*

Removal

1 Remove the exhaust system and the pulse secondary air (PAIR) valve assembly (see Chapter 4).
2 Drain the coolant (see Chapter 1).
3 Slacken the clip and disconnect the coolant hose from the left-hand side of the cooler housing.
4 Drain the engine oil (see Chapter 1) and remove the oil filter **(see illustrations)**. **Note:** *If the filter is damaged on removal it must be renewed.*
5 Undo the retaining bolts, then remove the oil cooler housing from the front of the crankcase and discard the seal from the top of the housing as a new one must be fitted on reassembly **(see illustrations)**.
6 Remove the collars from the crankcase/cooler housing as applicable, noting which way round they are fitted **(see illustration)**. Discard the O-rings as new ones must be fitted on reassembly.

Installation

7 Fit a new O-ring to the groove in each collar

18.5b Pull the housing away from the crankcase . . .

and fit a second new O-ring to the thinner end of each collar. Smear each O-ring with clean engine oil to ease installation.
8 Fit both collars into the crankcase thick end first.
9 Smear the new housing seal with clean engine oil and fit it into the groove in the housing **(see illustration)**.
10 Install the cooler housing on the front of the crankcase, making sure the seal remains seated in its groove. Align the housing with the collars and push it firmly into position.
11 Fit the mounting bolts and tighten them securely.
12 Connect the coolant hose and tighten its retaining clip securely, then fit the oil filter (a new oil filter is recommended).
13 Install the remaining components in the reverse order of removal. **Note:** *Fill the engine*

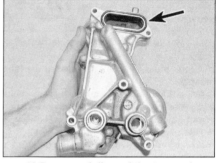

18.5c . . . and discard the top seal (arrowed)

with the correct amount and type of oil and coolant (see Chapter 1), then start the engine and check for leaks before riding the motorcycle.

19 Oil cooler –
disassembly and reassembly

Disassembly

1 Remove the oil cooler housing (see Section 18).
2 Unscrew the housing cover bolts, noting the sealing washer on the lower bolt **(see illustration)**. Discard the sealing washer if it is damaged and fit a new one on reassembly.
3 Lift off the cover and discard the seal as a

2

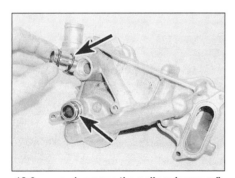

18.6 . . . and remove the collars (arrowed)

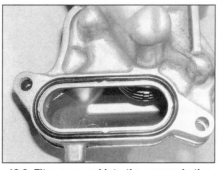

18.9 Fit a new seal into the groove in the housing

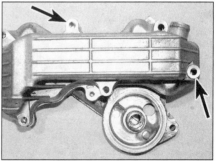

19.2 Cover bolt locations (arrowed)

19.3 Renew the seal (arrowed) on reassembly

19.4a Undo the cooler retaining bolts (arrowed) . . .

new one must be fitted on reassembly **(see illustration)**.

4 Undo and remove the cooler retaining bolts and washers and remove the cooler, noting how it fits **(see illustrations)**.

5 Remove the two collars from the back of the housing and discard the O-rings as new ones must be fitted on reassembly.

6 Clean all the components in solvent and dry them thoroughly.

7 Check the cooler housing for cracks and dents and any evidence of coolant/oil leakage and replace it with a new one, if necessary. Check the coolant hose for splits,

cracks and deterioration and fit a new one if required.

Reassembly

8 Fit the collars into the back of the cooler housing.

9 Smear the new O-rings with clean engine oil and fit them on the collars **(see illustration)**.

10 Install the oil cooler in the housing, making sure the arrow on the cooler is pointing in the same direction as the arrow on the back of the housing **(see illustration)**. Fit the cooler mounting bolts and washers and tighten them securely.

11 Fit a new seal into the groove in the cooler cover, then fit the cover on the housing making sure the seal remains correctly seated **(see illustration 19.3)**. Install the cover bolts, with a new sealing washer on the lower bolt if required, and tighten them securely **(see illustration)**.

12 Install the oil cooler (see Section 18).

20 Gearchange mechanism – removal, inspection and installation

Note: *This procedure can be carried out with the engine in the frame. If the engine has been removed, ignore the steps that do not apply.*

Removal

1 Remove the clutch (see Section 15).

2 Make sure the transmission is in neutral. There should be a punch mark on the end of the gearchange shaft which aligns with the slot in the gearchange linkage lever; if not, make a mark to aid reassembly, then undo the pinch bolt and disconnect the linkage lever from the shaft **(see illustration)**.

3 On the right-hand side of the engine, note how the gearchange shaft return spring ends fit on each side of the locating pin in the

19.4b . . . and remove the cooler

19.9 Fit the collars and new O-rings into the housing

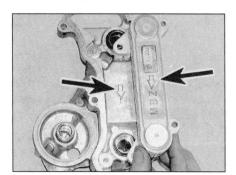

19.10 Arrows on cooler and housing should point in the same direction

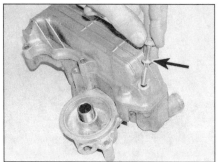

19.11 Check the condition of the sealing washer on the lower cover bolt (arrowed)

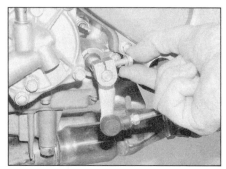

20.2 Disconnect the gearchange linkage lever

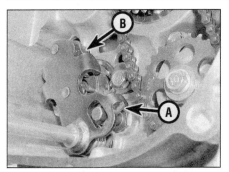

20.3 Note the location of the return spring ends (A) and selector arm pawls (B)

20.4 Withdraw the gearchange shaft and thrust washer (arrowed)

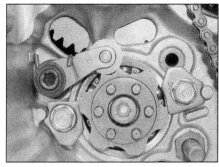

20.5a Note the arrangement of the stopper arm and cam

casing, and how the shaft selector arm pawls engage with the pins on the gearchange cam **(see illustration)**.

4 Withdraw the gearchange shaft and its thrust washer from the casing **(see illustration)**.

5 Note where the ends of the gearchange stopper arm return spring locate and how the roller on the arm rests in the neutral detent on the gearchange cam **(see illustration)**. Unscrew the stopper arm bolt and remove the stopper arm, washer and spring, noting their correct fitted positions **(see illustration)**.

6 If required, unscrew the selector drum centre bolt and remove the bolt and the selector drum cam **(see illustration)**. Remove the locating pin from the selector drum and store it with the cam for safe-keeping (see Section 30).

Inspection

7 Inspect the stopper arm return spring and the gearchange shaft return spring. If they are fatigued, worn or damaged they must be renewed. The shaft return spring is retained by a circlip. To remove the circlip, slide it down the length of the shaft, do not stretch it over the shaft **(see illustration)**. Ensure the circlip is correctly located in its groove.

8 Check that the shaft return spring locating pin in the casing is securely tightened. If it is loose, remove it and apply a suitable non-permanent thread-locking compound, then tighten it to the torque specified at the beginning of this Chapter.

9 Check the gearchange shaft for straightness and damage to the splines. If the shaft is bent you can attempt to straighten it,

but if the splines are damaged the shaft must be renewed.

10 Check the condition of the gearchange shaft oil seal in the engine casing and renew it if it is damaged or deteriorated. Undo the retaining bolt for the seal retaining plate and remove the plate, then lever the old seal out using a flat bladed screwdriver **(see illustrations)**. Press the new seal in squarely with a suitably sized socket. Check the condition of the gearchange shaft needle roller bearing behind the seal; the bearing on the machine we stripped pulled out easily with the seal removed, but if the bearing is a tight fit refer to *Tools and Workshop Tips* in the Reference Section. If the bearing is worn or damaged it must be replaced. Install the seal retaining plate and tighten the bolt securely.

11 Inspect the gearchange shaft selector arm

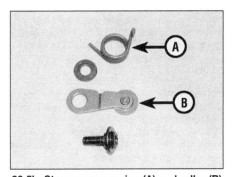

20.5b Stopper arm spring (A) and roller (B) should be checked for wear

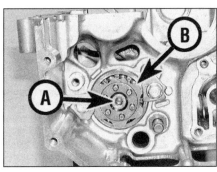

20.6 Undo bolt (A) and remove the cam (B)

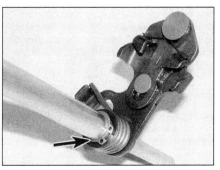

20.7 Gearchange shaft return spring is retained by circlip (arrowed)

2

20.10a Remove the retaining plate . . .

20.10b . . . then lever out the seal

20.10c Check the condition of the bearing

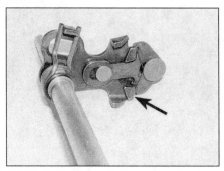

20.11 Gearchange shaft pawl mechanism (arrowed)

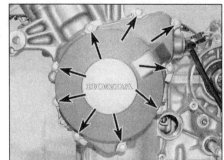

21.2 Unscrew the bolts (arrowed) to remove the engine cover

21.3 Check the operation of the starter clutch by rotating the idle gear (arrowed)

for wear where it bears on the return spring. Also inspect the selector arm pawl mechanism and spring for wear or damage **(see illustration)**. The gearchange shaft and selector arm mechanism must be replaced as one assembly.

12 Check for wear on the gearchange cam pins and cam lobes, and the stopper arm and the stopper arm roller. If they are worn or damaged they must be renewed.

Installation

13 If removed, fit the pin in the end of the gear selector drum, then install the gear selector cam, locating the pin in the recess in the back of the cam. Clean the threads of the centre bolt, then apply a suitable non-permanent thread-locking compound. Install the bolt and tighten it to the torque setting specified at the beginning of this Chapter.

14 Fit the stopper arm, washer and spring to the retaining bolt, noting that the spring should be positioned to hold the stopper arm against the cam. Screw the stopper arm bolt into the crankcase. Lift the arm into position on the selector drum cam, then tighten the bolt securely **(see illustration 20.5a)**. Check the operation of the arm before proceeding.

15 Check that the gearchange shaft return spring is properly positioned and that the circlip is in its groove, then slide the thrust washer onto the shaft. Lightly grease the inside of the gearchange shaft oil seal and slide the shaft into place from the right-hand side of the engine **(see illustration 20.4)**.

16 Locate the selector arm pawls onto the

pins on the selector cam and the ends of the return spring onto each side of the locating pin **(see illustration 20.3)**.

17 Align the gearchange linkage lever with the punch mark on the gearchange shaft and refit the lever. Tighten the lever pinch bolt to the torque setting specified at the beginning of this Chapter.

18 Install the clutch (see Section 15).

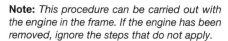

21 Starter clutch and idle gear – removal, inspection and installation

Note: *This procedure can be carried out with the engine in the frame. If the engine has been removed, ignore the steps that do not apply.*

Removal

1 Remove the air filter housing (see Chapter 4), then trace the alternator wiring from the left-hand side of the engine and disconnect it at the white 3-pin connector. Release the wiring from any clips or ties, and feed it through to the left-hand engine cover, noting its routing.

2 Unscrew the bolts securing the left-hand engine cover and remove the cover, being prepared to catch any residual oil **(see illustration)**. If the cover will not lift away easily, break the gasket seal by tapping gently around the sides with a rubber hammer or block of wood. Discard the gasket as a new one must be fitted on reassembly. Remove the dowel from either the cover or the crankcase if it is loose.

3 The operation of the starter clutch can be checked while it is in place. Remove the starter motor (see Chapter 9). The idle gear should rotate freely anti-clockwise as you look at it from the left-hand side of the bike, but lock when rotated clockwise **(see illustration)**. If not, the starter clutch is faulty and should be removed for inspection.

4 Withdraw the idle gear shaft from the crankcase and remove the gear **(see illustration)**.

5 Remove the alternator rotor – the starter clutch is mounted on the back of it (see Chapter 9, Section 33).

Note: *Before removing the alternator rotor, loosen the starter clutch bolts while holding the rotor centre bolt. If the rotor has already been removed from the bike, hold the rotor with a strap wrench to loosen the bolts.*

6 Withdraw the starter driven gear from the starter clutch **(see illustration)**. If the gear appears stuck, rotate it anti-clockwise as you withdraw it to free it from the starter clutch. If the starter driven gear does not come away with the alternator rotor, slide it off the crankshaft.

Inspection

7 Inspect the teeth on the idle gear and replace it if any are chipped or worn. Check the idle gear shaft and bearing surfaces for signs of wear or damage, and replace if necessary **(see illustration)**.

8 Lay the alternator rotor face down and fit the starter driven gear into the starter clutch, rotating it anti-clockwise as you do so to

21.4 Withdraw the shaft and remove the gear

21.6 Withdraw the gear from the clutch and inspect it for wear or damage

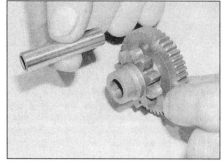

21.7 Inspect the idle gear and gear shaft

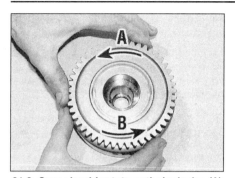

21.8 Gear should rotate anti-clockwise (A) and lock clockwise (B)

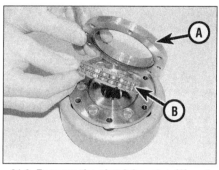

21.9 Remove the clutch housing (A) and clutch (B)

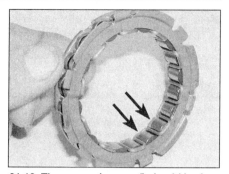

21.10 The sprags (arrowed) should be free in the cage

spread the clutch sprags to allow the gear hub to enter. Check that the starter driven gear rotates freely in an anti-clockwise direction and locks against the rotor in a clockwise direction **(see illustration)**. If it doesn't, the starter clutch should be dismantled.

9 Unscrew the bolts and remove the clutch housing and the clutch from the back of the alternator rotor **(see illustration)**.

10 Inspect the condition of the sprags and the sprag cage inside the clutch assembly **(see illustration)**. If they are damaged or worn at any point, the starter clutch should be renewed.

11 Inspect the driven gear internal bearing surface for signs of wear and scoring and inspect the needle roller bearing on the crankshaft for loose or damaged rollers **(see illustration)**. See *Tools and Workshop Tips* in the *Reference* section if the bearing needs replacing. Wear on the driven gear boss can be assessed by measuring the outside diameter of the boss and comparing it to the service limit listed in this Chapter's Specifications. Inspect the teeth of the driven gear and replace the gear if they are worn or damaged.

Installation

12 Clean the starter clutch bolts and apply a drop of locking compound to their threads.

13 Fit the clutch assembly and the clutch housing to the back of the rotor, then turn the rotor over and install the bolts and tighten them to the torque setting specified at the beginning of this Chapter **(see illustrations)**.

Note: *If a strap wrench is not available to hold the alternator rotor, final tightening of the bolts can take place once the rotor has been fitted to the crankshaft.*

14 Lubricate the hub of the starter driven gear with clean engine oil, then fit it into the starter clutch and check the operation of the clutch **(see illustration 21.6)**.

15 Install the alternator (see Chapter 9).

16 Lubricate the idle gear shaft with clean engine oil. Position the idle gear, making sure the teeth of the smaller pinion mesh correctly with the teeth of the starter driven gear, then slide the shaft through the gear into the crankcase **(see illustration)**.

17 Install the starter motor (see Chapter 9).

18 Apply a smear of suitable sealant across the crankcase joint, make sure the locating

21.11 Inspect the bearing (arrowed) on the crankshaft

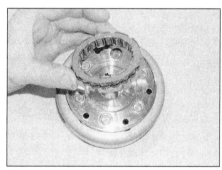

21.13a Install the clutch assembly . . .

21.13b . . . and the clutch housing . . .

2

21.13c . . . then fit the bolts . . .

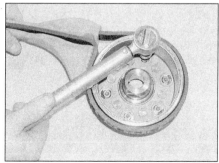

21.13d . . . and tighten them to the specified torque

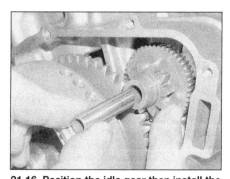

21.16 Position the idle gear then install the shaft

21.18 Fit the dowel (arrowed) and a new gasket

21.19 Ensure the cover aligns with the idle gear shaft (arrowed)

With all the relevant components removed proceed as follows.

4 Remove the oil jet which is located in the right-hand side of the crankcase behind the ignition rotor cover (see Section 13). Remove the O-ring from the jet and discard it as a new one must be fitted on reassembly.

5 With the crankcase the right way up, unscrew the seven upper crankcase bolts a 1/4 turn at a time in a criss-cross pattern until they are finger-tight, then remove them **(see illustration)**. Note the sealing washers on the bolts marked with an arrow on the crankcase; discard the washers as new ones must be fitted on reassembly **(see illustration)**.

dowel is in position and fit a new gasket to the crankcase **(see illustration)**.

19 Install the alternator cover, making sure it locates correctly onto the dowel and the idle gear shaft **(see illustration)**. Install the cover bolts and tighten them evenly in a criss-cross sequence to the torque setting specified at the beginning of this Chapter **(see illustration 21.2)**.

20 Feed the alternator wiring back to its connector, making sure it is correctly routed and secured, and reconnect it.

21 Check the engine oil level before riding the motorcycle (see *Daily (pre ride) checks*).

22 Crankcase – separation and reassembly

Separation

1 To gain access to the crankshaft, pistons and connecting rods and transmission components, the crankcase must be split into two parts.

2 To enable the crankcase to be split the engine must be removed from the frame (see Section 5) and the following components removed:
● Camshafts (Section 9)
● Cylinder head (Section 10)
● Camchain and guide (Section 13)
● Clutch (Section 15)
● Oil pump sprockets and chain (Section 17)
● Alternator rotor (Chapter 9)
● Pulse secondary air (PAIR) valve (see Chapter 4)
● Oil cooler (Section 18)
● Oil sump (Section 16)
Note: *If the crankcase halves are being separated purely to examine the transmission shafts or crankshaft, then there is no need to remove the cylinder head.*

3 If the crankcases are being separated as part of a complete engine overhaul, remove the following components:
● Oil pump (Section 17)
● Gearchange mechanism (Section 20)
● Starter motor (see Chapter 9)
● Water pump (see Chapter 3)

> **HAYNES HiNT** *Make a cardboard template of the crankcase and punch a hole for each bolt location. Number the holes. As each bolt is removed, store it in its relative position, with its washer where applicable, in the template. This will ensure all bolts are installed correctly on reassembly – this is important, as some bolts differ slightly in length.*

6 Turn the crankcase upside down, and unscrew the single 10 mm bolt from the left rear corner of the crankcase **(see illustration)**.

7 Working in a criss-cross pattern, unscrew the 6 mm lower crankcase bolts and store them on your template **(see illustration)**.

8 Starting from the outside and working inwards in a criss-cross pattern, unscrew the ten 8 mm main bearing journal bolts a 1/4 turn at a time. Once all the bolts are finger-tight remove them and store them on your template. **Note:** *The right-hand rear journal bolt fitted inside the sump is 88 mm long, the other bolts fitted inside the sump are 75 mm long. The journal bolts fitted outside the sump are all 100 mm long.*

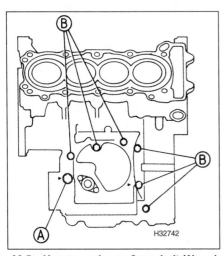

22.5a Upper crankcase 8 mm bolt (A) and 6 mm bolts (B)

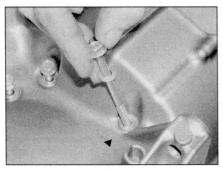

22.5b Note the sealing washers on bolts marked with an arrow

22.6 Undo the lower crankcase 10 mm bolt (arrowed) first

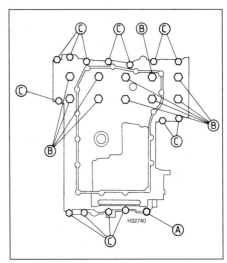

22.7 Lower crankcase 10 mm (A), 8 mm (B) and 6 mm (C) bolts

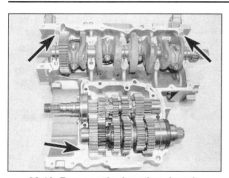

22.10 Remove the locating dowels (arrowed)

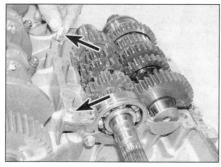

22.11a Remove the oil jets (arrowed) . . .

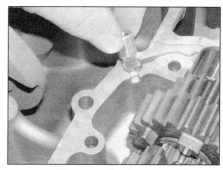

22.11b . . . noting how they fit

9 Carefully lift the lower crankcase half off the upper half. If necessary, use a soft-faced hammer or block of wood to tap around the joint to initially separate the halves. As the upper half is lifted away take care not to dislodge or lose any main bearing inserts. **Note:** *If the halves do not separate easily, make sure all fasteners have been removed. Do not try and separate the halves by levering between the sealing surfaces as they are easily damaged and will leak oil on reassembly.*

10 Remove the three locating dowels from the upper crankcase half **(see illustration)**.

11 Remove the two oil jets from the upper crankcase half, noting which way around they are fitted **(see illustrations)**.

12 Refer to Sections 23 to 30 for the removal and installation of the components housed within the crankcases.

Reassembly

13 Remove all traces of sealant from the crankcase mating surfaces and ensure the oilways are clear (see *Tools and Workshop Tips* in the *Reference* section).

14 Ensure that all components and their bearings are in place in the upper and lower crankcase halves. If the transmission shafts have not been removed, check the condition of the oil seal on the left-hand end of the

output shaft and replace it with a new one if it is damaged, deformed or deteriorated (see Section 28). It is sound practice to renew this seal anyway. Apply some grease to the inside of the new seal on installation.

15 Make sure the selector drum and forks and the transmission shafts are in the neutral position (see Section 30). You should be able to rotate each transmission shaft independently of the other one.

16 Lubricate the crankshaft, transmission shafts and selector drum and forks with clean engine oil, particularly around the bearings, then use a rag soaked in high flash-point solvent to wipe over the mating surfaces of both crankcase halves to remove all traces of oil.

17 Make sure the oil jet holes are clear then fit both jets into the upper crankcase half ensuring that they are the correct way up **(see illustrations 22.11a and b)**.

18 Fit the three locating dowels into the upper crankcase half **(see illustration 22.10)**.

19 Apply a thin coating of suitable sealant to the mating surface of the lower crankcase half **(see illustration)**.

Caution: Do not apply an excessive amount of sealant as it will ooze out when the case halves are assembled and may obstruct oil passages. Do not apply the sealant on or too close (within 2 to 3 mm) to any of the bearing inserts or surfaces.

20 Make sure that the main bearing shells are in position in the lower crankcase half, then fit the lower crankcase half onto the upper half. Engage the selector forks with their respective

slots in the transmission gears as the halves are joined and make sure that the dowels locate correctly.

21 Check that the lower crankcase half is seated correctly. **Note:** *The crankcase halves should fit together without being forced. If the casings are not correctly seated, remove the lower crankcase half and investigate the problem. Do not attempt to pull them together using the crankcase bolts as the casing will crack and be ruined.*

22 Lubricate the threads and undersides of the heads of the ten 8 mm main bearing journal bolts with clean engine oil and install the bolts in their original locations **(see illustration)** (see Step 8).

23 Starting from the centre and working outwards in a criss-cross pattern, tighten the main bearing journal bolts to approximately half the torque specified at the beginning of this Chapter. Go around a second time in the same sequence and tighten them to the full torque setting **(see illustration)**.

24 Fit the single 10 mm crankcase bolt and tighten it to the specified torque setting **(see illustration 22.6)**.

25 Fit the 6 mm bolts in their original locations and tighten them in a criss-cross pattern to the specified torque setting **(see illustration 22.7)**.

26 Turn the crankcase over so that it is the right way up and install the seven upper crankcase bolts. Note that new sealing washers must be fitted on the bolts marked with an arrow on the crankcase **(see illustration 22.5b)**. Working in a criss-cross

2

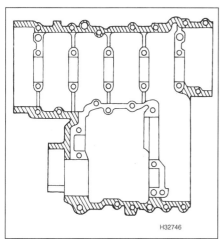

H32746

22.19 Apply sealant to the lower crankcase half as illustrated

22.22 Install the crankshaft main bearing journal bolts first . . .

22.23 . . . then tighten them as described

pattern, tighten the 6 mm bolts to the specified torque, then tighten the 8 mm bolt to the specified torque.

27 With all crankcase bolts tightened, check that the crankshaft and transmission shafts rotate smoothly and easily. Check that all gears can be selected and that the shafts rotate freely in every gear. If there are any signs of undue stiffness, rough spots or of any other problem, the fault must be rectified before proceeding further.

28 Fit a new O-ring to the oil jet. Apply a smear of oil to the O-ring to ease installation and insert the jet into position in the crankcase (see Section 13).

29 Install all other removed assemblies in the reverse of the sequence given in Steps 2 and 3.

23 Connecting rod and main bearings – general information

1 Even though main and connecting rod bearings are generally replaced with new ones during the engine overhaul, the old bearings should be carefully examined as they may reveal valuable information about the condition of the engine.

2 Bearing failure occurs mainly because of lack of lubrication, the presence of dirt or other foreign particles, overloading the engine and/or corrosion. Regardless of the cause of bearing failure, it must be corrected before the engine is reassembled to prevent it from happening again.

3 When examining the bearings, match them with their corresponding journal on the crankshaft to help identify the cause of any problem.

4 Dirt and other foreign particles get into the engine in a variety of ways. They may be left in the engine during assembly or they may pass through filters or breathers, then get into the oil and from there into the bearings. Metal chips from machining operations and normal engine wear are often present. Abrasives are sometimes left in engine components after reconditioning operations, especially when parts are not thoroughly cleaned using the proper cleaning methods. Whatever the source, foreign objects often end up imbedded in the soft bearing material and are easily recognised. Large particles will not imbed in the bearing and will score or gouge the bearing and journal. The best prevention for this type of bearing failure is to clean all parts thoroughly and keep everything spotlessly clean during engine reassembly. Regular oil and filter changes are also essential.

5 Lack of lubrication or lubrication breakdown have a number of interrelated causes. Excessive heat (which thins the oil), overloading (which squeezes the oil from the bearing face) and oil leakage or throw off (from excessive bearing clearances, a worn oil pump or high engine speeds) all contribute to a breakdown of the protective lubricating film. Blocked oil

passages will starve a bearing of lubrication and destroy it. When lack of lubrication is the cause of bearing failure, the bearing material is wiped or extruded from the steel backing of the bearing. Temperatures may increase to the point where the steel backing and the journal turn blue from overheating.

> **HAYNES HINT** *Refer to Tools and Workshop Tips (Section 5) in the Reference section for bearing fault finding.*

6 Riding habits can have a definite effect on bearing life. Full throttle low speed operation, or lugging (labouring) the engine, puts very high loads on bearings, which tend to squeeze out the oil film. These loads cause the bearings to flex, which produces fine cracks in the bearing face (fatigue failure). Eventually the bearing material will loosen in pieces and tear away from the steel backing. Short trip riding leads to corrosion of bearings, as insufficient engine heat is produced to drive off the condensed water and corrosive gases produced. These products collect in the engine oil, forming acid and sludge. As the oil is carried to the engine bearings, the acid attacks and corrodes the bearing material.

7 Incorrect bearing installation during engine assembly will lead to bearing failure as well. Tight fitting bearings which leave insufficient bearing oil clearances result in oil starvation. Dirt or foreign particles trapped behind a bearing insert result in high spots on the bearing which lead to failure.

8 To avoid bearing problems, clean all parts thoroughly before reassembly, double check all bearing clearance measurements and lubricate the new bearings with clean engine oil during installation.

24 Connecting rods and bearings – removal, inspection and installation

Note: *To remove the connecting rods the engine must be removed from the frame.*

Removal

1 Separate the crankcase halves (see Section 22).

2 Before detaching the rods from the crankshaft, measure the side clearance of each rod with a feeler gauge **(see illustration)**. If the clearance on any rod is greater than the service limit listed in the Specifications at the beginning of this Chapter, replace the rod with a new one.

3 Using paint or a marker pen, mark the cylinder identity on the top of each piston and on each connecting rod and cap **(see illustration)**. Cylinders are numbered 1 to 4, numbering from the left-hand side of the motorcycle. **Note:** *The number and letter already written on the rod and cap are the rod size and weight code respectively, not the cylinder number.*

4 Working on one connecting rod at a time, unscrew the two cap nuts and remove the cap, complete with the lower bearing shell, from the crankpin **(see illustration)**. Detach

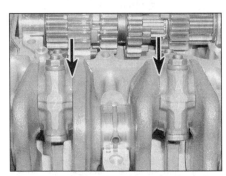

24.2 Measure the clearance between the connecting rods and the crankshaft

24.3a Mark the cylinder identity on each piston . . .

24.3b . . . and each connecting rod and cap

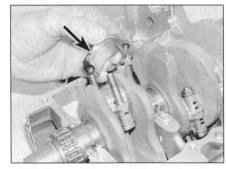

24.4 Remove the cap and lower bearing shell (arrowed)

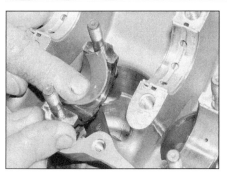

24.6a Only remove the upper shells if they are loose

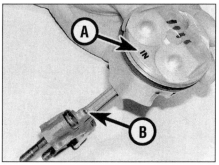

24.6b Note the IN mark (A) on the piston and the oil hole (B) in the rod

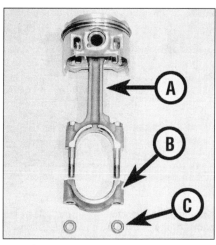

24.7 Keep the piston and rod (A), bearing cap (B) and cap nuts (C) together as an assembly

the rod, complete with the upper bearing shell, from the crankpin. Repeat the procedure on the other three connecting rod assemblies.

5 If required, the crankshaft can be lifted out of the upper crankcase half, taking care not to dislodge the main bearing shells (see Section 27).

6 Remove the upper bearing shells if they are loose but keep them in order **(see illustration)**. Push each piston/connecting rod assembly to the top end of the cylinder bore and remove it, making sure the rod does not mark the bore walls. Note the IN mark on the top of each piston which should face the back (inlet side) of the engine and the oil hole in the big end of each connecting rod which should also face the back **(see illustration)**.

 HAYNES HINT *To ease removal of the pistons, carefully remove any ridge of carbon built up on the top of each cylinder bore using a scraper. If there is a pronounced wear ridge, remove it using a ridge reamer.*

Caution: Do not try to remove the piston/connecting rod from the bottom of the cylinder bore. The piston will not pass the crankcase main bearing webs. If the piston is pulled right to the bottom of the bore the oil control ring will expand and lock the piston in position. If this happens it is likely the ring will be broken.

7 Fit the related bearing shells (if removed), bearing cap and nuts on each connecting rod assembly so that they are all kept together as a matched set **(see illustration)**.

8 Do not remove the bolts from the connecting rods. **Note:** *It is not necessary to renew the big-end bolts when the connecting rods are removed. If, for any reason, the bolts have to be renewed, drive the old bolts out of the rods by tapping gently with a hammer. Because the bolts are a tight fit in the rods, take care to align the bolt heads with the machined insets in the rod shoulders before pressing them into place* **(see illustration)**.

9 Remove the pistons from the connecting rods (see Section 25).

Inspection

10 Check the connecting rods for cracks and other obvious damage.

11 Apply clean engine oil to the piston pin, insert it into its connecting rod small-end and check for any freeplay between the two **(see illustration)**. If there is freeplay, measure the pin external diameter and compare the result to the Specifications at the beginning of this Chapter **(see illustration)**. Replace the pin with a new one if it is worn beyond its specified limits. If the pin diameter is within specifications, replace the connecting rod with a new one. Repeat the measurements for all the rods. **Note:** *If a connecting rod is to replaced, it is essential that the new rod is of the same weight to minimise vibration. The*

weight code is indicated by a letter marked on the big-end cap of each rod. This letter together with the connecting rod size (see Step 25) should be quoted when purchasing new connecting rod(s).

12 Refer to Section 23 and examine the connecting rod bearing shells. If they are scored, badly scuffed or appear to have seized, new shells must be installed. Always renew the shells in the connecting rods as a set. If they are badly damaged, check the corresponding crankpin. Evidence of extreme heat, such as bluing, indicates that lubrication failure has occurred. Be sure to thoroughly check the oil pump and pressure relief valve as well as all oil holes and passages before reassembling the engine. Have the rods checked by a Honda dealer if you are in doubt about their straightness.

Oil clearance check

13 Whether new bearing shells are being fitted or the original ones are being re-used, the connecting rod big-end bearing oil clearance should be checked prior to reassembly. Bearing oil clearance is measured with a product known as Plastigauge.

14 Remove the bearing shells from the rods

2

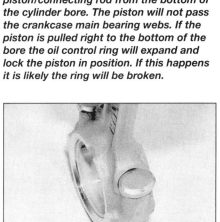

24.8 Bolt head must fit into recess in connecting rod shoulder

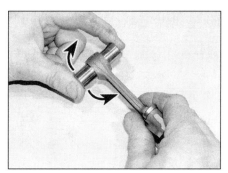

24.11a Rock the piston pin back and forth to check for freeplay

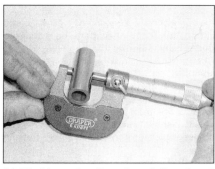

24.11b Measuring the external diameter of the pin

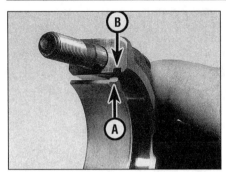

24.15 Ensure tab (A) locates in notch (B)

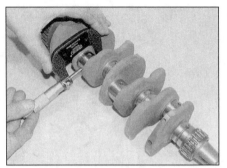

24.22 Measuring the diameter of the crankpin journal

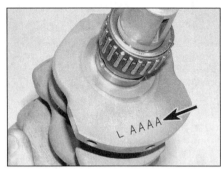

24.25a Crankpin journal size codes (arrowed)

and caps, keeping them in order. Clean the backs of the shells, the bearing locations in both the connecting rod and cap, and the crankpin journal with a suitable solvent.

15 Press the bearing shells into their locations, ensuring that the tab on each shell engages the notch in the connecting rod or cap **(see illustration)**. Make sure the bearings are fitted in the correct locations and take care not to touch any shell's bearing surface with your fingers.

16 Support the crankshaft. Cut an appropriate size length of Plastigauge (it should be slightly shorter than the width of the crankpin) and place it on the crankpin journal to be checked **(see illustration 27.12)**. Do not place Plastigauge over the oil holes in the journal.

17 Apply molybdenum disulphide oil to the bolt shanks and threads and to the seats of the cap nuts. Fit the connecting rod and cap onto the crankpin **(see illustrations 24.33a and b)**. Make sure the oil hole in the rod is facing the right way (see Step 6) and that the cap is fitted the correct way around so the previously made markings align (see Step 3).

18 Fit the nuts and tighten them evenly, in two or three stages, to the specified torque setting. **Note:** *It is essential that, throughout this procedure, the connecting rod does not rotate on the crankshaft.*

19 Undo the cap nuts and remove the cap and connecting rod from the crankshaft, again ensuring that the rod does not rotate on the crankshaft.

20 Compare the width of the crushed Plastigauge on the crankpin to the scale printed on the Plastigauge envelope to obtain the connecting rod bearing oil clearance **(see illustration 27.18)**. Compare the reading to the specifications at the beginning of this Chapter. If the clearance is within the range specified and the bearings are in perfect condition, they can be reused.

21 Carefully clean away all traces of the Plastigauge from the crankpin journal and bearing shells using a fingernail or other object which will not score the bearing surfaces.

22 If the clearance is beyond the service limit, measure the diameter of the crankpin journal with a micrometer and compare the

result with the appropriate figure in the table for connecting rod bearing shell selection **(see illustration)**. For example, if the journal being measured is code A, the table indicates that the service limit for that journal is 31.492 mm. If the journal diameter is larger than the service limit, new bearing shells can be fitted (see Steps 25 and 26). If the journal diameter is smaller than the service limit, the crankshaft should be renewed.

23 Repeat the oil clearance check for the remaining connecting rods. Always renew all of the shells (on all four rods) at the same time.

24 Install the new shells and check the oil clearance once again.

Bearing shell selection

25 Replacement bearing shells for the big-end bearings are supplied on a selected fit basis. Codes for the crankshaft journals are stamped on the outside of the crankshaft web on the left-hand end of the crankshaft **(see illustration)**. The lower block of four letters is the size codes for the crankpin bearing journals (the upper block of five numbers is the size codes for the main bearing journals). The first letter of the block is for the left-hand (No. 1 cylinder) journal, and so on. Each connecting rod size code number is marked

on the flat face of the connecting rod and cap **(see illustration)**.

26 A corresponding range of bearing shells is available. To select the correct shells, use the table below to cross-reference the crankpin journal code letter with the connecting rod code number to determine the colour code of the shells required. For example, if the connecting rod size is 2, and the crankpin size is A, then the bearing shells required are Green. The colour is marked on the side of the shell **(see illustration)**.

Installation

27 Fit the pistons onto the connecting rods (see Section 25).

28 Ensure that the backs of the bearing shells, the bearing seats in the caps and rods and the crankpin journals are clean. If new shells are being fitted, ensure that all traces of protective grease are removed using paraffin (kerosene). Dry the shells, caps, rods and journals with a clean, lint-free cloth. Install the shells, making sure the tab on each shell engages the notch in the cap or rod **(see illustration 24.15)**.

29 Make sure the bearings are fitted in their correct locations and take care

	Crankpin code	
Connecting rod code	**A** (31.492 to 31.500 mm)	**B** (31.484 to 31.492 mm)
1 (34.000 to 34.008 mm)	Yellow	Green
2 (34.008 to 34.016 mm)	Green	Brown

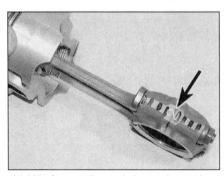

24.25b Connecting rod size code number (arrowed)

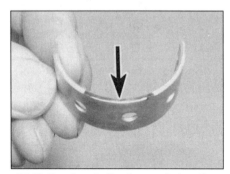

24.26 Bearing shell colour code location (arrowed)

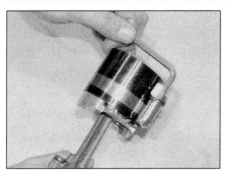

24.30 Fit the piston ring compressor over the piston and rings

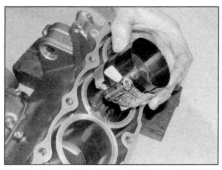

24.31a Lower the piston/rod assembly into the bore . . .

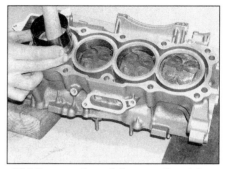

24.31b . . . and carefully press the piston into the bore

not to touch any bearing surfaces with your fingers. Lubricate the shells with clean engine oil.

30 Lubricate the pistons, rings and cylinder bore with clean engine oil. Stagger the piston ring end gaps as described in Section 26. If available, use a piston ring compressor to aid installation **(see illustration)**.

31 Insert the piston/connecting rod assembly into the top of its bore, taking care not to allow the connecting rod to mark the bore **(see illustration)**. Make sure the IN mark on the top of the piston faces the back (inlet side) of the engine and the oil hole in the rod also faces the back of the engine (see Step 6). Insert the piston into the bore so that its crown is flush with the top of the bore **(see illustration)**; if a ring compressor is not available, carefully compress and feed each

piston ring into the bore as the piston is inserted **(see illustration)**.

32 If the crankshaft has been removed, lower it into position in the upper crankcase, making sure all the bearing shells remain in place (see Section 27).

33 Working on one connecting rod at a time, lubricate the crankpin journal and the shells in the connecting rod and cap with clean engine oil. Apply molybdenum disulphide grease to the shanks and threads of the big-end bolts. Pull the rod onto the crankpin and fit the cap onto the rod **(see illustrations)**. Make sure the cap is fitted the correct way around so the previously made markings align (see Step 3).

34 Apply molybdenum disulphide oil to the threads and seats of the cap nuts, then fit the nuts and tighten them finger-tight **(see illustration)**. Check that all components have

been returned to their original locations using the marks made on disassembly.

35 Tighten the cap nuts, in two or three stages, to the specified torque setting **(see illustration)**.

36 Lubricate the cylinder bore liberally with clean engine oil and check that the crankshaft rotates smoothly and freely. If there are any signs of roughness or tightness, detach the rod and recheck the assembly. Sometimes tapping the bottom of the connecting rod cap will relieve tightness.

37 Install the remaining piston/connecting rod assemblies in the same way, then reassemble the crankcase halves (see Section 22).

25 Pistons – removal, inspection and installation

Note: *To remove the connecting rods the engine must be removed from the frame.*

Removal

1 Separate the crankcase halves (see Section 22) and remove the piston/connecting rod assemblies (see Section 24).

2 Before removing the piston from the connecting rod, ensure it is marked with its cylinder identity. Cylinders are numbered 1 to 4, numbering from the left-hand side of the motorcycle. If the piston is going to be cleaned, scratch the identity lightly on the

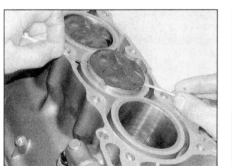

24.31c Feed the rings into the bore with care

24.33a Pull the rod onto the crankpin . . .

2

24.33b . . . then fit the cap onto the rod

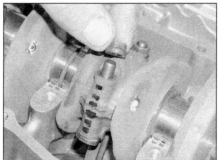

24.34 Install the nuts finger-tight . . .

24.35 . . . then tighten them to the specified torque

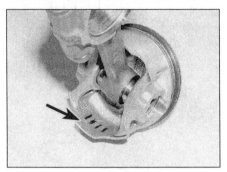

25.2a Mark the piston identity on the inside of the skirt (arrowed) . . .

25.2b . . . or on the top

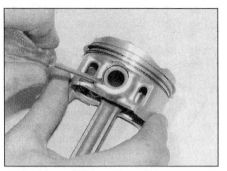

25.3a Prise out the circlip . . .

inside of the piston skirt **(see illustrations)**. Each piston must be installed in its original cylinder on reassembly. Note the IN mark on the top of each piston that faces the back (inlet side) of the engine. If this is not visible, mark the piston accordingly so that it can be installed the correct way round.

3 Carefully prise out the circlips on each side of the piston pin using needle-nose pliers or a small flat-bladed screwdriver inserted into the notch **(see illustration)**. Check for burring around the circlip grooves and remove any with a very fine file or penknife blade, then push the piston pin out to free the piston from the connecting rod **(see illustration)**. Discard the circlips as new ones must be used on reassembly. When the piston has been removed from the rod, keep the piston and its pin together so that related parts do not get mixed up.

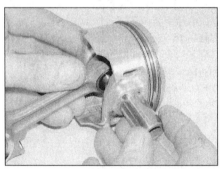

25.3b . . . then push out the pin and remove the piston

HAYNES HiNT *If a piston pin is a tight fit in the piston, soak a rag in boiling water then wring it out and wrap it around the piston – this will expand the alloy piston sufficiently to release its grip on the pin. If the piston pin is particularly stubborn, extract it using a drawbolt tool, but be careful to protect the piston's working surfaces.*

4 Using your thumbs or a piston ring removal and installation tool, carefully remove the rings from the pistons, working on one piston at a time **(see illustrations)**. Do not nick or gouge the pistons in the process. Note which way up each ring fits and in which groove, as they must be installed in their original positions if being re-used. The upper surface of the top two rings should have a manufacturer's mark or letter at one end – if the mark on each ring is different, note which mark is for the top ring and which is for the second **(see illustration)**. **Note:** *It is good practice to renew the piston rings when an engine is being overhauled. Ensure that the pistons and bores are serviceable before purchasing new rings.*

5 Clean all traces of carbon from the tops of the pistons. A hand-held wire brush or a piece of fine emery cloth can be used once most of the deposits have been scraped away. Do not, under any circumstances, use a wire brush mounted in a drill motor; the piston material is soft and is easily damaged.

6 Use a piston ring groove cleaning tool to remove any carbon deposits from the ring grooves. If a tool is not available, a piece broken off an old ring will do the job. Be very careful to remove only the carbon deposits. Do not remove any metal and do not nick or gouge the sides of the ring grooves.

7 Once the carbon has been removed, clean the pistons with a suitable solvent and dry them thoroughly. Make sure the oil return holes at the back of the oil ring groove are clear. If the identification previously marked on the piston is cleaned off, be sure to re-mark it correctly **(see illustration 25.2a and b)**.

Inspection

8 Inspect each piston for cracks around the skirt, at the pin bosses and at the ring lands. Normal piston wear appears as even, vertical wear on the thrust surfaces of the piston and slight looseness of the top ring in its groove. If the skirt is scored or scuffed, the engine may have been suffering from overheating and/or abnormal combustion, resulting in excessively high operating temperatures.

9 A hole in the top of the piston, in one extreme, or burned areas around the edge of the piston crown, indicate that pre-ignition or knocking under load have occurred. If you find evidence of any problems the cause must be corrected or the damage will occur again (see *Fault Finding* in the *Reference* section).

10 Check the piston-to-bore clearance by measuring the bore (see Section 31) and the piston diameter. Make sure each piston is

25.4a Take care removing the piston rings by hand . . .

25.4b . . . or with a ring removal and installation tool

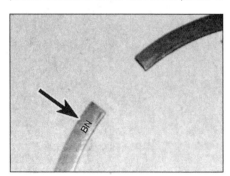

25.4c Note the mark on the end of the top two rings

25.10 Measuring the piston skirt diameter

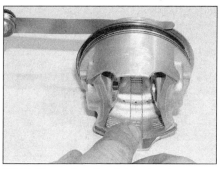

25.11 Measuring the piston ring-to-groove clearance

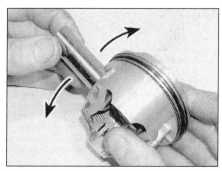

25.12a Insert the pin into the piston and rock it back and forth. If the pin is loose . . .

matched to its correct cylinder. Measure the piston 11 mm up from the bottom of the skirt and at 90° to the piston pin axis **(see illustration)**. Subtract the piston diameter from the bore diameter to obtain the clearance. If it is greater than the figure specified at the beginning of this Chapter, check whether it is the bore or piston that is worn beyond its service limit. If the bores are good, install new pistons and rings and have the bores honed (see Section 31). If the bores are worn, the cylinder block must be rebored and an oversize set of pistons fitted.

11 Measure the piston ring-to-groove clearance by laying each piston ring in its groove and slipping a feeler gauge in beside it **(see illustration)**. Make sure you have the correct ring for the groove (see Step 4). Check the clearance at three or four locations around the groove. If the clearance is greater than specified, renew both the piston and rings as a set. If new rings are being used (see Section 26), measure the clearance using the new rings. If the clearance is greater than that specified, the piston is worn and must be renewed.

12 Apply clean engine oil to the piston pin, insert it part way into the piston and check for any freeplay between the two **(see illustration)**. Measure the pin external diameter, and the pin bore in the piston **(see illustrations)**. Subtract the bore diameter

from the pin diameter to obtain the clearance. If it is greater than the specified figure, check whether it is the bore or pin that is worn beyond its service limit and renew them as required. Repeat the checks between the pin and the connecting rod small-end (see Section 24).

Note: *If the pistons are to be replaced, ensure the correct size of piston is ordered. Honda produces four oversizes of piston as well as standard pistons. The piston oversizes available are: +0.25 mm, +0.50 mm, +0.75 mm and +1.0 mm. Oversize pistons have their size stamped on top of the piston crown, e.g. a 0.25 mm oversize piston will be marked 0.25.*

Installation

13 Inspect and install the piston rings (see Section 26).

14 Install a **new** circlip into one side of the piston (never re-use old circlips), then lubricate the piston pin, the piston pin bore and the connecting rod small-end bore with clean engine oil.

15 Fit the piston on its connecting rod so that the IN mark on the top of the piston aligns with the oil hole in the rod. Insert the piston pin from the side without the circlip. Secure the pin with the other **new** circlip. When installing the circlips, compress them only just

enough to fit them in the piston, and make sure they are properly seated in their grooves with the open end away from the removal notch **(see illustration)**.

16 Install the piston/connecting rod assembly (see Section 24).

26 Piston rings –
inspection and installation

1 Before installing the piston rings, the ring end gaps must be checked.

Inspection

2 Lay out each piston with its ring set so the rings will be matched with the same piston and cylinder during the measurement procedure. The upper surface of the top two rings should have a manufacturer's mark or letter at one end – if the mark on each ring is different, note which mark is for the top ring and which is for the second **(see illustration 25.4c)**.

3 To measure the ring end gap, insert the ring into the top of the cylinder bore and square it up with the cylinder walls by pushing it in with the top of the piston. The ring should be about 25 mm below the top edge of the cylinder. Slip a feeler gauge between the ends of the ring to measure the gap and compare the

2

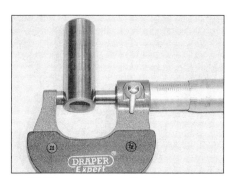

25.12b . . . measure the pin external diameter . . .

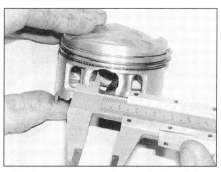

25.12c . . . and the pin bore in the piston

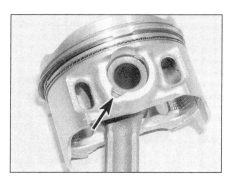

25.15 Fit the circlip with the open end away from the removal notch (arrowed)

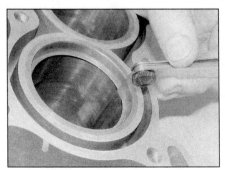

26.3 Measuring piston ring end gap

26.7a Fit the oil ring expander in its groove . . .

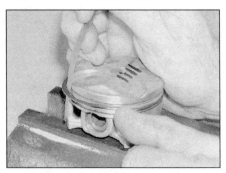

26.7b . . . then fit the side rails as described

measurement to the specifications at the beginning of this Chapter **(see illustration)**.

4 If the gap is larger than specified, double check to make sure that you have the correct rings before proceeding; excess end gap is not critical unless it exceeds the service limit. If the service limit is exceed with new rings, check the bore for wear (see Section 31).

5 Repeat the procedure for each ring and each cylinder in turn. Note that the end gaps differ between the top, second and oil control ring, and that only the side-rails of the oil control ring can be checked in this way. To check the expander ring, fit it into its groove in the piston and check that the ends touch but do not overlap. Remember to keep the rings together with their matched pistons.

Installation

6 Once the ring end gaps have been checked and corrected as necessary, the rings can be installed on the pistons.

7 The oil control ring (lowest on the piston) is

26.9 Old pieces of feeler gauge blade can be used to guide the ring over the piston

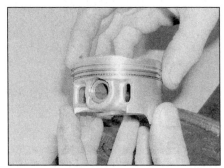

26.11a Ensure that the rings move freely in their grooves . . .

installed first. It is composed of three separate components; the expander and the upper and lower side rails. Slip the expander into the ring groove, then install the lower side rail **(see illustrations)**. Do not use a piston ring installation tool on the oil ring side rails as they may be damaged. Instead, place one end of the side rail into the groove between the expander and the ring land. Hold it firmly in place and slide a finger or thin blade around the piston while pushing the rail into the groove **(see illustration)**. Next, install the upper side rail in the same manner.

8 With the oil control ring installed, check that both the upper and lower side rails can be turned smoothly in the ring groove.

9 Fit the second ring into the middle groove in the piston with its mark or letter facing up (see Step 2). Note that the second ring is wider than the top ring. Do not expand the ring any more than is necessary to slide it into place. To avoid breaking the ring, use a piston ring installation tool **(see illustration 25.4b)**, or pieces of old feeler gauge blade **(see illustration)**.

10 Fit the top ring in the same manner into the top groove in the piston.

11 Once the rings are installed, check they move freely without snagging and stagger their end gaps as shown **(see illustrations)**.

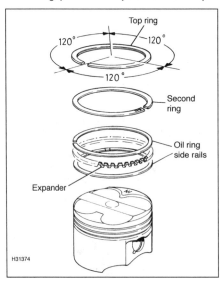

26.11b . . . then stagger the ring end gaps as shown

27 Crankshaft and main bearings – removal, inspection and installation

Note: *To remove the crankshaft the engine must be removed from the frame.*

Removal

1 Separate the crankcase halves (see Section 22) and disconnect the piston/connecting rod assemblies from the crankshaft (see Section 24). There is no need to remove piston/connecting rod assemblies from the cylinders; push them up the bores so that the connecting rod ends are clear of the crankshaft and rap clean rag around the rods to prevent damage to the bores.

2 Lift the crankshaft out of the upper crankcase half, taking care not to dislodge the bearing shells **(see illustration)**.

Inspection

3 Clean the crankshaft with a suitable solvent, paying particular attention to flush out the oil passages. If available, blow the crank dry with compressed air. Inspect the starter clutch needle roller bearing (see Section 21).

4 Refer to Section 23 and examine the main bearing shells **(see illustration)**. If they are scored, badly scuffed or appear to have seized, new bearings must be installed. Always renew the main bearings as a set. If they are badly damaged, check the corresponding crankshaft journals. Evidence of extreme heat, such as bluing, indicates that

27.2 Lift the crankshaft out of the crankcase carefully

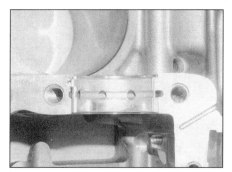

27.4 Examine the main bearing shells . . .

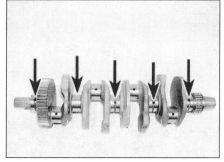

27.5 . . . and the crankshaft journals (arrowed)

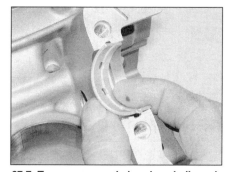

27.7 To remove a main bearing shell, push it sideways and lift it out

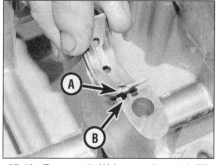

27.10 Ensure tab (A) locates in notch (B)

lubrication failure has occurred. Be sure to thoroughly check the oil pump and pressure relief valve as well as all oil holes and passages before reassembling the engine.

5 Give the crankshaft journals a close visual examination (see illustration). Pay particular attention where damaged bearings have been discovered. If the journals are scored or pitted in any way, a new crankshaft will be required. Note that undersized bearing shells are not available, precluding the option of re-grinding the crankshaft.

6 Place the crankshaft on V-blocks and check the runout with a dial indicator touching the centre main bearing journal (see *Tools and Workshop Tips* in the *Reference* section). Compare the reading to the maximum specified at the beginning of this Chapter. If the runout exceeds the limit, the crankshaft must be renewed.

7 If required, remove the bearing shells from the crankcase halves by pushing their centres to the side, then lifting them out (see illustration). Keep the shells in order so that they can be fitted in their original locations for the oil clearance check.

Oil clearance check

8 Whether new bearing shells are being fitted or the original ones are being re-used, the main bearing oil clearance should be checked before the engine is reassembled. Bearing oil clearance is measured with a product known as Plastigauge.

9 If not already done, remove the bearing shells from the crankcase halves (see Step 7).

Clean the backs of the shells and the bearing seats in both crankcase halves, and the main bearing journals on the crankshaft.

10 Press the bearing shells into their seats, ensuring that the tab on each shell engages in the notch in the crankcase (see illustration). Make sure the bearings are fitted in the correct locations and take care not to touch the bearing surfaces with your fingers.

11 Ensure the shells and crankshaft are clean and dry, then lay the crankshaft in position in the upper crankcase (see illustration). If removed, fit the dowels into the crankcase (see illustration 22.10).

12 Cut five appropriate size lengths of Plastigauge (they should be slightly shorter than the width of the crankshaft journals). Place a strand of Plastigauge on each journal (see illustration). Do not place Plastigauge over the oil holes in the crankshaft. Note: *It is essential that, throughout this procedure, the crankshaft does not rotate in the crankcase.*

13 Carefully fit the lower crankcase half onto the upper half. Make sure that the selector forks engage with their respective slots in the transmission gears as the halves are joined and that the Plastigauge is not disturbed.

14 Make sure that the dowels locate correctly and that the lower crankcase half is correctly seated. Note: *Do not tighten the crankcase bolts if the casing is not correctly seated.*

15 Lubricate the threads and undersides of the heads of the ten 8 mm crankshaft main bearing journal bolts with clean engine oil and install the bolts in their original locations (see Section 22).

16 Starting from the centre and working outwards in a criss-cross pattern, tighten the crankshaft journal bolts to approximately half the torque specified at the beginning of this Chapter. Go around a second time in the same sequence and tighten them to the full torque setting.

17 Working in a criss-cross pattern from the outside in, loosen and remove the crankcase bolts and store them on your template, then carefully lift off the lower crankcase half, making sure the Plastigauge is not disturbed.

18 Compare the width of the crushed Plastigauge on each crankshaft journal to the scale printed on the Plastigauge envelope to obtain the main bearing oil clearance (see illustration). Compare the reading to the specifications at the beginning of this Chapter. If the clearance is within the range

2

27.11 Lay the crankshaft in the crankcase

27.12 Place a strip of Plastigauge on each bearing journal

27.18 Measure the crushed Plastigauge using the scale on the pack. Be sure to use the correct scale as both metric and Imperial are used

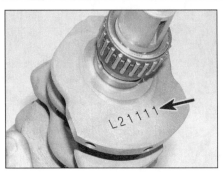

27.22a Main bearing journal size codes (arrowed)

27.22b Main bearing bore size codes (arrowed)

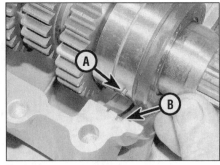

28.2a Note how pin (A) locates in notch (B)

specified and the bearings are in perfect condition, they can be reused.

19 Carefully clean away all traces of the Plastigauge from the journals and bearing shells using a fingernail or other object which will not score the bearing surfaces.

20 If the clearance is beyond the service limit, measure the diameter of each crankshaft journal with a micrometer **(see illustration 27.5)** and compare the result with the appropriate figure in the table for main bearing shell selection. For example, if the journal being measured is code 2, the table indicates that the service limit for that journal is 32.986 mm. If the journal diameter is larger than the service limit, new bearing shells can be fitted (see Steps 22 and 23). If the journal diameter is smaller than the service limit the crankshaft should be renewed.

21 Always renew all of the shells at the same time. Install the new shells and check the oil clearance once again.

Bearing shell selection

22 Replacement bearing shells for the main bearings are supplied on a selected fit basis. Codes for the crankshaft journals are stamped on the outside of the crankshaft web on the left-hand end of the crankshaft **(see illustration)**. The upper block of five numbers is the size codes for the main bearing journals (the lower block of four letters is the size codes for the crankpin bearing journals). The first number of the block is for the left-hand (No. 1 cylinder) journal, and so on. The corresponding main bearing bore size codes are stamped into the upper crankcase half and will be either an A, B or C **(see illustration)**. The left-hand letter corresponds to the left-hand journal, and so on from left to right respectively.

23 A range of bearing shells is available. To select the correct shells for a particular journal, use the table below to cross-reference the main bearing journal code with the main bearing bore code to determine the colour code of the shells required. For example, if the journal code is 2, and the bore code is B, then the bearing shells required are Green. The colour is marked on the side of the shell **(see illustration 25.26)**.

Crankshaft main bearing journal code	Crankcase bore code		
	A (36.000 to 36.007 mm)	B (36.007 to 36.014 mm)	C (36.014 to 36.021 mm)
1 (32.993 to 33.000 mm)	Pink	Yellow	Green
2 (32.986 to 32.993 mm)	Yellow	Green	Brown

Installation

24 Ensure the backs of the bearing shells, the bearing seats in both crankcase halves, and the main bearing journals on the crankshaft are clean. If new shells are being fitted, ensure that all traces of the protective grease are cleaned off using paraffin (kerosene). Wipe the shells and crankcase halves dry with a lint-free cloth. Make sure all the oil passages and holes are clear, and blow them through with compressed air if it is available.

25 Press the bearing shells into their seats. Make sure the tab on each shell engages in the notch in the casing **(see illustration 27.10)**. Make sure the bearings are fitted in the correct locations and take care not to touch any bearing surfaces with your fingers. Lubricate the shells with clean engine oil.

26 Lower the crankshaft into position in the upper crankcase, making sure all bearing shells remain in place.

27 Refer to Section 24 and fit the connecting rods onto the crankshaft.

28 Reassemble the crankcase halves (see Section 22).

28 Transmission shafts – removal and installation

Note: *To remove the transmission shafts the engine must be removed from the frame.*

Removal

1 Separate the crankcase halves as described in Section 22.

2 Note how the pin on the outer race of the output shaft left-hand bearing locates in the notch in the upper crankcase half **(see illustration)**. Lift the output shaft out of the crankcase; if it is stuck, use a soft-faced hammer and gently tap on the ends of the shaft to free it. Remove the end plate from the right-hand end of the output shaft for safe-keeping **(see illustration)**.

3 Remove the bearing half-ring retainer from the crankcase or bearing on the output shaft, noting how it fits **(see illustration)**. Remove the dowel from the bearing seat in the upper crankcase half (see

28.2b Remove the output shaft end plate

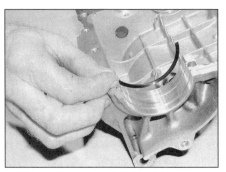

28.3a Remove the bearing retainer . . .

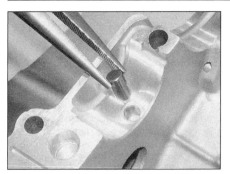

28.3b . . . and the dowel from the bearing seat

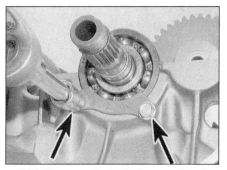

28.4 Unscrew the bolts (arrowed) and remove the retainer plate

28.8 Fit the output shaft seal with the lip (arrowed) on the inside

illustration). Discard the oil seal from the left-hand end of the shaft as a new one must be fitted on reassembly.

4 Unscrew the input shaft bearing retaining plate bolts and remove the plate, noting which way round it fits (see illustration).

5 Lift the input shaft out of the crankcase.

6 If necessary, the transmission shafts can be disassembled and inspected for wear or damage (see Section 29).

Installation

7 Install the output shaft bearing half ring and dowel pin in the upper crankcase.

8 Grease the inside of the new output shaft oil seal and install the seal, making sure it is fitted with its sealing lip facing inwards (see illustration).

9 Install the output shaft end plate and lower the shaft into position in the upper crankcase (see illustration). Make sure the right-hand bearing locates on the dowel in the bearing seat, and the left-hand bearing locates on the half-ring retainer with the pin on the bearing outer race in the notch in the upper crankcase. Ensure the lip on the oil seal locates in the groove in the crankcase.

Caution: If the output shaft bearing locating pin and/or output shaft half ring or dowel pin are not correctly engaged, the crankcase halves will not seat correctly.

10 Install the input shaft (see illustration).

11 Clean the threads of the input shaft bearing retaining plate bolts and apply a suitable non-permanent thread-locking compound.

12 Fit the plate making sure the OUT SIDE mark is facing outwards. Install the bolts and tighten them securely (see illustration 28.4).

13 Position the gears in the neutral position and check the shafts are free to rotate easily and independently of each other before reassembling the crankcase halves (see Section 22).

---

29 Transmission shafts –
disassembly, inspection and reassembly

1 Remove the transmission shafts from the casing (see Section 28). Always disassemble the transmission shafts separately to avoid mixing up the components.

> **HAYNES HiNT** *When disassembling the transmission shafts, place the parts on a long rod or thread a wire through them to keep them in order and facing in the proper direction.*

Input shaft

Disassembly

2 Slide the needle roller bearing cage and bearing off the left-hand end of the shaft (see illustration 29.23b and a).

3 Slide the thrust washer and the 2nd gear pinion off the shaft, noting which way around it is fitted (see illustrations 29.22b and a).

4 Note how the tabs on the lock washer fit into the slotted splined washer and remove the lockwasher (see illustration 29.21b).

5 Turn the slotted splined washer to align it with the splines on the shaft and slide it off the shaft (see illustration 29.21a).

6 Slide the 6th gear pinion and its bush, and the splined washer off the shaft (see illustrations 29.20c, b and a).

7 Remove the circlip securing the combined 3rd/4th gear pinion. Do not expand the ends of the circlip any further than is necessary to slide it down the length of the shaft, then slide the pinion off the shaft (see illustrations 29.19b and a).

8 Remove the circlip securing the 5th gear pinion, then slide the splined washer, the pinion and its bush, and the thrust washer off the shaft (see illustrations 29.18e, d, c, b and a). The 1st gear pinion is integral with the shaft.

9 If necessary, press the caged ball bearing

2

28.9 Install the output shaft . . .

28.10 . . . and then the input shaft

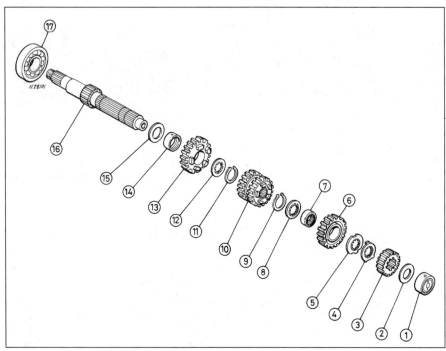

29.16a Transmission input shaft components

1 Bearing
2 Thrust washer
3 2nd gear pinion
4 Tabbed lockwasher
5 Slotted splined washer
6 6th gear pinion
7 6th gear pinion bush
8 Splined washer
9 Circlip
10 3rd/4th gear pinion
11 Circlip
12 Splined washer
13 5th gear pinion
14 5th gear pinion bush
15 Thrust washer
16 Input shaft
17 Bearing

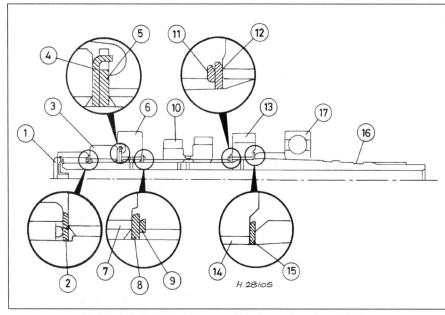

29.16b Input shaft washers and circlips – direction of fitting

1 Bearing
2 Thrust washer
3 2nd gear pinion
4 Tabbed lockwasher
5 Slotted splined washer
6 6th gear pinion
7 6th gear pinion bush
8 Splined washer
9 Circlip
10 3rd/4th gear pinion
11 Circlip
12 Splined washer
13 5th gear pinion
14 5th gear pinion bush
15 Thrust washer
16 Input shaft
17 Bearing

off the shaft using a suitable tool (see *Tools and Workshop Tips* in the Reference section of this manual).

Inspection

10 Wash all of the components in clean solvent and dry them off.

11 Check the gear teeth for cracking, chipping, pitting and other obvious wear or damage. Any pinion that is damaged must be renewed. Inspect the dogs and the dog holes in the gears for cracks, chips, and excessive wear especially in the form of rounded edges. Make sure mating gears engage properly. Renew the paired gears as a set if necessary.

12 Check for signs of scoring or bluing on the pinions, bushes and shaft. This could be caused by overheating due to inadequate lubrication. Check that all the oil holes and passages are clear. Renew any damaged pinions or bushes.

13 Check that each pinion moves freely on the shaft or bush but without undue freeplay. Check that each bush moves freely on the shaft but without undue freeplay. If the necessary measuring equipment is available, the gear, bush and shaft dimensions can be checked and compared with the Specifications at the beginning of this chapter. The shaft is unlikely to sustain damage unless the engine has seized, placing an unusually high loading on the transmission, or the machine has covered a very high mileage. Check the surface of the shaft, especially where a pinion turns on it, and renew the shaft if it has scored or picked up, or if there are any cracks or wear. Damage of any kind can only be cured by renewal.

14 Check the washers and circlips and renew any that are bent or appear weakened or worn. Use new ones if in any doubt. It is good practice to renew the washers and circlips as a matter of course when overhauling the gearshaft.

15 Check the bearings referring to *Tools and Workshop Tips* (Section 5) in the Reference Section.

Reassembly

16 During reassembly, apply clean engine oil to the mating surfaces of the shaft, pinions and bushes, and to the bearings. When installing the circlips, do not expand the ends any further than is necessary to slide them along the shaft. Install them so that their chamfered side faces the pinion they secure **(see illustrations 29.16a and b)**.

17 If removed, press the caged ball bearing onto the right-hand end of the shaft **(see illustration)**.

18 Slide the thrust washer onto the left-hand end of the shaft, followed by the 5th gear pinion bush, aligning the oil hole in the bush with the hole in the shaft, and the 5th gear pinion, with the pinion dogs facing away from the integral 1st gear **(see illustrations)**. Slide the splined washer onto the shaft, then fit the

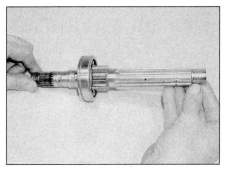

29.17 Fit the bearing onto the shaft

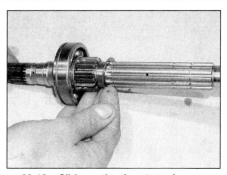

29.18a Slide on the thrust washer . . .

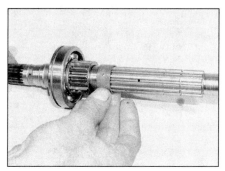

29.18b . . . 5th gear pinion bush . . .

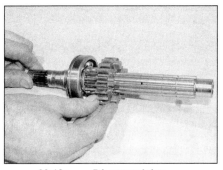

29.18c . . . 5th gear pinion . . .

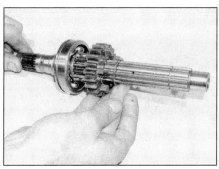

29.18d . . . and splined washer . . .

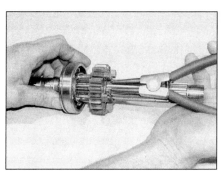

29.18e . . . and secure them with the circlip

circlip, making sure that it locates correctly in the groove on the shaft **(see illustrations)**.

19 Slide the combined 3rd/4th gear pinion onto the shaft with the larger 4th gear pinion facing the 5th gear pinion. Ensure the oil hole in the pinion aligns with the oil hole in the shaft **(see illustration)**. Fit the circlip, making sure it is locates correctly in its groove on the shaft **(see illustration)**.

20 Slide the splined washer onto the shaft, followed by the 6th gear pinion bush, aligning the oil hole in the bush with the hole in the shaft, and the 6th gear pinion, making sure the dogs on the pinion face the 3rd/4th gear pinion **(see illustrations)**.

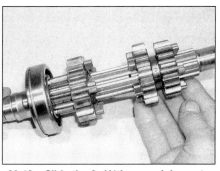

29.19a Slide the 3rd/4th gear pinion onto the shaft . . .

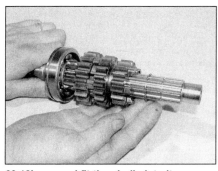

29.19b . . . and fit the circlip into its groove

2

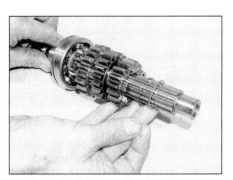

29.20a Install the splined washer . . .

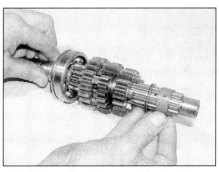

29.20b . . . the 6th gear pinion bush . . .

29.20c . . . and slide on the 6th gear pinion

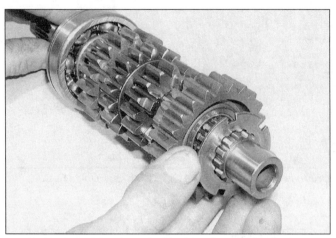

29.21a Install the slotted splined washer as described ...

29.21b ... then slide on the tabbed lockwasher

29.22a Slide on the 2nd gear pinion ...

29.22b ... and the thrust washer ...

21 Slide the slotted splined washer onto the shaft and locate it in its groove, then turn it in the groove so that the splines on the washer align against the splines on the shaft and secure the washer in the groove. Slide the lock washer onto the shaft so that the tabs on the lockwasher locate in the slots on the outside edge of the splined washer (see illustrations).
22 Slide the 2nd gear pinion onto the shaft, ensuring it is fitted the same way around as noted on removal (see illustration). Install the thrust washer (see illustration).
23 Fit the needle roller bearing and its cage over the end of the shaft (see illustrations).
24 Check that all components have been correctly installed (see illustration 29.16a).

Output shaft

Disassembly

25 Slide the needle roller bearing cage and bearing off the right-hand end of the shaft (see illustrations 29.42b and a).
26 Slide the thrust washer off the shaft, followed by the 1st gear pinion and its needle roller bearing, the thrust washer and the 5th gear pinion (see illustrations 29.41c, b and a, and 29.40b and a).
27 Remove the circlip securing the 4th gear pinion, then slide the splined washer, the pinion and its splined bush off the shaft (see illustrations 29.39d, c, b and a).
28 Slide the lockwasher off the shaft. Note

how the tabs on the lock washer fit into the slotted splined washer. Turn the slotted splined washer to align it with the splines on the shaft and slide it off the shaft (see illustration 29.38b and a).
29 Slide the 3rd gear pinion and its splined bush, followed by the splined washer, off the shaft (see illustration 29.37c, b and a).
30 Remove the circlip securing the 6th gear pinion, then slide the pinion off the shaft (see illustrations 29.36b and a).
31 Remove the circlip securing the 2nd gear pinion, then slide the splined washer, the pinion and its bush off the shaft (see illustrations 29.35d, c, b and a).
32 The remaining caged ball bearing is an integral part of the output shaft and cannot be removed (see illustration).

Inspection

33 Refer to Steps 10 to 15 above.

Reassembly

34 During reassembly, apply clean engine oil to the mating surfaces of the shaft, pinions and bushes, and to the bearings. When installing the circlips, do not expand the ends any further than is necessary to slide them along the shaft. Install them so that the chamfered side faces the pinion they secure (see illustrations 29.34a and b).
35 Slide the 2nd gear pinion bush, the 2nd

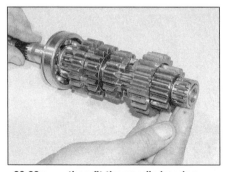

29.23a ... then fit the needle bearing ...

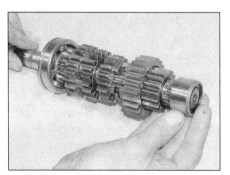

29.23b ... and its cage

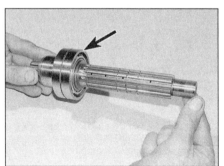

29.32 The caged bearing (arrowed) is an integral part of the output shaft

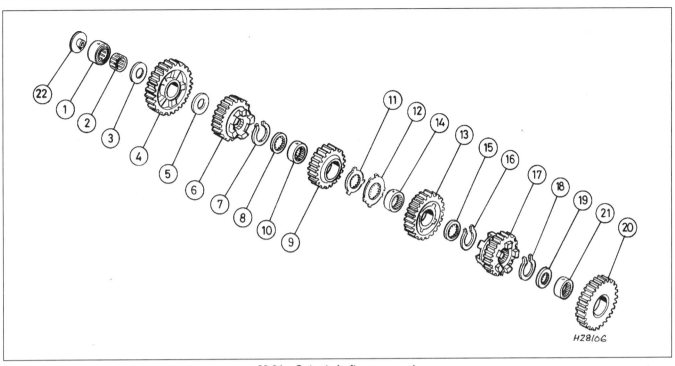

29.34a Output shaft components

1 Bearing
2 1st gear pinion bearing
3 Thrust washer
4 1st gear pinion
5 Thrust washer
6 5th gear pinion

7 Circlip
8 Splined washer
9 4th gear pinion
10 4th gear pinion bush
11 Tabbed lockwasher
12 Slotted splined washer

13 3rd gear pinion
14 3rd gear pinion bush
15 Splined washer
16 Circlip
17 6th gear pinion

18 Circlip
19 Thrust washer
20 2nd gear pinion
21 2nd gear pinion bush
22 End plate

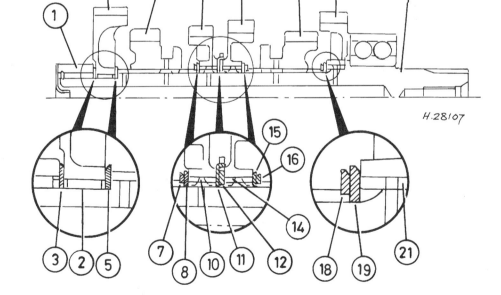

1 Bearing
2 1st gear pinion bearing
3 Thrust washer
4 1st gear pinion
5 Thrust washer
6 5th gear pinion
7 Circlip
8 Splined washer
9 4th gear pinion
10 4th gear pinion bush
11 Tabbed lockwasher
12 Slotted splined washer
13 3rd gear pinion
14 3rd gear pinion bush
15 Splined washer
16 Circlip
17 6th gear pinion
18 Circlip
19 Thrust washer
20 2nd gear pinion
21 2nd gear pinion bush
22 Output shaft

29.34b Output shaft washers and circlips – direction of fitting

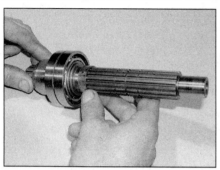

29.35a Slide the 2nd gear pinion bush . . .

29.35b . . . the 2nd gear pinion . . .

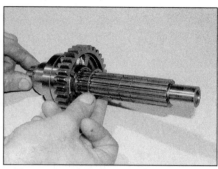

29.35c . . . and the splined washer onto the shaft . . .

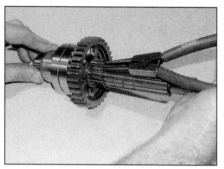

29.35d . . . and secure them with the circlip

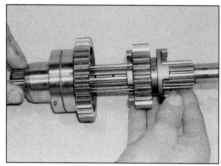

29.36a Slide on the 6th gear pinion . . .

29.36b . . . and secure it with the circlip (arrowed)

29.37a Install the splined washer . . .

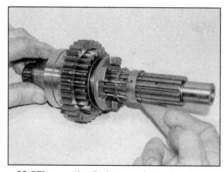

29.37b . . . the 3rd gear pinion bush . . .

29.37c . . . and the 3rd gear pinion

29.38a Install the slotted splined washer as described . . .

29.38b . . . then slide on the tabbed lockwasher . . .

29.38c . . . and engage its tabs (arrowed) in the slots

gear pinion (with its dog holes facing away from the bearing) and the splined washer onto the shaft, then fit the circlip, making sure it is locates correctly in its groove on the shaft **(see illustrations)**.

36 Slide the 6th gear pinion with its selector fork groove facing away from the 2nd gear pinion, onto the shaft. Ensure that the oil hole in the pinion aligns with the hole in the shaft, then fit the circlip, making sure it is locates correctly in its groove on the shaft **(see illustrations)**.

37 Slide the splined washer and the 3rd gear pinion bush onto the shaft, making sure the oil hole in the bush aligns with the hole in the shaft, followed by the 3rd gear pinion. The dog holes of the 3rd gear pinion must face the 6th gear pinion **(see illustrations)**.

38 Slide the slotted splined washer onto the shaft and locate it in its groove **(see illustration)**. Turn it in the groove so that the splines on the washer locate against the splines of the shaft and secure the washer in the groove. Slide the lockwasher onto the shaft, so that the tabs on the lockwasher locate into the slots on the outside edge of the splined washer **(see illustrations)**.

39 Slide the 4th gear pinion bush onto the shaft, making sure the oil hole in the bush aligns with the hole in the shaft, followed by the 4th gear pinion (dog holes facing away from the 3rd gear pinion) and the splined washer. Fit the circlip, making sure it is locates correctly in its groove on the shaft **(see illustrations)**.

40 Slide the 5th gear pinion onto the shaft with its selector fork groove facing the 4th gear pinion. Ensure that the oil hole in the pinion aligns with the hole in the shaft. Fit the thrust washer **(see illustrations)**.

41 Slide the 1st gear pinion needle roller bearing onto the shaft, followed by the 1st gear pinion (dog holes facing the 5th gear pinion) and the thrust washer **(see illustrations)**.

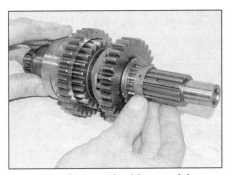

29.39a Slide on the 4th gear pinion bush . . .

29.39b . . . the 4th gear pinion . . .

29.39c . . . and the splined washer . . .

29.39d . . . and secure them with the circlip

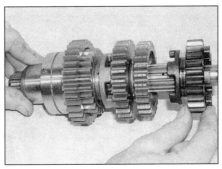

29.40a Slide the 5th gear pinion onto the shaft . . .

29.40b . . . and fit the thrust washer

2

29.41a Install the 1st gear pinion bearing . . .

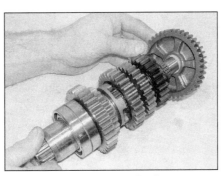

29.41b . . . then slide the first gear pinion . . .

29.41c . . . and the thrust washer onto the shaft

29.42a Install the bearing . . .

29.42b . . . and the bearing cage

42 Fit the needle roller bearing and its cage over the end of the shaft **(see illustrations)**.
43 Check that all components have been correctly installed **(see illustration 29.34a)**.
44 Install the transmission shafts in the casing (see Section 28).

30 Selector drum and forks – removal, inspection and installation

Note: *To remove the selector drum and forks, ideally the engine must be removed from the*

frame. It is possible to remove the selector drum and forks with the engine in the frame, having removed the clutch and oil sump, however working access is very restricted.

Removal

1 Remove the clutch (see Section 15), then turn the engine upside down (if removed from the frame) and remove the oil sump (see Section 16).
2 Ensure the transmission is in the neutral position with the gearchange stopper arm resting in the neutral detent on the gearchange cam. Note the position of the

selector drum against the neutral switch pin inside the crankcase **(see illustration)**.
3 Remove the gearchange mechanism (see Section 20).
4 Before removing the selector forks, note that each fork is lettered for identification. The right-hand fork has an R, the centre fork a C, and the left-hand fork an L **(see illustration 30.6c)**. These letters face the right-hand side of the engine. If no letters are visible, mark them using a felt pen.
5 Note how the forks locate in the grooves on the input shaft 3rd/4th gear pinion and output shaft 5th and 6th gear pinions. Note how the guide pins on the forks locate in the grooves in the selector drum.
6 Unscrew the bolt securing the selector fork shaft retainer plate, located next to the gearchange cam **(see illustration)**. Note how the retainer plate fits. Support the selector forks and withdraw the shaft from the casing, then remove the forks **(see illustration)**. Once removed, slide the forks back onto the shaft in their correct order and way round **(see illustration)**.
7 Unscrew the bolt securing the gear selector drum retainer plate and note how the retainer plate fits. Slide the selector drum out of he crankcase **(see illustration)**.
8 If the gearchange cam has not been removed from the end of the gear selector drum, pass a steel rod through the drum to

30.2 Note the position of the neutral detent (arrowed) on the end of the selector drum

30.6a Remove the selector fork shaft retainer plate . . .

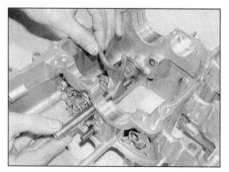

30.6b . . . then remove the shaft and forks

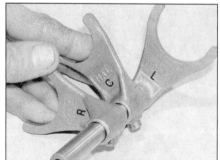

30.6c Note the letter on each fork denoting its position

30.7 Withdraw the selector drum

30.8a Unscrew the cam retaining bolt . . .

30.8b . . . and remove the cam locating pin (arrowed) for safekeeping

30.9 Remove the bearing if necessary

hold it while unscrewing the cam retaining bolt **(see illustration)**. The cam locates on a pin in the end of the selector drum. Remove the pin for safekeeping **(see illustration)**.

9 If necessary, pull the caged ball bearing off the end of the selector drum **(see illustration)**.

Inspection

10 Inspect the selector forks for any signs of wear or damage, especially around the fork ends where they engage with the groove in the pinion. Check that each fork fits correctly in its pinion groove. Check closely to see if the forks are bent. If the forks are in any way damaged they must be renewed.

11 Measure the thickness of the fork ends and compare the readings to the specifications at the beginning of this Chapter **(see illustration)**. Renew the forks if they are worn beyond their specifications.

12 Check that the forks fit correctly on their shaft. They should move freely with a light fit but no appreciable freeplay. Measure the internal diameter of the fork bores and the corresponding diameter of the fork shaft. Renew the forks and/or shaft if they are worn beyond their specifications. Check that the fork shaft holes in the casing are not worn or damaged.

13 The selector fork shaft can be checked for trueness by rolling it along a flat surface. A bent rod will cause difficulty in selecting gears and make the gearchange action heavy. Renew the shaft if it is bent.

14 Inspect the selector drum grooves and

selector fork guide pins for signs of wear or damage. If either component shows signs of wear or damage the selector fork(s) and drum must be renewed.

15 Check the selector drum bearing referring to *Tools and Workshop Tips (Section 5)* in the Reference Section.

Installation

16 If removed, press the selector drum bearing onto the drum. Install the pin in the end of the gear selector drum and install the cam, locating the pin in the cut-out in the back of the cam. Clean the threads of the centre bolt, then apply a suitable non-permanent thread-locking compound. Install the bolt and tighten it to the specified torque setting.

17 Slide the selector forks off their shaft and locate the forks in the grooves of their correct gear pinions (see Steps 4 and 5). Push the forks forward and slide the selector drum into position in the crankcase. Make sure the drum end locates into its bore in the casing, and position it so that the neutral contact is against the neutral switch **(see illustration)**.

18 Apply a suitable non-permanent thread-locking compound to the selector drum bearing retainer plate bolt, then fit the plate with the OUT mark facing outwards and tighten the bolt to the specified torque setting.

19 Lubricate the selector fork shaft with clean engine oil and slide it through the crankcase and each fork in turn, locating the guide pin on the end of each fork into its

groove in the selector drum as you do. Ensure the inner end of the shaft locates in its bore.

20 Apply a suitable non-permanent thread-locking compound to the selector fork shaft retainer plate bolt, then fit the plate with the OUT mark facing outwards and tighten the bolt to the torque setting specified at the beginning of this Chapter.

21 Lubricate the selector forks and fork grooves with a 50/50 mixture of molybdenum disulphide grease and clean engine oil. Lubricate the gears, shafts and bushings with clean engine oil.

22 Ensure the gears are in the neutral position and check the shafts are free to rotate easily and independently of each other **(see illustration 30.2)**.

23 Install the gearchange mechanism (see Section 20) and check gearchange operation while turning the input shaft.

24 Install the remaining components in the reverse order of removal.

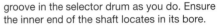

31 Crankcase halves and cylinder bores – inspection and servicing

Crankcase halves

1 After the crankcase halves have been separated, remove the crankshaft, connecting rods and pistons, bearings, transmission shafts, selector drum and forks, and any other components or assemblies (see Steps 2 and 3 in Section 22).

2 Remove the oil pressure switch, the neutral switch and, on CB600FS models, the speed sensor switch (see Chapter 9).

3 Clean the crankcases thoroughly with a suitable solvent and dry them with compressed air. Remove any oil passage plugs that haven't already been removed and blow out all oil passages with compressed air.

4 All traces of old gasket sealant should be removed from the mating surfaces. Minor damage to the surfaces can be cleaned up with a fine sharpening stone.

Caution: Be very careful not to nick or gouge the crankcase mating surfaces or leaks will result. Check both crankcase halves very carefully for cracks and other damage.

30.11 Measuring the selector fork end thickness

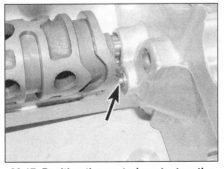

30.17 Position the neutral contact on the drum against the neutral switch (arrowed)

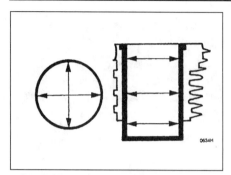

31.12 Measure the cylinder bore in the directions shown with a telescoping gauge

5 Before proceeding further, check the cylinder bores (see Steps 11 to 13).

6 Inspect the bearing seats for signs of damage, especially if an engine or transmission bearing has overheated or seized (see Section 22).

7 Small cracks or holes in aluminium castings may be repaired with an epoxy resin adhesive as a temporary measure. Permanent repairs can only be effected by argon-arc welding, and only a specialist in this process is in a position to advise on the economy or practical aspect of such a repair. If any damage is found that can't be repaired, replace the crankcase halves as a set.

8 Damaged threads can be economically reclaimed by using a diamond section wire insert of the Heli-Coil type, which is easily fitted after drilling and re-tapping the affected thread. Most motorcycle dealers and small engineering firms offer a service of this kind.

9 Sheared studs or screws can usually be removed with stud or screw extractors; if you are in any doubt consult your Honda dealer or a specialist motorcycle engineer.

Refer to Tools and Workshop Tips (Section 2) in the Reference section for details of how to fit a thread insert and use screw extractors.

10 Always clean the crankcases thoroughly (see Step 3) after any repair work to ensure no dirt or metal swarf is trapped inside when the engine is rebuilt.

Cylinder bores

Caution: Do not attempt to separate the liners from the cylinder block.

11 Check the cylinder walls carefully for scratches and score marks.

12 Using telescoping gauges and a micrometer (see *Tools and Workshop Tips* in the Reference Section), check the dimensions

of each cylinder to assess the amount of wear, taper and ovality. Measure near the top (but below the level of the top piston ring at TDC), the centre and bottom (but above the level of the oil ring at BDC) of the bore. Measure both parallel to and across the crankshaft axis in each case and calculate the average cylinder dimension at each point **(see illustration)**. Compare the results to the specifications at the beginning of this Chapter.

13 If precision measuring tools are not available, take the crankcase to a Honda dealer or specialist motorcycle engineer for assessment and advice.

14 If the cylinders are tapered, out-of-round, worn beyond the specified limits, or badly scuffed or scored, have them rebored by a dealer service department or a motorcycle repair shop. If a rebore is done, oversize pistons and rings will be required as well. Honda produce four sizes of oversize pistons (see Section 25).

15 If the cylinders are in good condition and the piston-to-bore clearance is within specifications (see Section 25), the cylinders should be honed (de-glazed). To perform this operation you will need the proper size flexible hone with fine stones (see Specialist Tools in *Tools and Workshop Tips* in the Reference Section), or a bottle-brush type hone, plenty of light oil or honing oil, some clean rags and an electric drill motor.

16 Clamp the cylinder block securely so that the bores are horizontal rather than vertical. Mount the hone in the drill motor, compress the stones and insert the hone into the cylinder. Thoroughly lubricate the cylinder, then turn on the drill and move the hone up and down in the cylinder at a pace which produces a fine cross-hatch pattern on the cylinder wall with the lines intersecting at an angle of approximately 60°. Be sure to use plenty of lubricant and do not take off any more material than is necessary to produce the desired effect. Do not withdraw the hone from the cylinder while it is still turning. Switch off the drill and continue to move it up and down in the cylinder until it has stopped turning, then compress the stones and withdraw the hone. Wipe the oil from the cylinder and repeat the procedure on the next cylinder. Remember, do not take too much material from the cylinder wall.

17 Wash the cylinders thoroughly with warm soapy water to remove all traces of the abrasive grit produced during the honing operation. After rinsing, dry the cylinders thoroughly and clear the oil and coolant passages with compressed air. Apply a thin coat of light, rust-preventative oil to all machined surfaces.

18 If you do not have the equipment or desire to perform the honing operation, take the crankcase to a Honda dealer or specialist motorcycle engineer.

32 Initial start-up after overhaul

1 Make sure the engine oil and coolant levels are correct (see 'Daily (pre-ride) checks').

2 Turn the engine kill switch to the ON position and shift the gearbox into neutral. Turn the ignition ON. Set the choke enough to encourage the bike to start, but not so much as to allow it to race.

3 Start the engine and allow it to run at a moderately fast idle until it reaches operating temperature.

 Warning: If the oil pressure warning light doesn't go off, or it comes on while the engine is running, stop the engine immediately.

4 Check carefully for oil leaks and make sure the transmission and controls, especially the brakes, function properly before road testing the machine. Refer to Section 33 for the recommended running-in procedure.

5 Upon completion of the road test, and after the engine has cooled down completely, recheck the valve clearances (see Chapter 1) and check the engine oil and coolant levels (see 'Daily (pre-ride) checks').

33 Recommended running-in procedure

1 Treat the machine gently for the first few miles to allow the oil to circulate throughout the engine and any new parts installed to seat.

2 Great care is necessary if the engine has been extensively overhauled – the bike will have to be run in as when new. This means greater use of the transmission and a restraining hand on the throttle until at least 300 miles (500 km) have been covered. There's no point in keeping to any set speed limit – the main idea is to keep from labouring the engine and to gradually increase performance up to the 300 mile (500 km) mark. Experience is the best guide, since it's easy to tell when an engine is running freely.

3 If a lubrication failure is suspected, stop the engine immediately and find the cause. If an engine is run without oil pressure, even for a short period of time, severe damage will occur.

Chapter 3
Cooling system

Contents

Degrees of difficulty

Easy, suitable for novice with little experience	Fairly easy, suitable for beginner with some experience	Fairly difficult, suitable for competent DIY mechanic	Difficult, suitable for experienced DIY mechanic	Very difficult, suitable for expert DIY or professional

Specifications

Coolant
Mixture type and capacity . . . . see Chapter 1

Radiator cap
Cap valve opening pressure . . . . 16 to 20 psi (1.1 to 1.4 Bar)

Fan switch
Switch comes on . . . . 98 to 102°C
Switch goes off . . . . 93 to 97°C

Coolant temperature sender
Resistance @ 80°C . . . . 2.1 to 2.6 K-ohms
Resistance @ 120°C . . . . 0.62 to 0.76 K-ohms

Thermostat
Opening temperature . . . . 80 to 84°C
Valve lift . . . . 8 mm (min) @ 95°C

Torque settings
Cooling fan switch . . . . 18 Nm
Coolant temperature sender . . . . 10 Nm
Thermostat housing bolt . . . . 12 Nm
Water pump drain bolt . . . . 12 Nm
Water pump cover bolt . . . . 13 Nm

3

1 General information

The cooling system uses a water/antifreeze coolant to carry excess energy away from the engine in the form of heat. The cylinders are surrounded by a water jacket through which the coolant is circulated by thermo-syphonic action in conjunction with a water pump. The pump is mounted on the lower left-hand side of the engine. Hot coolant flows upwards to the thermostat and then to the radiator where it is cooled by the passing air. It then flows through the water pump and back to the engine where the cycle is repeated.

Coolant from the pump also flows through the oil cooler which is mounted on the front of the engine crankcases.

A thermostat is fitted in the system to prevent the coolant flowing through the radiator when the engine is cold, thus allowing the engine to reach normal operating temperature quickly. A thermostatically-controlled cooling fan is fitted behind the radiator to aid cooling in extreme conditions.

Coolant temperature information is supplied to the gauge in the instruments by a sender unit mounted in the thermostat housing.

The cooling system is partially sealed and pressurised, the pressure being controlled by a spring-loaded valve contained in the pressure cap. By pressurising the coolant the boiling point is raised, preventing premature boiling in adverse conditions. The overflow pipe from the system is connected to a reservoir into which excess coolant is expelled under pressure. The discharged coolant automatically returns to the radiator when the engine cools.

 Warning: Do not remove the pressure cap from the radiator when the engine is hot. Scalding hot coolant and steam may be blown out under pressure, which could cause serious injury. When the engine has cooled, place a heavy cloth, like a towel, over the pressure cap; slowly rotate the cap anti-clockwise and allow any residual pressure to escape before removing the cap completely.

Warning: Do not allow antifreeze to come in contact with your skin or painted surfaces of the motorcycle. Rinse off any spills immediately with plenty of water. Antifreeze is highly toxic if ingested. Never leave antifreeze lying around in an open container or in puddles on the floor; children and pets are attracted by its sweet smell and may drink it. Check with the local authorities about disposing of used antifreeze. Many communities will have collection centres which will see that antifreeze is disposed of safely.

Caution: At all times use the specified type of antifreeze, and always mix it with distilled water in the correct proportion. The antifreeze contains corrosion inhibitors which are essential to avoid damage to the cooling system. A lack of these inhibitors could lead to a build-up of corrosion which would block the coolant passages, resulting in overheating and severe engine damage. Distilled water must be used as opposed to tap water to avoid a build-up of scale which would also block the passages.

2 Radiator cap – check

1 If problems such as overheating or loss of coolant occur, check the entire system as described in Chapter 1. The radiator cap opening pressure should be checked by a Honda dealer with the special tester required to do the job. If the cap is defective, renew it.

3 Coolant reservoir – removal and installation

Removal

1 The coolant reservoir is located under the frame behind the rear shock absorber **(see illustration)**. Remove the seat cowling (see Chapter 8).
2 Release the clip securing the breather hose on the right-hand side of the reservoir and detach the hose **(see illustration)**.
3 Unclip the fusebox and secure it away from the coolant reservoir, then drain the reservoir (see Chapter 1, Section 25) .
4 Unscrew the reservoir mounting bolt, then pull the reservoir off its mounting bracket and remove it from the motorcycle **(see illustration)**.

Installation

5 Installation is the reverse of removal. Make sure the hoses are correctly installed and secured with their clips **(see illustration)**. On completion refill the reservoir as described in Chapter 1.

4 Cooling fan switch and cooling fan – check and replacement

Cooling fan switch

Check

1 If the engine is overheating and the cooling fan isn't coming on, first check the coolant level (see *Daily (pre-ride) checks*). If the level is correct, check the cooling fan circuit fuse (see Chapter 9). If the fuse is blown, check the fan circuit for a short to earth (see the wiring diagrams at the end of this book).

3.1 Coolant reservoir location behind the shock absorber

3.2 Disconnect the breather hose (arrowed)

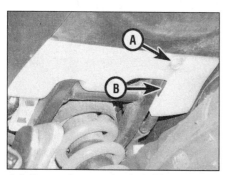

3.4 Reservoir mounting bolt (A) and frame bracket (B)

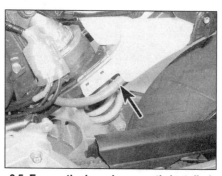

3.5 Ensure the hose is correctly installed and secured with its clip (arrowed)

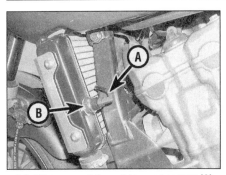

4.2 Disconnect the wiring connector (A) from the fan switch (B)

2 If the fuse is good, disconnect the wiring connector from the fan switch on the left-hand side of the radiator **(see illustration)**. Using a jumper wire, connect the wire to earth (ground) and turn the ignition ON. If the fan comes on, the switch connection or the switch is defective and must be renewed (see Steps 6 to 9). If it does not come on, the fan motor should be tested (see Steps 10 to 12).

3 If the fan stays on all the time, turn the ignition OFF, then disconnect the fan switch wiring connector and turn the ignition ON. The fan should stop. If it does, the switch is defective and must be renewed. If it doesn't, check the wiring between the switch and the fan for a short to earth.

4 If the fan works but is suspected of cutting in at the wrong temperature, a more comprehensive test of the switch can be made as follows. Remove the switch (see Steps 6 to 7). Fill a small heatproof container with coolant and place it on a stove. Connect the positive (+ve) probe of an ohmmeter to the terminal of the switch and the negative (-ve) probe to the switch body, then, using some wire or other support, suspend the switch in the coolant so that just the sensing portion and the threads are submerged **(see illustration)**. Also place a thermometer capable of reading temperatures up to 110°C

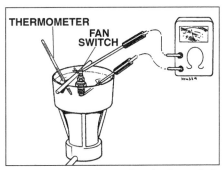

4.4 Arrangement for testing the fan switch and temperature gauge sender

in the coolant so that its bulb is close to the switch. **Note:** *None of the components should be allowed to directly touch the container.*

5 Initially the ohmmeter reading should be very high indicating that the switch is open (OFF). Heat the coolant, stirring it gently.

 Warning: This must be done very carefully to avoid the risk of personal injury.

When the temperature reaches around 98 to 102°C the meter reading should drop to around zero ohms, indicating that the switch has closed (ON). Now turn the heat off. As the temperature falls below 93 to 97°C the meter reading should show infinite (very high) resistance, indicating that the switch has opened (OFF). If the meter readings obtained are different, or they are obtained at different temperatures, then the fan switch is faulty and must be renewed.

Replacement

 Warning: The engine must be completely cool before carrying out this procedure.

6 Drain the cooling system (see Chapter 1).
7 Disconnect the wiring connector from the fan switch on the left-hand side of the radiator **(see illustration 4.2)**. Unscrew the switch and withdraw it from the radiator. Discard the O-ring as a new one must be used.

8 Apply a suitable sealant to the switch threads, then install the switch using a new O-ring and tighten it to the torque setting specified at the beginning of this Chapter. Take care not to overtighten the switch as the radiator could be damaged.

9 Reconnect the switch wiring and refill the cooling system (see Chapter 1).

Cooling fan

Check

10 If the engine is overheating and the cooling fan isn't coming on, first check the coolant level (see *Daily (pre-ride) checks*). If the level is correct, check the cooling fan circuit fuse (see Chapter 9) and then the fan switch (see Steps 2 and 3).

11 If the fan switch is good, the fault lies in either the cooling fan motor or the relevant wiring. Test all the wiring and connections as described in Chapter 9.

12 To test the cooling fan motor, remove the fuel tank (see Chapter 4). Trace the fan motor wiring from the motor and disconnect it at the 2-pin connector **(see illustration)**. Using a 12 volt battery and two jumper wires, connect the battery positive (+ve) lead to the black/blue wire terminal on the fan side of the connector and the battery negative (-ve) lead to the green terminal. Once connected the fan should operate. If it does not, then the motor is faulty. The fan motor is available as a separate item.

Replacement

 Warning: The engine must be completely cool before carrying out this procedure.

13 Remove the radiator (see Section 7).
14 Disconnect the wiring connector from the fan switch then unscrew the three bolts securing the fan shroud and fan assembly to the radiator, noting that one bolt also secures the earth (ground) wire, and remove the fan **(see illustration)**.

 3

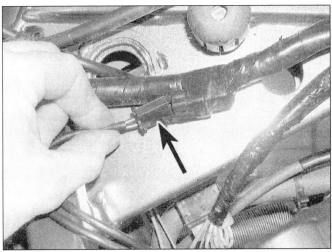

4.12 Disconnect the fan motor wiring connector (arrowed)

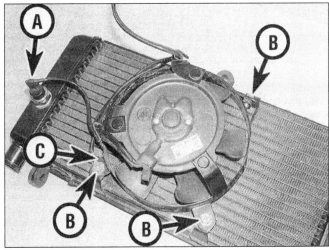

4.14 Fan switch wiring connector (A), fan mounting bolts (B) and earth wire (C)

15 Unscrew the three nuts securing the fan assembly to the shroud.

16 Hold the fan with a rag to prevent damage to the blades and unscrew the fan centre nut. Remove the fan from the motor shaft, noting how it fits on the shaft.

17 Installation is the reverse of removal, noting the following:

● Align the flat on the fan motor shaft with the flat in the fan hub.

● Apply a suitable non-permanent locking compound to the threads of the fan retaining nut.

● Attach the earth (ground) wire to the lower left-hand fan shroud bolt.

5 Coolant temperature gauge and sender – check and replacement

Coolant temperature gauge

Check

1 The circuit consists of the sender mounted in the thermostat housing on the right-hand side of the engine, and the gauge mounted in the instrument cluster. If the gauge malfunctions, first check the coolant level (see *Daily (pre-ride) checks*). If the level is correct, check that the battery is fully charged and that the fuses are all good.

2 If the gauge is still not working, disconnect the wire from the sender and connect it to earth (ground) with a jumper wire **(see illustration)**. Turn the ignition switch ON; the temperature gauge needle should swing over to the 'H' on the gauge.

Caution: If the needle moves, turn the ignition OFF immediately to avoid damaging the gauge.

If the needle moves as described, check the operation of the sender (see Steps 5 to 8). **Note:** *It is possible for a faulty gauge to register a reading in this check, but not when connected to the sender. Only renew the sender if it fails the check described below.*

3 If the needle movement is still faulty, or if it does not move at all, the fault lies in the wiring or the gauge itself. Check all the relevant wiring and wiring connectors (see Chapter 9). If all appears to be well, the gauge is defective and must be renewed.

Replacement

4 See Chapter 9. **Note:** *On CB600F models, the temperature gauge is integral with the tachometer and cannot be renewed as a separate item.*

Temperature gauge sender

Check

5 The sender is mounted in the thermostat housing. Unscrew the thermostat housing shield bolts and remove the shield **(see illustration 6.4)**.

6 Disconnect the sender wiring connector **(see illustration)**.

5.2 Coolant temperature sender (arrowed)

7 Remove the sender (see Steps 9 to 11 below). Fill a small heatproof container with coolant and place it on a stove. Connect the positive (+ve) probe of an ohmmeter to the terminal on the sender and the negative (-ve) probe to the sender body, then, using some wire or other support, suspend the sender in the coolant so that just the sensing portion and the threads are submerged **(see illustration 4.4)**. Also place a thermometer capable of reading temperatures up to 120°C in the coolant so that its bulb is close to the sender. **Note:** *None of the components should be allowed to directly touch the container.*

8 Heat the coolant to approximately 40°C and keep the temperature constant for 3 minutes before continuing the test. Then increase the heat gradually, stirring the coolant gently.

⚠ *Warning: This must be done very carefully to avoid the risk of personal injury.*

As the temperature of the coolant rises, the resistance of the sender should fall. Check that the correct resistance is obtained at the temperatures specified at the beginning of this Chapter. If the meter readings obtained are different, or they are obtained at different temperatures, then the sender is faulty and must be renewed.

Replacement

⚠ *Warning: The engine must be completely cool before carrying out this procedure.*

9 Drain the cooling system (see Chapter 1) and remove the fuel tank (see Chapter 4).

10 Disconnect the sender wiring connector.

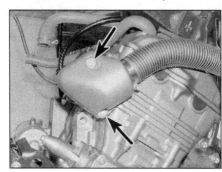

6.4 Undo the bolts (arrowed) and remove the shield

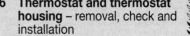

5.6 Disconnect the sender wiring connector

Unscrew the sender and remove it from the thermostat housing.

11 Apply a suitable sealant to the sender threads, then install it into the thermostat housing and tighten it to the torque setting specified at the beginning of this Chapter. Connect the sender wiring.

12 Refill the cooling system (see Chapter 1).

6 Thermostat and thermostat housing – removal, check and installation

Removal

⚠ *Warning: The engine must be completely cool before carrying out this procedure.*

1 The thermostat is automatic in operation and should give many years service without requiring attention. In the event of a failure, the valve will probably jam open, in which case the engine will take much longer than normal to warm up. Conversely, if the valve jams shut, the coolant will be unable to circulate and the engine will overheat. Neither condition is acceptable, and the fault must be investigated promptly.

2 The thermostat is located in the thermostat housing on the right-hand side of the engine.

3 Drain the cooling system (see Chapter 1).

4 Unscrew the thermostat housing shield bolts and remove the shield **(see illustration)**.

5 If required, note the index mark for the coolant hose, then loosen the clip securing the hose to the thermostat housing and disconnect the hose **(see illustrations)**.

6.5a Note the index mark (arrowed) for the coolant hose . . .

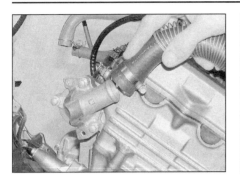

6.5b . . . then disconnect the coolant hose . . .

6.6a . . . undo the cover bolts (arrowed) . . .

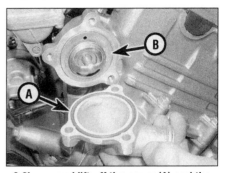

6.6b . . . and lift off the cover (A) and the thermostat (B)

6 Unscrew the two thermostat cover bolts and lift the cover off the housing. Discard the cover O-ring as a new one must be used on reassembly. Withdraw the thermostat, noting how it fits (see illustrations).

Check

7 Examine the thermostat visually before carrying out the test. If it remains in the open position at room temperature, it should be renewed.
8 Fill a small, heatproof container with cold water and place it on a stove. Using a piece of wire, suspend the thermostat in the water. Place a thermometer in the water so that the bulb is close to the thermostat (see illustration). Heat the water, noting the temperature when the thermostat opens, and compare the result with the specifications given at the beginning of this Chapter. Also check the amount the valve opens after it has been heated at 95°C for a few minutes and compare the measurement to the specifications. If the readings obtained differ from those given, the thermostat is faulty and must be renewed.
9 In the event of thermostat failure, as an emergency measure only, it can be removed and the machine used without it. Note: Take care when starting the engine from cold as it will take much longer than usual to warm up. Ensure that a new unit is installed as soon as possible.

Installation

10 Installation is the reverse of removal, noting the following:

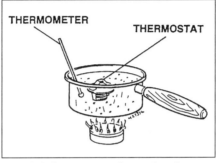

6.8 Arrangement for testing the thermostat

● Fit a new O-ring to the thermostat cover.
● Smear the O-ring with grease and ensure it fits correctly in the groove in the cover.
● Install the thermostat with the air bleed hole at the top (see illustration).
● Refill the cooling system (see Chapter 1).

7 Radiator – removal and installation

Removal

Warning: The engine must be completely cool before carrying out this procedure.

6.10 Install the thermostat with the air bleed hole (arrowed) at the top

1 Remove the fuel tank (see Chapter 4) and, on CB600FS models, the fairing (see Chapter 8).
2 Trace the cooling fan motor wiring from the motor and disconnect it at the 2-pin connector (see illustration 4.12).
3 Drain the cooling system (see Chapter 1).
4 Loosen the clips securing the main hoses to the top right-hand side and bottom left-hand side of the radiator and detach the hoses, then loosen the clip securing the overflow hose to the radiator filer neck and detach the hose (see illustrations).
5 Unscrew the radiator lower mounting bolt, noting the arrangement of the collar and bushes (see illustration overleaf). Support the radiator, then unscrew the upper mounting bolt, noting the arrangement of the collar and bushes, and pull the radiator off the

3

7.4a Detach the radiator top hose . . .

7.4b . . . bottom hose . . .

7.4c . . . and overflow hose

7.5a Undo the lower mounting bolt

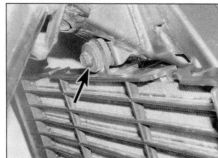

7.5b Undo the upper mounting bolt . . .

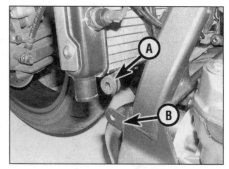

7.5c . . . then pull the mounting bush (A)
off the frame lug (B)

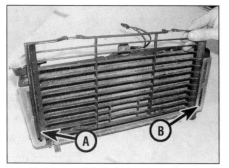

7.6 Stone guard is held by clips (A) and (B)

8.2 Check for signs of coolant leakage
underneath the water pump

mounting lug on the lower, left-hand side of the frame (see illustrations).

6 Unclip the stone guard from the front of the radiator and, if necessary, separate the cooling fan (see Section 4) from the radiator (see illustration).

7 Check the radiator for signs of damage and clear any dirt or debris that might obstruct air flow and inhibit cooling (see Chapter 1). If the fins are badly damaged or broken the radiator must be renewed. Also check the mounting bushes, and renew them if necessary.

Installation

8 Installation is the reverse of removal, noting the following.

● Ensure the stone guard is held securely by its mounting clips.

● Ensure the bushes and collars are correctly installed with the mounting bolts.

● Ensure the coolant hoses are in good

condition (see Chapter 1), and are securely retained by their clips, using new ones if necessary.

● Refill the cooling system (see Chapter 1).

8 Water pump – check, removal and installation

Check

1 The water pump is located on the lower left-hand side of the engine. Visually check the area around the pump for signs of leakage.

2 To prevent leakage of water from the cooling system to the lubrication system a mechanical seal is fitted to the water pump shaft inside the pump body. If the seal fails, a drain hole in the underside of the pump body allows the coolant to escape (see illustration).

Look for telltale signs of leakage around the drain hole.

3 The pump body is only available as a complete assembly. Therefore, if on inspection the drainage hole shows signs of leakage, the pump must be removed and the body renewed.

4 To check the pump impeller bearing, first remove the pump (see Steps 5 to 11). Rock the impeller back-and-forth and spin it by hand (see illustration). If there is excessive movement, or the bearing is noisy or rough when turned, the pump must be renewed.

Removal

5 Drain the cooling system (see Chapter 1) and place a suitable container below the water pump to catch any residual coolant or oil as the pump is removed.

6 Unscrew the four bolts securing the cover to the pump (the upper and lower bolts also secure the pump to the crankcase), noting how they fit, and remove the cover (see illustration). There is no need to detach the hoses unless you want to remove the cover from the machine. Discard the cover O-ring as a new one must be used on reassembly.

7 Loosen the clip securing the coolant hose to the pump body and detach the hose. Carefully draw the pump out of the crankcase, noting how it fits. Discard the O-ring from the rear of the pump body as a new one must be fitted on reassembly.

8 To remove the whole pump as an assembly, first loosen the clip on the bypass hose and detach the hose (see illustration).

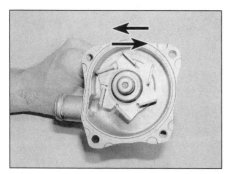

8.4 Rock the impeller back and forth to
check for wear in the bearing

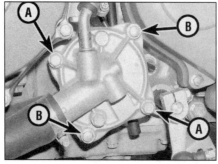

8.6 Pump cover bolts (A), pump-to-
crankcase bolts (B)

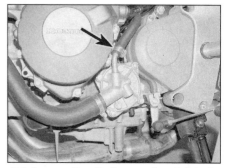

8.8 Loosen the clip (arrowed) and detach
the bypass hose

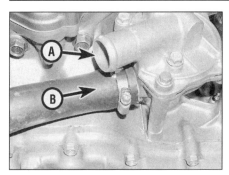

8.9 Detach the hose from the radiator (A) and to the oil cooler (B)

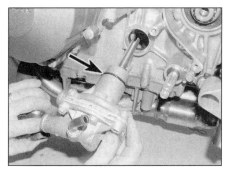

8.10 Withdraw the pump and discard the O-ring (arrowed)

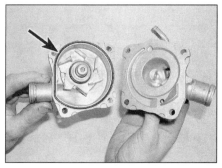

8.11 Remove the pump cover and discard the O-ring (arrowed)

9 Loosen the clips securing the coolant hoses to the pump cover and body and detach the hoses, noting which fits where **(see illustration)**.

10 Unscrew the upper and lower bolts securing the pump to the crankcase and pull the pump out, noting how it fits. Discard the O-ring from the rear of the pump body as a new one must be fitted on reassembly **(see illustration)**.

11 Separate the cover from the pump if required and discard the cover O-ring **(see illustration)**.

Installation

12 Clean any corrosion or scale build-up from inside the pump cover and body.

13 Smear the new pump body O-ring with grease and fit it onto the rear of the pump body, then carefully install the pump body in the crankcase, making sure the slot in the impeller shaft aligns with the peg on the oil pump spindle **(see illustrations)**.

14 Attach the coolant hose to the pump body and secure it with its clip.

15 Install a new cover O-ring into its groove in the pump body and smear it with grease **(see illustration 8.11)**.

16 Fit the pump cover onto the pump, then install the bolts and tighten them to the torque settings specified at the beginning of this

Chapter. Make sure the different bolts are in their correct locations **(see illustration 8.6)**.

17 If the pump was removed as an assembly, install the two bolts securing the pump to the crankcase and tighten them to the torque setting specified at the beginning of this Chapter **(see illustrations)**. Attach the coolant hoses to the pump and secure them with their clips **(see illustrations 8.8 and 8.9)**.

18 Refill the cooling system (see Chapter 1).

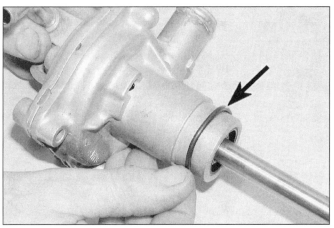

8.13a Fit a new O-ring on the pump body . . .

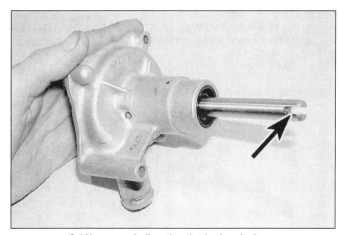

8.13b . . . and align the slot in the shaft . . .

3

8.13c . . . with the oil pump spindle (arrowed)

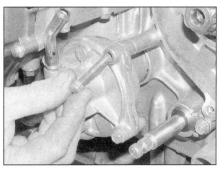

8.17a Fit the upper (shorter) pump mounting bolt . . .

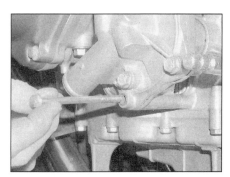

8.17b . . . and the lower (longer) pump mounting bolt

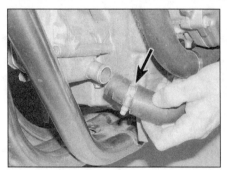

9.4a First slide the clip (arrowed) onto the hose . . .

9.4b . . . then fit the hose onto the union as far as the shoulder (arrowed) . . .

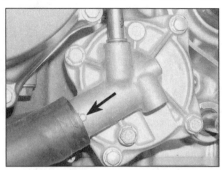

9.4c . . . or index mark (arrowed) . . .

9 Coolant hoses – removal and installation

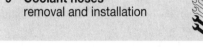

Removal

1 Before removing a hose, drain the cooling system (see Chapter 1).

2 Use a screwdriver or small socket to slacken the larger-bore hose clips, then slide them back along the hose and clear of the union spigot. The smaller-bore hoses are secured by spring clips which can be expanded by squeezing their ends together with pliers.

Caution: The radiator unions are fragile. Do not use excessive force when attempting to remove the hoses.

3 If a hose proves stubborn, release it by rotating it on its union before working it off. If all else fails, cut the hose with a sharp knife then slit it lengthways at the union so that it can be peeled off (see *Tools and Workshop Tips* in the Reference Section). Whilst this means renewing the hose, it is preferable to buying a new radiator.

Installation

4 Slide the clip onto the hose first and then work the hose all the way onto its union as far as the shoulder or index mark **(see illustrations)**.

HAYNES HiNT *If the hose is difficult to push on its union, it can be softened by soaking it in very hot water, or alternatively a little soapy water can be used as a lubricant.*

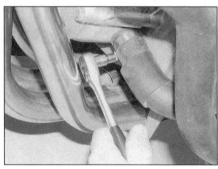

9.5 . . . and tighten the clip securely

5 Rotate the hose on its unions to settle it in position before sliding the clip into place and tightening it securely **(see illustration)**.

6 Refill the cooling system (see Chapter 1).

Chapter 4
Fuel and exhaust systems

Contents

Degrees of difficulty

Easy, suitable for novice with little experience	Fairly easy, suitable for beginner with some experience	Fairly difficult, suitable for competent DIY mechanic	Difficult, suitable for experienced DIY mechanic	Very difficult, suitable for expert DIY or professional

Specifications

Fuel
Grade	Unleaded, minimum 91 RON (Research Octane Number)
Fuel tank capacity	16 litres (inc. reserve of 3 litres)

Carburettors
Type	Keihin VP 49A
Throttle bore	34 mm
Idle speed	1,300 rpm (± 100 rpm)
Pilot screw setting (turns out)	1¾ turns out
Main jet	100 (carbs 1 and 4), 102 (carbs 2 and 3)
Pilot jet	40
Jet needle	J7SL
Float height	13.7 mm (non-adjustable)

Torque settings
Carburettor connecting stud nuts (6 mm)	10 Nm
Carburettor connecting stud nuts (5 mm)	5 Nm
Exhaust downpipe nuts	20 Nm
Exhaust pipe and silencer mounting bolts	22 Nm
Fuel tank mounting bolt nut	12 Nm

4

1 General information and precautions

General information

The fuel system consists of the fuel tank, fuel tap and filter, carburettors, fuel hoses and control cables.

The fuel filter is part of the tap and is fitted inside the fuel tank.

The carburettors used on all models are CV types with one carburettor for each cylinder. For cold starting, a choke lever is mounted on the left-hand handlebar, and is connected to the carburettors by a cable.

Air is drawn into the carburettors through an air filter which is housed behind the carburettors.

The exhaust system is a four-into-one design.

Many of the fuel system service procedures are considered routine maintenance items and for that reason are included in Chapter 1.

Precautions

⚠️ **Warning: Petrol (gasoline) is extremely flammable, so take extra precautions when you work on any part of the fuel system. Don't smoke or allow open flames or bare light bulbs near the work area, and don't work in a garage where a natural gas-type appliance is present. If you spill any fuel on your skin, rinse it off immediately with soap and water. When you perform any kind of work on the fuel system, wear safety glasses and have a fire extinguisher suitable for a class B type fire (flammable liquids) on hand.**

Always perform service procedures in a well-ventilated area to prevent a build-up of fumes.

Never work in a building containing a gas appliance with a pilot light, or any other form of naked flame. Ensure that there are no naked light bulbs or any sources of flame or sparks nearby.

Do not smoke (or allow anyone else to smoke) while in the vicinity of petrol (gasoline) or of components containing it.

2.2a Undo the bolt at the back of the tank . . .

Remember the possible presence of vapour from these sources and move well clear before smoking.

Check all electrical equipment belonging to the house, garage or workshop where work is being undertaken (see the Safety first! section of this manual). Remember that certain electrical appliances such as drills, cutters etc. create sparks in the normal course of operation and must not be used near petrol (gasoline) or any component containing it. Again, remember the possible presence of fumes before using electrical equipment.

Always mop up any spilt fuel and safely dispose of the rag used.

Any stored fuel that is drained off during servicing work must be kept in sealed containers that are suitable for holding petrol (gasoline), and clearly marked as such; the containers themselves should be kept in a safe place. Note that this last point applies equally to the fuel tank if it is removed from the machine; also remember to keep its filler cap closed at all times.

Read the Safety first! section of this manual carefully before starting work.

2 Fuel tank, fuel tap and filter – removal and installation

⚠️ **Warning: Refer to the precautions given in Section 1 before starting work.**

2.2b . . . and detach the hoses from the fuel tap (arrowed)

Fuel tank

Removal

1 Make sure the fuel filler cap is secure and fuel tap is in the OFF position. Remove the seat and the frame side panels (see Chapter 8).

2 Unscrew the nut and bolt securing the rear of the tank to the frame, then lift the rear of the tank to gain access to the clips securing the fuel hose and the fuel tap vacuum hose **(see illustration)**. Place a rag under the fuel tap to catch any residual fuel as the hose is detached. Release the clips securing the fuel hose and the vacuum hose and detach the hoses **(see illustration)**.

Note: *If it is necessary to drain the tank , connect a length of fuel hose to the tap and place the free end of the hose in a suitable container below the level of the fuel in the tank. Turn the tap to the RES position and draw vacuum in the vacuum hose; fuel should flow from the tank. Clamp the vacuum hose until sufficient fuel has been drawn from the tank, then turn the tap OFF and disconnect the fuel hose.*

3 Remove the tank; note the routing of the breather hose under the right-hand side of the tank **(see illustration)**. Note the position of the two bushes on the front mounting brackets and the two bushes in the rear mounting bracket **(see illustrations)**. Inspect the bushes for signs of damage or deterioration and renew them if necessary.

2.3a Note the routing of the breather hose

2.3b Check the condition of the front . . .

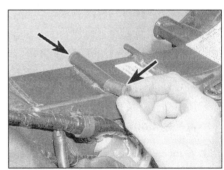

2.3c . . . and rear mounting bushes

2.4 Support the rear of the tank . . .

2.5 . . . while the hoses are secured

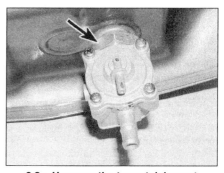

2.8a Unscrew the tap retaining nut (arrowed) . . .

Installation

4 Check that the tank mounting bushes are in place, then carefully lower the tank into position on the front mounting bushes. Support the rear of the tank with a block of wood **(see illustration)**.

5 Ensure the breather hose is correctly routed down behind the engine unit to a point above the water pump. Fit the vacuum hose to the tap and secure it with its clip. Fit the fuel hose to the tap and secure it with its clip **(see illustration)**.

6 Lower the rear of the tank carefully, ensuring none of the hoses are trapped against the carburettors, then install the rear tank mounting nut and bolt and tighten them to the torque setting specified at the beginning of this Chapter.

7 Turn the fuel tap ON, start the engine and check that there is no sign of fuel leakage, then install the seat and the frame side panels (see Chapter 8).

Fuel tap

8 The tap should not be removed from the tank unnecessarily to avoid the possibility of damaging the O-ring or the filter. If the fuel tap to tank joint is leaking, first ensure that the tap retaining nut is tight. Hold the tap to prevent it twisting while tightening the nut. If leakage persists, the tank must be drained of fuel, the tap removed by unscrewing the retaining nut and the O-ring replaced with a new one **(see illustrations)**.

9 If fuel flow problems are experienced, first check that the tank breather hose is clear and that the tap vacuum hose is in good condition and its connections are air tight, then check the tap filter (see Step 16).

10 If the filter is clean and in good condition, check the operation of the tap diaphragm which is actuated by vacuum drawn through the hose from the no.1 cylinder inlet manifold. With the tank off the motorcycle, connect lengths of hose to the fuel and vacuum outlets on the tap and place the free end of the fuel hose into a suitable container below the level of fuel in the tank. When vacuum is drawn in the vacuum hose, fuel should flow from the tank. Check the tap operation in both the ON and RES positions.

11 If there is no fuel flow, or fuel flow in only one tap position, disassemble the tap and check for an internal blockage.

12 Undo the tap body fixing screws and remove the tap cover, the diaphragm spring and the diaphragm assembly, noting how it fits **(see illustrations)**.

13 If a fault with the tap body cannot be corrected, replace the tap assembly with a new one.

14 If fuel flows from the tank with no vacuum in the vacuum hose, the diaphragm is faulty and must be replaced with a new one.

Fuel filter

15 Cleaning or renewal of the fuel filter is advised after a particularly high mileage has been covered. It is also necessary if fuel starvation is suspected. The fuel filter is

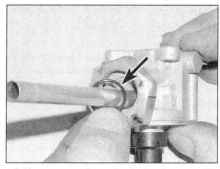

2.8b . . . to replace the O-ring (arrowed)

mounted in the tank and is integral with the fuel tap.

16 Remove the fuel tank (see Steps 1 to 3) and the fuel tap (see Step 8), and carefully pull the filter off the fuel reserve supply tube **(see illustration)**. Once the filter is dry, clean the gauze with a soft brush or low pressure compressed air to remove all traces of dirt and fuel sediment. Check the gauze for holes. If any are found, a new filter should be fitted (it is available separately). A damaged filter will allow dirt particles to enter the tap body. Disassemble the body (see Step 12) and check that it is clean inside before replacing the tap.

17 Check the condition of the tap O-ring and renew it if it is in any way damaged or deteriorated **(see illustration 2.8b)**. It is advisable to renew the O-ring as a matter of course.

4

2.12a Remove the tap cover and diaphragm spring. . .

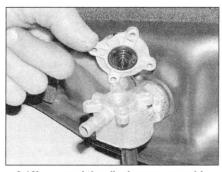

2.12b . . . and the diaphragm assembly

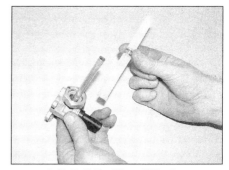

2.16 Pull the filter off the tap

3 Fuel tank –
cleaning and repair

1 All repairs to the fuel tank should be carried out by a professional who has experience in this critical and potentially dangerous work. Even after cleaning and flushing of the fuel system, explosive fumes can remain and ignite during repair of the tank.

2 If the fuel tank is removed from the bike, it should not be placed in an area where sparks or open flames could ignite the fumes coming out of the tank. Be especially careful inside garages where a natural gas-type appliance is located, because the pilot light could cause an explosion.

4 Idle fuel/air mixture –
pilot screw adjustment

⚠ **Warning: Refer to the precautions given in Section 1 before starting work.**

1 If the engine runs extremely roughly at idle or continually stalls, and if a carburettor overhaul does not cure the problem (see Section 5), the pilot screws may require adjustment. The pilot screws are set to their correct position by the manufacturer and should not normally be adjusted or removed. It is also worth noting at this point that unless you have the experience to carry this out, it is best to entrust the task to a motorcycle dealer, tuner or fuel systems specialist. An angled screwdriver, with flexible drive, is required to turn the pilot screws; use either the Honda service tool (pt. No. 07908-4730002) or a commercially available alternative – note that the pilot screw heads on Swiss market models require a different service tool. Additionally, Honda advise the use of an auxiliary tachometer with graduations of 50 rpm, rather than relying on the motorcycle's own tachometer. **Note:** *Before adjusting the pilot screws, ensure that*

the carburettors are synchronised (see Chapter 1).

2 Turn each pilot screw clockwise until it seats lightly, then back it out the number of turns specified at the beginning of this Chapter **(see illustration)**. This is the base position for adjustment.

Caution: The pilot screw seat is easily damaged if the screw is tightened against it.

3 Warm the engine up to normal operating temperature and set the idle speed with the idle speed adjuster (see Chapter 1).

4 Working on the carburettor for cylinder No. 3 first, turn the pilot screw by a small amount either side of the base position to find the point at which the highest consistent idle speed is obtained. Now do the same for the other three cylinders. Blip the throttle open a couple of times, then readjust the idle speed to the specified figure.

5 Turn the pilot screw on cylinder No. 3 carburettor in gradually so that the idle speed drops by 50 rpm, then readjust the idle speed to the specified figure. Now turn the pilot screw in so that the idle speed again drops by 50 rpm, then turn the pilot screw 7/8 of a turn out from this position.

6 Repeat Step 5 on the pilot screws for the other three cylinders.

7 When all four carburettors have been adjusted, snap the throttle open two or three times and make a final check of the idle speed.

Restrictions

8 Due to the increased emphasis on controlling exhaust emissions in certain world markets, regulations have been formulated which prevent adjustment of the air/fuel mixture. On such models the pilot screw positions are pre-set at the factory and in some cases have a limiter cap fitted to prevent tampering. Where adjustment is possible, it can only be made in conjunction with an exhaust gas analyser to ensure that the machine does not exceed the emissions regulations.

5 Carburettor overhaul –
general information

1 Poor engine performance, hesitation, hard starting, stalling, flooding and backfiring are all signs that carburettor maintenance may be required.

2 Keep in mind that many so-called carburettor problems are really not carburettor problems at all, but mechanical problems within the engine or ignition system malfunctions. Try to establish for certain that the carburettors are in need of maintenance before beginning a major overhaul.

3 Check the fuel tap and filter, the fuel hoses, the inlet manifold joint clamps, the air filter, the ignition system, the spark plugs and carburettor synchronisation before assuming that a carburettor overhaul is required.

4 Most carburettor problems are caused by dirt particles, varnish and other deposits which build up in and block the fuel and air passages. Also, in time, gaskets and O-rings shrink or deteriorate and cause fuel and air leaks which lead to poor performance.

5 When overhauling the carburettors, disassemble them completely and clean the parts thoroughly with a carburettor cleaning solvent and dry them with filtered, unlubricated compressed air. Blow through the fuel and air passages with compressed air to force out any dirt that may have been loosened but not removed by the solvent. Once the cleaning process is complete, reassemble the carburettors using new gaskets and O-rings.

6 Before disassembling the carburettors, make sure you have all necessary gaskets and O-rings, some carburettor cleaner, a supply of clean rag, some means of blowing out the carburettor passages and a clean place to work. It is recommended that only one carburettor be overhauled at a time to avoid mixing up parts.

6 Air filter housing –
removal and installation

Removal

1 Remove the fuel tank (see Section 2), and the battery (see Chapter 9).

2 Remove air filter element (see Chapter 1).

3 Undo the screw securing the sub-air cleaner clamp to the right-hand side of the filter housing and remove the clamp. Release the clips securing the pulse secondary air (PAIR) system hose and the crankcase breather hose to the filter housing and detach the hoses **(see illustrations)**.

4.2 Pilot screw on No 1 carburettor (arrowed)

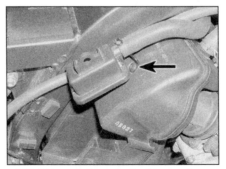

6.3a Unscrew the sub-air cleaner clamp (arrowed) . . .

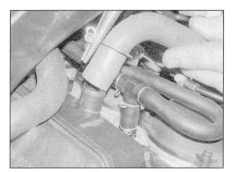

6.3b . . . then detach the PAIR system hose . . .

6.3c . . . and the crankcase breather hose

6.4 Loosen the housing-to-carburettor clamps

6.5 Housing rests on the swingarm bracket

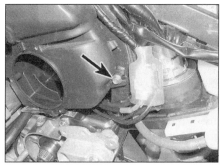

6.6a Unscrew the mounting bolt (arrowed) . . .

6.6b . . . and remove the housing

4 Loosen the clamps securing the housing to the carburettor intakes **(see illustration)**.

5 Note the location of the carburettor vent hose where it rests on the top of the housing, and how the housing rests on the right-hand swingarm bracket **(see illustration)**.

6 Unscrew the housing mounting bolt and remove the housing from the left-hand side of the motorcycle **(see illustrations)**.

Installation

7 Installation is the reverse of removal, noting the following:

● Ensure the carburettor intake clamps are positioned with the screws at the top before installing the housing onto the carburettors.

● Ensure the wiring loom is not trapped between the housing and the frame **(see illustration 6.6a)**.

● Install the open end of the carburettor vent hose in the recess on the top of the housing **(see illustration)**.

● Check the condition of the breather hoses and clips and renew them if necessary.

---

7 Carburettors –
removal and installation

> ⚠️ *Warning: Refer to the precautions given in Section 1 before starting work.*

Removal

1 Remove the air filter housing (see Section 6).

2 Connect a length of hose to the drain outlet underneath the float chamber of No. 1 carburettor. Loosen the drain screw and drain any residual fuel into a suitable container, then tighten the screw and drain the other carburettors **(see illustration)**.

3 Release the clip securing the sub-air cleaner hose to the carburettor union and detach the hose and sub-air cleaner **(see illustration)**.

4 Unclip the throttle position sensor

6.7 Carburettor vent hose location (arrowed)

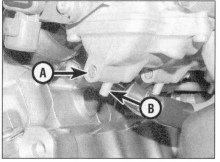

7.2 Drain screw (A) and outlet (B) on No 1 carburettor

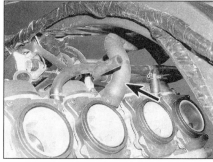

7.3 Detach the sub-air cleaner hose (arrowed)

7.4a Unclip the cover . . .

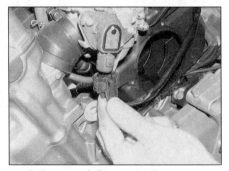

7.4b . . . and disconnect the sensor

7.5 Loosen the throttle cable locknuts

connector cover and disconnect the connector **(see illustrations)**.

5 Loosen the lock nuts securing the throttle cables in the bracket on the carburettors **(see illustration)**.

6 Unclip the choke outer cable from its bracket and detach the inner cable from the choke linkage **(see illustration)**.

7 Loosen the clamps on the cylinder head inlet stubs, then ease the carburettors off the inlet stubs **(see illustration)**. **Note:** *Keep the carburettors as upright as possible to prevent the possibility of the piston diaphragms being damaged*

8 Detach the throttle cables from the carburettor throttle cam, noting how they fit **(see illustration)**.

Caution: Stuff clean rag into each cylinder head inlet after removing the carburettors to prevent anything from falling in.

9 If necessary, slacken the clamps securing the inlet stubs to the cylinder head and

remove the stubs. The stubs are clearly marked; note which way round they fit and the location lugs on the underside of the head **(see illustrations)**.

Installation

10 Installation is the reverse of removal, noting the following.

● Check for cracks or splits in the cylinder head inlet stubs, and renew them if necessary.

● If removed, make sure the inlet stubs are installed so that the slot in the underside of the stub locates over the lug on the underside of the head **(see illustration 7.9b)**.

● Connect the throttle cables to the throttle cam before fitting the carburettors to the engine.

● Make sure the carburettors are fully engaged with the inlet stubs and the clamps are securely tightened.

● Make sure all cables and hoses are correctly routed and secured and not trapped or kinked .

● Refer to Section 11 for installation of the throttle cables and Section 12 for the choke cable. Check the operation of the cables and adjust them as necessary (see Chapter 1).

● Check idle speed and carburettor synchronisation (if the carburettors have been overhauled) and adjust as necessary (see Chapter 1).

8 Carburettors – disassembly, cleaning and inspection

⚠️ **Warning: Refer to the precautions given in Section 1 before starting work.**

Disassembly

1 Remove the carburettors (see Section 7). **Note:** *Do not separate the carburettors unless absolutely necessary; each carburettor can be dismantled sufficiently for all normal cleaning and adjustments while in place on the mounting brackets. Dismantle the carburettors separately to avoid interchanging parts* **(see illustration)**.

2 If required, release the clips securing the carburettor air vent hoses and fuel hoses and detach the hoses **(see illustration)**.

3 Unscrew and remove the screws securing the linkage bar to the carburettors and remove the plastic washers. Unhook the choke linkage bar return spring, noting how it fits **(see illustrations)**.

4 Remove the linkage bar, noting how the forked tabs locate on the choke plungers, and remove the second set of plastic washers and the return spring **(see illustrations)**.

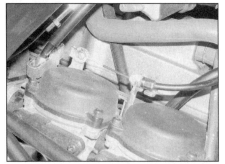

7.6 Detach the choke cable

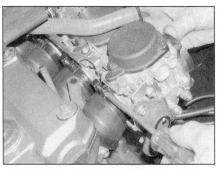

7.7 Loosen the carburettor-to-cylinder head clamps

7.8 Detach the cables from the throttle cam (arrowed)

7.9a Note the markings on the inlet stubs . . .

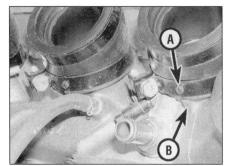

7.9b . . . and the lugs for the clamps (A) and the stubs (B)

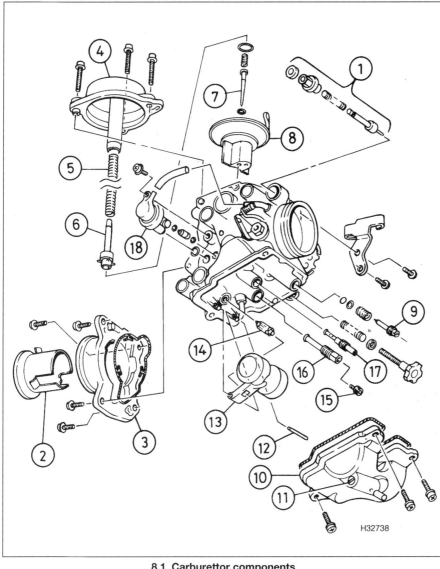

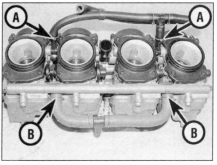

8.2 Air vent hose clips (A) and fuel hose clips (B)

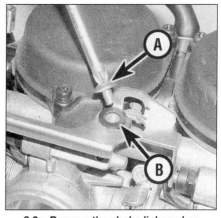

8.3a Remove the choke linkage bar screws (A) and washers (B)

8.3b . . . then unhook the return spring (arrowed)

8.1 Carburettor components

1 Choke plunger assembly
2 Intake venturi
3 Intake venturi holder
4 Top cover
5 Spring
6 Jet needle holder
7 Needle
8 Diaphragm/piston
9 Pilot screw assembly
10 Float chamber
11 Drain bolt
12 Float pivot pin
13 Float
14 Needle valve
15 Main jet
16 Emulsion tube
17 Pilot jet
18 Air cut-off valve

H32738

4

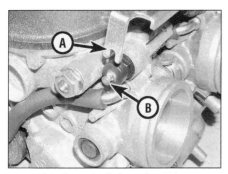

8.4a Note how the linkage bar (A) locates on the choke plungers (B)

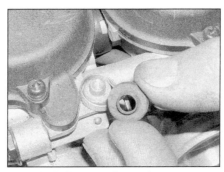

8.4b Remove the washers . . .

8.4c . . . and the return spring

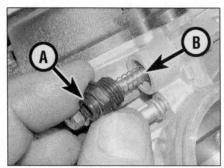

8.5a Remove the cover (arrowed) . . .

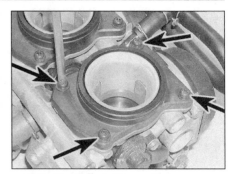

8.5b . . . and remove the choke plunger nut (A) and plunger assembly (B)

8.6a Undo the intake venturi screws (arrowed) . . .

8.6b . . . then lift off the venturi and holder . . .

8.6c . . . and the O-ring

5 Remove the cover, then unscrew the choke plunger nut, using a pair of thin-nosed pliers if access is too restricted for a spanner, and withdraw the spring and plunger from the carburettor body **(see illustrations)**.

6 Unscrew and remove the intake venturi holder retaining screws. Lift off the holder and the venturi, noting how they fit together **(see illustrations)**. Carefully lift the O-ring out of the groove in the carburettor body **(see illustration)**.

7 Unscrew and remove the top cover retaining screws. Lift off the cover and remove the spring from inside the piston **(see illustration)**.

8 Note how the tab on the piston diaphragm locates around the air passage in the carburettor body **(see illustration)**. Carefully peel the rim of the diaphragm out of its sealing groove and withdraw the piston assembly, noting how the piston and slide locate in the carburettor body **(see illustration)**.

Caution: Do not use a sharp instrument to displace the diaphragm as it is easily damaged.

9 To remove the jet needle holder from the piston, thread a 4 mm screw into the top of the holder (one of the top cover retaining screws is ideal), then grasp the screw with a pair of pliers and carefully draw the holder out of the piston **(see illustrations)**. Note the

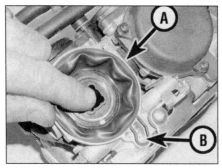

8.7 Lift off the top cover and remove the spring

8.8a Diaphragm sealing groove (A) and tab recess (B)

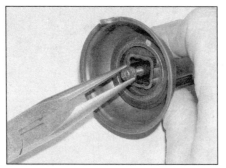

8.8b Note how the piston fits in the carburettor body

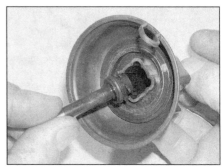

8.9a Thread a screw into the needle holder . . .

8.9b . . . and pull it out as described

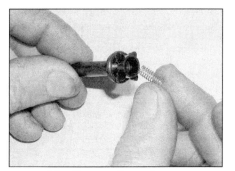

8.9c Remove the spring . . .

8.9d . . . and discard the O-ring

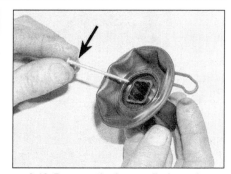

8.10 Remove the jet needle from the piston with the washer (arrowed)

8.11a Undo the float chamber retaining screws . . .

8.11b . . . and remove the float chamber

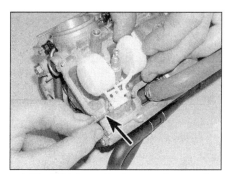

8.12a Withdraw the float pin (arrowed)

spring that fits inside the holder. Discard the O-ring on the holder as a new one must be fitted on reassembly **(see illustrations)**.

Caution: Do not push the needle holder out of the piston by pushing up on the needle.

10 Push the jet needle up from the bottom of the piston and withdraw it from the top **(see illustration)**. Note the washer that fits on the needle between the head of the needle and the piston.

11 Remove the screws securing the float chamber to the carburettor body and remove the float chamber **(see illustrations)**. Discard the gasket as a new one must be fitted on reassembly.

12 Carefully withdraw the float pin **(see illustration)**. Remove the float and unhook the float valve, noting how it fits onto the tab on the float **(see illustration)**.

13 Unscrew and remove the pilot jet **(see illustration)**.

14 Unscrew and remove the main jet **(see illustration)**.

15 Unscrew and remove the emulsion tube **(see illustration)**.

16 The pilot screw assembly can be removed if required, but note that its setting will be

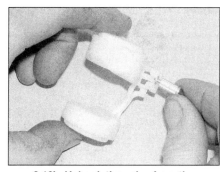

8.12b Unhook the valve from the float tab

4

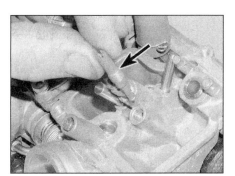

8.13 Remove the pilot jet . . .

8.14 . . . the main jet . . .

8.15 . . . and the emulsion tube

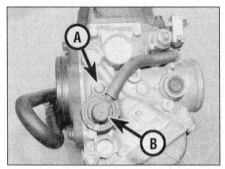

8.17a Undo the screw (A) and withdraw the valve (B)

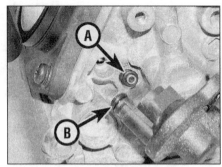

8.17b Discard the O-rings on the air jet (A) and valve body (B)

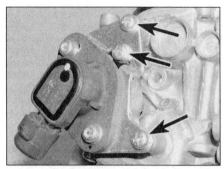

8.18 Throttle position sensor mounting bracket screws (arrowed)

disturbed **(see Haynes Hint)**. Unscrew and remove the pilot screw along with its spring, washer and O-ring **(see illustration 8.1)**. Discard the O-ring as a new one must be fitted on reassembly.

> **To record the pilot screw's current setting, turn the screw in until it seats lightly, counting the number of turns necessary to achieve this, then fully unscrew it. On installation, the screw is simply backed out the number of turns you've recorded.**

17 An air cut-off valve is located on the right-hand side of each carburettor. Unscrew and remove the valve retaining screw and carefully pull the valve and the valve air jet out of the carburettor body **(see illustration)**. Discard the O-rings on the valve body and the air jet as new ones must be fitted on reassembly **(see illustration)**. Detach the cut-off valve hose from the carburettor body.
18 A throttle position sensor is mounted on the outside of No. 1 carburettor **(see illustration)**. Note that the sensor is not available separately from the carburettor body and should not be disturbed unless attention to the throttle shaft components is required. If necessary, remove the three screws which retain the sensor mounting bracket to the carburettor – do not disturb the two screws which secure the sensor to its mounting bracket.

Cleaning
Caution: Use only a dedicated carburettor cleaner or petroleum-based solvent for carburettor cleaning. Do not use caustic cleaners.
19 Soak the carburettor body and individual components in the cleaner to loosen and dissolve the varnish and other deposits (always check the directions for use of solvent products, especially when applying them to non-metallic items). Then use a nylon-bristle brush to remove the stubborn deposits, rinse, and dry the components with compressed air.
20 Use compressed air to blow out all the fuel and air passages in the carburettor body and the jets and emulsion tube. **Note:** *The float valve seat has an integral fuel filter; clean the filter by blowing air through from the float chamber side only.*
Caution: Never clean the jets or passages with a piece of wire or a drill bit, as they will be enlarged, causing the fuel and air metering rates to be upset.

Inspection
21 Check the carburettor body, float chamber and top cover for cracks, distorted sealing surfaces and other damage. If any defects are found, renew the faulty component.
22 Operate the throttle shaft to make sure the throttle butterfly valve opens and closes smoothly. If it doesn't, cleaning the throttle linkage may help. Otherwise, renew the carburettor.
23 Check the piston diaphragm for splits,

holes, creases and general deterioration **(see illustration)**. Holding it up to a light will help to reveal defects of this nature. Renew the piston/diaphragm assembly if necessary.
24 Insert the piston in the carburettor body and check that it moves up-and-down smoothly. Check the surface of the piston and slide for wear **(see illustration 8.23)**. If it is worn excessively or doesn't move smoothly in the body, replace it with a new one.
25 Check the operation of the choke plunger assembly. If it doesn't move smoothly, inspect the needle on the end of the plunger, the spring and the plunger linkage bar **(see illustration 8.1)**. Replace the plunger assembly with a new one if any component is worn, damaged or bent – individual parts are not available.
26 If removed, check the tapered portion of the pilot screw and the spring and O-ring for wear or damage. Replace the assembly with a new one if necessary – individual parts are not available.
27 Check the jet needle for straightness by rolling it on a flat surface such as a piece of glass. Replace it with a new one if it is bent, or if the tip is worn.
28 Check the tip of the float valve for grooves or scratches or other signs of wear. Gently push down on the plunger on the top of the valve then release it – it should spring back immediately **(see illustration)**. If any defects are found, replace the valve with a new one.
29 Check the float for damage. This will usually be apparent by the presence of fuel inside the float. If the float is damaged, replace it with a new one.

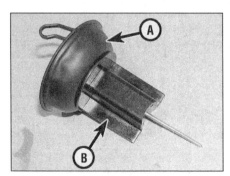

8.23 Inspect the piston diaphragm (A) and the slide (B)

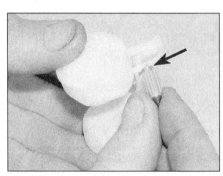

8.28 Check the operation of the float valve plunger (arrowed)

9 Carburettors – reassembly and float height check

> ⚠ **Warning: Refer to the precautions given in Section 1 before proceeding.**

Note: *When reassembling the carburettors, be sure to use new O-rings and gaskets. Do not overtighten the carburettor jets and screws as they are easily damaged.*
1 If removed, install the pilot screw along with its spring, washer and O-ring, turning it in until it seats lightly. Now, turn the screw out the

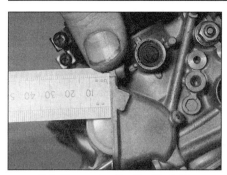

9.6 Measuring the float height

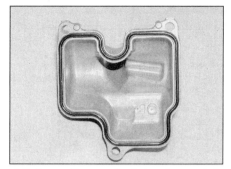

9.7 Ensure the new float chamber gasket is properly seated

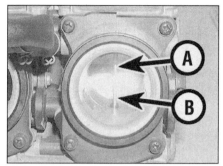

9.10 Ensure the needle (A) is aligned with the jet (B)

number of turns previously recorded, or as specified at the beginning of this Chapter.

2 Install the emulsion tube **(see illustration 8.15)**.

3 Install the main jet **(see illustration 8.14)**.

4 Install the pilot jet **(see illustration 8.13)**.

5 Hook the float valve onto the tab on the float assembly, then position the float assembly in the carburettor, making sure the valve locates in its seat. Install the float pin **(see illustration 8.12b and 8.12a)**.

6 To check the float height, hold the carburettor so the float hangs down, then tilt it back until the needle valve is just seated, but not so far that the needle's spring-loaded tip is compressed. Measure the distance between the gasket face and the bottom of the float with an accurate ruler **(see illustration)**. The correct setting is given in the Specifications at the beginning of this Chapter. The float height is not adjustable, so if it is incorrect the float may be damaged and should be renewed.

7 Fit a new gasket onto the float chamber, making sure it is seated properly in its groove **(see illustration)**. Install the chamber on the carburettor and tighten its screws securely.

8 Fit the washer onto the jet needle and insert the needle into the piston **(see illustration 8.10)**.

9 Fit a new O-ring into the groove in the jet needle holder and install the spring into the holder. Using a 4 mm screw as on disassembly, insert the holder into the centre of the piston and push it down until the O-ring is felt to locate in its groove in the piston **(see illustration 8.9d, c, b and a)**. Remove the screw.

10 Slide the piston assembly into the carburettor body, making sure the needle is correctly aligned with the needle jet **(see illustration)**.

11 Align the tab on the piston diaphragm with the air passage in the carburettor body and press the rim of the diaphragm into its groove, making sure it is correctly seated **(see illustration 8.8a)**.

12 Carefully press the piston down into the carburettor body, then fit the spring into the piston and into the recess in the top cover. Ensure the cover is correctly aligned with the body, then fit the cover and tighten the retaining screws securely **(see illustration 8.7)**. Check that the piston moves smoothly in the carburettor body by pushing it up with your finger; note that the piston should descend slowly and smoothly as the diaphragm draws air into the chamber – it should not drop sharply under spring pressure.

13 Carefully fit the intake venturi O-ring into the groove in the carburettor body **(see**

9.13 Install the intake venturi in the carburettor body

illustration 8.6c), fit the venturi into the holder and install the assembly into the carburettor body **(see illustration)**. Install the holder screws and tighten them securely **(see illustration 8.6a)**.

14 Fit the choke plunger and spring into the carburettor body **(see illustrations)**. Tighten the retaining nut securely and fit the cover **(see illustrations 8.5b and a)**.

15 Install the return spring and plastic washers for the choke linkage bar, then fit the bar, making sure the tabs locate correctly on each choke plunger. Fit the second set of washers and install the screws, tightening them securely.

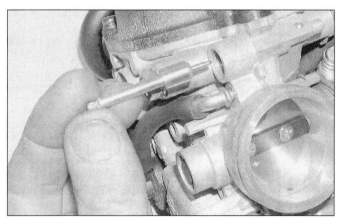

9.14a Install the choke plunger . . .

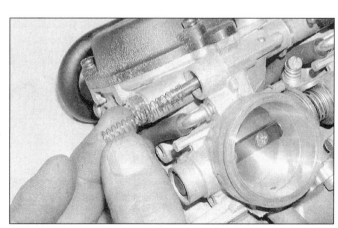

9.14b . . . and the plunger spring

4

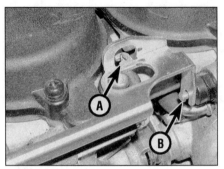

9.16a Ensure the linkage bar is engaged with the return spring (A) and the choke plungers (B) . . .

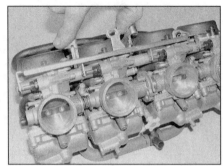

9.16b . . . then check the linkage bar operation

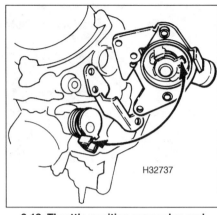

9.18 Throttle position sensor lug and corresponding tangs on throttle shaft

16 Engage the linkage bar return spring and check the operation of the mechanism **(see illustrations)**.
17 Fit new O-rings to the air cut-off valve jet and install the jet in the carburettor body **(see illustration 8.17b)**. Fit a new O-ring to the valve body, install the valve body and tighten

the retaining screw securely. Connect the valve hose to the carburettor.
18 If the throttle position sensor bracket was detached from No. 1 carburettor, ensure that its lug fits between the tangs on the end of the throttle shaft on installation **(see illustration)**. Tighten the three bracket screws securely.

19 If removed, install the carburettor air vent hoses and fuel hoses and secure them with their clips.
20 Install the carburettors (see Section 7).

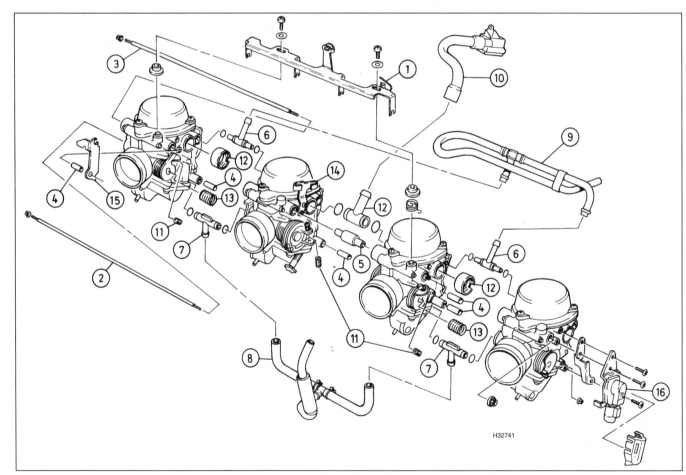

10.1 Carburettor assembly

1 Choke linkage bar	5 Shouldered dowel	9 Air vent hoses	13 Throttle linkage springs
2 Connecting bolt (5 mm)	6 Air vent joints	10 Sub-air cleaner hose	14 Throttle cable bracket
3 Connecting bolt (6 mm)	7 Fuel joints	11 Synchronising screw springs	15 Choke cable bracket
4 Plain dowels	8 Fuel feed hoses	12 Sub-air cleaner joints	16 Throttle position sensor

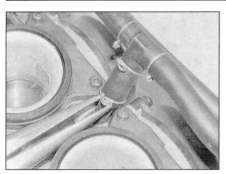

10.3 Release the clips securing the air vent and fuel hoses

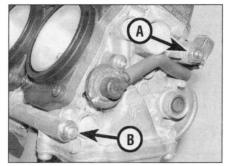

10.5 Carburettor upper (A) and lower (B) joining stud nuts

10.6a Note the arrangement of the synchronising springs (A) and linkage springs (B) . . .

10 Carburettors – separation and joining

⚠ *Warning: Refer to the precautions given in Section 1 before proceeding*

Separation

1 The carburettors do not need to be separated for normal overhaul. If you need to separate them (to fit a new carburettor body, for example), refer to the following procedure **(see illustration)**.

2 Remove the carburettors (see Section 7). Mark the body of each carburettor with its cylinder location to ensure that it is positioned correctly on reassembly.

3 Release the clips securing the carburettor air vent hoses and fuel hoses and detach the hoses **(see illustration)**.

4 Remove the choke plunger linkage bar (see Section 8).

5 Alternately loosen the nuts on the right-hand end of the two threaded studs which join the carburettors together **(see illustration)**. Remove the nuts and withdraw the studs.

6 Make a careful note of how the carburettor synchronising screw springs and throttle linkage springs are arranged to ensure that they are fitted correctly on reassembly. Also note the arrangement of the sub air cleaner,

carburettor breather and fuel supply joint pipes **(see illustrations)**.

7 Carefully separate the carburettors, taking care not to damage the fuel and air joints between each carburettor. Keep a careful watch on all springs as the carburettors are separated; the synchronising springs should stay with the adjusting screw, but if they don't, refit them so that they are not lost.

8 Pull out the fuel and air vent joint pipes and discard the O-rings as new ones must be used.

9 Detach the carburettor joining dowels and spacers. Note how the choke cable bracket is held between No. 3 and 4 carburettors.

Joining

10 Assembly is the reverse of the disassembly procedure. Fit the fuel and air vent joint pipe, dowel and spacer to one carburettor first before joining the two together. Use new O-rings on the fuel and vent pipe fittings, and smear them with clean engine oil.

11 Tighten the nuts on the carburettor joining studs to the torque settings specified at the beginning of this Chapter. **Note:** *The upper joining nuts (nearest the engine) are 6 mm and the lower joining nuts are 5 mm. Take great care when tightening to avoid damaging the carburettors.*

12 Check the operation of the choke and throttle linkages ensuring that both operate smoothly and return quickly under spring

pressure before installing the carburettors on the bike.

13 Check carburettor synchronisation (see Chapter 1).

11 Throttle cables – removal and installation

Warning: Refer to the precautions given in Section 1 before proceeding.

Removal

1 Remove the fuel tank (see Section 2). Whilst it is possible to detach the throttle cables with the carburettors in place, there is a limited amount of space to work in. If required, displace the carburettors to improve access (see Section 7).

2 Turn the handlebars onto full left lock to provide the maximum freeplay in the cables. The opening cable is the front cable in the twistgrip, the closing cable is the rear one. Loosen the locknut on the opening cable adjuster and thread the adjuster fully in, then tighten the locknut against it **(see illustration)**. This resets the adjuster to the start of its range.

3 At the carburettor end, loosen the opening cable adjuster locknut (above the bracket) then unscrew the lower nut off the adjuster **(see illustration)**.

4 Slip the adjuster out of the bracket and

4

10.6b . . . and the carburettor joint pipes (arrowed)

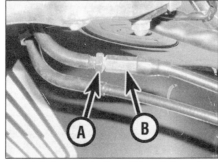

11.2 Loosen locknut (A) and thread adjuster (B) fully in

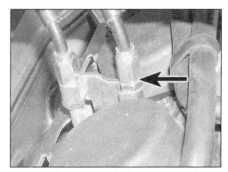

11.3 Loosen the locknut (arrowed)

11.4 Detach the opening cable nipple from the throttle cam

11.5a Unscrew the locknut fully . . .

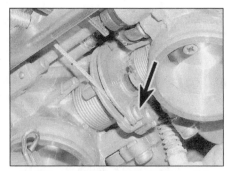

11.5b . . . and detach the closing cable nipple from the throttle cam

detach the inner cable from the carburettor throttle cam **(see illustration)**.

5 Unscrew the closing cable holder locknut fully and slip the holder out of the bracket and detach the inner cable from the throttle cam **(see illustrations)**. Withdraw the cables from the bike noting the correct routing of each cable.

6 At the throttle twistgrip, unscrew the opening cable elbow locknut from the twistgrip housing, then unscrew the closing cable nut **(see illustrations)**.

7 Remove the twistgrip housing screws, noting that the rear screw is longer then the front screw, and pull off the upper half of the housing, then detach the inner cables from the pulley **(see illustrations)**.

8 Detach the lower half of the housing from the handlebar, noting how it fits, and withdraw the opening cable and elbow from the housing. Thread the housing off the elbow

and withdraw the cable from the housing. Mark each cable to ensure it is connected correctly on installation.

Installation

9 Fit the opening cable elbow into the front socket of the lower half of the twistgrip housing and thread the housing onto it. Tighten the elbow locknut finger-tight. Lubricate the cable end fitting with multi-purpose grease and install it in the throttle pulley. Fit the closing cable into the rear socket and screw in the nut finger-tight. Lubricate the cable end fitting with multi-purpose grease and install it in the pulley. Fit the lower half of the housing over the pulley and onto the handlebar. Ensure the pin on the housing locates in the hole in the handlebar.

10 Fit the upper half of the twistgrip housing onto the handlebar, align it with the lower half and install the screws with the longest screw

at the rear of the housing. Tighten the screws securely and ensure the twistgrip turns freely, then adjust the alignment of the cable elbows and tighten the opening cable locknut and the closing cable nut **(see illustration)**.

11 Feed the cables through to the carburettors, making sure they are correctly routed. The cables must not interfere with any other component and should not be kinked or bent sharply.

12 Lubricate the opening cable end fitting with multi-purpose grease and fit it into the rear socket on the carburettor throttle cam then fit the cable adjuster into the bracket and thread the lower nut onto the adjuster. Turn the adjuster locknut (above the bracket) until the specified amount of cable freeplay is obtained **(see illustration 11.3)** (see Chapter 1). Tighten the lower nut against the bracket.

13 Lubricate the closing cable end fitting with multi-purpose grease and fit it into the front socket on the carburettor throttle cam, fit the cable holder into the bracket, thread the nut onto the holder below the bracket and tighten the nut against the bracket **(see illustration 11.5a)**.

14 Operate the throttle to check that it opens and closes freely. Turn the handlebars from lock to lock to make sure the cables don't cause the steering to bind.

15 Install the carburettors (if displaced), and the fuel tank (see Sections 7 and 2).

16 Start the engine and check that the idle speed does not rise as the handlebars are turned. If it does, the throttle cables are routed incorrectly. Correct the problem before riding the motorcycle.

11.6a Unscrew the opening cable locknut . . .

11.6b . . . and the closing cable gland nut

11.7a Remove the screws to split the housing . . .

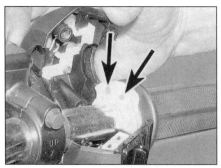

11.7b . . . and detach the cables (arrowed) from the pulley

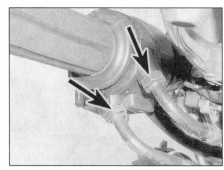

11.10 Adjust cable alignment before tightening the nuts (arrowed)

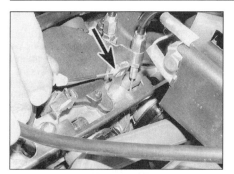

12.2 Unclip the outer cable from the bracket and detach the end fitting (arrowed)

12.3a Unscrew the cable nut . . .

12.3b . . . and remove the screws to split the housing

12 Choke cable –
removal and installation

Removal

1 Remove the fuel tank (see Section 2). Turn the handlebars onto full right lock to provide the maximum freeplay in the cable.
2 Unclip the choke outer cable from the bracket on the carburettors, then detach the inner cable end fitting from the choke linkage lever **(see illustration)**. Withdraw the cable from the machine noting the correct routing.
3 Unscrew the cable elbow nut from the left handlebar switch housing and remove the handlebar switch housing screws, noting that the rear screw is shorter then the front screw **(see illustrations)**. Separate the two halves of

12.4 Detach the cable (arrowed) from the pulley

the switch to gain access to the cable end fitting.
4 Detach the cable end fitting from the lever pulley and withdraw the cable from the housing **(see illustration)**.

Installation

5 Fit the choke cable elbow into the socket in the lower half of the left handlebar switch housing and tighten the nut finger-tight. Lubricate the cable end fitting with multi-purpose grease and install it in the lever pulley. Fit the lower half of the housing over the pulley and onto the handlebar. Ensure the pin on the housing locates in the hole in the handlebar.
6 Fit the upper half of the switch housing onto the handlebar, align it with the lower half and install the screws with the shortest screw at the rear of the housing. Tighten the screws securely and ensure the lever turns freely,

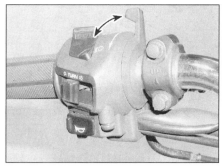

12.6 Check the choke lever turns freely with the housing assembled

then adjust the alignment of the cable elbow and tighten the gland nut **(see illustration)**.
7 Feed the cable through to the carburettors, making sure it is correctly routed. The cable must not interfere with any other component and should not be kinked or bent sharply.
8 Lubricate the cable end fitting with multi-purpose grease and attach it to the choke linkage lever then clip the outer cable into its bracket **(see illustration 12.2)**.
9 Check the operation of the choke cable (see Chapter 1).
10 Install the fuel tank (see Section 2).

13 Exhaust system –
removal and installation

⚠ **Warning: If the engine has been running the exhaust system will be very hot. Allow the system to cool before carrying out any work.**

Removal

Silencer

1 Remove the seat cowling (see Chapter 8).
2 Loosen the nut and bolt on the silencer clamp **(see illustration)**.
3 Unscrew the silencer mounting bolt **(see illustration)**. Support the silencer and remove the bolt and washer and pull the silencer off the exhaust pipe. Note the bushes in the silencer bracket.
4 Remove the gasket from inside the end of the silencer pipe **(see illustration)**.

4

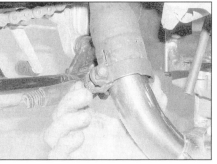

13.2 Loosen the silencer clamp

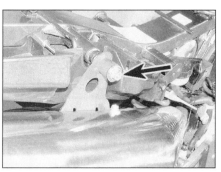

13.3 Unscrew the mounting bolt (arrowed)

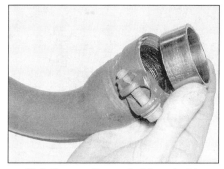

13.4 Remove the gasket from inside the pipe

13.6 Undo the exhaust pipe flange nuts

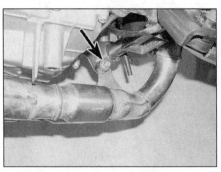

13.7a Disconnect the pipe from the support bracket (arrowed)

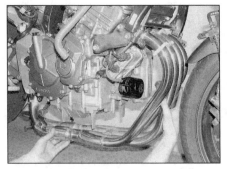

13.7b Lift the pipes away carefully

13.8 Remove the old exhaust port gaskets

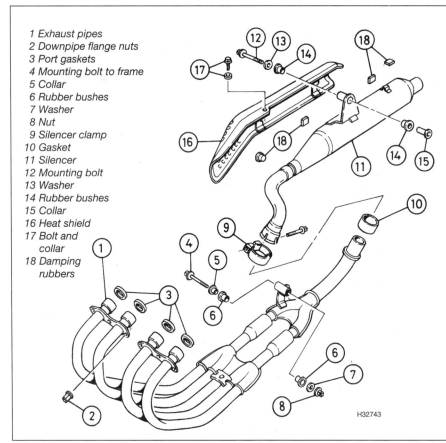

1 Exhaust pipes
2 Downpipe flange nuts
3 Port gaskets
4 Mounting bolt to frame
5 Collar
6 Rubber bushes
7 Washer
8 Nut
9 Silencer clamp
10 Gasket
11 Silencer
12 Mounting bolt
13 Washer
14 Rubber bushes
15 Collar
16 Heat shield
17 Bolt and collar
18 Damping rubbers

13.9 Exhaust system

Exhaust pipes

5 Remove the radiator (see Chapter 3).

6 Unscrew the nuts securing the downpipe flanges to the cylinder head **(see illustration)**.

7 Unscrew the nut and remove the washer from the bolt securing the exhaust pipe to the frame bracket **(see illustration)**. Support the pipes, then withdraw the bolt and manoeuvre them away from the cylinder head **(see illustration)**. Note the bushes in the bracket.

8 Remove the gaskets from the exhaust ports and discard them as new ones must be fitted on reassembly **(see illustration)**.

Installation

9 Installation is the reverse of removal, noting the following **(see illustration)**:

● Clean the jointing surfaces of the exhaust ports and the downpipes. Smear the port gaskets with grease to hold them in place while fitting the exhaust system.

● Use new gaskets in each exhaust port and between the exhaust pipe and the silencer **(see illustrations 13.4 and 13.8)**.

● Clean the cylinder head studs and lubricate them with a suitable copper-based grease before reassembly.

● Check the condition of the bushings on the exhaust pipe and silencer brackets and renew them if they are damaged or deteriorated.

● Leave all fasteners finger-tight until the entire system has been installed, making alignment easier. Tighten the mounting nuts and bolts to the torque settings specified at the beginning of this Chapter. Tighten the downpipe nuts first.

● Run the engine and check that there are no exhaust gas leaks.

14 Pulse secondary air (PAIR) system – removal and installation

General information

1 To reduce the amount of unburned hydrocarbons released in the exhaust gases, a pulse secondary air (PAIR) system is fitted. The system consists of the control valve mounted on the front of the crankcase and the hoses linking the valve to the cylinders, air filter housing and intake manifold. The control valve is actuated by engine vacuum.

2 Under certain operating conditions, the vacuum opens up the PAIR control valve which then allows filtered air to be drawn from the air filter housing to the exhaust ports. The air mixes with the exhaust gases, causing any unburned particles of the fuel in the mixture to be burnt in the exhaust port/pipes. This process changes a considerable amount of hydrocarbons and carbon monoxide into relatively harmless carbon dioxide and water.

Note: The system is not adjustable and can only be tested by a Honda dealer. Checks which can be performed by the owner are given in Chapter 1.

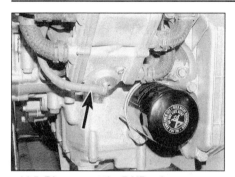

14.5 Disconnect the PAIR valve vacuum hose (arrowed)

14.6 Release the hoses from the clip on the frame

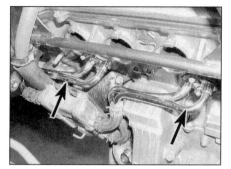

14.7a Disconnect the pipes (arrowed) from the cylinder head . . .

Warning: If the engine has been running the exhaust system will be very hot. Allow the system to cool before carrying out any work.

Removal

3 Remove the fuel tank (see Section 2) and the exhaust pipes (see Section 13).
4 Release the clip securing the PAIR valve air intake hose to the air filter housing and disconnect the hose (see Section 6).
5 Release the clip securing the PAIR valve vacuum hose to the valve and disconnect the hose **(see illustration)**.

6 Release the hoses from the clip on the front right-hand frame tube **(see illustration)**.
7 Unscrew the nuts securing the secondary air pipes to the cylinder head and disconnect the pipes. Remove the gaskets from the pipe flanges and discard them as new ones must be fitted on reassembly **(see illustrations)**.
8 Undo the bolts securing the PAIR valve mounting bracket to the engine unit and remove the bracket with the valve attached **(see illustration)**. If required, undo the screws securing the valve to the bracket and remove the valve.
9 Release the clip securing the air intake hose

to the back of the valve and detach the hose **(see illustration)**.
10 Inspect the PAIR valve assembly (see Chapter 1).

Installation

11 Installation is the reverse of removal, noting the following:
● Ensure the secondary air pipe and cylinder head mating surfaces are clean.
● Ensure the gaskets are fitted to the cylinder head unions the right way round.
● Route the air intake hose and the vacuum hose through the clip on the front right-hand frame tube.

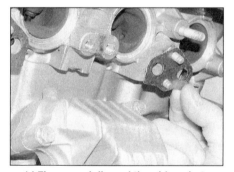

14.7b . . . and discard the old gaskets

14.8 Undo the bracket mounting bolts (arrowed) and remove the valve

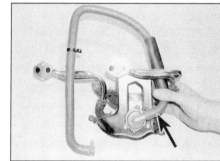

14.9 Detach the air intake hose (arrowed)

4

Notes

Chapter 5
Ignition system

Contents

Degrees of difficulty

Easy, suitable for novice with little experience		Fairly easy, suitable for beginner with some experience		Fairly difficult, suitable for competent DIY mechanic		Difficult, suitable for experienced DIY mechanic		Very difficult, suitable for expert DIY or professional	

Specifications

General information
Cylinder numbering (from left-hand to right-hand side of the bike) 1-2-3-4
Firing order 1-2-4-3
Spark plugs .... see Chapter 1

Ignition timing
At idle .... 7° BTDC

Ignition pulse generator coil
Resistance .... 460 to 580 ohms @ 20°C

Ignition HT coils
Primary winding resistance .... 2.5 to 3.2 ohms @ 20°C
Secondary winding resistance
  with plug caps and leads .... 21 to 25 K-ohms @ 20°C
  without plug caps and leads .... 11 to 15 K-ohms @ 20°C

Throttle position sensor
Input voltage .... 4.7 to 5.3 volts
Resistance .... 4 to 6 K-ohms @ 20°C

Torque settings
Ignition rotor cover centre cap .... 18 Nm

5

1 General information

All models are fitted with a fully transistorised electronic ignition system, which due to its lack of mechanical parts is totally maintenance free. The system comprises a rotor, pulse generator coil, ignition control unit, throttle position sensor and ignition HT coils (refer to the wiring diagrams at the end of Chapter 9 for details).

The ignition triggers, which are on the rotor mounted on the right-hand end of the crankshaft, magnetically operate the pulse generator coil as the crankshaft rotates. The pulse generator coil sends a signal to the ignition control unit which then supplies the ignition HT coils with the power necessary to produce a spark at the plugs.

The system uses two HT coils which are mounted on the frame underneath the fuel tank. The left-hand coil supplies Nos. 1 and 4 cylinder spark plugs and the right-hand coil supplies Nos. 2 and 3 cylinder spark plugs.

The ignition control unit incorporates an electronic advance system controlled by signals generated by the ignition triggers and the throttle position sensor.

The ignition system incorporates a safety interlock circuit which will cut the ignition if the sidestand is put down whilst the engine is running and in gear, or if a gear is selected whilst the engine is running and the sidestand is down. It also prevents the engine from being started if the sidestand is down and the engine is in gear unless the clutch lever is pulled in.

Because of their nature, the individual ignition system components can be checked but not repaired. If ignition system troubles occur, and the faulty component can be isolated, the only cure for the problem is to renew the part. Keep in mind that most electrical parts, once purchased, cannot be

TOOL TiP

A simple spark gap testing tool can be made from a block of wood, a large alligator clip and two nails, one of which is fabricated so that a spark plug cap or bare HT lead end can be connected to its end. Make sure the gap between the two nail ends is 6 mm.

returned. To avoid unnecessary expense, make very sure the faulty component has been positively identified before buying a new part.

Note that there is no provision for adjusting the ignition timing on these models.

2 Ignition system – check

⚠️ **Warning: The energy levels in electronic systems can be very high. On no account should the ignition be switched on whilst the plugs or plug caps are being held. Shocks from the HT circuit can be most unpleasant. Secondly, it is vital that the engine is not turned over or run with any of the plug caps removed, and that the plugs are soundly earthed (grounded) when the system is checked for sparking. The ignition system components can be seriously damaged if the HT circuit becomes isolated.**

1 As no means of adjustment is available, any failure of the system can be traced to failure of a system component or a simple wiring fault. Of the two possibilities, the latter is by far the most likely. In the event of failure, check the system in a logical fashion, as described below.

2 Disconnect the HT leads from the spark plugs. Connect each lead to a spare spark plug and lay each plug on the engine with the threads earthed (grounded) **(see illustration)**. If necessary, hold each spark plug with an insulated tool.

⚠️ **Warning: Do not remove any of the spark plugs from the engine to perform this check – atomised fuel being pumped out of the open spark plug hole could ignite, causing severe injury!**

3 Having observed the above precautions, check that the kill switch is in the RUN position and the transmission is in neutral, then turn the ignition switch ON and turn the engine over on the starter motor. If the system is in good condition a regular, fat blue spark

2.2 Earth the spark plug and operate the starter – sparks should be visible at the electrode (arrowed)

should be evident at each plug electrode. If the spark appears thin or yellowish, or is non-existent, further investigation will be necessary. Before proceeding further, turn the ignition OFF and remove the key as a safety measure.

4 The ignition system must be able to produce a spark which is capable of jumping a particular size gap. Honda do not provide a specification, but a healthy system should produce a spark capable of jumping at least 6 mm. A simple tool can be made to test the maximum gap across which the spark will jump (see **Tool Tip**) or alternatively it is possible to buy an ignition spark gap tester tool **(see illustration)** some of which are adjustable to set the exact spark gap specified.

5 Connect an HT lead from to the protruding electrode on the test tool, and clip the tool to a good earth (ground) on the engine or frame **(see illustration)**. Check that the kill switch is in the RUN position, turn the ignition switch ON and turn the engine over on the starter motor. If the system is in good condition a regular, fat blue spark should be seen to jump the gap between the nail ends. Repeat the test for the other HT leads. If the test results are good the entire ignition system can be considered good. If the spark appears thin or yellowish, or is non-existent, further investigation will be necessary.

6 Ignition faults can be divided into two categories, namely those where the ignition

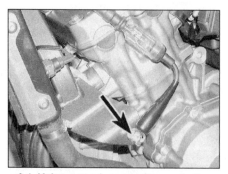

2.4 Using a spark gap tester – note the earth connection (arrowed)

2.5 Connect the tester as shown – when the engine is cranked sparks should jump the gap between the nails

system has failed completely, and those which are due to a partial failure. The likely faults are listed below, starting with the most probable source of failure. Work through the list systematically, referring to the subsequent sections for full details of the necessary checks and tests. **Note:** *Before checking the following items ensure that the battery is fully charged and that all fuses are in good condition.*

● Loose, corroded or damaged wiring connections, broken or shorted wiring between any of the component parts of the ignition system (see Chapter 9).
● Faulty HT lead or spark plug cap, faulty spark plug, dirty, worn or corroded plug electrodes, or incorrect gap between electrodes.
● Faulty ignition (main) switch or engine kill switch (see Chapter 9).
● Faulty neutral, clutch or sidestand switch (see Chapter 9).
● Faulty pulse generator coil or damaged rotor.
● Faulty ignition HT coil(s).
● Faulty ignition control unit.

7 If the above checks don't reveal the cause of the problem, have the ignition system tested by a Honda dealer equipped with a special diagnostic tester.

3 Ignition HT coils – check, removal and installation

Check

1 In order to determine conclusively that the ignition HT coils are defective, they should be tested by a Honda dealer equipped with a peak voltage tester.

2 However, the coils can be checked visually (for cracks and other damage) and the primary and secondary coil resistance can be measured with a multimeter. If the coils are undamaged, and if the resistance readings

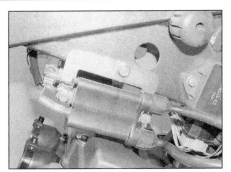

3.3 Location of the ignition coils

are as specified at the beginning of this Chapter, they are probably capable of proper operation.

3 Remove the fuel tank (see Chapter 4) and disconnect the battery negative (-ve) lead. The coils are mounted to the frame **(see illustration)**.

4 Disconnect the primary circuit electrical connectors from the coil being tested and the HT leads from the spark plugs. Note the locations of all wires before disconnecting them.

5 Set the multimeter to the ohms x 1 scale and measure the resistance between the primary circuit terminals **(see illustration)**. This will give a resistance reading for the primary windings of the coil and should be consistent with the value given in the Specifications at the beginning of this Chapter.

6 To check the condition of the secondary windings, set the multimeter to the K-ohm scale and connect the meter to the spark plug caps **(see illustration)**. If the reading obtained is not within the range shown in the Specifications, unscrew the HT leads from the coil and measure the resistance between the HT terminals. If the reading is now as specified, renew the HT leads. If the reading is still outside the specified range, it is likely that the coil is defective.

7 Should any of the above checks not

3.5 Measuring resistance between the coil primary circuit terminals (arrowed)

produce the expected result, have your findings confirmed by a Honda dealer (see Step 1). If the coil is confirmed to be faulty, it must be renewed; the coil is a sealed unit and cannot be repaired.

Removal and installation

8 Remove the fuel tank (see Chapter 4) and disconnect the battery negative (-ve) lead. The coils are mounted to the frame **(see illustration)**.

9 Disconnect the primary circuit electrical connectors from the coil and disconnect the HT leads from the spark plugs. Mark the locations of all wires before disconnecting them.

10 Unscrew the nuts and bolts securing the coil to the mounting and remove the coil **(see illustration 3.8)**.

11 Installation is the reverse of removal. Make sure the wiring connectors and HT leads are securely connected.

4 Ignition pulse generator coil – check, removal and installation

Check

1 In order to determine conclusively that the pulse generator coil is defective, it should be

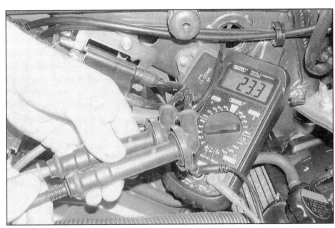

3.6 Measuring resistance in the coil secondary windings

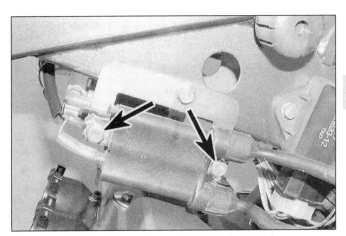

3.8 Ignition coil mounting bolts (arrowed)

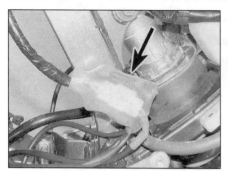

4.2a Pulse generator wiring connector is inside the boot (arrowed)

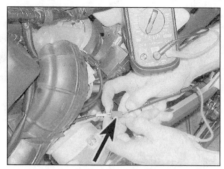

4.2b Measuring resistance between the terminals of the pulse generator coil connector (arrowed)

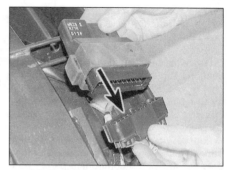

4.6 Identify the pulse generator coil terminals (arrowed) inside the connector

tested by a Honda dealer equipped with a peak voltage tester. It is, however, possible to gain an indication of the coil's condition by performing the following checks using a multimeter.

2 Remove the seat and side panels (see Chapter 8) and disconnect the battery negative (-ve) lead.Trace the pulse generator coil wiring back from the right-hand engine cover and disconnect it at the blue 2-pin connector inside the boot on the left-hand side of the frame **(see illustration)**. Using a multimeter set to the ohms x 100 scale, measure the resistance between the white/yellow and yellow wire terminals on the pulse generator coil side of the connector **(see illustration)**.

3 Compare the reading obtained with that given in the Specifications at the beginning of this Chapter. The pulse generator coil must be renewed if the reading obtained differs greatly from that given, particularly if the meter indicates a short circuit (no measurable resistance) or an open circuit (infinite, or very high resistance).

4 If the pulse generator coil is thought to be faulty, first check that this is not due to a damaged or broken wire from the coil to the connector; pinched or broken wires can usually be repaired.

5 If the reading is satisfactory, reconnect the connector and check the wiring between the connector and the ignition control unit.

Remove the seat cowling (see Chapter 8); the ignition control unit is secured to the left-hand side of the frame (see Section 6).

6 Disconnect the ignition control unit multi-pin connector and identify the pulse generator wire terminals (white/yellow and yellow) in the connector **(see illustration)**. Measure the resistance between the terminals as before. If the reading is not within the specifications renew the wiring between the connector and the ignition control unit.

Removal

7 Remove the seat and side panels (see Chapter 8) and disconnect the battery negative (-ve) lead. Remove the air filter housing (see Chapter 4).

8 Trace the pulse generator coil wiring back from the ignition rotor cover and disconnect it at the blue 2-pin connector inside the boot on the left-hand side of the frame **(see illustration 4.2)**. Free the wiring from any ties and feed it through to the cover, noting its routing **(see illustration)**.

9 Remove the ignition rotor cover (see Chapter 2, Section 13).

10 Unscrew the bolts securing the pulse generator coil in the cover and pull the coil wiring grommet out of its recess **(see illustration)**. While the cover is off, examine the triggers on the timing rotor for signs of damage and renew it if necessary (see Chapter 2, Section 13).

Installation

11 Installation is the reverse of removal, noting the following:
● Apply a suitable non-permanent locking compound to the bolts securing the pulse generator coil and tighten them securely.
● Apply a suitable sealant to the wiring grommet and fit it into its recess.
● Refit the ignition rotor cover (see Chapter 2, Section 13).
● Ensure all wiring connections are clean and tight.

5 Throttle position sensor –
check, removal and installation

Check

1 The throttle position sensor is mounted on the left-hand (No. 1) carburettor. To check if the sensor system is working, unclip the sensor connector cover and disconnect the connector **(see illustration)**.

2 Start the engine and increase engine speed to 3,500 rpm. Now connect the sensor connector; engine speed should increase. If engine speed does not increase, stop the engine and check the system as follows.

3 Disconnect the sensor connector and turn the ignition ON. Using a multimeter set to volts, connect the meter positive (+ve) probe

4.8 Free the wiring from the cable tie (arrowed)

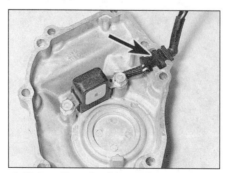

4.10 Location of pulse generator coil and wiring grommet (arrowed)

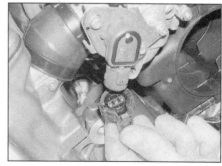

5.1 Disconnect the throttle position sensor connector

5.3 Measuring the throttle position sensor input voltage

5.4 Measuring throttle position sensor resistance at the ICU connector

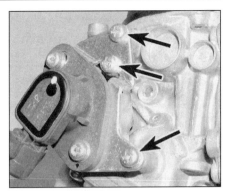

5.7 Throttle position sensor mounting bracket screws (arrowed)

to the yellow/red wire terminal in the connector and the negative (-ve) probe to the blue/green wire terminal **(see illustration)**. The voltage reading should be consistent with the value given in the Specifications at the beginning of this Chapter. If the reading is incorrect, or there is no voltage, remove the seat cowling (see Chapter 8) and check the wiring between the sensor and the ignition control unit for damage and check the terminal connections at the ignition control unit. **Note:** *The ignition control unit is secured to the mudguard on the left-hand side of the motorcycle (see Section 6).*

4 Connect the sensor connector and disconnect the multi-pin wiring connector from the ignition control unit. Set the multimeter to the K-ohm scale and connect the meter probes to the yellow/red and blue/green wire terminals in the multi-pin connector **(see illustration)**. Recorded resistance should be consistent with the value given in the Specifications. Now connect the meter probes to the red/yellow and blue/green wire terminals and open and close the throttle. Resistance should increase as the throttle is opened and decrease as the throttle is closed.

5 If the correct readings cannot be obtained, disconnect the sensor connector and check for resistance at the corresponding terminals on the sensor. If the readings at the ignition control unit are incorrect, but they are correct at the sensor, then check for a fault in the

wiring or a poor connection at a terminal. If both sets of readings are incorrect, then the throttle position sensor is faulty.

Removal and installation

6 The sensor is not available separately from the No. 1 cylinder carburettor body – its wiring connector cover is the only item listed as a replacement part.

7 The sensor can be detached from the carburettor by removing the three screws which retain its mounting bracket to the carburettor **(see illustration)**. Do not detach the sensor from its mounting bracket because its position is pre-set and secured by the two screws.

8 On installation, ensure that the sensor's lug fits between the tangs on the end of the throttle shaft **(see illustration)**. Tighten the three bracket screws securely.

6 Ignition control unit – check, removal and installation

Check

1 If the tests shown in the preceding Sections have failed to isolate the cause of an ignition fault, it is possible that the ignition control unit itself is faulty. No details are available for testing the unit on home workshop equipment. Take the motorcycle to a Honda dealer for examination on a diagnostic tester.

Removal

2 Remove the seat cowling (see Chapter 8) and disconnect the battery negative (-ve) lead.

3 The ignition control unit is secured to the mudguard on the left-hand side of the motorcycle **(see illustration)**.

4 Disconnect its multi-pin wiring connector, then remove the ignition control unit from its rubber sleeve.

Installation

5 Installation is the reverse of removal. Make sure the wiring connector is correctly and securely connected and that the rubber sleeve is securely fixed to the mudguard.

7 Ignition timing – general information and check

General information

1 Since no provision exists for adjusting the ignition timing and since no component is subject to mechanical wear, there should be no need for regular checks; only if investigating a fault such as a loss of power or a misfire, should the ignition timing be checked.

2 The ignition timing is checked dynamically (engine running) using a stroboscopic lamp. The inexpensive neon lamps should be adequate in theory, but in practice may produce a pulse of such low intensity that the timing mark remains indistinct. If possible, one of the more precise xenon tube lamps should be used, powered by an external source of the appropriate voltage. **Note:** *Do not use the motorcycle's own battery as an incorrect reading may result from stray impulses within the machine's electrical system.*

Check

3 Warm the engine up to normal operating temperature then stop it.

4 Unscrew the centre cap from the ignition rotor cover on the right-hand side of the

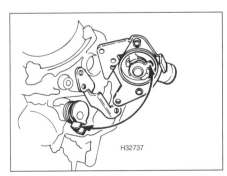

5.8 Throttle position sensor lug and corresponding tangs on throttle shaft

6.3 Location of the ignition control unit

5

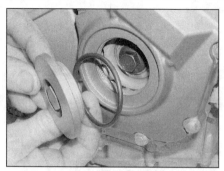

7.4 Unscrew the ignition rotor centre cover cap (arrowed)

engine **(see illustration)**. Discard the cover O-ring if it is damaged and obtain a new one.
5 The position on the ignition rotor which indicates the firing point at idle speed for the No. 1 cylinder is mid-way between the set of two punch marks and the set of three punch marks; the static timing mark with which this should align is the notch in the timing inspection hole **(see illustration)**.

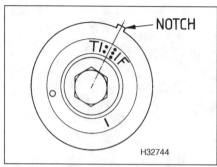

7.5 Ignition timing alignment marks at idle speed

 HAYNES HiNT *The timing marks can be highlighted with white paint to make them more visible under the stroboscope light.*

6 Connect the timing light to the No. 1 cylinder HT lead as described in the manufacturer's instructions.

7 Start the engine and aim the light at the static timing mark.
8 With the engine idling at the specified speed (see Chapter 1), the mid-way point between the two sets of punch marks should align with the static timing mark.
9 Slowly increase the engine speed whilst observing the timing mark; the punch marks should appear to move anti-clockwise as the ignition timing advances electronically. **Note:** *The ignition timing should begin to advance at approximately 1500 rpm.*
10 If the ignition timing is incorrect, or suspected of being incorrect, one of the ignition system components is at fault, and the system must be tested as described in the preceding Sections of this Chapter.
11 Ensure the O-ring is in position on the centre cap, then smear the cap threads and O-ring with oil and refit the cap to the ignition rotor cover. Tighten the cap to the specified torque setting.

Chapter 6
Frame, suspension and final drive

Contents

Degrees of difficulty

| Easy, suitable for novice with little experience | | Fairly easy, suitable for beginner with some experience | | Fairly difficult, suitable for competent DIY mechanic | | Difficult, suitable for experienced DIY mechanic | | Very difficult, suitable for expert DIY or professional | |

Specifications

Front forks

Fork oil type	Honda fork oil
Fork oil capacity	
CB600F	486 cc
CB600FS	467 cc
Fork oil level*	
CB600F	102 mm
CB600FS	120 mm
Fork spring free length	
CB600F	
Standard	309.2 mm
Service limit	303.0 mm
CB600FS	
Standard	310.8 mm
Service limit	304.6
Fork tube runout limit	0.2 mm

Oil level is measured from the top of the tube with the fork spring removed and the leg fully compressed.

Final drive

Chain type	RK525R or DID525M2 (110 links)
Joining link pin projection from side plate (unstaked)	
RK type chain	1.2 to 1.4 mm
DID type chain	1.15 to 1.55 mm
Joining link staked ends diameter (RK and DID type)	5.50 to 5.80 mm

6

Torque settings

Brake lever pivot bolt	1 Nm
Brake lever pivot nut	6 Nm
Fork bottom yoke clamp bolts	39 Nm
Fork top bolt	23 Nm
Fork top yoke clamp bolts	23 Nm
Fork damper rod Allen bolt	20 Nm
Front brake master cylinder clamp bolts	12 Nm
Front sprocket bolt	54 Nm
Handlebar clamp bolts	26 Nm
Rear sprocket nuts	108 Nm
Rider's footrest bracket bolts	26 Nm
Shock absorber lower mounting bolt	37 Nm
Shock absorber upper mounting bolt	37 Nm
Sidestand pivot bolt	15 Nm
Sidestand pivot locknut	39 Nm
Sidestand switch bolt	10 Nm
Steering head bearing adjuster nut	25 Nm
Steering stem nut	103 Nm
Swingarm pivot bolt nut	88 Nm

1 General information

All models use a single spar backbone frame which incorporates the engine unit as a stressed member. The frame is constructed in box section steel.

Front suspension is by a pair of oil-damped telescopic forks.

At the rear, an aluminium, box-section swingarm acts on a single shock absorber. The shock absorber is adjustable for spring pre-load.

The drive to the rear wheel is by chain.

2 Frame – inspection and repair

1 The frame should not require attention unless accident damage has occurred. In most cases, frame renewal is the only satisfactory remedy for such damage. A few frame specialists have the jigs and other equipment necessary for straightening the frame to the required standard of accuracy, but even then there is no simple way of assessing to what extent the frame may have been over stressed.

2 On a high mileage bike, the frame should be examined closely for signs of cracking or splitting at the welded joints. Loose engine mount bolts can cause ovaling or fracturing of the mounting points. Minor damage can often be repaired by specialist welding, depending on the extent and nature of the damage.

3 Remember that a frame which is out of alignment will cause handling problems. If misalignment is suspected as the result of an accident, it will be necessary to strip the machine completely so the frame can be thoroughly checked.

3 Footrests, brake pedal and gearchange lever – removal and installation

Rider's footrests

1 Remove the split pin and washer from the footrest pivot pin, then withdraw the pivot pin and remove the footrest, noting the fitting of the return spring (see illustrations). The footrest rubbers are secured by two bolts on the underside of the footrest and can be renewed separately.

2 Installation is the reverse of removal. Apply a small amount of copper-based grease to the pivot pin. Use a new split pin and bend its ends securely.

Passenger's footrests

3 Remove the split pin and washer from the footrest pivot pin, then withdraw the pivot pin and remove the footrest, noting the fitting of the washer on the end of the footrest (see illustration). The footrest rubbers are a push fit on the footrest and can be replaced separately.

4 Installation is the reverse of removal. Apply a small amount of copper-based grease to the pivot pin. Use a new split pin and bend its ends securely.

Brake pedal

Removal

5 Remove the seat and the frame side panels (see Chapter 8).

6 Trace the wiring from the brake light switch and disconnect it at the white 2-pin connector. Feed the wiring back to the right-hand side of the motorcycle.

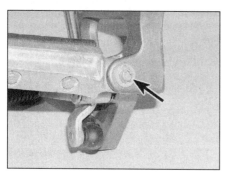

3.1a Remove the split pin and washer (arrowed) to withdraw pivot pin

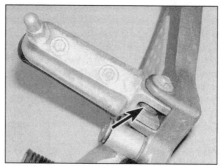

3.1b Note the spring (arrowed)

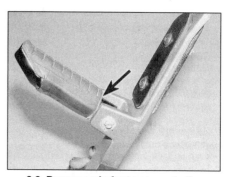

3.3 Passenger's footrest – note the position of the washer (arrowed)

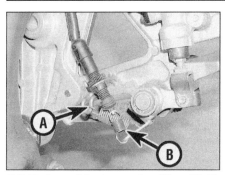

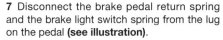

3.7 Brake pedal return spring (A) and light switch spring (B)

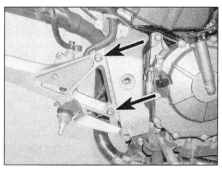

3.8 Unscrew the right-hand footrest bracket bolts (arrowed)

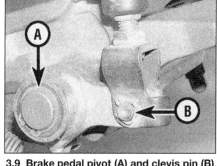

3.9 Brake pedal pivot (A) and clevis pin (B)

7 Disconnect the brake pedal return spring and the brake light switch spring from the lug on the pedal **(see illustration)**.

8 Unscrew the right-hand footrest bracket bolts **(see illustration)**. Lift the bracket away from the bike, taking care not to strain the hoses to the brake caliper and the hydraulic reservoir.

9 Remove the split pin from the clevis pin securing the brake pedal to the brake master cylinder pushrod. Remove the clevis pin and separate the rod from the pedal **(see illustration)**.

10 Remove the circlip and washer from the pedal pivot and remove the pedal **(see illustration 3.9)**.

Installation

11 Installation is the reverse of removal, noting the following:
● Apply molybdenum disulphide or copper-based grease to the brake pedal pivot.
● Ensure the circlip is a firm fit in its groove on the brake pedal pivot. Don't forget the washer.
● Use a new split pin on the clevis pin securing the brake pedal to the master cylinder pushrod and bend the split pin ends securely.
● Tighten the footrest bracket bolts to the torque setting specified at the beginning of this Chapter.
● Check the operation of the rear brake and the brake light switch (see Chapter 1).

Gearchange lever

Removal

12 Note the alignment punch mark on the gearchange shaft **(see illustration)**. If no mark is visible, make your own so that the gearchange linkage lever can be correctly aligned with the shaft on installation. Unscrew the linkage lever pinch bolt and remove the lever from the shaft.

13 Unscrew the gearchange lever pivot bolt and remove the bolt and the lever assembly **(see illustration)**. Note the washer between the lever and the footrest bracket.

14 Note the position of the locknut at the lever end of the gearchange linkage rod, then loosen the locknut and unscrew the rod and separate it from the lever. If required, loosen

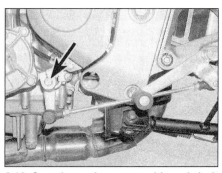

3.12 Gearchange lever assembly and shaft (arrowed)

the locknut at the other end of the rod and unscrew the rod from the linkage lever.

Installation

15 Installation is the reverse of removal. Adjust the gear lever position by moving the linkage lever around the splined gearchange shaft. **Note:** *Ensure the linkage rod is screwed fully into the couplings at both ends before tightening the locknuts.*

16 Ensure the linkage lever pinch bolt is tightened securely.

4 Sidestand – removal and installation

Removal

1 The sidestand is attached to a bracket on the left-hand side of the frame. Two springs,

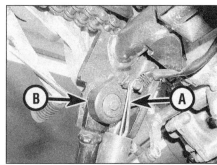

4.2 Sidestand springs (A) and switch (B)

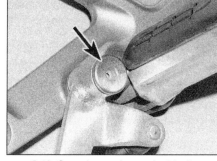

3.13 Gearchange lever pivot bolt

one inside the other, ensure that the stand is held in the retracted or extended position.

2 Support the bike on an auxiliary stand and unhook the stand springs from the frame **(see illustration)**.

3 Unscrew the sidestand switch retaining bolt and free the sidestand switch from the stand pivot, noting how it fits **(see illustration 4.2)**.

4 Unscrew the nut securing the stand on the pivot bolt then unscrew the pivot bolt from the inside of the bracket and remove the stand **(see illustration)**.

Installation

5 Apply grease to the stand bracket and the pivot bolt shank. Fit the stand to the bracket then fit the pivot bolt, tightening it to the specified torque setting. Fit the locknut to the pivot bolt and tighten it to the specified torque setting.

6 Locate the tab on the inside of the sidestand switch in the hole in the stand and

6

4.4 Sidestand pivot bolt nut (arrowed)

5.2 Brake master cylinder clamp bolts (arrowed)

5.4 Clutch lever clamp bolts (arrowed)

5.6 Remove the handlebar end weights

align the switch body with the stand spring post. Either fit a new bolt or apply locking compound to the original bolt (having first cleaned its threads), then tighten the switch bolt to the specified torque setting.

7 Reconnect the sidestand springs and check that they hold the stand up securely when not in use – an accident is almost certain to occur if the stand extends while the machine is in motion.

8 Check the operation of the sidestand switch (see Chapter 1, Section 15).

5 Handlebars and levers – removal and installation

Handlebars

Removal

1 On CB600F models, lift the cover, where fitted, on the rear view mirror mounting locknuts, loosen the locknuts and unscrew the mirrors from the handlebar brackets.

2 Ensure the front brake fluid reservoir cover is secure. Unscrew the master cylinder clamp bolts and remove the back of the clamp, noting how it fits (see illustration). Position the assembly clear of the handlebar, making sure no strain is placed on the hydraulic hose and the brake light switch wiring. Keep the master cylinder reservoir upright to prevent fluid loss and air entering the hydraulic

system. Note the alignment mark on the handlebar for the clamp.

3 Displace the throttle twistgrip housing from the handlebar and detach both cable end fittings from the throttle pulley (see Chapter 4).

4 Unscrew the clutch lever clamp bolts and remove the back of the clamp, noting how it fits (see illustration). Position the lever clear of the handlebar, making sure the cable and the clutch switch wiring is not unduly bent or strained. Note the alignment mark on the handlebar for the clamp.

5 Displace the handlebar switch housing (see Chapter 9) and the choke lever (see Chapter 4).

6 Unscrew the handlebar end-weight retaining screws, then remove the end-weights (see illustration). Slide the throttle grip off the right-hand end of the bar and the hand grip off the left-hand end. If the left-hand grip is stuck in place, slit the grip open using a sharp blade and replace it with a new one on reassembly. Slide the choke lever pulley off the handlebar, noting how it fits.

7 The internal handlebar weight assemblies are held in place by spring retainers. Thread the end-weight screw into the internal weight assembly, depress the spring retainer through the hole in the handlebar with a small screwdriver and withdraw the assembly.

8 Unscrew the handlebar clamp bolts and remove the clamp and the handlebars. Note the punch marks on the clamp and the handlebars for reassembly (see illustrations).

Installation

9 Installation is the reverse of removal, noting the following:

● Align the punch mark on the handlebars with the split in the clamp (see illustration 5.8b). Fit the handlebar clamp with the punch marks to the front (see illustration 5.8a). Tighten the front handlebar clamp bolts before the rear ones.

● Do not forget to install the choke lever pulley on the left-hand end of the bar before the hand grip.

● Make sure the front brake and clutch lever clamps are installed with the UP mark facing up. Tighten the upper bolt first, then the lower bolt (see illustrations 5.2 and 5.4).

● Lubricate the right-hand bar before sliding on the throttle twistgrip. Apply grease to the clutch, throttle and choke cable ends.

● Make sure the pin on the lower half of each switch housing locates in the hole in the handlebar.

● If removed, apply a suitable non-permanent locking compound to the handlebar end-weight retaining screws. If new grips are being fitted, secure them using a suitable adhesive to the handlebar (left-hand grip) or to the throttle twistgrip (right-hand grip).

● Tighten all bolts to the torque settings specified at the beginning of this Chapter.

Handlebar levers

10 To remove the clutch lever, unscrew the lever pivot bolt locknut (see illustration).

5.8a Handlebar clamp punch marks . . .

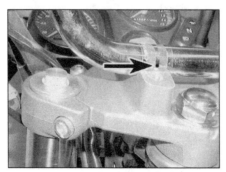

5.8b . . . and handlebar index mark (arrowed)

5.10a Lever pivot bolt locknut (arrowed)

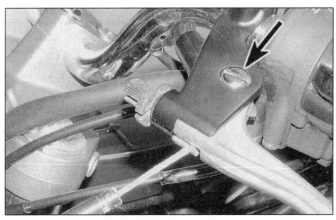

5.10b Disconnect the cable from the bracket and unscrew the bolt (arrowed)

5.11 Unscrew the locknut (arrowed) then unscrew the pivot bolt

Loosen the clutch cable adjuster and disconnect the cable from the bracket, then withdraw the pivot bolt and remove the lever, detaching the cable end fitting as you do so **(see illustration)**.

11 To remove the front brake lever, unscrew the lever pivot bolt locknut, then withdraw the pivot bolt and remove the lever **(see illustration)**.

12 Installation is the reverse of removal, noting the following:
● Grease the pivot bolt shafts, the contact areas between the lever and its bracket, and the clutch cable end fitting.
● Adjust the clutch cable freeplay (see Chapter 1).

6 Forks – removal and installation

Removal

Caution: Although not strictly necessary, it is recommended that the fairing is removed from CB600FS models (see Chapter 8) before removing the forks. This will prevent accidental damage to the paintwork.

1 Remove the front wheel (see Chapter 7) and the front mudguard (see Chapter 8).

2 Displace the front brake calipers (see Chapter 7). There is no need to disconnect the brake hoses but secure the calipers to the motorcycle with cable ties to prevent straining the hoses.

3 Work on each fork leg individually. Note the routing of the various cables and hoses around the forks.

4 Loosen but do not remove the fork clamp bolt in the top yoke **(see illustration)**; if the fork legs are going to be disassembled or the fork oil is going to be changed, loosen the fork top bolt while the leg is still clamped in the bottom yoke **(see illustration)**.

5 Support the fork leg, then loosen but do not remove the fork clamp bolt in the bottom yoke **(see illustration)**. Remove the fork leg by twisting it and pulling it downwards. Note which fork leg fits on which side and mark them if necessary.

> **HAYNES HINT** *Haynes hint If the fork legs are seized in the yokes, spray the area with penetrating oil and allow time for it to soak in before trying again.*

Installation

6 Remove all traces of corrosion from the fork tubes and the yokes. Slide the fork leg up through the bottom yoke into the top yoke until the top edge of the fork tube is level with the top edge of the yoke. Make sure the wiring, cables and hoses are the correct side of the leg as noted on removal.

7 Tighten the fork clamp bolt in the bottom yoke to the torque setting specified at the beginning of this Chapter.

8 If the fork legs have been disassembled or the fork oil changed, tighten the fork top bolt to the specified torque setting, and then tighten the fork clamp bolt in the top yoke to the specified torque setting.

9 Install the remaining components in the reverse order of removal.

10 Check the operation of the front forks and brakes before taking the machine out on the road.

7 Forks – disassembly, inspection and reassembly

Disassembly

1 Always dismantle the fork legs separately to avoid interchanging parts. Store all

6

6.4a Loosen the fork clamp bolt

6.4b Fork top bolt (arrowed)

6.5 Support the leg and loosen the clamp bolt (arrowed)

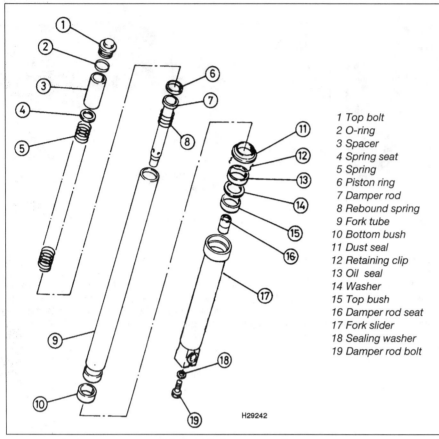

1 Top bolt
2 O-ring
3 Spacer
4 Spring seat
5 Spring
6 Piston ring
7 Damper rod
8 Rebound spring
9 Fork tube
10 Bottom bush
11 Dust seal
12 Retaining clip
13 Oil seal
14 Washer
15 Top bush
16 Damper rod seat
17 Fork slider
18 Sealing washer
19 Damper rod bolt

H29242

7.1 Front fork components

components in separate, clearly marked containers (see illustration).

2 Before dismantling the fork leg, it is advised that the damper rod bolt be loosened at this stage. Invert the fork leg and compress the fork tube in the slider so that the spring exerts maximum pressure on the damper rod head, then loosen the damper rod bolt in the base of the fork slider (see illustration).

3 If the fork top bolt was not loosened with the fork on the motorcycle, carefully clamp the fork tube in a vice equipped with soft jaws, taking care not to overtighten the vice or score the tube's surface, and loosen the top bolt.

4 Unscrew the top bolt and discard the O-ring as a new one must be fitted on reassembly (see illustration).

⚠️ Warning: The fork spring is pressing on the fork top bolt with considerable pressure. Unscrew the bolt very carefully, keeping a downward pressure on it and release it slowly as it is likely to spring clear. It is advisable to wear some form of eye and face protection when carrying out this operation.

5 Slide the fork tube down into the slider and withdraw the spacer, spring seat and the spring from the tube (see illustrations 26c, b and a). Note which way up the spring is fitted.

6 Invert the fork leg over a suitable container and pump the fork vigorously to expel as much fork oil as possible.

7 Remove the previously slackened damper rod bolt and its copper sealing washer from the bottom of the slider (see Step 2). Discard the sealing washer as a new one must be used on reassembly. If the damper rod bolt was not slackened before dismantling the fork, it may be necessary to re-install the spring, spring seat, spacer and top bolt to prevent the damper rod from turning. Alternatively, a long metal bar passed down through the fork tube and pressed hard into the damper rod head quite often suffices.

8 Tip out the damper rod from inside the fork tube and remove the rebound spring from the damper rod (see illustration).

9 Carefully prise out the dust seal from the top of the slider to gain access to the oil seal retaining clip (see illustration). Discard the dust seal as a new one must be used.

10 Compress the fork tube into the slider and

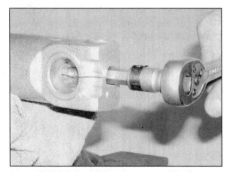

7.2 Loosen the damper rod bolt

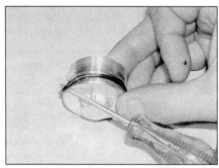

7.4 Discard the top bolt O-ring

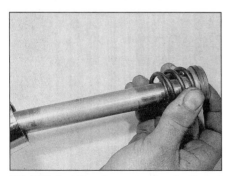

7.8 Withdraw the damper rod and rebound spring from the tube

7.9 Prise out the dust seal . . .

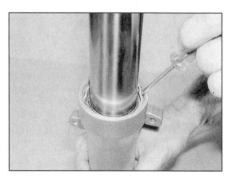

7.10 . . . and carefully remove the oil seal retaining clip

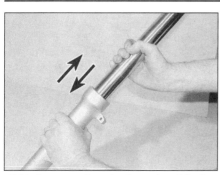

7.11 Separate the tube from the slider by pulling them apart firmly several times

7.12 Oil seal (A), washer (B), top bush (C) and bottom bush (D)

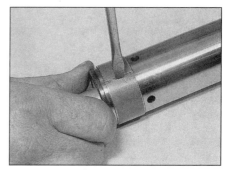

7.17 Prise the bottom bush off with a flat-bladed screwdriver

carefully remove the retaining clip, taking care not to scratch the surface of the tube **(see illustration)**.

11 To separate the tube from the slider it is necessary to displace the oil seal and top bush in the slider. The bottom bush will not pass through the top bush, and this can be used to good effect. Push the tube gently inwards until it stops against the damper rod seat. Take care not to do this forcibly or the seat may be damaged. Then pull the tube sharply outwards until the bottom bush strikes the top bush **(see illustration)**. Repeat this operation until the seal, seal washer and top bush are tapped out of the slider and the tube can be fully withdrawn from the slider.

12 With the tube removed, slide off the oil seal and its washer, noting which way up they fit **(see illustration)**. Discard the oil seal as a new one must be fitted on reassembly. The top bush can then be slid off the upper end of the tube.

Caution: Do not remove the bottom bush from the tube unless it is to be renewed.

13 Tip the damper rod seat out of the slider, noting which way up it fits.

Inspection

14 Clean all parts in solvent and blow them dry with compressed air, if available. Check the fork tube for score marks, scratches, flaking of the chrome finish and excessive or abnormal wear. Look for dents in the tube and renew the tube in both forks if any are found. Check the fork seal seat for nicks, gouges and scratches. If damage is evident, leaks will occur. Also check the oil seal washer for damage or distortion and renew it if necessary.

15 Check the fork tube for runout using V-blocks and a dial gauge, or have it done by a Honda dealer (see *Tools and Workshop Tips* in the Reference Section). If the amount of runout exceeds the service limit specified, the tube should be renewed.

 Warning: If the tube is bent or exceeds the runout limit, it should not be straightened; renew it.

16 Check the spring for cracks and other damage. Measure the spring free length and compare it to the specifications at the beginning of this Chapter. If it is defective or has sagged below the service limit, renew the springs in both forks. Never renew only one spring. Also check the rebound spring.

17 Examine the working surfaces of the two bushes; if worn or scuffed they must be renewed. Honda recommend that if the Teflon coating is worn so that the copper surface of the bush is visible over _ or more of its surface, the bush should be renewed. To remove the bottom bush from the fork tube, prise it apart at the slit using a flat-bladed screwdriver and slide it off **(see illustration)**. Make sure the new bush seats properly.

18 Check the damper rod and its piston ring for damage and wear, and renew them if necessary **(see illustration)**. Do not remove the ring from the piston unless it requires renewal.

Reassembly

19 If removed, install the new piston ring into the groove in the damper rod, then slide the rebound spring onto the rod **(see illustration)**. Insert the damper rod into the fork tube and slide it into place so that it projects fully from the bottom of the tube, then install the seat on the bottom of the damper rod **(see illustration)**.

20 Oil the fork tube and bottom bush with the specified fork oil and insert the tube into the slider **(see illustration)**. Fit a new copper sealing washer to the damper rod bolt and apply a few drops of a suitable non-permanent thread-locking compound, then install the bolt into the bottom of the slider. Tighten the bolt to the specified torque setting. If the damper rod rotates inside the

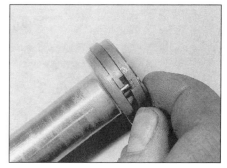

7.18 Inspect the damper rod and piston ring for wear

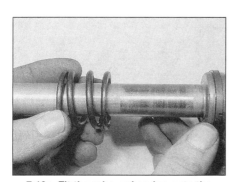

7.19a Fit the rebound spring onto the damper rod

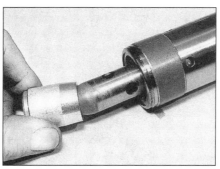

7.19b Install the rod in the fork tube and fit the seat onto the bottom of the rod

7.20 Insert the tube into the slider

6

7.21 Install the top bush . . .

7.22a Install the oil seal washer . . .

7.22b . . . and the oil seal with markings facing up

tube, hold the rod with spring pressure or a metal bar as on disassembly (see Step 7).
21 Push the fork tube fully into the slider, then oil the top bush and slide it down over

the tube **(see illustration)**. Press the bush squarely into its recess in the slider. Use a hammer and a suitable piece of tubing to tap the bush lightly into place; note that excessive

force should be unnecessary and will damage the bush.
Note: *Take care not to scratch the fork tube during reassembly; if the fork tube is pushed fully into the slider any accidental scratching is confined to the area above the oil seal.*
22 Install the oil seal washer, then lubricate the new oil seal with fork oil and slide it down over the tube with its markings facing upwards **(see illustrations)**. Press the seal squarely into the slider and tap it lightly into place (either as described in Step 21or using Honda service tools 07947–KF00100 and 07947–KFA50100) until the retaining clip groove is visible above the seal.
23 Fit the retaining clip, making sure it is correctly located in its groove **(see illustration)**.
24 Lubricate the inside of the new dust seal then slide it down the fork tube and press it into position **(see illustration)**.
25 Slowly pour in the correct quantity of the specified grade of fork oil and carefully pump the fork at least ten times to distribute it evenly **(see illustration)**. Stand the leg upright and allow the oil to settle, then fully compress the fork tube into the slider and measure the fork oil level from the top of the tube **(see illustration)**. Add or subtract fork oil until it is at the level specified at the beginning of this Chapter.
26 Pull the fork tube out of the slider to its full extension and install the spring with its closer-wound coils at the bottom, followed by the spring seat and the spacer **(see illustrations)**.

7.23 Fit the oil seal retaining clip . . .

7.24 . . . and the dust seal

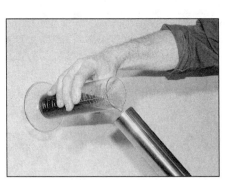

7.25a Pour the oil into the top of the tube . . .

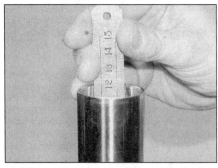

7.25b . . . then measure the oil level with the fork leg fully compressed

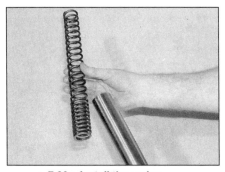

7.26a Install the spring . . .

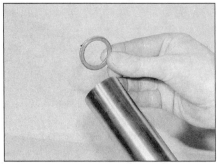

7.26b . . . the spring seat . . .

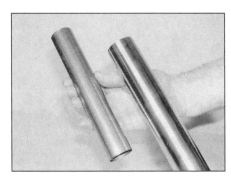

7.26c . . . and the spacer

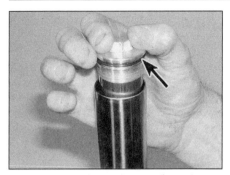

7.27 Fit a new O-ring (arrowed) and install the top bolt

8.2 Bolt (arrowed) secures the horn and brake hose on CB600F models

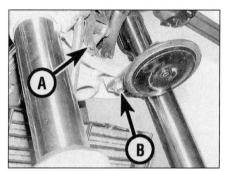

8.3 Bolts securing the brake hose (A) and horn (B) on CB600FS models

27 Lubricate a new O-ring with fork oil and fit it onto the top bolt, then thread the bolt into the top of the fork tube making sure it is not cross-threaded **(see illustration).**

 Warning: It will be necessary to compress the spring by pressing it down with the top bolt in order to engage the threads of the top bolt with the fork tube. This is a potentially dangerous operation and should be performed with care, using an assistant if necessary. Wipe off any excess oil before starting to prevent the possibility of slipping.

Note: *The top bolt can be tightened to the specified torque setting when the fork has been installed in the bike and is securely held in the bottom yoke.*

28 Install the fork leg (see Section 6).

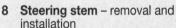

8 Steering stem – removal and installation

Removal

Caution: Although not strictly necessary, it is recommended that the fuel tank and fairing (where fitted) are removed (see Chapters 4 and 8) before removing the forks. This will improve access and prevent accidental damage to the paintwork. You may also wish to remove the fuel tank to prevent accidental damage.

1 Remove the front fork legs (see Section 6).
2 On CB600F models, remove the headlight assembly and instrument cluster (see Chapter 9). Disconnect the wiring connectors to the horn and the front turn indicators and unscrew the bolt securing the front brake hose clamp and horn to the headlight bracket **(see illustration).**
3 On CB600FS models, unscrew the bolt securing the front brake hose clamp to the bottom yoke and remove the clamp, then disconnect the wiring connectors to the horn, unscrew the bolt securing the horn to the bottom yoke and remove the horn **(see illustration).**
4 Trace the wiring from the ignition switch and disconnect it at the connector (see Chapter 9).
5 Remove the handlebar clamp and displace the bars (see Section 5). **Note:** *It is not*

necessary to disconnect any of the handlebar controls when displacing the bars but ensure no strain is placed on the wiring or hydraulic hose and keep the brake fluid reservoir upright.
6 Unscrew and remove the steering stem nut, then remove the washer and lift off the top yoke **(see illustrations).**
7 On CB600F models, the headlight and turn signal bracket locates in sockets in the top and bottom yoke. Lift the bracket clear of the bottom yoke, making sure the mounting bushes are secure on the ends of the bracket stays **(see illustration).**
8 Prise the lockwasher tabs out of the notches in the locknut and unscrew the locknut using either a C-spanner or a suitable drift located in one of the notches **(see illustration).** Remove the lockwasher and discard it as a new one must be used on reassembly.

8.6a Remove the steering stem nut . . .

8.6b . . . and washer . . .

8.6c . . . then lift off the top yoke

8.7 Note the bushes (arrowed) on CB600F models

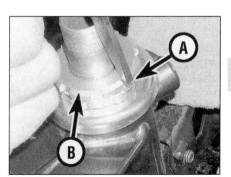

8.8 Lockwasher tab (A) and locknut (B)

6

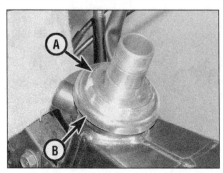

8.9 Unscrew the adjuster nut (A) and remove the bearing cover (B)

9 Supporting the bottom yoke, unscrew the adjuster nut using either a C-spanner, a peg-spanner, a drift located in one of the notches or the Honda service tool (see Chapter 1, Section 19), then remove the adjuster nut and the bearing cover from the steering stem **(see illustration)**.

10 Gently lower the bottom yoke and steering stem out of the steering head.

11 Remove the inner bearing race and bearing from the top of the steering head and remove the bearing from the base of the steering stem **(see illustration)**. **Note:** *Do not attempt to remove the outer races from the steering head or the inner race*

on the steering stem unless they are to be renewed.

Installation

12 Grease the bearing outer races in the steering head and on the inner race on the steering stem and work grease well into the upper and lower bearings.

13 Fit the lower bearing on the inner race on the steering stem, then lift the bottom yoke and steering stem up through the steering head. Install the upper bearing and its inner race in the top of the steering head, then install the bearing cover and thread the adjuster nut onto the steering stem **(see illustration 8.9)**.

14 Adjust the bearings, then install a new lockwasher and tighten the locknut (see Chapter 1, Section 19). **Note:** *If new bearings have been fitted you may need to carry out the adjustment procedure several times to allow them to settle properly.*

15 Install the remaining components in the reverse order of removal.

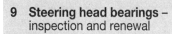

9 Steering head bearings – inspection and renewal

Inspection

1 Remove the steering stem (see Section 8).
2 Remove all traces of old grease from the bearings and the races. Check the bearings and races for wear and damage (see *Tools and Workshop Tips* in the *Reference* section).
3 If there are any signs of wear or damage on any of the components, both upper and lower bearing sets must be renewed at the same time.

Renewal

4 The outer races are an interference fit in the steering head and can be tapped out with a suitable drift **(see illustration)**. Tap firmly and evenly around each race to ensure that it is driven out squarely. It may prove advantageous to curve the end of the drift slightly to improve access.
5 Alternatively, the races can be removed

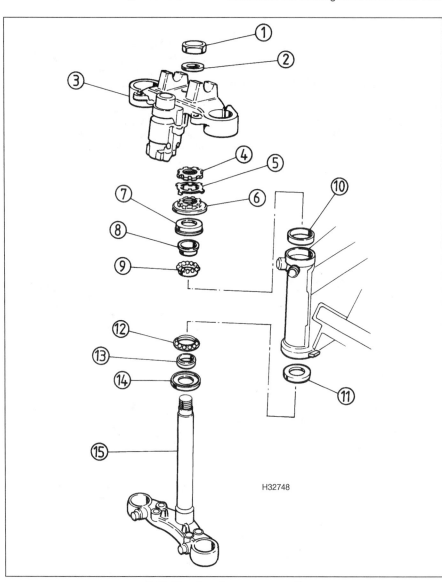

H32748

8.11 Steering stem components

1 Steering stem nut	7 Bearing cover	12 Lower bearing
2 Steering stem washer	8 Upper bearing inner race	13 Lower bearing inner race
3 Top yoke	9 Upper bearing	14 Dust seal
4 Locknut	10 Upper bearing outer race	15 Steering stem and bottom
5 Lockwasher	11 Lower bearing outer race	yoke
6 Adjuster nut		

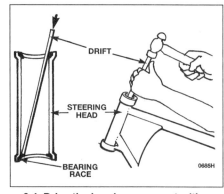

9.4 Drive the bearing races out with a brass drift as shown

9.6 Drawbolt arrangement for fitting steering stem races

1 Long bolt or threaded bar
2 Thick washer
3 Guide for lower race

using a slide-hammer type bearing extractor; these can often be hired from tool shops.

6 The new outer races can be installed in the steering head using a drawbolt arrangement **(see illustration)**, or by using a large diameter tubular drift. Ensure that the drawbolt washer or drift (as applicable) bears only on the outer edge of the race and does not contact the working surface and that the race fits all the way into its seat. Alternatively, have the races installed by a Honda dealer.

> **HAYNES HiNT** *Installation of new bearing outer races is made much easier if the races are left overnight in the freezer. This causes them to contract slightly making them a looser fit.*

7 To remove the inner race from the steering stem, use two screwdrivers placed on opposite sides to work it free, using blocks of wood to improve leverage and protect the yoke, or tap under it using a cold chisel **(see**

9.7a Lever the lower race off the steering stem . . .

illustration). If the race is firmly in place it will be necessary to use a puller **(see illustration)**. Check the condition of the dust seal that fits under the race – it is good practice to renew this seal as a matter of course.

8 Fit the new dust seal and new bearing race onto the steering stem. A length of tubing with an internal diameter slightly larger than the steering stem will be needed to tap the new race into position **(see illustration)**. Ensure that the tube bears only on the inner edge of the bearing race and does not contact its working surface.

9 Install the steering stem (see Section 8).

---

10 Rear shock absorber – removal, inspection and installation

> ⚠ *Warning: Do not attempt to disassemble this shock absorber. It is nitrogen-charged under high pressure. Improper disassembly could result in serious injury. Take the shock to a Honda dealer or suspension specialist for disposal.*

Removal

1 Support the motorcycle securely in an upright position using an auxiliary stand so that all weight is off the rear suspension.

2 Remove the side panels (see Chapter 8) and the rear wheel (see Chapter 7).

3 Unscrew the shock absorber lower mounting nut and bolt, then support the swingarm and remove the bolt **(see**

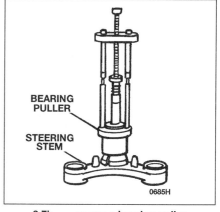

9.7b . . . or use a bearing puller

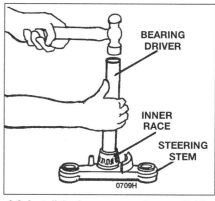

9.8 Install the lower race using a suitable driver of length of tubing

illustration). Pull the lower end of the shock away from its mounting on the swingarm.

4 Unscrew the upper shock absorber mounting nut and bolt, then support the shock and remove the bolt. Lift the shock away from the motorcycle **(see illustration)**.

Inspection

5 Inspect the body of the shock absorber for obvious physical damage and the coil spring for looseness, cracks or signs of fatigue.

6 Displace the dust cover and inspect the damper rod for signs of bending, corrosion and oil leakage **(see illustration)**. Damage to

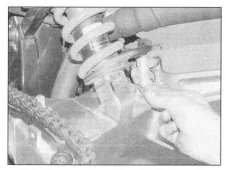

10.3 Unscrew the nut and withdraw the shock lower mounting bolt

10.4 Support the shock and withdraw the upper bolt

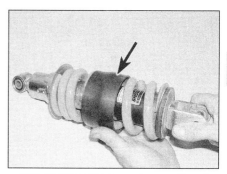

10.6 Displace the cover (arrowed) and inspect the damper rod

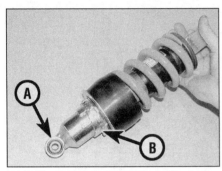

10.7 Check the mounting bush (A) and the pre-load mechanism (B)

10.9a Withdraw the bearing sleeve . . .

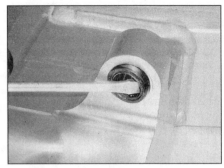

10.9b . . . and carefully remove the seals . . .

the surface of the rod will wear the oil seal and lead to oil loss and lack of suspension damping.

7 Check the bush in the mounting at the upper end of the shock; if it is worn or deteriorated the shock absorber should be renewed **(see illustration)**.

8 Ensure that the spring pre-load adjusting ring is clean and free to rotate; inspect the indents on the ring for wear **(see illustration 10.7)**.

9 Remove the sleeve from the bearing in the shock absorber's lower mounting on the swingarm and inspect the bearing seals and needle bearing **(see illustrations)**. The bearing can be pressed out with a suitably sized socket if a new one has to be fitted (see *Tools and Workshop Tips* in the *Reference* section). If necessary, remove the swingarm to renew the bearing (see Section 12). When a new bearing is installed it should be positioned centrally in the bearing housing to allow space for fitting the seals on either side – the depth on each side should be 5.0 to 5.5 mm from the face of the casting. Install a new seal each side of the bearing.

Installation

10 Installation is the reverse of removal, noting the following.
● Ensure the dust cover is correctly positioned at upper end of the spring.
● Apply molybdenum disulphide or copper-based grease to the spring pre-load adjuster.

● Lubricate the needle bearing with lithium-based grease.
● Tighten the mounting bolts to the torque settings specified at the beginning of this Chapter.

11 Suspension – adjustments

Front forks

1 The front forks are not adjustable. If the suspension is poor, check the forks thoroughly (see Chapter 1, Section 17). After a high mileage it may be necessary to change the fork oil (see Chapter 1, Section 31) or renew the fork springs (see Section 7).

Rear shock absorber

2 The rear shock absorber is adjustable for spring pre-load. Adjustment is made using a suitable C-spanner (one is provided in the toolkit) to turn the spring seat on the top of the shock absorber **(see illustration)**. There are seven positions. Position 1 is the softest setting, position 7 is the hardest. Standard setting is position 3. Align the setting required with the adjustment stopper.

3 To increase the pre-load, turn the spring seat anti-clockwise; to decrease the pre-load, turn the spring seat clockwise **(see illustration 11.2)**.

12 Swingarm – removal and installation

Removal

1 Support the motorcycle securely in an upright position using an auxiliary stand so that all weight is off the rear suspension. Unscrew the bolts securing the chainguard to the swingarm and remove the guard **(see illustration)**. Note how the front edge of the chainguard engages the lug on the swingarm.

2 Remove the rear wheel (see Chapter 7). Remove the front sprocket cover (see Section 15) and lift the drive chain off the front sprocket so that it rests on the drive chain slider.

3 Unscrew the bolts securing the rear brake hose clamps to the right-hand side of the swingarm and displace the rear brake caliper, noting how the caliper bracket locates onto the swingarm **(see illustrations)**. Secure the caliper to the motorcycle with a cable tie to prevent straining the hose.

4 Remove the chain tensioners from the ends of the swingarm **(see illustration)**.

5 Disconnect the gearchange linkage lever from the gearchange shaft (see Section 3).

6 Unscrew the shock absorber lower mounting nut and bolt, then support the swingarm and remove the bolt **(see illustration 10.3)**. Pull the lower end of the

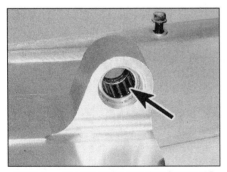

10.9c . . . to check the bearing (arrowed)

11.2 Adjusting the pre-load on the rear shock

12.1 Unscrew the bolts (arrowed) and remove the chainguard

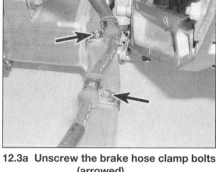

12.3a Unscrew the brake hose clamp bolts (arrowed) . . .

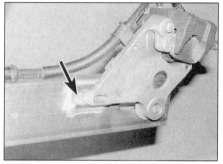

12.3b . . . and displace the caliper bracket from the swingarm lug (arrowed)

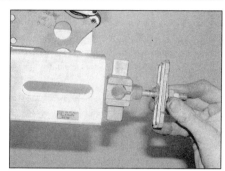

12.4 Remove the chain tensioners

shock away from its mounting on the swingarm.

7 Unscrew the bolts securing the left-hand footrest bracket to the swingarm left-hand bracket and remove the footrest bracket **(see illustration)**.

8 Counter-hold the swingarm pivot bolt and unscrew the nut on the right-hand end of the bolt but do not remove the bolt. Unscrew the bolts securing the swingarm left-hand bracket and remove the bolts.

9 Support the swingarm and withdraw the swingarm pivot bolt and remove it together with the left-hand bracket **(see illustration)**. Ease the swingarm out of the back of the frame and remove it together with the drive chain. Ensure the right-hand pivot bolt sleeves are retained inside the swingarm bearing seals (see Section 13).

10 If necessary, unscrew the bolts securing the drive chain slider to the swingarm, remove the shouldered washers and unclip the slider from the swingarm **(see illustrations)**.

Installation

11 Clean the frame around the swingarm mountings and check that the pivot bolt is a good fit in the frame **(see illustrations)**. Any wear in the pivot bolt mountings will cause poor handling and must be rectified before the motorcycle is ridden on the road. Consult your Honda dealer or a specialist repair shop.

12 Lubricate the bearings, seals, sleeves and the pivot bolt with lithium-based grease. If removed, install the drive chain slider and tighten the bolts to the specified torque setting.

13 Position the drive chain on the swingarm, then install the swingarm, ensuring it is correctly aligned with the mountings for the pivot bolt **(see illustration)**. If removed, fit the left-hand swingarm bracket on the pivot bolt

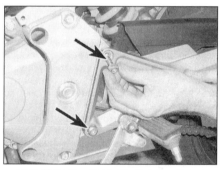

12.7 Unscrew the bolts (arrowed) and remove the footrest bracket

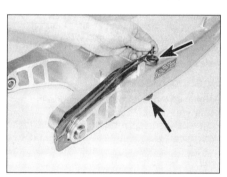

12.10a Unscrew the chain slider bolts (arrowed) . . .

and install the pivot bolt **(see illustration 2.9)**. Align the holes for the swingarm bracket bolts and install the bolts finger tight.

14 Fit the nut on the pivot bolt, then counter-hold the bolt and tighten the nut to the

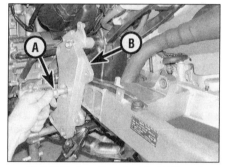

12.9 Withdraw the pivot bolt (A) and bracket (B)

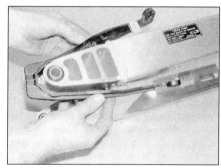

12.10b . . . and unclip the slider from the swingarm

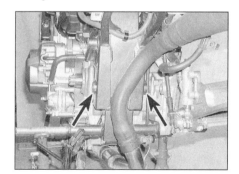

12.11a Clean the swingarm mounting points (arrowed) thoroughly . . .

12.11b . . . and check the pivot bolt location (arrowed)

12.13 Install the swingarm with the chain (arrowed) in place

6

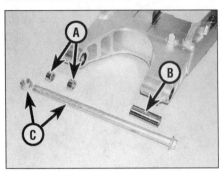

13.2 Right-hand pivot bolt sleeves (A), left-hand pivot bolt sleeve (B), pivot bolt and nut (C)

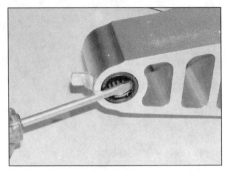

13.3 Prise the bearing seals out of the swingarm

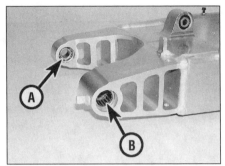

13.8 Swingarm ball bearings (A) and needle bearings (B)

specified torque setting. Tighten the bolts for the left-hand swingarm bracket securely.

15 Install the remaining components in the reverse order of removal, noting the following:
● Tighten the footrest bracket bolts and the lower shock absorber mounting bolt to the specified torque settings.
● Ensure the rear brake caliper bracket is correctly located in the lug on the swingarm.
● Ensure the rear brake hose is correctly routed along the swingarm and secured with its clamps.

16 Check the operation of the rear suspension and brakes before taking the machine out on the road.

13 Swingarm – inspection and bearing renewal

Inspection

1 Remove the swingarm (see Section 12).
2 Remove the two small right-hand and one large left-hand pivot bolt sleeves from the swingarm bearings **(see illustration)**.
3 Prise out the seals from each side of the swingarm bearings **(see illustration)**. Obtain new seals for use on refitting.
4 Thoroughly clean all components with solvent, removing all traces of dirt, corrosion and grease. Inspect all components closely, looking for obvious signs of wear such as heavy scoring,

and cracks or distortion due to accident damage. Check that the two arms of the swingarm are aligned with each other. Any damaged or worn component must be renewed.
5 Lay the swingarm on the work surface and support it so that the pivot bolt end is level (check this with a spirit level). Install the chain adjusters and the axle and check the level of the axle. If the axle is not level, the swingarm is out of true and must be renewed, although seek the advice of a frame specialist to confirm your findings.
6 Check the swingarm pivot bolt for wear especially where it passes through the frame. Check the bolt for straightness by rolling it on a flat surface such as a piece of plate glass (first wipe off all old grease and remove any corrosion using steel wool). If the pivot bolt is bent, renew it.
7 Clean the bearings with solvent and dry them with compressed air. Inspect the bearings (see *Tools and Workshop Tips (Section 5)* in the Reference Section) and the bearing sleeves.

Bearing renewal

8 Remove the pivot bolt sleeves and the dust seals (see Steps 2 and 3). There are two caged ball bearings retained by a circlip in the right-hand side of the swingarm and two needle roller bearings in the left-hand side **(see illustration)**. Refer to *Tools and Workshop Tips* in the Reference Section before removing the bearings.

9 To remove the needle bearings, support the bearing housing and press both the bearings out from the left-hand side of the housing **(see illustration)**. Take care not to damage the internal surface of the bearing housing.
10 Press the new inner needle bearing into the bearing housing from the same (left-hand) side with the markings on the bearing facing out. Press the bearing in to a depth of 28 – 29 mm **(see illustration)**. Now press the new outer needle bearing into the housing with the markings on the bearing facing out. Press the bearing in to a depth of 4 – 5 mm.
11 To remove the ball bearings, first remove the circlip from right-hand side of the bearing housing **(see illustration)**. Support the housing circlip side down and press both the bearings out from the inside of the swingarm. Note the bearing seat inside the housing.
12 Turn the swingarm over and support the bearing housing. Press the new inner ball bearing into the bearing housing from the right-hand (circlip) side until it is up against the seat, then press the new outer ball bearing into the housing until it is up against the inner bearing. With the bearings correctly installed the circlip groove should be visible. If the old circlip is in good condition it can be reused, otherwise replace it with a new one.
13 Lubricate the new bearings with lithium-based grease. Install the new seals followed by the bearing sleeves.

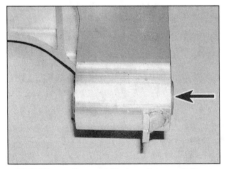

13.9 Press the needle bearings out from the left-hand side

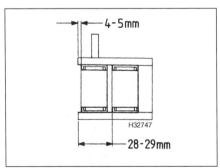

13.10 Swingarm needle bearing installation depths

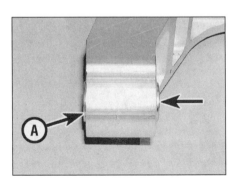

13.11 Remove the circlip (A) and press the bearings out from the other end

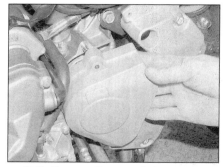

14.6 Ensure that the ends of the joining link are properly staked

15.1a On CB600F models, disconnect the speedometer cable

15.1b Remove the sprocket cover . . .

14 Drive chain – removal and installation

Removal

Note: The original equipment drive chain fitted to these models has a staked-type joining link which can be disassembled using either Honda service tool, Pt. No. 07HMH-MR10103, or one of several commercially-available drive chain splitting/staking tools. Such chains can be recognised by the joining link side plate's identification marks (and usually its different colour), as well as by the staked ends of the link's two pins which look as if they have been deeply centre-punched, instead of peened over as with all the other pins.

> ⚠ *Warning: Use ONLY the correct service tools to disassemble and assemble the staked-type of master link – if you do not have access to such tools or do not have the skill to operate them correctly, have the old chain removed and a new one fitted by a Honda dealer or motorcycle repair shop.*

1 Remove the front sprocket cover (see Section 15) and place the joining link in a convenient position to work on by rotating the back wheel.
2 Slacken the drive chain (see Chapter 1).
3 Split the chain at the joining link using the chain splitter, carefully following the manufacturer's operating instructions (see also *Tools and Workshop Tips (Section 8)* in

the Reference Section). Remove the chain from the bike.

Installation

> ⚠ *Warning: If you do not have access to a chain riveting tool, have the chain fitted by a Honda dealer or motorcycle repair shop.*

4 Install the chain through the chainguard and around the front and rear sprockets, leaving the two ends in a convenient position to work on.
5 Refer to Section 8 in *Tools and Workshop Tips* in the Reference Section. Fit an O-ring onto each pin on the new joining link, then slide the link through from the inside and fit the other two O-rings. Install the new side plate with its identification marks facing out. Measure the amount that the joining link pins project from the side plate and check they are within the measurements specified at the beginning of this Chapter (RK and DID chains). Stake the new link using the drive chain splitting/staking tool, following the instructions of both the chain manufacturer and the tool manufacturer carefully. DO NOT re-use old joining link components.
6 After staking, check the joining link and staking for any signs of cracking **(see illustration)**. If there is any evidence of cracking, the joining link, O-rings and side plate must be renewed. Measure the diameter of the staked ends in two directions and check that they are evenly staked and within the measurements specified at the beginning of this Chapter (RK and DID chains).

7 Install the front sprocket cover (see Section 15).
8 On completion, adjust and lubricate the chain (see Chapter 1).

15 Sprockets – check and renewal

Check

1 On CB600F models, remove the screw retaining the speedometer cable in the speedometer gearbox and disconnect the cable **(see illustration)**. On all models, unscrew the two bolts securing the front sprocket cover to the engine unit, then remove the cover, the drive chain guide plate and, if they are loose, the two dowels **(see illustrations)**.
2 Check that the front sprocket bolt is tightened to the torque setting specified at the beginning of this Chapter **(see illustration)**.
3 Check that the rear wheel sprocket nuts are tightened to the torque setting specified at the beginning of this Chapter **(see illustration)**.
4 Check the wear pattern on the front and rear wheel sprockets **(see illustration 1.7 in Chapter 1)**. Whenever the sprockets are inspected, the drive chain should also be inspected. If the sprocket teeth are worn excessively, or you are fitting a new chain, renew the chain and sprockets as a set.

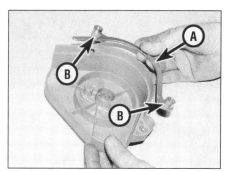

15.1c . . . with the chain guide plate (A) and dowels (B)

15.2 Front sprocket bolt . . .

15.3 . . . and rear sprocket nuts should be tightened to the specified torque

6

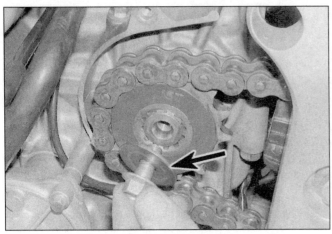

15.6 Remove the bolt and washer (arrowed)

15.7a Slide the sprocket and chain off the shaft together

15.7b Sprocket size is stamped on the outside face (arrowed)

Renewal

Front sprocket

5 Remove the front sprocket cover (see Step 1).

6 Have an assistant apply the rear brake, then unscrew the sprocket bolt and remove the washer **(see illustration)**.

7 Slacken the drive chain (see Chapter 1), then slide the sprocket and chain off the shaft and slip the sprocket out of the chain **(see illustration)**. **Note:** *The size of the sprocket (i.e. the number of teeth) is stamped on the outside face of the sprocket **(see illustration)**.*

8 Engage the new sprocket with the chain and slide it on the shaft. Install the sprocket bolt and washer and hand tighten. Adjust the chain tension (see Chapter 1).

9 Have an assistant apply the rear brake, then tighten the sprocket bolt to the torque setting specified at the beginning of this Chapter.

10 Install the front sprocket cover.

Rear sprocket

11 Remove the rear wheel (see Chapter 7). Loosen the sprocket nuts before pulling the sprocket coupling out of the hub.

Caution: Don't lay the wheel down and allow it to rest on the disc or the sprocket – they could become warped. Set the wheel on wood blocks so the wheel rim supports the weight of the wheel. Don't operate the brake pedal with the wheel removed.

12 Unscrew the nuts securing the sprocket to the hub assembly and remove the sprocket **(see illustration)**. **Note:** *The size of the sprocket (i.e. the number of teeth) is stamped on the outside face of the sprocket **(see illustration)**.*

13 Fit the sprocket onto the hub, then install the nuts and tighten them evenly and in a criss-cross sequence to the torque setting specified at the beginning of this Chapter.

14 Install the rear wheel (see Chapter 7).

16 Sprocket coupling/rubber damper – check and renewal

1 Remove the rear wheel (see Chapter 7). *Caution: Don't lay the wheel down and allow it to rest on the disc or the sprocket – they could become warped. Set the*

15.12a Unscrew the sprocket nuts (arrowed)

15.12b Sprocket size is stamped on the outside face (arrowed)

16.2 Pull the coupling out of the hub

16.3 Check the condition of the rubber dampers

16.4 Check the condition of the O-ring (arrowed)

wheel on wood blocks so the wheel rim supports the weight of the wheel. Don't operate the brake pedal with the wheel removed.

2 Pull the sprocket coupling out of the hub, taking care not to lose the inner spacer if it is loose **(see illustration)**. The coupling should be a press fit between the rubber dampers with no freeplay. Check the coupling for cracks and damage, and renew it if necessary.
3 Remove the rubber dampers from the hub and check them for cracks, hardening and general deterioration and renew them if

necessary **(see illustration)**. Always renew the dampers as a set.
4 Check the condition of the coupling O-ring and renew it if it is damaged or deteriorated **(see illustration)**. Smear the O-ring with grease before installing the sprocket coupling onto the hub.
5 Checking and renewal procedures for the coupling bearing are in Chapter 7.
6 Installation is the reverse of removal. Check the dampers are fitted the correct way round in the hub **(see illustration)** and that the inner spacer is in position.

16.6 Ensure the dampers are fitted correctly before installing the hub

6

Notes

Chapter 7
Brakes, wheels and tyres

Contents

Degrees of difficulty

Easy, suitable for novice with little experience	Fairly easy, suitable for beginner with some experience	Fairly difficult, suitable for competent DIY mechanic	Difficult, suitable for experienced DIY mechanic	Very difficult, suitable for expert DIY or professional

Specifications

Front brake

Brake fluid type	DOT 4
Brake pad minimum thickness	see Chapter 1
Caliper bore ID	
Standard	27.000 to 27.050 mm
Service limit	27.060 mm
Caliper piston OD	
Standard	26.935 to 26.968 mm
Service limit	26.910 mm
Disc thickness	
Standard	4.5 mm
Service limit	3.5 mm
Disc maximum runout	0.30 mm
Master cylinder bore ID	
Standard	14.000 to 14.043 mm
Service limit	14.055 mm
Master cylinder piston OD	
Standard	13.957 to 13.984 mm
Service limit	13.945 mm

7

Rear brake

Brake fluid type	DOT 4
Pad minimum thickness	see Chapter 1
Caliper bore ID	
Standard	38.18 to 38.23 mm
Service limit	38.24 mm
Caliper piston OD	
Standard	38.098 to 38.148 mm
Service limit	38.090
Disc thickness	
Standard	5.0 mm
Service limit	4.0 mm
Disc maximum runout	0.30 mm
Master cylinder bore ID	
Standard	14.000 to 14.043 mm
Service limit	14.055 mm
Master cylinder piston OD	
Standard	13.957 to 13.984 mm
Service limit	13.945 mm

Wheels

Rim size	
Front	
CB600F-W and X models	16 x MT3.50
CB600F-Y onwards and CB600FS models	17 x MT3.50
Rear	
CB600F- W models	17 x MT5.00
CB600F-X onwards and CB600FS models	17 x MT5.50
Maximum wheel runout (front and rear)	
Axial (side-to-side)	2.00 mm
Radial (out-of-round)	2.00 mm
Maximum axle runout (front and rear)	0.20 mm

Tyres

Tyre pressures	see Daily (pre-ride) checks
Tyre sizes*	
Front	
CB600F-W and X models	130/70-ZR16 (61W)
CB600F-Y onwards and CB600FS models	120/70-ZR17 (61W)
Rear	180/55-ZR17 (73W)

Refer to the owners handbook, the tyre information label on the chainguard, or your Honda dealer for approved tyre brands.

Torque wrench settings

Brake pad pin	18 Nm
Brake hose banjo bolts	34 Nm
Bleed valves	6 Nm
Front axle bolt	59 Nm
Front axle pinch bolt	23 Nm
Front brake caliper mounting bolts	30 Nm
Front brake caliper slider pin on bracket	23 Nm
Front brake caliper slider pin on caliper	27 Nm
Front brake disc bolts	20 Nm
Front brake hose clamp bolt	12 Nm
Front brake master cylinder clamp bolts	12 Nm
Rear brake caliper mounting bolt	23 Nm
Rear brake caliper slider pin	27 Nm
Rear brake disc bolts	42 Nm
Rear brake hose clamp bolt	9 Nm
Rear brake master cylinder mounting bolts	12 Nm
Rear axle nut	88 Nm

1 General information

All models are equipped with hydraulically-operated disc brakes. The front brakes are twin discs with twin-piston calipers, the rear brake is a single disc with a single-piston caliper.

Wheels on all models are cast alloy designed for tubeless tyres only.

Caution: Disc brake components rarely require disassembly. Do not disassemble components unless absolutely necessary. If a hydraulic brake line is loosened, the entire system must be disassembled, drained, cleaned and then properly filled and bled upon reassembly. Do not use solvents on internal brake components. Solvents will cause the seals to swell and distort. Use only clean brake fluid or denatured alcohol for cleaning. Use care when working with brake fluid as it can injure your eyes and it will damage painted surfaces and plastic parts.

2 Front brake pads – renewal

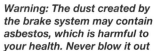

Warning: The dust created by the brake system may contain asbestos, which is harmful to your health. Never blow it out with compressed air and don't inhale any of it. An approved filtering mask should be worn when working on the brakes.

1 If new pads are being installed, displace the caliper from the disc (see Section 3) – this makes it easier to push the pistons back into the caliper to allow for the extra thickness of new pads. Otherwise, the pads can be removed with the caliper in place.

2 Unscrew the pad retaining pin plug then unscrew the pad retaining pin and withdraw the pin, noting how it fits **(see illustrations)**.

3 Withdraw the pads from the bottom of the caliper, noting how they fit **(see illustrations)**. **Note:** *Do not operate the brake lever while the pads are out of the caliper.*

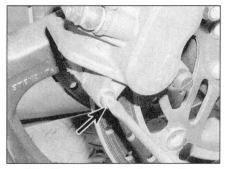

2.2a Remove the plug (arrowed) . . .

2.2b . . . then unscrew the pin

4 Inspect the surface of each pad for contamination and check that the friction material has not worn down to or beyond its wear limit (see Chapter 1, Section 3). If either pad is worn down to or beyond the wear limit indicator, is fouled with oil or grease, or is heavily scored or damaged by dirt and debris, both pads in each caliper must be renewed. **Note:** *It is not possible to degrease the friction material; if the pads are contaminated in any way they must be renewed.*

5 Check that each pad has worn evenly at each end, and that each has the same amount of wear as the other. If uneven wear is noticed, one of the pistons is probably sticking in the caliper, in which case the caliper must be overhauled (see Section 3).

6 If the pads are in good condition, clean them carefully using a fine wire brush which is completely free of oil and grease to remove all traces of road dirt and corrosion. Using a pointed instrument, clean out the grooves in the friction material and dig out any embedded particles of foreign matter. Remove any areas of glazing using emery cloth. Spray the caliper with a dedicated brake cleaner to remove any dust and remove any traces of corrosion which might cause sticking of the caliper/pad operation.

7 Check the condition of the brake disc (see Section 4).

8 Remove all traces of corrosion from the pad retaining pin. Check it for signs of wear and renew it if necessary.

9 If new pads are being installed, push the pistons as far back into the caliper as possible, using hand pressure or a piece of

wood as leverage. This will displace brake fluid back into the hydraulic reservoir, so it may be necessary to remove the reservoir cap, plate and diaphragm and siphon out some fluid (depending on how much fluid was in there in the first place and how far the pistons have to be pushed in). If the pistons are difficult to push back, attach a length of clear hose to the bleed valve and place the open end in a suitable container, then open the valve and try again. Take great care not to draw any air into the system and don't forget to tighten the valve once the pistons have been sufficiently displaced. If in doubt, bleed the brakes afterwards (see Section 11). **Note:** *If the caliper is still in place, under no circumstances must you lever against the brake disc to push the pistons back into the caliper as damage to the disc will result.*

10 Smear the backs of the pads and the pad pin lightly with copper-based grease, making sure that none gets on the front or sides of the pads.

11 Make sure the pad spring is in place in the lower end of the caliper (see Section 3). Insert the pads into the caliper so that the friction material faces the disc. Push the pads hard against the pad plate in the top end of the caliper and against the pad spring in the lower end of the caliper **(see illustration)**. Align the holes for the pad retaining pin and install the pin.

12 Tighten the pad retaining pin to the torque setting specified at the beginning of this Chapter. Install the pad pin plug and tighten it securely.

13 If displaced, install the caliper (see

2.3a Remove the pads from the bottom of the caliper . . .

2.3b . . . noting how they fit

2.11 Push the pads against the pad plate (arrowed)

7

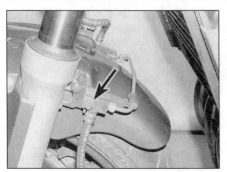

3.2 Unscrew the bolt (arrowed) and detach the hose assembly from the fork slider

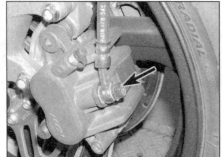

3.3 Front brake hose banjo bolt (arrowed)

3.5 Remove the front caliper and bracket

Section 3). Operate the brake lever several times to bring the pads into contact with the disc. Repeat the procedure on the other caliper.
14 Check the level of fluid in the hydraulic reservoir and top-up if necessary (see *Daily (pre-ride) checks*).
15 Check the operation of the brake before riding the motorcycle.

3 Front brake calipers –
removal, overhaul and installation

⚠️ *Warning: If a caliper is in need of an overhaul all old brake fluid should be flushed from the system. Also, the dust created by the brake system may contain asbestos, which is harmful to your health. Never blow it out with compressed air and do not inhale any of it. An approved filtering mask should be worn when working on the brakes. Disassembly, overhaul and reassembly of the brake caliper must be done in a spotlessly clean work area to avoid contamination and possible failure of the brake hydraulic system components. Do not, under any circumstances, use petroleum-based solvents to clean brake parts. Use clean brake fluid of the type specified, dedicated brake cleaner or denatured alcohol only, as described. To prevent damage from spilled brake fluid, always cover paintwork when working on the braking system.*

Removal

Note*: If the caliper is being overhauled (usually due to sticking pistons or fluid leaks) read through the entire procedure first and make sure that you have obtained all the new parts required, including some new DOT 4 brake fluid.*
1 If the caliper is just being displaced, the brake pads can be left in place. If the caliper is being overhauled, remove the brake pads (see Section 2).
2 Unscrew and remove the bolts securing the brake hose assembly to the front fork sliders **(see illustration)**.
3 If the caliper is just being displaced, do not

disconnect the brake hose from the caliper. If the caliper is being completely removed or overhauled, unscrew the brake hose banjo bolt and detach the banjo fitting, noting its alignment with the caliper **(see illustration)**. **Note:** *If you are planning to overhaul the caliper and do not have a source of compressed air to blow out the pistons, just loosen the banjo bolt at this stage and retighten it lightly. The hydraulic system can then be used to force the pistons out of the caliper once the pads have been removed. Disconnect the hose when the pistons have been sufficiently displaced.*
4 Once disconnected, clamp the hose and secure it in an upright position to minimise fluid loss. Wrap a clean plastic bag tightly around the end to prevent dirt entering the system. Discard the sealing washers, as new ones must be fitted on reassembly.
5 Unscrew the caliper bracket mounting bolts and slide the caliper off the disc **(see**

illustration). **Note:** *Honda recommend using new caliper bolts when the old ones are removed. This is because the bolts are pre-treated with a locking compound. It is possible, however, to clean up the old bolts and reinstall them using a suitable non-permanent thread locking compound that is commercially available.*
6 If the caliper is just being displaced, secure it to the motorcycle with a cable tie to avoid straining the brake hose. **Note:** *Do not operate the brake lever while the caliper is off the disc.*

Overhaul

7 Slide the caliper off its mounting bracket and clean the exterior of the caliper with denatured alcohol or brake system cleaner.
8 Remove the rubber boots from the slider pins, then remove the pad spring and pad plate from inside the caliper, noting how they fit **(see illustration)**.

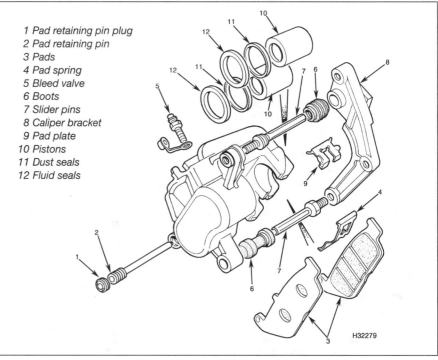

1 Pad retaining pin plug
2 Pad retaining pin
3 Pads
4 Pad spring
5 Bleed valve
6 Boots
7 Slider pins
8 Caliper bracket
9 Pad plate
10 Pistons
11 Dust seals
12 Fluid seals

H32279

3.8 Front brake caliper components

3.11 Remove the dust seal carefully to avoid damage to the bore and seal groove

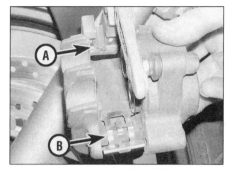

3.18 Install the pad plate (A) and pad spring (B)

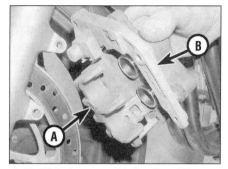

3.19 Slide the assembled caliper (A) onto its bracket (B)

9 Mark each piston and the caliper body to ensure that the pistons can be matched to their original bores on reassembly. Displace the pistons from their bores using either compressed air or by carefully operating the front brake lever to pump them out. Ensure that all the pistons are moving freely and evenly.

10 If the pistons are being displaced hydraulically, it may be necessary to top-up the hydraulic reservoir during the procedure. Also, have some clean rag ready to catch any spilled brake fluid when the pistons reach the end of their bores. **Note:** *If the compressed air method is used, direct the air into the fluid inlet on the caliper. Use only low pressure to ease the pistons out and make sure both pistons are displaced at the same time. If the air pressure is too high and the pistons are forced out, the caliper and/or pistons may be damaged – pad the caliper mouth with rag to cushion the pistons as they come free.*

⚠ **Warning: Never place your fingers in front of the pistons in an attempt to catch or protect them when applying compressed air, as serious injury could result.**

Caution: Do not try to remove the pistons by levering them out, or by using pliers or any other grips.

11 Remove the dust seals and the piston seals from the piston bores using a soft wooden or plastic tool to avoid scratching the bores **(see illustration)**. Discard the seals as new ones must be fitted on reassembly.

12 Clean the pistons and bores with clean brake fluid of the specified type. If compressed air is available, blow it through the fluid galleries in the caliper to ensure they are clear and use it to dry the parts thoroughly (make sure it is filtered and unlubricated).

Caution: Do not, under any circumstances, use a petroleum-based solvent to clean brake parts.

13 Inspect the caliper bores and pistons for signs of corrosion, nicks and burrs and loss of plating. If surface defects are present, the caliper assembly must be renewed. If the necessary measuring equipment is available, compare the dimensions of the caliper bores and pistons to those specified at the beginning of this Chapter, and install a new caliper if necessary. If the caliper is in poor condition, the master cylinder should also be checked.

14 Clean all traces of corrosion off the slider pins and their bores in the caliper and bracket. Replace the pins with new ones if they are worn. If the pins are loose, remove them and clean the threads. Apply a suitable non-permanent thread locking compound and tighten them to the specified torque. It is advisable to renew the rubber dust boots, particularly if they are damaged or deteriorated.

15 Lubricate the new piston seals with clean brake fluid and install them in their grooves in the caliper bores.

16 Lubricate the new dust seals with clean brake fluid and install them in their grooves in the caliper bores.

17 Lubricate the pistons with clean brake fluid and install them, closed-end first, into the caliper bores. Using your thumbs, push the pistons all the way in, making sure they enter the bores squarely.

18 Clean the pad plate and pad spring and ensure they fit firmly in the caliper, otherwise replace them with new ones **(see illustration)**.

19 Apply a smear of copper-based grease to the slider pins, fit the slider pin boots and then slide the caliper onto the bracket and check that it is able to move freely **(see illustration)**.

Installation

20 Slide the caliper onto the brake disc. If they weren't removed, make sure the pads sit squarely in the caliper before installing it **(see illustration)**.

21 Install the new caliper mounting bolts (or clean the threads of the original bolts and apply fresh locking compound) and tighten them to the torque setting specified at the beginning of this Chapter **(see illustration)**.

22 If removed, connect the brake hose to the caliper, using new sealing washers on each side of the banjo fitting. Align the fitting as noted on removal **(see illustration 3.3)**. Tighten the banjo bolt to the torque setting specified at the beginning of this Chapter.

23 Install the bolts securing the brake hose assembly to the front fork sliders and tighten them to the specified torque setting.

24 If removed, install the brake pads (see Section 2).

25 Top-up the hydraulic reservoir with DOT 4 brake fluid (see *Daily (pre-ride) checks*) and bleed the system as described in Section 11. Check that there are no fluid leaks and thoroughly test the operation of the brake before riding the motorcycle.

---

4 Front brake discs – inspection, removal and installation

7

Inspection

Note: *Renew the front brake discs as a pair, never singly, and always fit new brake pads if new discs are fitted.*

1 Visually inspect the surface of the disc for

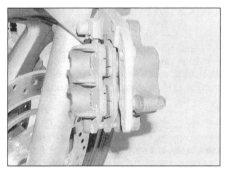

3.20 Ensure the pads sit squarely in the caliper

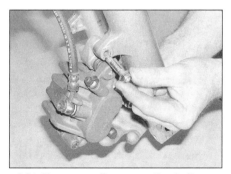

3.21 Use new caliper mounting bolts on reassembly, or apply a locking compound to the originals

4.2a The minimum disc thickness is marked on the disc

4.2b Measuring the disc thickness

4.3 Checking the brake disc runout

score marks and other damage. Light scratches are normal after use and will not affect brake operation, but deep grooves and heavy score marks will reduce braking efficiency and accelerate pad wear. If a disc is badly grooved it must be machined, or a new one fitted.

2 The disc must not be machined or allowed to wear down to a thickness less than the service limit as listed in this Chapter's Specifications. The minimum thickness is also stamped on the disc **(see illustration)**. Check the thickness of the disc with a micrometer and renew it if necessary **(see illustration)**.

3 To check disc runout, support the bike on an auxiliary stand with the front wheel is raised off the ground. Mount a dial gauge to a fork leg, with the gauge plunger touching the surface of the disc about 10 mm from the outer edge **(see illustration)**. Rotate the wheel and watch the gauge needle, comparing the reading with the limit listed in the Specifications at the beginning of this Chapter. If the runout is greater than the service limit, check the wheel bearings for play (see Chapter 1). If the bearings are worn, install new ones (see Section 16) and repeat this check. If the disc runout is still excessive, the disc will have to be renewed.

Removal

4 Remove the wheel (see Section 14).
Caution: Don't lay the wheel down and allow it to rest on the disc – the disc could become warped. Set the wheel on wood blocks so the wheel rim supports the weight of the wheel.

4.5 Directional arrow stamped on the front disc

5 Note the direction of rotation indicated by the arrow stamped on the disc **(see illustration)**. Left and right-hand discs are not interchangeable. If you are not replacing the disc with a new one, mark the relationship of the disc to the wheel so that it can be installed in the same position. Unscrew the disc retaining bolts, loosening them evenly and a little at a time in a criss-cross pattern to avoid distorting the disc, then remove the disc from the wheel. **Note:** *Honda recommend using new bolts when the old ones are removed. This is because the bolts are pre-treated with a locking compound. It is possible, however, to clean up the old bolts and reinstall them using a suitable non-permanent thread locking compound that is commercially available.*

Installation

6 Before installing the disc, make sure there is no dirt or corrosion where the disc seats on the hub, particularly right in the angle of the seat. If the disc does not sit flat when it is bolted down, it will appear to be warped when checked or when the front brake is used.

7 Ensure the directional arrow is pointing the right way and install the disc on the wheel. Align the previously applied register marks if you are reinstalling the original disc.

8 Install the new bolts (or clean the threads of the original bolts and apply fresh locking compound) and tighten them evenly and a little at a time in a criss-cross pattern to the torque setting specified at the beginning of this Chapter. Clean the brake disc using acetone or brake system cleaner. If a new brake disc has been installed, remove any

5.2 Brake master cylinder clamp bolts (arrowed)

protective coating from its working surfaces.
9 Install the front wheel (see Section 14).
10 Operate the brake lever several times to bring the pads into contact with the disc. Check the operation of the brakes carefully before riding the motorcycle.

---

5 Front brake master cylinder
  – removal, overhaul and
  installation

 Warning: If the brake master cylinder is in need of an overhaul all old brake fluid should be flushed from the system. Disassembly, overhaul and reassembly of the brake master cylinder must be done in a spotlessly clean work area to avoid contamination and possible failure of the brake hydraulic system components. Do not, under any circumstances, use petroleum-based solvents to clean brake parts. Use clean brake fluid of the type specified, dedicated brake cleaner or denatured alcohol only, as described. To prevent damage from spilled brake fluid, always cover paintwork when working on the braking system.

Removal

Note: *If the master cylinder is being overhauled (usually due to sticking or poor action, or fluid leaks) read through the entire procedure first and make sure that you have obtained all the new parts required, including some new DOT 4 brake fluid.*

1 On CB600F models, lift the cover, where fitted, on the rear view mirror mounting locknut, then loosen the locknut and unscrew the mirror from the handlebar bracket.

2 If the master cylinder is just being displaced, ensure the fluid reservoir cover is secure. Unscrew the master cylinder clamp bolts and remove the back of the clamp, noting how it fits **(see illustration)**. Position the assembly clear of the handlebar, making sure no strain is placed on the brake hose and the brake light switch wiring. Keep the fluid reservoir upright to prevent air entering the hydraulic system.

3 Disconnect the brake light switch wiring connectors.

5.4 Note the alignment of the brake hose (arrowed) before removal

4 Unscrew the brake hose banjo bolt and detach the banjo fitting, noting its alignment with the master cylinder **(see illustration)**. Once disconnected, clamp the hose and secure it in an upright position to minimise fluid loss. Wrap a clean plastic bag tightly around the end to prevent dirt entering the system. Discard the sealing washers as new ones must be fitted on reassembly.

5 Unscrew the master cylinder clamp bolts and remove the back of the clamp, noting how it fits **(see illustration 5.2)**, then lift the master cylinder away from the handlebar.

6 Unscrew the reservoir cover retaining screws and lift off the cover, the diaphragm plate and the diaphragm **(see illustration)**. Drain the brake fluid into a suitable container. Wipe any remaining fluid out of the reservoir with a clean rag.

7 If necessary, remove the screw securing the brake light switch to the bottom of the master cylinder and remove the switch.

Overhaul

8 Unscrew the brake lever pivot bolt locknut, then withdraw the pivot bolt and remove the lever. Carefully remove the dust boot from the master cylinder to reveal the pushrod retaining circlip **(see illustration)**.

9 Depress the pushrod and use circlip pliers to remove the circlip, then slide out the piston assembly and the spring, noting how they fit **(see illustration 5.6)**. If they are difficult to remove, apply low pressure compressed air to the brake fluid outlet. Lay the parts out in the

5.8 Remove the boot from the end of the master cylinder piston

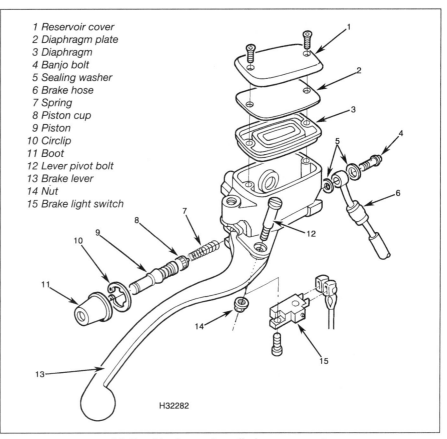

1 Reservoir cover
2 Diaphragm plate
3 Diaphragm
4 Banjo bolt
5 Sealing washer
6 Brake hose
7 Spring
8 Piston cup
9 Piston
10 Circlip
11 Boot
12 Lever pivot bolt
13 Brake lever
14 Nut
15 Brake light switch

H32282

5.6 Front brake master cylinder components

proper order to prevent confusion during reassembly.

10 Clean all parts with clean brake fluid. If compressed air is available, blow it through the fluid galleries to ensure they are clear and use it to dry the parts thoroughly (make sure the air is filtered and unlubricated).

Caution: Do not, under any circumstances, use a petroleum-based solvent to clean brake parts.

11 Check the master cylinder bore for corrosion, scratches, nicks and score marks. If the necessary measuring equipment is available, compare the diameter of the bore and the piston to that given in the Specifications at the beginning of this Chapter. If damage or wear is evident, the master cylinder must be replaced with a new one. If the master cylinder is in poor condition, then the calipers should be checked as well.

12 The dust boot, circlip, piston assembly and spring are included in the master cylinder rebuild kit. Use all of the new parts, regardless of the apparent condition of the old ones. Fit them according to the layout of the old piston assembly **(see illustration 5.6)**.

13 Fit the spring into the master cylinder with its narrow end facing out. Lubricate the piston assembly with clean brake fluid and fit the assembly into the master cylinder, making sure it is the correct way round. Make sure the lips on the cup do not turn inside out when

they are slipped into the bore. Depress the piston and install the new circlip, making sure it is properly located in the groove.

14 Install the dust boot, making sure the lip is seated properly in the groove **(see illustration 5.8)**.

15 Inspect the reservoir cover, diaphragm plate and diaphragm and renew any parts if they are damaged or deteriorated.

Installation

16 Installation is the reverse of removal, noting the following points:

● Make sure the master cylinder clamp is installed with the UP mark facing up. Tighten the upper bolt first, then the lower bolt.

● Connect the brake hose to the master cylinder, using new sealing washers on each side of the banjo fitting. Align the fitting as noted on removal (see illustration 5.4). Tighten the banjo bolt to the torque setting specified at the beginning of this Chapter.

● Fill the fluid reservoir with new DOT 4 brake fluid as described in Daily (pre-ride) checks. Refer to Section 11 of this Chapter and bleed the air from the system.

● Ensure the reservoir diaphragm is correctly seated, and that the cover screws are tightened securely.

● Check the operation of the brake before riding the motorcycle.

7

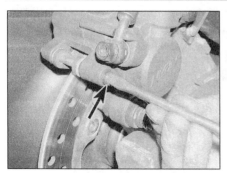

6.2a Remove the plug (arrowed) . . .

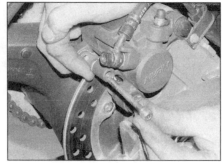

6.2b . . . then unscrew the pin

6 Rear brake pads – renewal

⚠️ **Warning: The dust created by the brake system may contain asbestos, which is harmful to your health. Never blow it out with compressed air and do not inhale any of it. An approved filtering mask should be worn when working on the brakes.**

1 If new pads are being installed, displace the caliper from the disc (see Section 7) – this makes it easier to push the piston back into the caliper to allow for the extra thickness of new pads. Otherwise, the pads can be removed with the caliper in place.

2 Unscrew the pad retaining pin plug then unscrew the pad retaining pin and withdraw the pin, noting how it fits **(see illustrations)**.

3 Withdraw the pads from the bottom of the caliper, noting how they fit **(see illustration)**. An insulating pad and shim are fitted to the rear of each brake pad; remove these, noting how they fit **(see illustration)**. **Note:** Do not operate the brake lever while the pads are out of the caliper.

4 Inspect the surface of each pad for contamination and check that the friction material has not worn down to or beyond its wear limit (see Chapter 1, Section 3). If either pad is worn down to or beyond the wear limit indicator, is fouled with oil or grease, or is heavily scored or damaged by dirt and debris, both pads must be renewed together. **Note:** It

is not possible to degrease the friction material; if the pads are contaminated in any way they must be renewed.

5 Check that both pads have worn evenly, and that each has the same amount of wear as the other. If uneven wear is noticed, the piston is probably sticking in the caliper, in which case the caliper must be overhauled (see Section 7).

6 If the pads are in good condition, clean them carefully using a fine wire brush which is completely free of oil and grease to remove all traces of road dirt and corrosion. Using a pointed instrument, clean out the grooves in the friction material and dig out any embedded particles of foreign matter. Remove any areas of glazing using emery cloth. Spray the caliper with a dedicated brake cleaner to remove any dust and remove any traces of corrosion which might cause sticking of the caliper/pad operation.

7 Check the condition of the brake disc (see Section 8).

8 Remove all traces of corrosion from the pad retaining pin. Check it for signs of wear and renew it if necessary.

9 If new pads are being installed, push the piston as far back into the caliper as possible, using hand pressure or a piece of wood as leverage. This will displace brake fluid back into the hydraulic reservoir, so it may be necessary to remove the reservoir cap, plate and diaphragm and siphon out some fluid (depending on how much fluid was in there in the first place and how far the pistons have to be pushed in). If the piston is difficult to push

back, attach a length of clear hose to the bleed valve and place the open end in a suitable container, then open the valve and try again. Take great care not to draw any air into the system and don't forget to tighten the valve once the piston has been sufficiently displaced. If in doubt, bleed the brake afterwards (see Section 11). **Note:** If the caliper is still in place, under no circumstances must you lever against the brake disc to push the pistons back into the caliper as damage to the disc will result.

10 Assemble the insulating pad and shim on the back of each pad and smear the pad pin lightly with copper-based grease.

11 Make sure the pad spring is in place inside the caliper (see Section 7). Insert the pads into the caliper so that the friction material faces the disc **(see illustration 6.3a)**. Push the pads hard against the pad spring to align the holes for the pad retaining pin and install the pin.

12 Tighten the pad retaining pin to the torque setting specified at the beginning of this Chapter. Install the pad pin plug and tighten it securely.

13 If displaced, install the caliper (see Section 7). Operate the brake lever several times to bring the pads into contact with the disc.

14 Check the level of fluid in the hydraulic reservoir and top-up if necessary (see Daily (pre-ride) checks).

15 Check the operation of the brake before riding the motorcycle.

7 Rear brake caliper – removal, overhaul and installation

⚠️ **Warning: If a caliper indicates the need for an overhaul (usually due to leaking fluid or sticky operation), all old brake fluid should be flushed from the system. Also, the dust created by the brake system may contain asbestos, which is harmful to your health. Never blow it out with compressed air and do not inhale any of it. An approved filtering mask should be worn when working on the brakes. Do not, under any circumstances, use petroleum-based solvents to clean brake parts. Use the specified clean brake fluid, dedicated brake cleaner or denatured alcohol only, as described.**

Removal

Note: If the caliper is being overhauled (usually due to sticking pistons or fluid leaks) read through the entire procedure first and make sure that you have obtained all the new parts required, including some new DOT 4 brake fluid.

1 If the caliper is just being displaced, the brake pads can be left in place. If the caliper is being overhauled, remove the brake pads (see Section 6).

6.3a Remove the pads from the bottom of the caliper

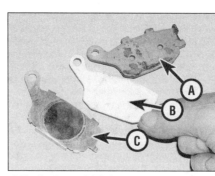

6.3b Brake pad (A), insulating pad (B) and shim (C)

7.2 **Unscrew the brake hose clip bolt (arrowed)**

7.3 **Note the alignment of the fitting, then unscrew the banjo bolt (arrowed)**

7.5 **Unscrew the caliper mounting bolt (arrowed)**

2 Unscrew and remove the bolt securing the brake hose to the caliper bracket and, if necessary, the swingarm **(see illustration)**.

3 If the caliper is just being displaced, do not disconnect the brake hose from the caliper. If the caliper is being completely removed or overhauled, unscrew the brake hose banjo bolt and detach the banjo fitting, noting its alignment with the caliper **(see illustration)**. **Note:** *If you are planning to overhaul the caliper and do not have a source of compressed air to blow out the piston, just loosen the banjo bolt at this stage and retighten it lightly. The hydraulic system can then be used to force the pistons out of the caliper once the pads have been removed. Disconnect the hose when the pistons have been sufficiently displaced.*

4 Once disconnected, clamp the hose and secure it in an upright position to minimise fluid loss. Wrap a clean plastic bag tightly around the end to prevent dirt entering the system. Discard the sealing washers, as new ones must be fitted on reassembly.

5 Unscrew the caliper mounting bolt **(see illustration)**. Pivot the caliper up to clear the brake disc and then slide the caliper off its bracket. **Note:** *Honda recommend using a new caliper bolt when the old one is removed. This is because the bolt is pre-treated with a locking compound. It is possible, however, to clean up the old bolt and reinstall it using a suitable non-permanent thread locking compound that is commercially available. If the caliper is just being displaced, secure it to the motorcycle with a cable tie to avoid straining the brake hose.* **Note:** *Do not operate the brake lever while the caliper is off the disc.*

Overhaul

6 Clean the exterior of the caliper with denatured alcohol or brake system cleaner.

7 Remove the rubber boots from the slider pin sleeve in the caliper bracket and the mounting bolt sleeve in the caliper **(see illustration)**.

8 Remove the pad spring from inside the

caliper and the pad retainer from the caliper bracket, noting how they fit.

9 Displace the piston from its bore using either compressed air or by carefully operating the rear brake pedal to pump it out. If the piston is being displaced hydraulically, it may be necessary to top-up the hydraulic reservoir during the procedure. Also, have some clean rag ready to catch any spilled hydraulic fluid when the piston reaches the end of its bore. **Note:** *If the compressed air method is used, direct the air into the fluid inlet on the caliper. Use only low pressure to ease the piston out – if the air pressure is too high and the piston is forced out, the caliper and/or piston may be damaged.*

⚠ **Warning: Never place your fingers in front of the piston in an attempt to catch or protect it when applying compressed air, as serious injury could result.**

10 If the piston sticks in its bore and cannot be displaced, the caliper will have to be replaced with a new one.

Caution: Do not try to remove the piston by levering it out, or by using pliers or any other grips.

11 Remove the dust seal and the piston seal from the piston bore using a wooden or plastic tool to avoid scratching the bore **(see illustration 3.11)**. Discard the seals as new ones must be fitted on reassembly.

12 Clean the piston and bore with clean brake fluid of the specified type. If compressed air is available, blow it through the fluid galleries in the caliper to ensure they are clear and use it to dry the parts thoroughly (make sure it is filtered and unlubricated).

Caution: Do not, under any circumstances, use a petroleum-based solvent to clean brake parts.

13 Inspect the caliper bore and pistons for signs of corrosion, nicks and burrs and loss of plating. If surface defects are present, the caliper assembly must be renewed. If the necessary measuring equipment is available, compare the dimensions of the caliper bore and piston to those specified at the beginning of this Chapter, and install a new caliper if necessary. If the caliper is in poor condition, the master cylinder should also be checked.

14 Clean all traces of corrosion off the slider

7

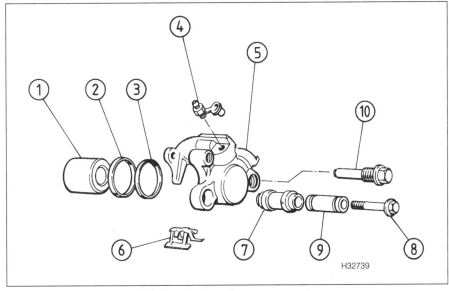

7.7 **Rear brake caliper components**

1 Piston
2 Dust seal
3 Fluid seal
4 Bleed valve
5 Caliper body
6 Pad spring
7 Boot
8 Slider pin
9 Sleeve
10 Caliper mounting bolt

H32739

7.18 Install the pad spring in the caliper

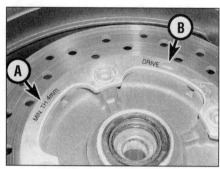
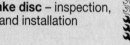

8.1 Disc minimum thickness (A) and direction of rotation arrow (B)

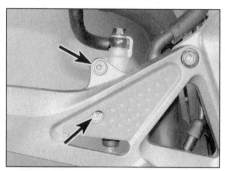

9.2 Master cylinder mounting bolts

pin and its bore in the caliper sleeve. Replace the pin with new one if it is worn. If the pin is loose, remove it and clean the threads. Apply a suitable non-permanent thread locking compound and tighten it to the specified torque. It is advisable to renew the rubber dust boots, particularly if they are damaged or deteriorated.

15 Lubricate the new piston seal with clean brake fluid and install it in its groove in the caliper bore.

16 Lubricate the new dust seal with clean brake fluid and install it in its groove in the caliper bore.

17 Lubricate the piston with clean brake fluid and install it, closed-end first, into the caliper bore. Using your thumbs, push the piston all the way in, making sure it enters the bore squarely.

18 Clean the pad spring and ensure it fits firmly in the caliper, otherwise replace it with a new one **(see illustration)**.

19 Fit the slider pin sleeve boot on the caliper bracket and the mounting bolt sleeve boot on the caliper. Apply a smear of copper-based grease to the slider pin.

Installation

20 Slide the caliper onto the bracket, pivot it down over the brake disc and install the new caliper mounting bolt **(see illustration 7.5)**; or clean the threads of the original bolt and apply fresh locking compound. If they weren't removed, make sure the pads sit squarely each side of the disc.

21 Tighten the caliper mounting bolt to the specified torque setting.

22 If removed, connect the brake hose to the caliper, using new sealing washers on each side of the banjo fitting. Align the fitting as noted on removal **(see illustration 7.3)**. Tighten the banjo bolt to the torque setting specified at the beginning of this Chapter.

23 Install the bolts securing the brake hose to the caliper bracket and swingarm and tighten them to the specified torque setting.

24 If removed, install the brake pads (see Section 6).

25 Top-up the hydraulic reservoir with DOT 4 brake fluid (see *Daily (pre-ride) checks*) and bleed the system as described in Section 11. Check that there are no fluid leaks and

thoroughly test the operation of the brake before riding the motorcycle.

8 Rear brake disc – inspection, removal and installation

Inspection

1 Refer to Section 4 of this Chapter, noting that the dial gauge should be attached to the swingarm. The disc minimum thickness and direction of rotation arrow are stamped on the disc **(see illustration)**.

Removal

2 Remove the rear wheel (see Section 15). *Caution: Don't lay the wheel down and allow it to rest on the disc or the sprocket – they could become warped. Set the wheel on wood blocks so the wheel rim supports the weight of the wheel.*

3 If you are not replacing the disc with a new one, mark the relationship of the disc to the wheel so that it can be installed in the same position. Unscrew the disc retaining bolts, loosening them evenly and a little at a time in a criss-cross pattern to avoid distorting the disc, then remove the disc from the wheel. *Note: Honda recommend using new bolts when the old ones are removed. This is because the bolts are pre-treated with a locking compound. It is possible, however, to clean up the old bolts and reinstall them using a suitable non-permanent thread locking compound that is commercially available.*

Installation

4 Before installing the disc, make sure there is no dirt or corrosion where the disc seats on the hub, particularly right in the angle of the seat. If the disc does not sit flat when it is bolted down, it will appear to be warped when checked or when the rear brake is used.

5 Install the disc on the wheel; align previously applied register marks if you are reinstalling the original disc.

6 Install the new bolts (or clean the threads of the original bolts and apply fresh locking compound) and tighten them evenly and a little at a time in a criss-cross pattern to the

torque setting specified at the beginning of this Chapter. Clean the brake disc using acetone or brake system cleaner. If a new brake disc has been installed, remove any protective coating from its working surfaces.

7 Install the rear wheel (see Section 15).

8 Operate the brake pedal several times to bring the pads into contact with the disc. Check the operation of the brake carefully before riding the motorcycle.

9 Rear brake master cylinder – removal, overhaul and installation

Warning: If the brake master cylinder is in need of an overhaul all old brake fluid should be flushed from the system. Disassembly, overhaul and reassembly of the brake master cylinder must be done in a spotlessly clean work area to avoid contamination and possible failure of the brake hydraulic system components. Do not, under any circumstances, use petroleum-based solvents to clean parts. Use clean brake fluid of the type specified, dedicated brake cleaner or denatured alcohol only, as described. To prevent damage from spilled brake fluid, always cover paintwork when working on the braking system.

Removal

Note: *If the master cylinder is being overhauled (usually due to sticking or poor action, or fluid leaks) read through the entire procedure first and make sure you have obtained all the new parts required, including some new DOT 4 brake fluid.*

1 Remove the seat and frame side panels (see Chapter 8).

2 Loosen the bolts securing the master cylinder to the right-hand footrest bracket but leave them finger-tight **(see illustration)**.

3 Remove the two bolts which retain the right-hand footrest bracket to the frame and carefully turn the bracket around avoiding any strain on the brake light switch wiring (if necessary disconnect the wiring at the connector under the seat) or hydraulic hoses.

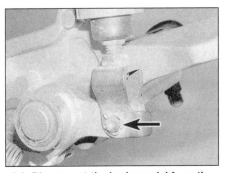

9.3 Disconnect the brake pedal from the master cylinder at the clevis (arrowed)

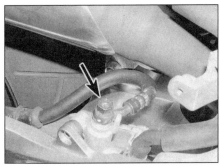

9.4 Brake hose banjo bolt (arrowed). Note the alignment of the hose

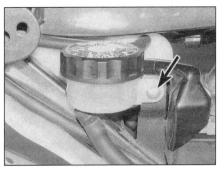

9.5 Fluid reservoir mounting bolt (arrowed)

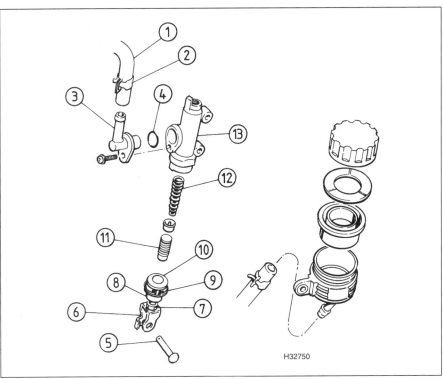

9.9 Rear master cylinder components

1 Reservoir hose	6 Clevis	10 Pushrod
2 Hose clamp	7 Locknut	11 Piston/seal
3 Hose union	8 Boot	12 Spring
4 O-ring	9 Circlip	13 Master cylinder
5 Clevis pin		

H32750

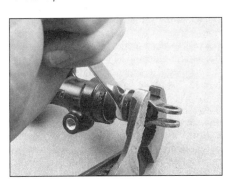

9.10a Loosen the locknut and unscrew the clevis . . .

9.10b . . . then remove the boot from the pushrod

Remove the split pin from the clevis pin securing the brake pedal to the master cylinder pushrod. Remove the clevis pin and separate the clevis from the pedal **(see illustration)**. Temporarily refit the footrest bracket to the frame and tighten the mounting bolts finger-tight.

4 Unscrew the brake hose banjo bolt and detach the banjo fitting, noting its alignment with the master cylinder **(see illustration)**. Once disconnected, secure the hose in an upright position to minimise fluid loss, and wrap a clean plastic bag tightly around the end to prevent dirt entering the system. Discard the sealing washers as new ones must be fitted on reassembly.

5 Ensure the fluid reservoir cap is secure, then remove the bolt securing the reservoir to the frame **(see illustration)**.

6 Support the master cylinder, then fully unscrew the bolts securing the master cylinder to the footrest bracket and remove them. Lift the master cylinder and the fluid reservoir away from the motorcycle.

7 Remove the reservoir cap, diaphragm plate and diaphragm and drain the brake fluid into a suitable container.

8 Release the clip securing the reservoir hose to the union on the master cylinder and detach the hose. Wipe any remaining fluid out of the reservoir with a clean rag and replace the diaphragm, diaphragm plate and cap temporarily.

Overhaul

9 Remove the reservoir hose union retaining screw and washer, then remove the union from the master cylinder; discard the O-ring as a new one must be used on reassembly **(see illustration)**. Inspect the reservoir hose for cracks or splits and renew it if necessary. Check the hose clips; renew them if they are sprained or corroded.

10 If required, measure the position of the clevis on the pushrod, then loosen the locknut and thread the clevis and nut off the pushrod **(see illustration)**. Carefully remove the boot from the end of the master cylinder to reveal the pushrod retaining circlip **(see illustration)**.

11 Depress the pushrod and use circlip pliers to remove the circlip, then slide out the pushrod, piston assembly and spring, noting

7

9.11 Depress the pushrod and remove the circlip

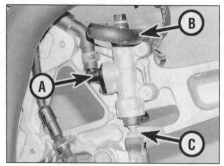

9.21 Ensure the reservoir hose (A), brake hose (B) and pushrod clevis (C) are properly connected

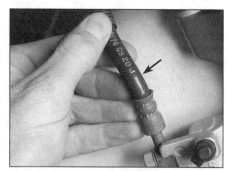

10.2 Flex the brake hoses and check for cracks, bulges and leaks

how they fit **(see illustration)**. If they are difficult to remove, apply low pressure compressed air to the brake fluid outlet. Lay the parts out in the proper order to prevent confusion during reassembly.

12 Clean all parts with clean brake fluid. If compressed air is available, blow it through the fluid galleries to ensure they are clear and use it to dry the parts thoroughly (make sure the air is filtered and unlubricated).

Caution: Do not, under any circumstances, use a petroleum-based solvent to clean brake parts.

13 Check the master cylinder bore for corrosion, scratches, nicks and score marks. If the necessary measuring equipment is available, compare the diameter of the bore and piston to that given in the Specifications at the beginning of this Chapter. If damage or wear is evident, the master cylinder must be replaced with a new one. If the master cylinder is in poor condition, then the caliper should be checked as well.

14 The boot, circlip, piston assembly and spring are included in the master cylinder rebuild kit. Use all of the new parts, regardless of the apparent condition of the old ones. Fit them according to the layout of the old piston assembly **(see illustration 9.9)**.

15 Fit the spring into the master cylinder with its narrow end facing out. Lubricate the piston assembly with clean brake fluid and fit the assembly into the master cylinder, making sure it is the correct way round. Make sure the lips on the cup do not turn inside out when they are slipped into the bore. Install the pushrod.

16 Depress the pushrod and install the circlip, making sure it is properly located in its groove **(see illustration 9.11)**.

17 Install the boot, making sure the lip is seated properly in the groove.

18 If removed, thread the clevis locknut and the clevis onto the pushrod. Position the clevis as noted on removal (see Step 10), then tighten the locknut securely.

19 Fit a new O-ring onto the reservoir hose union, then press the union into the master cylinder and secure it with the washer and screw.

20 Inspect the reservoir cap, diaphragm plate

and diaphragm and renew any parts if they are damaged or deteriorated.

Installation

21 Installation is the reverse of removal, noting the following:
● Fit the master cylinder onto the footrest bracket and tighten its mounting bolts to the torque setting specified at the beginning of this Chapter.
● Secure the master cylinder pushrod clevis pin with a new split pin.
● Connect the brake hose to the master cylinder, using new sealing washers on each side of the banjo fitting. Align the fitting as noted on removal **(see illustration 9.4)**.
● Tighten the banjo bolt to the specified torque setting.
● Fill the fluid reservoir with new DOT 4 brake fluid (see *Daily (pre-ride) checks*). Refer to Section 11 of this Chapter and bleed the air from the system.
● Ensure the reservoir diaphragm is correctly seated, and that the cap is tightened securely.
● Check the operation of the rear brake before riding the motorcycle.

10 Brake hoses and unions – inspection and renewal

Inspection

1 Brake hose condition should be checked regularly and the hoses renewed every four years.

2 Twist and flex the hoses while looking for cracks, bulges and seeping hydraulic fluid **(see illustration)**. Check extra carefully around the areas where the hoses connect with the banjo fittings, as these are common areas for hose failure.

3 Check the banjo fittings connected to the brake hoses. If the fittings are rusted, scratched or cracked, fit new hoses.

Renewal

4 The brake hoses have banjo fittings on each end. Cover the surrounding area with plenty of rags and unscrew the banjo bolt at

each end of the hose, noting the alignment of the fitting with the master cylinder or brake caliper **(see illustrations 5.4 and 7.3)**. Free the hose from any clips or guides and remove it, noting its routing. Discard the sealing washers. **Note:** *Do not operate the brake lever or pedal while a brake hose is disconnected.*

5 Position the new hose, making sure it is not twisted or otherwise strained, and ensure that it is correctly routed through any clips or guides and is clear of all moving components.

6 Check that the fittings align correctly, then install the banjo bolts, using new sealing washers on both sides of the fittings. Tighten the banjo bolts to the torque setting specified at the beginning of this Chapter.

7 Flush the old brake fluid from the system, refill with new DOT 4 brake fluid (see *Daily (pre-ride) checks*) and bleed the air from the system (see Section 11).

8 Check the operation of the brakes before riding the motorcycle.

11 Brake system – bleeding and fluid change

Air bleeding

1 Bleeding the brakes is simply the process of removing air from the brake fluid reservoir, the hose and the brake caliper. Bleeding is necessary whenever a brake system hydraulic connection is loosened, after a component or hose is renewed, or when the master cylinder or caliper is overhauled. Leaks in the system may also allow air to enter, but leaking brake fluid will reveal their presence and warn you of the need for repair.

2 To bleed the brakes, you will need some new DOT 4 brake fluid, a length of clear vinyl or plastic hose, a small container partially filled with clean brake fluid, some rags and a spanner to fit the brake caliper bleed valve.

3 Cover the fuel tank and other painted components to prevent damage in the event that brake fluid is spilled.

4 Remove the reservoir cover or cap, diaphragm plate and diaphragm and slowly pump the brake lever (front brake) or pedal

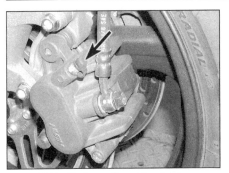

11.5a Brake caliper bleed valve

11.5b Attach one end of the hose to the bleed valve, submerge the other in the fluid container

brake lever or pedal gradually. Keep the reservoir topped-up with new fluid to above the LOWER level at all times or air may enter the system and greatly increase the length of the task. Repeat the process until new fluid can be seen emerging from the bleed valve.

14 Disconnect the hose, then tighten the

HAYNES HiNT	*Old brake fluid is invariably much darker in colour than new fluid, making it easy to see when all old fluid has been expelled from the system.*

(rear brake) a few times, until no air bubbles can be seen floating up from the holes in the bottom of the reservoir. This bleeds the air from the master cylinder end of the line. Temporarily refit the reservoir cap.

5 Pull the dust cap off the bleed valve then attach one end of the clear vinyl or plastic hose to the bleed valve and submerge the other end in the clean brake fluid in the container **(see illustrations)**. **Note:** *To avoid damaging the bleed valve during the procedure, loosen it and then tighten it temporarily with a ring spanner before attaching the hose. With the hose attached, the valve can then be opened and closed with an open-ended spanner.*

6 Check the fluid level in the reservoir. Do not allow the fluid level to drop below the lower mark during the procedure **(see illustrations)**.

7 Carefully pump the brake lever or pedal three or four times and hold it in (front) or down (rear) while opening the caliper bleed valve. When the valve is opened, brake fluid will flow out of the caliper into the clear tubing, and the lever will move toward the handlebar, or the pedal will move down. If there is air in the system there should be air bubbles in the brake fluid coming out of the caliper.

8 Tighten the bleed valve, then release the brake lever or pedal gradually. Top-up the reservoir and repeat the process until no air bubbles are visible in the brake fluid leaving the caliper, and the lever or pedal is firm when applied. On completion, disconnect the hose, then tighten the bleed valve to the torque

setting specified at the beginning of this Chapter and install the dust cap. If bleeding the front brake, go on to bleed air from the other caliper.

9 Top-up the reservoir, install the diaphragm,

HAYNES HiNT	*If it is not possible to produce a firm feel to the lever or pedal, the fluid may be aerated. Let the brake*

fluid in the system stabilise for a few hours and then repeat the procedure when the tiny bubbles in the system have settled out.

diaphragm plate and cap, and wipe up any spilled brake fluid. Check the entire system for fluid leaks.

10 Check the operation of the brakes before riding the motorcycle.

Fluid change

11 Changing the brake fluid is a similar process to bleeding the brakes and requires the same materials plus a suitable tool for siphoning the fluid out of the reservoir. Also ensure that the container is large enough to take all the old fluid when it is flushed out of the system.

12 Follow Steps 3 and 5, then remove the reservoir cap, diaphragm plate and diaphragm and siphon the old fluid out of the reservoir. Fill the reservoir with new brake fluid, then follow Step 7.

13 Tighten the bleed valve, then release the

bleed valve to the specified torque setting and install the dust cap.

15 Top-up the reservoir, install the diaphragm, diaphragm plate and cap, and wipe up any spilled brake fluid. Attach the rear brake hydraulic reservoir to the frame and tighten the retaining screw securely. Check the entire system for fluid leaks.

16 Check the operation of the brakes before riding the motorcycle.

12 Wheels – inspection and repair

1 In order to carry out a proper inspection of the wheels, it is necessary to support the bike upright so that the wheel being inspected is raised off the ground. Position the motorcycle on an auxiliary stand. Clean the wheels thoroughly to remove mud and dirt that may interfere with the inspection procedure or mask defects. Make a general check of the wheels (see Chapter 1) and tyres (see *Daily (pre-ride) checks*).

2 Attach a dial gauge to the fork or the swingarm and position its tip against the side of the wheel rim. Spin the wheel slowly and check the axial (side-to-side) runout at the rim **(see illustration)**.

3 In order to accurately check radial (out of round) runout with the dial gauge, remove the wheel from the machine, and the tyre from the wheel. With the axle clamped in a vice and the dial gauge positioned on the top of the rim, the wheel can be rotated to check the runout.

4 An easier, though slightly less accurate,

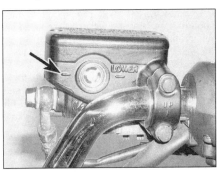

11.6a Do not allow the fluid to fall below the lower level mark (arrowed) in the front . . .

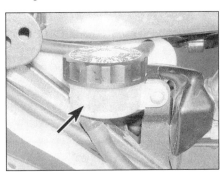

11.6b . . . or rear brake fluid reservoir

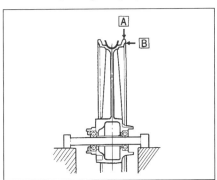

12.2 Check the wheel for radial (out-of-round) runout (A) and axial (side-to-side) runout (B)

7

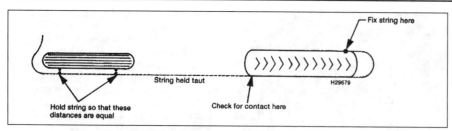

13.5 Wheel alignment check using string

method is to attach a stiff wire pointer to the fork or the swingarm and position the end a fraction of an inch from the edge of the wheel rim where the wheel and tyre join. If the wheel is true, the distance from the pointer to the rim will be constant as the wheel is rotated. **Note:** *If wheel runout is excessive, check the wheel bearings very carefully before renewing the wheel.*

5 The wheels should also be inspected for cracks, flat spots on the rim and other damage. Look very closely for dents in the area where the tyre bead contacts the rim. Dents in this area may prevent complete sealing of the tyre against the rim, which leads to deflation of the tyre over a period of time. If damage is evident, or if runout in either direction is excessive, the wheel will have to be replaced with a new one. Never attempt to repair a damaged cast alloy wheel.

13 Wheels – alignment check

1 Misalignment of the wheels due to a bent frame or forks can cause strange and possibly serious handling problems. If the frame or forks are at fault, repair by a frame specialist or replacement with new parts are the only options.
2 To check wheel alignment you will need an assistant, a length of string or a perfectly straight piece of wood and a ruler. A plumb bob or spirit level for checking that the wheels are vertical will also be required.
3 In order to make a proper check of the wheels it is necessary to support the bike in an upright position, using an auxiliary stand. First ensure that the chain adjuster markings coincide on each side of the swingarm (see Chapter 1, Section 1). Next, measure the width of both tyres at their widest points.

Subtract the smaller measurement from the larger measurement, then divide the difference by two. The result is the amount of offset that should exist between the front and rear tyres on both sides of the machine.
4 If a string is used, have your assistant hold one end of it about halfway between the floor and the rear axle, with the string touching the back edge of the rear tyre sidewall.
5 Run the other end of the string forward and pull it tight so that it is roughly parallel to the floor **(see illustration)**. Slowly bring the string into contact with the front edge of the rear tyre sidewall, then turn the front wheel until it is parallel with the string. Measure the distance from the front tyre sidewall to the string.
6 Repeat the procedure on the other side of the motorcycle. The distance from the front tyre sidewall to the string should be equal on both sides.
7 As previously mentioned, a perfectly straight length of wood or metal bar may be substituted for the string **(see illustration)**.
8 If the distance between the string and tyre is greater on one side, or if the rear wheel appears to be out of alignment, have your machine checked by a Honda dealer.
9 If the front-to-back alignment is correct, the wheels still may be out of alignment vertically.
10 Using a plumb bob or spirit level, check the rear wheel to make sure it is vertical. To do this, hold the string of the plumb bob against the tyre upper sidewall and allow the weight to settle just off the floor. If the string touches both the upper and lower tyre sidewalls and is perfectly straight, the wheel is vertical. If it is not, adjust the stand until it is.
11 Once the rear wheel is vertical, check the front wheel in the same manner. If both wheels are not perfectly vertical, the frame and/or major suspension components are bent.

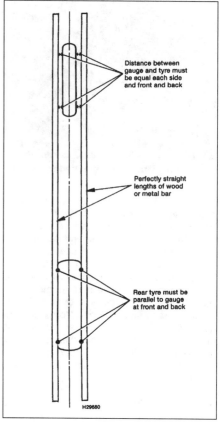

13.7 Wheel alignment check using a straight-edge

14 Front wheel – removal and installation

Removal

1 Using an auxiliary stand, support the motorcycle securely in an upright position with the front wheel off the ground.
2 Displace the left-hand front brake caliper (see Section 3). **Note:** *Do not operate the brake lever while the caliper is off the disc.*
3 Loosen the axle pinch bolt on the bottom of the right-hand fork slider, then unscrew the axle bolt and remove it **(see illustrations)**.
4 Unscrew the left-hand axle pinch bolt, then support the wheel and withdraw the axle from the left-hand side. **Note:** *Insert a suitable bar through the holes in the end of the axle to help pull it out* **(see illustration)**.
5 Remove the wheel from between the forks, then remove the axle spacers from each side of the wheel, noting how they fit inside the bearing seals **(see illustrations)**.
Caution: Don't lay the wheel down and allow it to rest on either of the brake discs – the disc could become warped. Set the wheel on wood blocks so the wheel rim supports the weight of the wheel, or keep the wheel upright. Don't operate the brake lever with the wheel removed.

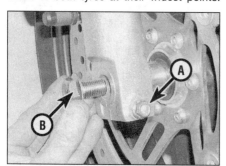

14.3 Loosen the pinch bolt (A) and unscrew the axle bolt (B)

14.4 Unscrew the pinch bolt and withdraw the axle

14.5a Remove the wheel spacer from the left . . .

14.5b . . . and right-hand sides

14.10 Install the axle from the left-hand side

Installation

9 The direction of wheel rotation is denoted by an arrow stamped into the brake disc (see Section 4). Apply lithium-based grease to the insides of the bearing seals, then fit the axle spacers into the seals. **Note:** *The right-hand spacer is longer than the left-hand spacer.*

10 Apply a thin coat of lithium-based grease to the axle, then lift the wheel into position between the forks, making sure the right-hand brake disc passes between the pads in the caliper, and slide the axle in from the left-hand side **(see illustration)**. Ensure the spacers remain in place.

11 Ensure the axle aligns correctly with the right-hand fork and tap it fully in with a soft-faced hammer **(see illustrations)**.

12 Fit the axle bolt, then hold the axle **(see illustration 14.4)** and tighten the bolt to the torque setting specified at the beginning of this Chapter.

13 Tighten the right-hand axle pinch bolt to the specified torque setting.

14 Install the left-hand brake caliper (see Section 3).

15 Apply the front brake to bring the pads back into contact with the discs. Move the motorcycle off its stand, apply the front brake and compress the front forks a few times to align the wheel and the suspension.

16 Tighten the left-hand axle pinch bolt to the specified torque setting

17 Check the operation of the front brake before riding the motorcycle.

14.11a Axle should be pressed fully in to the left . . .

14.11b . . . and right-hand fork sliders

6 Clean the axle and remove any corrosion using steel wool. Check the axle for straightness by rolling it on a flat surface such as a piece of plate glass. If available, place the axle in V-blocks and check for runout using a dial gauge. If the axle runout exceeds the service limit, renew it.

7 Wipe any old grease off the bearing seals and check the condition of the seals and the wheel bearings (see Section 16).

8 Clean the axle spacers and remove any corrosion with steel wool. The spacers should be perfectly smooth where they locate in the seals.

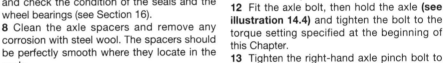

15 Rear wheel – removal and installation

Removal

1 Using an auxiliary stand, support the motorcycle securely in an upright position with the rear wheel off the ground.

2 Loosen the rear axle nut, then loosen the chain adjuster locknuts and turn the adjusters in to provide some slack in the chain **(see illustration)**.

3 Lift the chain off the sprocket **(see illustration)**.

4 Unscrew the axle nut and remove the nut, washer and right-hand chain adjuster plate **(see illustration)**.

15.2a Loosen the axle nut . . .

15.2b . . . and slacken the chain

15.3 Lift the chain off the sprocket

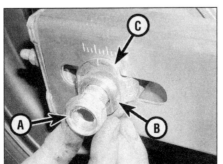

15.4 Remove the nut (A), washer (B) and chain adjuster plate (C)

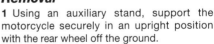

7

15.12a Install the left . . .

15.12b . . . and right-hand axle spacers

5 Support the wheel, then withdraw the axle along with the left-hand chain adjuster plate and lower the wheel to the ground. Slide the adjuster plate off the axle, noting how it fits.
6 Remove the wheel from inside the swingarm.
7 Note how the brake caliper bracket locates on a lug on the inside of the swingarm. Secure the caliper bracket with a cable tie to prevent it falling and straining the brake hose.
8 Remove the axle spacers from each side of the wheel, noting how they fit inside the bearing seals.
Caution: Don't lay the wheel down and allow it to rest on the disc or the sprocket – they could become warped. Set the wheel on wood blocks so the wheel rim supports the weight of the wheel, or keep the wheel upright. Don't operate the brake pedal with the wheel removed.
9 Clean the axle and remove any corrosion using steel wool. Check the axle for

straightness by rolling it on a flat surface such as a piece of plate glass. If available, place the axle in V-blocks and check for runout using a dial gauge (see *Tools and Workshop Tips* in the Reference Section. If axle runout exceeds the service limit, renew it.
10 Check the condition of the wheel bearings and seals (see Section 16).
11 Clean the axle spacers and remove any corrosion with steel wool. The spacers should be perfectly smooth where they locate in the seals.

Installation

12 Apply lithium-based grease to the insides of the bearing seals, then fit the axle spacers into the seals. **Note:** *The left-hand spacer has a flange on its outer edge, the right-hand spacer is plain* **(see illustrations)**.
13 Ensure that the brake caliper bracket is properly located on the swingarm and that the chain tensioners are correctly positioned in the ends of the swingarm **(see illustration)**.

Note: *The rounded corners of the tensioner end plates should face outwards.*
14 Manoeuvre the wheel into place in the swingarm ensuring the brake disc passes between the brake pads **(see illustration)**.
15 Slide the left-hand chain adjuster plate onto the axle and apply a thin coat of lithium-based grease to the axle.
16 Lift the wheel into position, making sure the axle spacers remain in place, and slide the axle through from the left-hand side **(see illustration)**. Ensure the axle passes through the chain tensioners and the caliper bracket.
17 Locate the tab on the front edge of the left-hand chain adjuster plate in the slot in the swingarm, then fit the right-hand chain adjuster plate with the tab on its front edge in the slot in the swingarm **(see illustration)**.
18 Fit the washer and the axle nut finger-tight **(see illustration 15.4)**. Engage the drive chain on the sprocket **(see illustration)**.
19 Adjust the chain tension as described in Chapter 1, then tighten the axle nut to the torque setting specified at the beginning of this Chapter.
20 Apply the rear brake to bring the pads into contact with the disc.
21 Check the operation of the rear brake before riding the motorcycle.

16 Wheel bearings – inspection, removal and installation

Caution: Don't lay the wheel down and allow it to rest on the disc or the sprocket – they could become warped. Set the wheel on wood blocks so the wheel rim supports the weight of the wheel, or keep the wheel upright. Don't operate the brake pedal with the wheel removed.
Note: *Always renew the wheel bearings in sets, never individually. Avoid using a high pressure cleaner on the wheel bearing area.*

Front wheel bearings

1 Remove the wheel (see Section 14).
2 Inspect the bearings – check that the inner race turns smoothly and that the outer race is a tight fit in the hub (see *Tools and Workshop Tips (Section 5)* in the Reference Section).

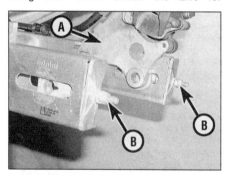

15.13 Ensure the brake caliper (A) and chain adjusters (B) are in place

15.14 Ensure the disc fits squarely between the brake pads

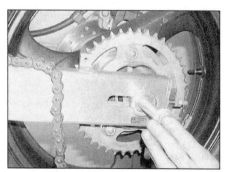

15.16 Install the axle

15.17 Locate the chain adjuster plate tabs (arrowed) in the swingarm slot

15.18 Lift the chain onto the sprocket

16.3 Lever the seals out carefully

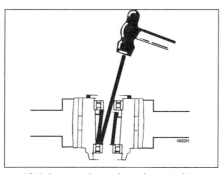

16.4 Locate the rod as shown when driving out the bearing

16.7 Driving in a new bearing

Note: *Honda recommends that the bearings are not removed unless they are going to be replaced with new ones.*

3 To renew the bearings, first lever out the grease seals from both sides of the hub using a large, flat-bladed screwdriver and a piece of wood. Take care not to damage the hub **(see illustration)**. Discard the seals and obtain new ones for refitting.

4 Use a metal rod (preferably a brass punch) inserted through the centre of the bearing on one side of the hub, to tap evenly around the outer race of the bearing on the other side **(see illustration)**. The bearing spacer will come out with the bearing.

5 Turn the wheel over and drive out the remaining bearing using the same procedure.

6 Thoroughly clean the hub area of the wheel with a suitable solvent and inspect the bearing seats for scoring and wear. If the seats are damaged, consult a Honda dealer before reassembling the wheel.

7 Install a new bearing into its seat in one side of the hub, with the marked or sealed side facing outwards. Using an old bearing, a bearing driver or a socket large enough to contact the outer race of the bearing, drive it in until it's completely seated **(see illustration)**.

8 Turn the wheel over, install the bearing spacer and drive the other new bearing into place.

9 Lubricate the new grease seals with lithium-based grease and press them into the hub,

using a bearing driver or a suitable socket, then level the seals with the inner rim of the hub with a small block of wood **(see illustrations)**.

10 Clean the brake discs using acetone or brake system cleaner, then install the wheel (see Section 14).

Rear wheel bearings

11 Remove the wheel (see Section 15) and lift the sprocket coupling out of the hub.

12 Inspect the bearings in both sides of the hub – check that the inner race turns smoothly and that the outer race is a tight fit in the hub (see *Tools and Workshop Tips (Section 5)* in the *Reference* section). **Note:** *Honda recommends that the bearings are not removed unless they are going to be replaced with new ones.*

13 To renew the bearings, first lever out the grease seal from the right-hand side of the hub using a large, flat-bladed screwdriver and a piece of wood. Take care not to damage the hub **(see illustration 16.3)**. Discard the grease seal and obtain a new one for refitting.

14 Use a metal rod (preferably a brass punch) inserted through the centre of the bearing on one side of the hub, to tap evenly around the outer race of the bearing on the other side **(see illustration 16.4)**. The bearing spacer will come out with the bearing.

15 Turn the wheel over and drive out the remaining bearing using the same procedure.

16 Thoroughly clean the hub area of the

wheel with a suitable solvent and inspect the bearing seats for scoring and wear. If the seats are damaged, consult a Honda dealer before reassembling the wheel.

17 Install a new bearing into its seat in the left-hand side of the hub, with the marked or sealed side facing outwards. Using an old bearing, a bearing driver or a socket large enough to contact the outer race of the bearing, drive it in until it's completely seated **(see illustration 16.7)**.

18 Turn the wheel over, install the bearing spacer and drive the new right-hand bearing into place.

19 Lubricate the new grease seal with lithium-based grease and press it into the hub, using a bearing driver or a suitable socket, then level the seal with the inner rim of the hub with a small block of wood **(see illustrations 16.9a and b)**.

20 Clean the brake disc using acetone or brake system cleaner, then install the wheel (see Section 15).

Sprocket coupling bearing

21 Remove the rear wheel (see Section 15) and lift the sprocket coupling out of the hub.

22 Lever out the grease seal using a large flat-bladed screwdriver and a piece of wood. Take care not to damage the rim of the coupling **(see illustration)**. Discard the seal and obtain a new one for refitting.

23 Remove the inner spacer from the sprocket coupling. If it's tight, place the

16.9a Press the seals into place . . .

16.9b . . . and level them with a block of wood

16.22 Remove the sprocket coupling bearing seal . . .

7

coupling sprocket side up on the work surface and tap out the spacer **(see illustration)**.

24 Inspect the bearing – check that the inner race turns smoothly and that the outer race is a tight fit in the coupling (see *Tools and Workshop Tips (Section 5)* in the Reference Section). **Note:** *Honda recommends that the bearing is not removed unless it is going to be replaced with a new one.*

25 To remove the bearing, support the coupling on blocks of wood, sprocket side down, and drive the bearing out using a bearing driver or socket **(see illustration)**.

26 Thoroughly clean the bearing seat with a suitable solvent and inspect the seat for scoring and wear. If the seat is damaged, consult a Honda dealer before installing a new bearing.

27 Before fitting the new bearing in the coupling, place the bearing marked or sealed side down on the work surface and press the bearing sleeve into the bearing.

28 Install the bearing into the coupling, with the marked or sealed side facing out (sprocket side). Using a bearing driver or a socket large enough to contact the outer race of the bearing, drive it in until it is completely seated **(see illustration 16.7)**.

29 Lubricate the new grease seal with lithium-base grease and press it into the coupling, using a bearing driver or a suitable socket, then level the seal with the inner rim of the coupling with a small block of wood **(see illustrations 16.9a and b)**.

30 Inspect the sprocket coupling rubber dampers and O-ring (see Chapter 6, Section 16). Smear the O-ring with grease before installing the sprocket coupling onto the hub.

16.23 . . . then tap out the inner spacer

16.25 Support the coupling off the work surface to drive out the bearing

31 Fit the inner spacer to the sprocket coupling bearing, then install the sprocket coupling assembly in the wheel. Clean the brake disc using acetone or brake system cleaner and install the wheel (see Section 15).

---

17 Tyres – general information and fitting

General information

1 The wheels fitted on all models are designed to take tubeless tyres only. Tyre sizes are given in the Specifications at the beginning of this chapter.

2 Refer to *Daily (pre-ride) checks* at the beginning of this manual for tyre maintenance.

Fitting new tyres

3 When selecting new tyres, refer to the tyre information in the Owner's Handbook. Ensure that front and rear tyre types are compatible,

and of the correct size and speed rating; if necessary, seek advice from a Honda dealer or motorcycle tyre specialist **(see illustration)**.

4 It is recommended that tyres are fitted by a motorcycle tyre specialist and that this is not attempted in the home workshop. This is particularly relevant in the case of tubeless tyres because the force required to break the seal between the wheel rim and tyre bead is substantial, and is usually beyond the capabilities of an individual working with normal tyre levers. Additionally, the specialist will be able to balance the wheels after tyre fitting.

5 Note that punctured tubeless tyres can in some cases be repaired. Seek the advice of a Honda dealer or a motorcycle tyre specialist concerning tyre repairs.

6 Ensure that the direction of tyre rotation marked on the tyre sidewall corresponds with the normal direction of rotation of the wheel.

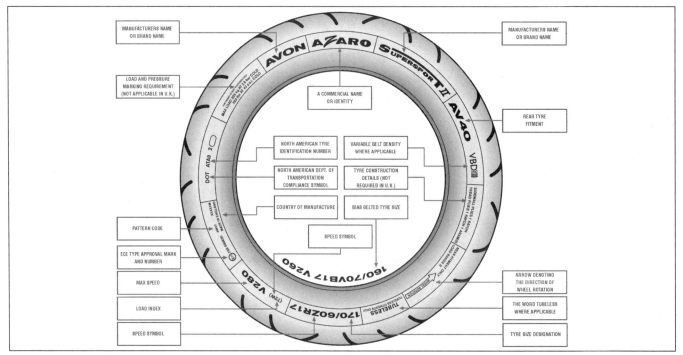

17.3 Common tyre sidewall markings

Chapter 8
Bodywork

Contents

Degrees of difficulty

| Easy, suitable for novice with little experience | | Fairly easy, suitable for beginner with some experience | | Fairly difficult, suitable for competent DIY mechanic | | Difficult, suitable for experienced DIY mechanic | | Very difficult, suitable for expert DIY or professional | |

Specifications

Torque settings

Front mudguard mounting bolts .... 12 Nm
Grab rail mounting bolt .... 26 Nm

1 General information

1 This Chapter covers the procedures necessary to remove and install the bodywork. Since many service and repair operations on these motorcycles require the removal of the bodywork, the procedures are grouped here and referred to from other Chapters.

2 In the case of damage to the bodywork, it is usually necessary to remove the broken component and renew it. The material that the body panels are composed of doesn't lend itself to conventional repair techniques. Note that there are however some companies that specialise in 'plastic welding' and there are a number of bodywork repair kits now available for motorcycles.

3 When attempting to remove any body panel, first study it closely, noting any fasteners and associated fittings, to be sure of returning everything to its correct place on installation. In some cases the aid of an assistant will be required when removing panels, to avoid the risk of damage to paintwork. Once the evident fasteners have been removed, try to withdraw the panel as described but DO NOT FORCE IT – if it will not release, check that all fasteners have been removed and try again.

4 To release trim clips, first push the centre of the head into the clip to release the spring pressure, then draw the complete clip out of

8

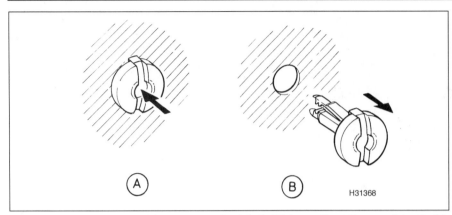

1.4 To release the clip, press its centre section fully in (A) then pull out the complete clip (B)

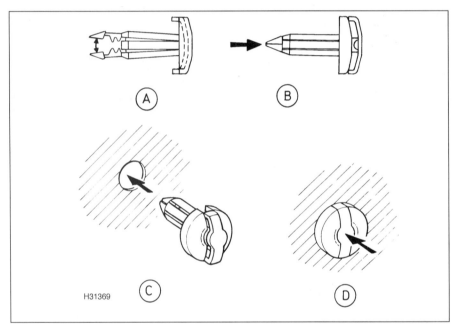

1.6 To install the clip, first get it ready for fitting by gently expanding and pushing its retaining tabs (A) into the clip until its centre section is fully extended (B). Fit the clip (C) and secure it in position by pressing the centre section in until it is flush with the clip body (D)

the panel **(see illustration)**. Where a panel engages another by means of tabs, be careful not to break the tab or its mating slot or to damage the paintwork. Remember that a few moments of patience at this stage will save you a lot of money in replacing broken panels!

5 When installing a body panel, first study it closely, noting any fasteners and associated fittings removed with it, to be sure of returning everything to its correct place. Check that all mounting brackets are straight and repair or renew them if necessary before attempting to install the panel. Check that all fasteners are in good condition, including all trim clips and rubber mounts; any of these must be renewed if faulty before the panel is reassembled.

6 To install trim clips, first ensure that the centre is pulled out of the clip head **(see illustration)**. Fit the clip into its hole, then push the centre in so that it is flush with the clip head. The clip should now be locked in place. Where assistance was required to remove a panel, make sure your assistant is on hand to help install it.

7 Tighten fasteners securely, but be careful not to overtighten any of them or the panel may break (not always immediately) due to the uneven stress.

2 Seat –
removal and installation

1 To remove the seat, insert the ignition key into the seat lock and turn the key clockwise. This will release the latch on the rear, underside of the seat.

2 Pull the seat backwards to disengage the seat hooks from the frame. Remove the seat, noting how the hooks engage the brackets on the frame **(see illustration)**.

3 Installation is the reverse of removal. Make sure the hooks locate under the brackets on the frame, then push down on the seat to engage the latch **(see illustration)**.

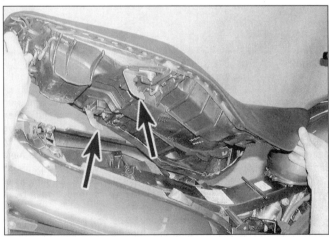

2.2 Hooks (arrowed) engage in brackets on the frame

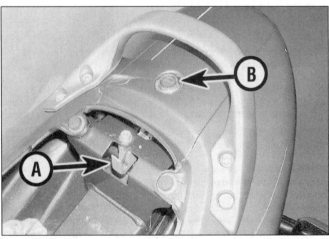

2.3 Latch (A) is released by lock (B)

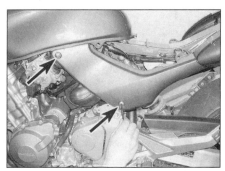

3.1a Undo the screws (arrowed) . . .

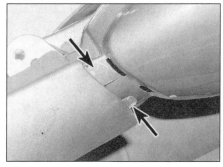

3.1b . . . and release the tabs (arrowed) from the seat cowling

4.2a Remove the caps from the bolts

3 Side panels –
removal and installation

1 Undo the panel retaining screws, then draw the panel forwards to release the tabs on the top rear corner from the slots in the seat cowling and remove the panel (see illustrations).
2 Installation is the reverse of removal. Note: *The upper retaining screw locates in a rubber mounted nut. If the screw is overtightened the nut will rotate in its mounting.*

4 Seat cowling –
removal and installation

Removal

1 Remove the seat (see Section 2) and the side panels (see Section 3).
2 Remove the caps from the grab rail mounting bolts, then unscrew the bolts securing the grab rail to the frame and remove the grab rail (see illustrations).
3 As described in Section 1, release the two trim clips from the underside of the seat cowling, either side of the rear mudguard (see illustration). Discard the clips if they are damaged and fit new ones on reassembly.
4 Remove the rubber caps from the rear cowling bolts, then unscrew the rear mounting

bolts and the front mounting bolts and remove them (see illustrations). Note the bushes in the bolt holes.
5 Carefully pull each side of the front of the cowling out away from the frame and draw the

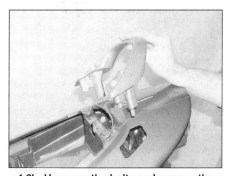

4.2b Unscrew the bolts and remove the grab rail

cowling rearwards and off the motorcycle, taking care not to bend the sides excessively (see illustration). Note how the arm on the seat lock engages the latch mechanism (see illustration).

4.3 Remove the trim clips

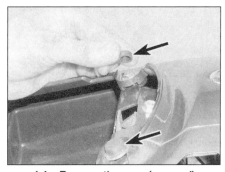

4.4a Remove the caps (arrowed)

4.4b Undo the rear mounting bolts . . .

4.4c . . . and the front mounting bolts (arrowed)

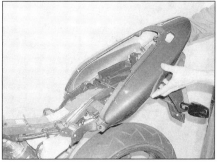

4.5a Ease the cowling rearwards off the bike

4.5b Note the position of the seat lock arm (arrowed)

8

4.6 Take care to locate the cowling correctly around the rear light

5.1 Lift the cover (A) and undo the locknut (B)

5.2 Unscrew the bolts (arrowed) to remove the mirror

Installation

6 Installation is the reverse of removal, noting the following:
● Take care not to pull the cowling sides apart excessively when locating it on the frame.
● Ensure the cowling is correctly located around the rear light unit (see illustration).
● Ensure that the bushes are in place in the mounting bolt holes and that the holes align with the threads in the frame without having to force the cowling into position.
● Fit the trim clips first and ensure they lock properly.
● Fit the rubber caps to the rear bolts to protect then underside of the seat.
● Tighten the grab rail mounting bolts to the torque setting specified at the beginning of this Chapter.

5 Rear view mirrors – removal and installation

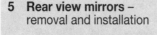

1 On CB600F models, lift the cover, where fitted, on the rear view mirror mounting locknut, loosen the locknut and unscrew the mirror from the handlebar bracket (see illustration).
2 On CB600FS models, unscrew the bolts retaining the mirror assembly to the upper fairing stay, then remove the bolts and the mirror (see illustration). Note: *The fairing and windshield are retained by the mirror assembly. Ensure that the insulating washers between the fairing stay and the windshield are in good condition and replace them if necessary to prevent damage to the windshield.*

3 Installation is the reverse of removal. On CB600F models, sit on the motorcycle and adjust the mirror before tightening the locknut. Final adjustment on all models can be made by tilting the mirror (see illustrations).

6 Fairing (CB600FS models) – removal and installation

Removal

1 Remove the rear view mirrors (see Section 5).
2 Undo the screws securing the windshield to the inside of the fairing and remove the screws and their washers (see illustration). Note: *Each screw is fitted with a plastic washer under the screw head and a rubber washer to protect the surface of the fairing.*
3 Undo the screws securing the fairing to the lower fairing stays and remove the screws, noting the arrangement of the collar and bushes (see illustration).
4 Pull the fairing forward carefully to disengage the pegs on the back of the headlight unit from the bushes in the fairing bracket (see illustrations). Disconnect the front turn signal wiring connectors on each side inside the fairing, the sidelight wiring connector and the headlight connector off the back of the headlight unit, then pull the fairing

5.3a On CB600F models, mirror head tilts

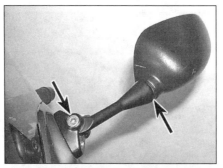

5.3b On CB600FS models, mirrors are adjustable in two places (arrowed)

6.2 Undo the windshield screws . . .

6.3 . . . and the lower fairing-to-bracket screws (arrowed)

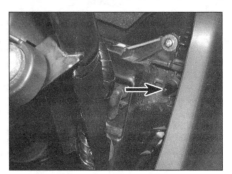

6.4a Pull the pegs (arrowed) . . .

6.4b . . . from the bushes (arrowed) in the fairing bracket

6.4c Disconnect the turn signal connectors . . .

6.4d . . . the sidelight connector . . .

forward and off the motorcycle **(see illustrations)**.

5 Lift each side of the windshield off the upper fairing stays and remove the windshield; remove the two insulating washers from each stay for safekeeping **(see illustrations)**.

6 If required, remove the turn signal assemblies (see Chapter 9).

7 If required, remove the headlight (see Chapter 9).

8 The fairing is constructed in three sections; left and right-hand panels and front panel. The individual sections of the fairing can be separated for replacement or repair by unscrewing the joining screws and easing the clips apart **(see illustration)**.

9 The fairing bracket is mounted on the steering head by two bolts. To remove the bracket, first remove the instrument cluster (see Chapter 9) and unclip the wiring loom for the instruments and the headlight. Unscrew the bracket mounting bolts and remove the bracket **(see illustrations)**.

10 The left and right-hand lower fairing stays can be removed from the frame by unscrewing the mounting bolts. Note

6.4e . . . and the headlight connector

6.4f Pull the fairing forward off the bike

6.5a Lift the windshield off the upper stays . . .

6.5b . . . and remove the washers (arrowed) for safekeeping

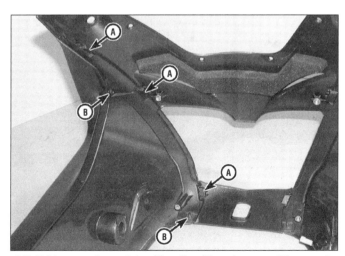

6.8 Fairing panels are joined by clips (A) and screws (B) on each side

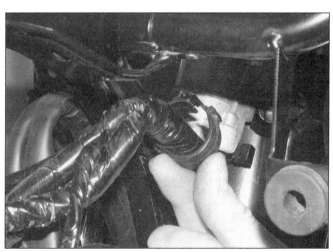

6.9a Unclip the wiring looms . . .

6.9b ... then unscrew the bolts (arrowed) ...

6.9c ... and remove the bracket

6.10 Remove the lower fairing stays

which way round the stays fit **(see illustration)**.

Installation

11 Installation is the reverse of removal, noting the following:
● Make sure the wiring looms are secured to the fairing frame.
● Make sure the wiring connectors are securely connected.
● When installing the fairing, ensure the two pegs on the back of the headlight unit locate in the bushes in the fairing bracket.
● Do not overtighten the fairing panel screws, especially the windshield screws.

● Turn the handlebars from lock to lock to ensure their movement is not restricted by the fairing.
● Test the operation of the lights before riding the motorcycle

7 Front mudguard – removal and installation

1 Unscrew and remove the bolts securing the brake hose assembly to the rear of the front fork sliders **(see illustration)**.

2 Unscrew and remove the bolts securing the mudguard to the fork sliders and remove the mudguard by withdrawing it forwards **(see illustration)**. Note the nuts for the brake hose assembly bolts are retained inside the mudguard **(see illustration)**.

3 Installation is the reverse of removal, noting the following:
● Ensure the brackets for the brake hose assembly are correctly aligned with the fork sliders.
● Tighten the mudguard mounting bolts to the torque setting specified at the beginning of this Chapter.

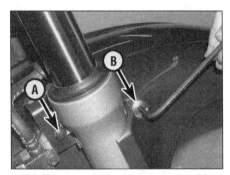

7.1 Unscrew the brake hose assembly bolts (A) and the mudguard bolts (B) ...

7.2a ... then withdraw the mudguard forwards

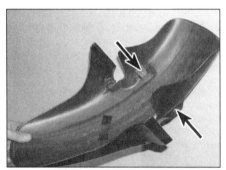

7.2b Nuts (arrowed) for the hose assembly are retained inside the mudguard

Chapter 9
Electrical system

Contents

Degrees of difficulty

Easy, suitable for novice with little experience		**Fairly easy,** suitable for beginner with some experience		**Fairly difficult,** suitable for competent DIY mechanic		**Difficult,** suitable for experienced DIY mechanic		**Very difficult,** suitable for expert DIY or professional	

Specifications

Battery

Capacity	12V, 6Ah
Voltage	
Fully charged @ 20°C	over 13.0V
Discharged @ 20°C	below 12.3V
Charging rate	
Normal	0.9A for 5 to 10 hrs
Quick	4.0A for 1 hr

Charging system

Current leakage	1.2 mA (max)
Regulated voltage output	13.0 to 15.5V @ 5,000 rpm
Alternator stator charging coil resistance	0.1 to 1.0 ohms

Starter motor

Brush length	
Standard	12.0 to 13.0 mm
Service limit (min)	4.5 mm

Fuses

Main	30A
Headlight	10A
Tail light, signal, brake light, horn	10A
Ignition, starter	10A
Fan	10A

Bulbs

Headlight	60/55W H4 halogen
Sidelight	4.0W
Brake/tail light	21/5W
Turn signal lights	21W
Warning lights	3.0W
Instrument lights	1.7W

Torque settings

Alternator rotor bolt	103 Nm
Alternator stator bolts	12 Nm
Alternator wiring clamp bolt	10 Nm
Ignition (main) switch bolts	25 Nm
Neutral switch	12 Nm
Oil pressure switch	12 Nm
Sidestand switch bolt	10 Nm

1 General information

All models have a 12-volt electrical system charged by a three-phase alternator with a separate regulator/rectifier.

The regulator maintains the charging system output within the specified range to prevent overcharging, and the rectifier converts the ac (alternating current) output of the alternator to dc (direct current) to power the lights and other components and to charge the battery. The alternator is mounted inside the left-hand engine cover

The starting system includes the starter motor, the relay, the battery and the various wires and switches. If the engine kill switch is in the RUN position and the ignition (main) switch is ON, the starting system will allow the starter motor to operate only if the transmission is in neutral (neutral light on) or, if the transmission is in gear, if the clutch lever is pulled into the handlebar and the sidestand is up. The starter motor is mounted on the engine unit behind the cylinders.

Note: *Keep in mind that electrical parts, once purchased, cannot be returned. To avoid unnecessary expense, make very sure the faulty component has been positively identified before buying a new part.*

2 Electrical system – fault finding

Warning: To prevent the risk of short circuits, the ignition (main) switch must always be OFF and the battery negative (-ve) terminal should be disconnected before any of the bike's other electrical components are disturbed. Don't forget to reconnect the terminal securely once work is finished or if battery power is needed for circuit testing.

1 A typical electrical circuit consists of an electrical component, the switches, relays, etc. related to that component and the wiring and connectors that hook the component to both the battery and the frame. To aid in locating a problem in any electrical circuit, refer to the wiring diagrams at the end of this Chapter.

2 Before tackling any faulty electrical circuit, first study the wiring diagram (see end of this Chapter) thoroughly to get a complete picture of what makes up that individual circuit. Trouble spots, for instance, can often be narrowed down by noting if other components related to that circuit are operating properly or not. If several components or circuits fail at one time, chances are the fault lies in the fuse or earth (ground) connection, as several circuits are often routed through the same fuse and earth (ground) connections.

3 Electrical problems often stem from simple causes, such as loose or corroded connections or a blown fuse. Prior to any electrical fault finding, always visually check the condition of the fuse, wires and connections in the problem circuit. Intermittent failures can be especially frustrating, since you can't always duplicate the failure when it's convenient to test. In such situations, a good practice is to clean all connections in the affected circuit, whether or not they appear to be good. All of the connections and wires should also be wiggled to check for looseness which can cause intermittent failure.

4 If testing instruments are going to be utilised, use the wiring diagram to plan where you will make the necessary connections in order to accurately pinpoint the trouble spot.

5 The basic tools needed for electrical fault finding include a battery and bulb test circuit, a continuity tester, a test light, and a jumper wire. A multimeter capable of reading volts, ohms and amps is also very useful as an alternative to the above, and is necessary for performing more extensive tests and checks.

Note: *The use of certain multimeters could lead to false readings being obtained, as could a low battery in the meter and contact between the meter probes and your fingers when the meter is in use.*

 Refer to Fault Finding Equipment in the Reference section for details of how to use electrical test equipment.

3 Battery – removal, installation, inspection and maintenance

Caution: Be extremely careful when handling or working around the battery. The electrolyte is very caustic and an explosive gas (hydrogen) is given off when the battery is charging.

Removal and installation

1 Remove the right-hand side panel (see Chapter 8) and unclip the battery strap **(see illustration)**.

3.1 Unclip the battery strap (arrowed)

3.2a Disconnect the negative (-ve) lead . . .

3.2b . . . then disconnect the positive (+ ve) lead

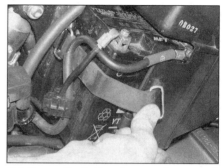

3.4 Ensure the battery is properly secured

2 Disconnect the battery negative (-ve) lead from the battery terminal and slide the battery rearwards to gain access to the positive (+ve) lead terminal, then disconnect the positive (+ve) lead **(see illustrations)**. Lift the battery from the bike, taking care not to loose the nuts from inside the terminal blocks when the battery is moved.

3 Before installation, clean the battery terminals, terminal screws, nuts and lead ends with a wire brush, knife or steel wool to ensure a good electrical connection. Reconnect the leads, connecting the positive (+ve) lead first.

HAYNES HINT *Battery corrosion can be kept to a minimum by applying a layer of petroleum jelly to the terminals after the cables have been connected.*

4 Replace the battery and secure the battery strap **(see illustration)**, then fit the right-hand side panel (see Chapter 8).

Inspection and maintenance

5 The battery fitted to the models covered in this manual is of the maintenance free (sealed) type and therefore does not require topping up. However, the following checks should still be regularly performed.

6 Check the battery terminals and leads for tightness and corrosion. If corrosion is evident, unscrew the terminal screws and disconnect the leads from the battery, disconnecting the negative (-ve) lead first. Wash the terminals and lead ends in a solution of baking soda and hot water and dry them thoroughly. If necessary, further clean the terminals and lead ends with a wire brush, knife or steel wool. Reconnect the leads, connecting the positive (+ve) lead first, and apply a thin coat of petroleum jelly to the connections to slow further corrosion.

7 The battery case should be kept clean to prevent current leakage, which can discharge the battery over a period of time (especially when it sits unused). Wash the outside of the case with a solution of baking soda and water. Rinse the battery thoroughly, then dry it.

8 Look for cracks in the case and renew the battery if any are found. If acid has been spilled on the frame or battery box, neutralise it with a baking soda and water solution, dry it thoroughly, then touch up any damaged paint.

9 If the motorcycle sits unused for long periods of time, disconnect the battery negative (-ve) terminal. Honda recommend that the battery is recharged once a month when the motorcycle is not being used (see Section 4).

10 The condition of the battery can be assessed by measuring the voltage present at the battery terminals with a multimeter. Connect the multimeter positive (+ve) probe to the battery positive (+ve) terminal, and the negative (-ve) probe to the battery negative (-ve) terminal. When fully charged there should be more than 13 volts present. If the voltage falls to 12.3 volts the battery must be removed, disconnecting the negative (-ve) lead first, and recharged (see Section 4).

4 Battery – charging

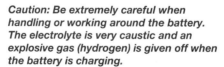

Caution: Be extremely careful when handling or working around the battery. The electrolyte is very caustic and an explosive gas (hydrogen) is given off when the battery is charging.

1 Ensure the charger is suitable for charging a 12V battery.

2 Remove the battery from the motorcycle (see Section 3). Connect the charger to the battery **BEFORE** switching the charger ON. Make sure that the positive (+ve) lead on the charger is connected to the positive (+ve) terminal on the battery, and the negative (-ve) lead is connected to the negative (-ve) terminal.

3 Few owners will have access to an expensive current controlled charger, so if a normal domestic charger is used check that after a possible initial peak, the charge rate falls to a safe level **(see illustration)**. If the battery becomes hot during charging **STOP**. Further charging will cause damage. **Note:** *In emergencies the battery can be charged at a high rate of up to 4.0 amps for a period of 1 hour. However, this is not recommended and the low amp (trickle) charge is by far the safer method of charging the battery.*

4 If the recharged battery discharges rapidly when left disconnected, it is likely that an internal short caused by physical damage or sulphation has occurred and a new battery will be required. A sound battery will tend to lose its charge at about 1% per day.

5 Install the battery (see Section 3).

6 If the motorcycle sits unused for long periods of time, Honda recommend recharging the battery once a month. If the battery is left on the motorcycle, disconnect the negative (-ve) lead, otherwise store the battery in a cool, dry place.

5 Fuses – check and renewal

1 The electrical system is protected by fuses of different ratings (see the Specifications at the beginning of this Chapter). All except the main fuse are housed in the fusebox which is

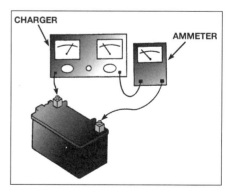

4.3 If the charger has no built-in ammeter, connect one in series as shown. DO NOT connect the ammeter between the battery terminals or it will be ruined

5.1a Location of the fusebox

5.1b Location of the main fuse

5.2a Unclip the lid to access the fuses

5.2b Disconnect the relay wiring connector to access the main fuse (arrowed)

5.3a Using the fuse puller to remove a fuse

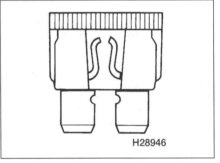

5.3b A blown fuse can be identified by a break in the element

located behind the left-hand side panel (see illustration). The main fuse is integral with the starter relay which is located behind the right-hand side panel (see illustration).

2 To access the fuses, remove the side panel (see Chapter 8) and unclip the fusebox lid (see illustration). To access the main fuse, remove the side panel (see Chapter 8) and disconnect the red starter relay wiring connector (see illustration).

3 The fuses can be removed and checked visually. Pull the fuse out with the puller supplied in the toolkit or a pair of suitable pliers (see illustration). A blown fuse is easily identified by a break in the element (see illustration). Each fuse is clearly marked with its rating and must only be replaced by a fuse of the correct rating. A spare fuse is housed in the fusebox, and a spare main fuse is housed in the bottom of the starter relay. If a spare fuse is used, always replace it with a new one so that a spare of each rating is carried on the motorcycle at all times.

 Warning: Never put in a fuse of a higher rating or bridge the terminals with any other substitute, however temporary it may be. Serious damage may be done to the circuit, or a fire may start.

4 If the new fuse blows, be sure to check the wiring circuit very carefully for evidence of a short-circuit. Look for bare wires and chafed, melted or burned insulation. If the fuse is renewed again without locating the cause, it will blow immediately.

5 Occasionally a fuse will blow or cause an open-circuit for no obvious reason. Corrosion of the fuse ends and fusebox terminals may occur and cause poor fuse contact. If this happens, remove the corrosion with a wire brush or steel wool, then spray the fuse ends and terminals with electrical contact cleaner.

6 Lighting system – check

1 The battery provides power for operation of the headlight, tail light, brake light and instrument cluster lights. If none of the lights operate, always check battery voltage before proceeding. Low battery voltage indicates either a faulty battery or a defective charging system. Refer to Section 3 for battery checks and Sections 31 and 32 for charging system tests. Also, check the condition of the fuses. When checking for a blown filament in a bulb, it is advisable to back up a visual check with a continuity test of the filament as it is not always apparent that a bulb has blown. When testing for continuity, remember that on tail light and turn signal bulbs it is often the metal body of the bulb that is the ground or earth.

Headlight

2 If the headlight fails to work, first check the bulb and bulb terminals (see Section 7) and then the fuse (see Section 5). Next check for voltage on the supply side of the headlight wiring connector with a test light or multimeter. Refer to *Wiring Diagrams* at the end of this Chapter, then connect the negative (-ve) probe

of the multimeter to earth (ground) and the positive (+ve) probe to first the high beam connector terminal (blue wire) and then the low beam connector terminal (white wire) with the ignition switch and light switch ON. Don't forget to select either high or low beam at the handlebar switch while conducting this test.

3 If no voltage is indicated at either terminal, check the wiring between the headlight connector, light switches and the ignition switch, then check the switches themselves (see Sections 19 and 25).

4 If voltage is indicated, check for continuity between the green wire connector terminal and earth (ground). If there is no continuity, check the earth (ground) circuit for a broken or poor connection.

Sidelight

5 If the sidelight fails to work, first check the bulb, the bulb terminals and wiring connector (see Section 7), then the fuse (see Section 5). Next check for voltage at the brown wire terminal on the supply side of the sidelight wiring connector, with the ignition switch and light switch ON.

6 If no voltage is indicated, check the wiring between the connector, the light switch and the ignition switch, then check the switches themselves (see Sections 19 and 25).

7 If voltage is indicated, check for continuity between the wiring connector terminal on the sidelight side of the wiring connector and the corresponding terminal in the bulbholder; no continuity indicates a break in the circuit. If continuity is present, check for continuity between the green wire terminal and earth

(ground). If there is no continuity, check the earth (ground) circuit for a broken or poor connection.

Tail light

8 If the tail light fails to work, first check the bulb, the bulb terminals and the wiring connector (see Section 10), then the fuse (see Section 5). Next check for voltage at the brown terminal on the supply side of the tail light wiring connector with the ignition switch and light switch ON.

9 If no voltage is indicated, check the wiring between the connector, the light switch and the ignition switch, then check the switches themselves (see Sections 19 and 25).

10 If voltage is indicated, check for continuity between the wiring connector terminal on the tail light side of the wiring connector and the corresponding terminal in the bulbholder; no continuity indicates a break in the circuit. If continuity is present, check for continuity between the green wire terminal and earth (ground). If there is no continuity, check the earth (ground) circuit for a broken or poor connection.

Brake light

11 If the brake light fails to work, first check the bulb, the bulb terminals and the wiring connector (see Section 10), then the fuse (see Section 5). Next check for voltage at the green/yellow terminal on the supply side of the brake light wiring connector, with the brake lever pulled in or the brake pedal depressed and the ignition switch ON.

12 If no voltage is indicated, check the wiring between the connector, the brake light

switches and the ignition switch, then check the brake light switches (see Section 11).

13 If voltage is indicated, check for continuity between the wiring connector terminal on the brake light side of the wiring connector and the corresponding terminal in the bulbholder; no continuity indicates a break in the circuit. If continuity is present, check for continuity between the green wire terminal and earth (ground). If there is no continuity, check the earth (ground) circuit for a broken or poor connection.

Turn signal lights

14 If one light fails to work, check the bulb, the bulb terminals and the wiring connector (see Section 18). If none of the turn signals work, first check the signal fuse.

15 If the fuse is good, check the turn signal circuit (see Section 12).

Instrument cluster lights

16 If one light fails to work, check the bulb and the bulb terminals (see Section 17). If none of the lights work, refer to *Wiring Diagrams* at the end of this Chapter, then disconnect the wiring connector for the instrument lights. Check for voltage at the brown wire terminal on the supply side of the wiring connector, with the ignition switch and light switch ON.

17 If no voltage is indicated, check the wiring between the connector, the light switch and the ignition switch, then check the switches themselves (see Sections 19 and 25).

18 If voltage is indicated, check for continuity between the wiring connector terminal on the

instrument cluster side of the wiring connector and the corresponding terminals in the light bulbholders; no continuity indicates a break in the circuit. If continuity is present, check for continuity between the green wire terminals and earth (ground). If there is no continuity, check the earth (ground) circuit for a broken or poor connection.

7 Headlight bulb and sidelight bulb – test and renewal

Note: *The headlight bulb is of the quartz-halogen type. Do not touch the bulb glass as skin acids will shorten the bulb's service life. If the bulb is accidentally touched, it should be wiped carefully when cold with a rag soaked in methylated spirit and dried before fitting.*

Warning: Allow the bulbs time to cool before removing them if the headlight has just been on.

Headlight bulb – CB600F models

1 Unscrew the three headlight rim retaining screws and remove the screws from the headlight shell **(see illustration)**. Pull the rim and headlight out of the shell, disconnect the wiring connector from the back of the headlight bulb and pull the sidelight bulbholder out of its socket in the headlight **(see illustration)**.

2 To test the headlight bulb, first ensure that the bulb terminals are clean and free of corrosion. Clean the terminals with a knife or steel wool, then use jumper wires to connect the bulb earth (ground) terminal to the battery negative (-ve) terminal, then alternately connect the bulb HI and LO beam terminals to the battery positive (+ve) terminal. If either of the bulb elements fails to illuminate, renew the bulb.

3 Remove the rubber cover from the back of the headlight bulb, noting how it fits **(see illustration)**.

4 Release the bulb retaining clip, noting how it fits, then remove the bulb **(see illustration)**.

5 Fit the new bulb, bearing in mind the information in the **Note** above. Make sure the tabs on the bulb fit correctly in the slots in the bulb housing, and secure the bulb in position with the retaining clip **(see illustration)**.

6 Install the rubber cover, making sure it is

7.1a Undo the rim retaining screws

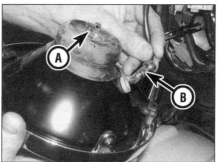
7.1b Disconnect the headlight bulb (A) and remove the sidelight (B)

7.3 Remove the cover (arrowed) ...

7.4 ... and release the retaining clip

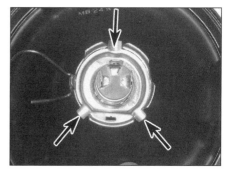
7.5 Ensure correct location of the tabs (arrowed)

9

7.10 Push and twist to remove the sidelight bulb

7.17 Remove the cover . . .

7.18a . . . then release the clip . . .

7.18b . . . and remove the bulb

16 To test the bulb see Step 2.
17 Remove the rubber cover from the back of the headlight unit, noting how it fits **(see illustration)**.
18 Release the bulb retaining clip, noting how it fits, then remove the bulb **(see illustrations)**.
19 Fit the new bulb, bearing in mind the information in the **Note** above. Make sure the tabs on the bulb fit correctly in the slots in the bulb housing, and secure the bulb in position with the retaining clip **(see illustration)**.
20 Install the rubber cover, making sure it is correctly seated with the arrow mark at the top **(see illustration 7.17)**.
21 Check that the contacts inside the wiring connector are clean and free from corrosion, then connect the wiring connector to the back of the headlight bulb.
22 Check the operation of the headlight.

Sidelight bulb – CB600FS models

23 Access to the sidelight bulb is gained through the hole in the underside of the fairing. Pull the sidelight bulbholder out of its socket in the underside of the headlight then pull the sidelight bulb out of the bulbholder **(see illustrations)**.
24 To test the bulb, use jumper wires to connect one of the bulb terminal wires to the battery positive (+ve) terminal and the other bulb terminal wire to the battery negative (-ve) terminal. If the bulb fails to illuminate, renew the bulb.
25 Check that the contacts inside the bulbholder are clean and free from corrosion. Install the new bulb in the bulbholder, then press the bulbholder into its socket in the headlight.
26 Check the operation of the sidelight.

correctly seated with the 'TOP' mark at the top. Check that the contacts inside the wiring connector are clean and free from corrosion, then connect the wiring connector. Press the sidelight bulbholder into its socket.
7 Install the rim and headlight in the headlight shell, fit the three retaining screws and tighten the screws securely.
8 Check the operation of the headlight.

Sidelight bulb – CB600F models

9 Remove the rim and headlight from its shell (see Step 1) and pull the sidelight bulbholder out of its socket in the headlight **(see illustration 7.1b)**.
10 Carefully push and twist to remove the sidelight bulb out of the bulbholder **(see illustration)**.
11 To test the bulb, first ensure that the metal

bulb body and the bottom terminal are clean and free of corrosion; clean them with a knife or steel wool. Use jumper wires to connect the bulb body to the battery negative (-ve) terminal and the bulb bottom terminal to the battery positive (+ve) terminal. If the bulb fails to illuminate, renew the bulb.
12 Check that the contacts inside the bulbholder are clean and free from corrosion. Install the new bulb in the bulbholder, then press the bulbholder into its socket.
13 Reconnect the headlight bulb and install the rim and headlight (see Step 6).
14 Check the operation of the sidelight.

Headlight bulb – CB600FS models

15 Disconnect the wiring connector from the back of the headlight bulb.

> **HAYNES HINT** *Always use a paper towel or dry cloth when handling new bulbs to prevent injury if the bulb should break and to increase bulb life.*

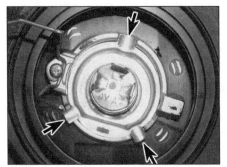

7.19 Ensure correct location of the tabs (arrowed)

7.23a Pull the bulbholder out of the headlight unit . . .

7.23b . . . and pull out the bulb

8.2 Note the arrangement of the wiring before freeing the clamps

8.3 Note headlight alignment marks (arrowed) before unscrewing the headlight bolts

8.7 Headlight is secured by screws (A). Note breather (B)

8 Headlight unit – removal and installation

CB600F models

1 Unscrew the three headlight rim retaining screws and remove the screws from the headlight shell. Pull the rim and headlight out of the shell, disconnect the wiring connector from the back of the headlight bulb and disconnect the wiring connectors for the sidelight (see illustrations 7.1a and b).

2 To remove the headlight shell, first note the arrangement of the wiring inside the shell, then free the wiring from any clamps and disconnect any wiring connectors as necessary (see illustration).

3 Unscrew the bolts securing the shell to the headlight brackets, noting the alignment marks on the shell and the brackets, and remove the shell, carefully easing the wiring out of the back of the shell (see illustration).

4 The headlight brackets are held in place between the top and bottom fork yokes and can only be removed by displacing the top yoke (see Chapter 6, Section 8).

5 Installation is the reverse of removal. Make sure that all the wiring is correctly connected and secured and that the marks on the shell and the brackets align (see illustration 8.3). Check the operation of the

headlight and sidelight. Check the headlight aim (see Chapter 1).

CB600FS models

6 Remove the fairing (see Chapter 8).

7 The headlight is secured to the fairing by four screws; undo the screws and remove the headlight, noting the breather tube in the right-hand top corner (see illustration).

8 Installation is the reverse of removal. Note the headlight is moulded to fit the opening in the fairing (see illustration). Take care not to overtighten the mounting screws. Check the operation of the headlight and sidelight. Check the headlight aim (see Chapter 1).

9 Brake/tail light bulbs – test and renewal

1 Remove the two screws securing the tail light lens and remove the lens, noting how it fits (see illustration).

2 Push the bulb into the socket and twist it anti-clockwise to remove it (see illustration).

3 To test the bulb, first ensure that the metal bulb body and the two bottom terminals are clean and free of corrosion; clean them with a knife or steel wool. Use jumper wires to connect the bulb body to the battery negative (-ve) terminal and then alternately connect the

8.8 Headlight is moulded to fit the fairing opening

bottom terminals (brake light and tail light) to the battery positive (+ve) terminal. If either of the bulb elements fails to illuminate, renew the bulb.

4 Check that the contacts inside the socket are clean and free from corrosion. Line up the pins on the bulb body with the slots in the socket, then push the bulb in and turn it clockwise until it locks into place. Note: The pins on the bulb are offset so it can only be installed one way. It is a good idea to use a paper towel or dry cloth when handling the new bulb to prevent injury if the bulb should break and to increase bulb life.

5 Check the condition of the lens sealing gasket and renew it if it is damaged. Install the lens and tighten the screws securely, but take care not to overtighten them (see illustration).

6 Check the operation of the brake/tail light.

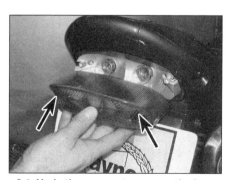

9.1 Undo the screws to remove the lens

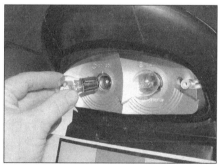

9.2 Push and twist to remove the bulb

9.5 Take care not to over-tighten the lens screws

9

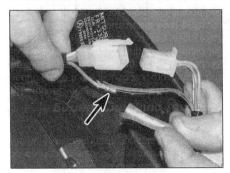

10.2 Disconnect the tail light connector and earth wire (arrowed)

10.3 Unscrew the mounting bolts (arrowed) . . .

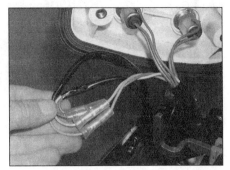

10.4 . . . and disconnect the turn indicators

10 Tail light assembly – removal and installation

Removal

1 Remove the seat cowling (see Chapter 8).
2 Trace the wiring loom back from the tail light and disconnect it at the wiring connector **(see illustration)**. Free the wiring loom, where it is clipped to the frame, back to the tail light .
3 Unscrew the two bolts securing the tail light assembly to the rear mudguard, remove the bolts and washers, noting how they fit through the bushes and spacers in the mudguard assembly, and displace the tail light **(see illustration)**.
4 Disconnect the wiring for the turn indicators from the wiring loom and remove the tail light **(see illustration)**.

Installation

5 Installation is the reverse of removal. Ensure that the turn signal wiring is connected before the tail light is installed and that the spacers for the tail light assembly bolts (see Step 3) are installed from the tail light side of the bushes.
6 Check the operation of the tail light and the brake light.

11 Brake light switches – check and replacement

Check

1 Before checking any electrical circuit, check the bulb (see Section 9) and fuse (see Section 5).
2 Using a multimeter or test light connected to a good earth (ground), with the ignition ON check for voltage at one of the terminals on the brake light switch wiring connector(s). **Note:** *The wiring connector for the rear brake light switch is located behind the left-hand side panel. Do not disconnect the wiring connectors for this test.*
3 There should be voltage at the black/brown wire terminal and no voltage at the green/yellow wire terminal with the lever/pedal at rest. If there's no voltage present, check the wiring between the switch and the fuse which supplies the tail light, signal, brake light, horn circuit (see the *Wiring Diagrams* at the end of this Chapter).
4 If there is voltage at the black/brown wire terminal of the switch, touch the test probe to the other terminal, then pull the brake lever in or depress the brake pedal. If no reading is obtained or the test light doesn't light up, renew the switch.
5 If a reading is obtained or the test light does light up, yet the brake light still does not come

on, check the wiring between the switch and the brake light bulb (see the *Wiring Diagrams* at the end of this Chapter).

Replacement

Front brake lever switch

6 The switch is mounted on the underside of the brake master cylinder; disconnect the wiring connectors from the switch **(see illustrations)**.
7 Remove the single screw securing the switch to the bottom of the master cylinder and remove the switch.
8 Installation is the reverse of removal. The switch is not adjustable.

Rear brake pedal switch

9 The switch is mounted on the inside of the right-hand footrest bracket **(see illustration)**.
10 Remove the seat (see Chapter 8). Trace the wiring from the brake light switch and disconnect it at the white 2-pin connector. Feed the wiring back to the right-hand side of the motorcycle.
11 Working from the inside of the footrest bracket, disconnect the brake light switch spring from the lug on the pedal. Pull the boot off the lower end of the switch and unscrew the switch from its mounting bracket. If necessary, press the switch sleeve out of the mounting bracket. If access proves too difficult, the footrest bracket can be detached from the frame by releasing its two bolts,

11.6a Front brake light switch (arrowed)

11.6b Disconnect the wiring connectors (arrowed)

11.9 Brake light switch mounting (arrowed)

12.3a Turn signal relay location

12.3b Disconnect the relay and test for voltage as described

although take care not to strain the hydraulic hoses.

12 Installation is the reverse of removal. Make sure the brake light is activated just before the brake takes effect. If adjustment is necessary, hold the switch and turn the adjusting sleeve until the light is activated as required.

12 Turn signal circuit – check

1 The battery provides power for operation of the turn signal lights, so if they do not operate, always check the battery voltage first. Low battery voltage indicates either a faulty battery or a defective charging system. Refer to Section 3 for battery checks and Sections 30 and 31 for charging system tests. Also, check the fuse (see Section 5) and the switch (see Section 24).

2 Most turn signal problems are the result of a failed bulb or corroded socket. This is especially true when the turn signals function properly in one direction, but not in the other. Check the bulbs and the sockets (see Section 13).

3 If the bulbs and sockets are good, remove the seat cowling (see Chapter 8) for access to the turn signal relay which is mounted on the left-hand side of the frame. Disconnect the

wiring connector then switch the ignition ON and check for voltage at the wiring connector black/brown terminal using a multimeter or test light connected to a good earth (ground) **(see illustrations)**. Turn the ignition OFF when the check is complete.

4 If there is no voltage, check the wiring between the connector and the fuse box (see *Wiring Diagrams* at the end of this Chapter).

5 If there is voltage at the black/brown terminal, reconnect the wiring connector and use the test light to check the output from the grey wire terminal on the relay. Ensure the test light is earthed and turn the ignition ON; the light should flash. If the light does not flash, renew the relay.

6 If the light flashes, check the wiring between the relay, the turn signal switch and the turn signal lights.

13 Turn signal bulb – test and renewal

1 Remove the screw on the front of the turn signal securing the signal lens and remove the lens, noting how it fits **(see illustration)**.

2 Push the bulb into the socket and twist it anti-clockwise to remove it **(see illustration)**.

3 To test the bulb, first ensure that the metal bulb body and the bottom terminal is clean

and free of corrosion; clean them with a knife or steel wool. Use jumper wires to connect the bulb body to the battery negative (-ve) terminal and the bottom terminal to the battery positive (+ve) terminal. If the bulb fails to illuminate, renew the bulb.

4 Check that the contacts inside the socket are clean and free from corrosion. Line up the pins on the bulb body with the slots in the socket, then push the bulb in and turn it clockwise until it locks into place. **Note:** *It is a good idea to use a paper towel or dry cloth when handling the new bulb to prevent injury if the bulb should break and to increase bulb life.*

5 Check the condition of the lens sealing gasket and renew it if it is damaged **(see illustration)**. **Note:** *There is a gap in the gasket to allow moisture to drain from the assembly.*

6 Install the lens, locating the tab on the side of the lens in the turn signal body, and tighten the screw securely **(see illustration 13.1)**.

7 Check the operation of the turn signal light.

14 Turn signals – removal and installation

Front

1 On CB600F models the connectors are

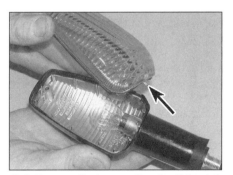

13.1 Remove the lens, noting the fixing tab (arrowed)

13.2 Push and twist to remove the bulb

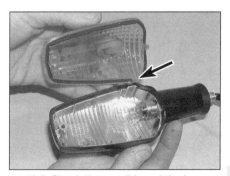

13.5 Check the condition of the lens gasket – note the drain hole

9

14.1a Removing the signal assembly on CB600F models . . .

14.1b . . . note the shaped hole (arrowed) to stop the assembly rotating

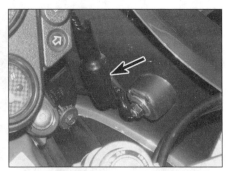

14.2a CB600FS front turn signal wiring connector (arrowed)

inside the headlight shell (see Section 8). Ease the wiring out of the back of the shell and disconnect the turn signal wiring connector. Unscrew the nut securing the signal assembly to the headlight bracket and thread the nut and washer off the wiring. Remove the signal assembly, noting how the hole for the signal assembly stem in the headlight bracket is shaped to prevent the assembly rotating (see illustrations).

2 On CB600FS models the wiring connectors are inside the fairing (see illustration). Disconnect the connector, then unscrew the nut securing the signal assembly to the fairing and thread the nut, washer and plate off the wiring. Withdraw the assembly from the fairing (see illustration). Note how the plate locates on the stem of the signal

assembly and against the inside of the fairing to prevent the turn signal rotating (see illustration).

3 Installation is the reverse of removal. On all models, ensure that the wiring connections are firm and that the wiring is securely clamped in place. On CB600FS models, ensure the plate on the assembly stem is correctly positioned inside the fairing.

4 Check the operation of the turn signals.

Rear

5 Remove the seat cowling (see Chapter 8) and displace the tail light assembly (see Section 10). Disconnect the wiring for the turn signal from the tail light wiring loom and feed it through to the underside of the mudguard (see illustration 10.4).

6 Unscrew the nut securing the signal assembly to the mudguard, thread the nut and washer off the wiring and remove the assembly (see illustration). Note how the hole for the signal assembly stem in the mudguard is shaped to prevent the assembly rotating.

7 Installation is the reverse of removal. Ensure that the wiring connections are firm.

8 Check the operation of the turn signals.

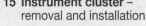

15 Instrument cluster – removal and installation

CB600F models

1 Remove the headlight (see Section 7)

2 Trace the wiring from the instrument cluster to the white 6-pin and red 6-pin connectors inside the headlight shell and disconnect the connectors (see illustration). Note the position of the wiring inside the shell then free the instrument wiring from the clamps and carefully ease it out of the back of the shell.

3 Unscrew the knurled ring securing the speedometer cable to the back of the speedometer and detach the cable (see illustration).

4 Unscrew the two bolts securing the

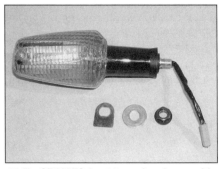

14.2b CB600FS front turn signal assembly and fittings

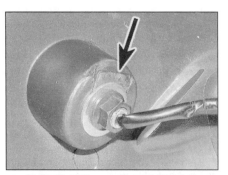

14.2c Note the position of the plate (arrowed) which prevents the signal from rotating

14.6 Nut (arrowed) securing rear turn signal assembly

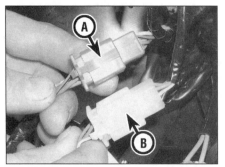

15.2 Instrument cluster red (A) and white (B) six-pin connectors

15.3 Detach the speedometer cable (arrowed)

15.4 Instrument cluster mounting bolts (arrowed)

15.7a Pull back the boot (arrowed) . . .

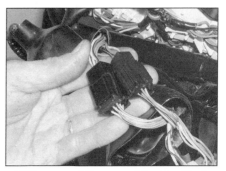

15.7b . . . and disconnect the two black connectors

15.8a Unscrew the mounting bolts (arrowed)

15.8b Remove the sleeved bolts . . .

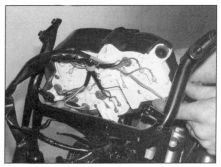

15.8c . . . and remove the instruments

instrument cluster to the top yoke and carefully remove it (see illustration).

5 Installation is the reverse of removal. Make sure that the speedometer cable and wiring are correctly routed and secured.

CB600FS models

6 Remove the fairing (see Chapter 8).
7 Pull back the rubber boot on the instrument wiring and disconnect the two black wiring connectors (see illustrations). Free the wiring from any clips on the fairing bracket.
8 Unscrew the three bolts securing the instrument cluster to the fairing bracket (see illustration). Note: *The bolt head between the speedometer and the tachometer is a dummy – do not try to unscrew it!* Remove the bolts and their sleeves and lift off the instrument

cluster (see illustrations). Note the bushes in the cluster mounting points.
9 Installation is the reverse of removal. Ensure the sleeves are fitted to the bolts before installing them (see illustration 15.8b).

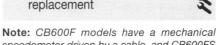

16 Speedometer cable/speed sensor – check and replacement

Note: *CB600F models have a mechanical speedometer driven by a cable, and CB600FS models have an electronic speedometer operated by a speed sensor.*

Speedometer cable – CB600F models

1 Remove the fuel tank (see Chapter 4).

2 To check the operation of the speedometer cable, unscrew the knurled ring securing the cable to the back of the speedometer and detach the cable (see illustration 15.3).
3 Turn the rear wheel in the normal direction of rotation and observe that the squared upper end of the inner cable rotates (see illustration).
4 To remove the cable, undo the screw that retains the lower end of the cable in the speedometer gearbox on the front sprocket cover and withdraw the cable (see illustrations). Remove the cable from the motorcycle, noting its routing between the carburettors and through the guide on the left-hand side of the frame.
5 If required, unscrew the bolts securing the speedometer gearbox to the front sprocket cover and remove the gearbox (see

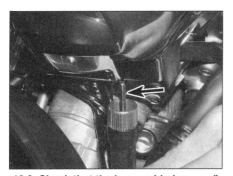

16.3 Check that the inner cable (arrowed) rotates

16.4a Undo the screw . . .

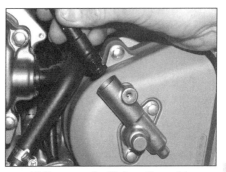

16.4b . . . and withdraw the cable

9

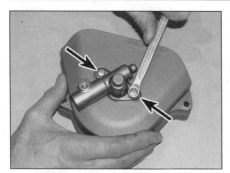

16.5 Unscrew the bolts (arrowed) to remove the speedometer gearbox

16.12 Speed sensor location (arrowed)

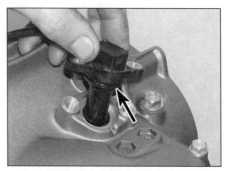

16.14 Withdraw the sensor and discard the O-ring (arrowed)

illustration). Check that the cable drive and the socket that locates on the sprocket bolt are in good condition.

6 Installation is the reverse of removal, having first checked the operation of the speedometer gearbox. Route the cable to avoid any tight bends or kinks and engage the forked lower end of the inner cable on the spade drive in the speedometer gearbox. Push the outer cable into the gearbox and tighten the retaining screw securely **(see illustration 16.4a)**.

7 Engage the squared upper end of the inner cable in the speedometer, then tighten the retaining ring securely.

8 Check that the cable doesn't restrict steering movement or interfere with any other components.

Speed sensor – CB600FS models

9 Remove the fairing (see Chapter 8).

10 Support the motorcycle on an auxiliary stand with the rear wheel off the ground and use a multimeter to test for an output signal on the wiring loom side of the instrument cluster wiring connectors (see Section 15).

11 Connect the multimeter positive (+ve) probe to the pink/green wire terminal and the negative (-ve) probe to the green/black wire

terminal, turn the ignition ON and slowly rotate the rear wheel by hand. If the speed sensor is working correctly the recorded voltage should pulse between 0 and 5 volts. Switch the ignition OFF.

12 If the test does not provide the specified result, remove the left-hand side panel and trace the wiring from the speed sensor and disconnect it at the black three-pin connector **(see illustration)**. Connect the multi-meter positive (+ve) probe to the black/brown wire terminal and the negative (-ve) probe to the green/black wire terminal on the wiring loom side of the connector and check for voltage with the ignition switched ON. If the wiring is good, full battery voltage should be present. Switch the ignition OFF.

13 If there is no voltage, check the wiring (see *Wiring Diagrams* at the end of this Chapter). If the wiring is good, replace the speed sensor with a new one.

14 Remove the air filter housing (see Chapter 4). Clean the area around the sensor then remove the bolts retaining the speed sensor and pull the sensor out of the crankcase **(see illustration)**. Discard the O-ring as a new one must be fitted on reassembly.

15 Lubricate the new O-ring with clean engine oil and fit it onto the sensor, then install

the sensor and its retaining bolts and tighten the bolts securely **(see illustration)**.

16 Connect the sensor wiring connector

17 Install the remaining components in the reverse order of removal.

17 Instruments – check and replacement

Speedometer
Check

1 Special equipment is required to check the operation of this meter. If it is believed to be faulty, take the speedometer to a Honda dealer for assessment. **Note:** *On CB600F models, first check the operation of the drive cable and gearbox (see Section 16).*

Replacement – CB600F models

2 Remove the instrument cluster (see Section 15).

3 Remove the five screws securing the instrument casing back and remove the back **(see illustration)**.

4 Undo the screw securing the wiring clip to the instrument mounting bracket and detach

16.15 Sensor wiring should face rearwards

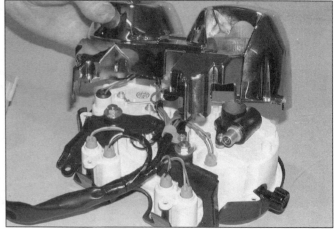

17.3 Remove the instrument casing back

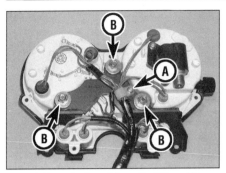

17.4 Detach the wiring clip (A) and the nuts securing the bracket (B)

the clip from the bracket, then unscrew the nuts securing the instrument cluster to the bracket and remove the nuts, washers and the bracket **(see illustration)**.

5 Remove the screw securing the instrument casing top cover and remove the cover **(see illustrations)**.

6 Using a very small Phillips screwdriver, remove the screw in the centre of the odometer trip knob and remove the knob **(see illustration)**.

7 Remove the two screws securing the speedometer gearbox and remove the gearbox, then remove the two screws securing the speedometer to the casing and carefully lift the speedometer out of the casing **(see illustration)**.

8 Installation is the reverse of removal.

Replacement – CB600FS models

9 Remove the instrument cluster (see Section 15).

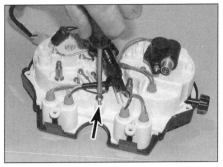

17.5a Remove the screw (arrowed) . . .

10 Remove the five screws securing the instrument casing top cover and remove the cover **(see illustration)**.

11 Remove the four screws securing the speedometer and trip assembly terminals to the casing and carefully lift the assembly out of the casing **(see illustrations)**. **Note:** *The speedometer and trip are not available separately.*

12 Installation is the reverse of removal. **Note:** *The terminals on the back of the instrument casing are marked with the colour coding for the wires.*

Tachometer

Check

13 Special equipment is required to check the operation of this meter. If it is believed to be faulty, take the tachometer to a Honda dealer or automotive electrician for assessment.

17.5b . . . and lift off the cover

Replacement – CB600F models

Note: *On these models, the tachometer and temperature gauge are an integral unit.*

14 Remove the instrument cluster (see Section 15) and follow Steps 3 to 5.

15 Remove the six screws securing the tachometer and temperature gauge terminals to the casing **(see illustration)**, then carefully lift the assembly out of the casing.

16 Installation is the reverse of removal. **Note:** *The terminals on the back of the instrument casing are marked with the colour coding for the wires.*

Replacement – CB600FS models

17 Remove the instrument cluster (see Section 15) and follow Step 10.

18 Remove the three screws securing the tachometer terminals to the casing and

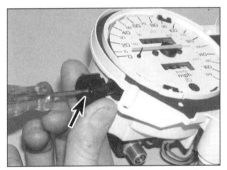

17.6 Odometer trip knob is retained by a central screw (arrowed)

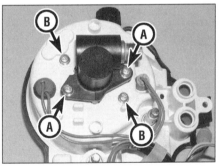

17.7 Screws securing the speedometer gearbox (A) and the speedometer (B)

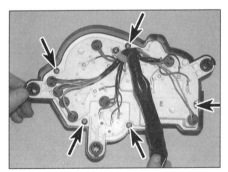

17.10 Top cover retaining screws (arrowed)

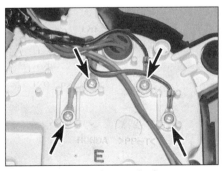

17.11a Undo the terminal screws (arrowed) . . .

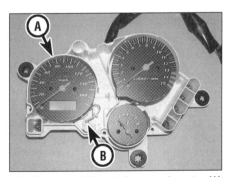

17.11b . . . and lift out the speedometer (A) and trip (B) assembly

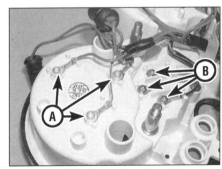

17.15 Undo the tachometer (A) and temperature gauge (B) terminal screws

9

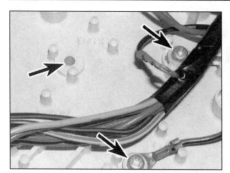

17.18a Undo the terminal screws . . .

17.18b . . . and lift out the tachometer

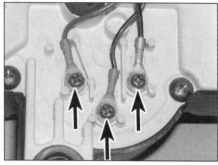

17.22 Undo the temperature gauge terminal screws

carefully lift the tachometer out of the casing **(see illustrations)**.

19 Installation is the reverse of removal. **Note:** *The terminals on the back of the instrument casing are marked with the colour coding for the wires.*

Coolant temperature gauge

Check

20 See Chapter 3.

Replacement – CB600F models

Note: *On these models, the tachometer and temperature gauge are an integral unit. Follow Steps 14 to 16.*

Replacement – CB600FS models

21 Remove the instrument cluster (see Section 15) and follow Step 10.

22 Remove the three screws securing the

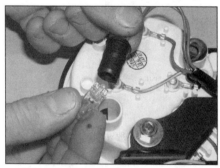

18.2a Replacing an instrument cluster light bulb . . .

18.2b . . . and a warning light bulb

temperature gauge terminals to the casing and carefully lift the gauge out of the casing **(see illustration)**.

23 Installation is the reverse of removal. **Note:** *The terminals on the back of the instrument casing are marked with the colour coding for the wires.*

---

18 Instrument and warning light bulbs – renewal

Note: *The neutral light is part of the safety circuit which prevents the engine from starting with the transmission in gear unless the clutch lever is pulled in and the sidestand is up, and prevents the engine from running with the sidestand down unless the transmission is in neutral. An apparent fault with the neutral light may be due to a defective diode (see Section 24).*

CB600F models

1 Disconnect the speedometer cable and detach the instrument cluster from the top yoke (see Section 15), then remove the back of the instrument casing (see Section 17).

2 Gently pull the bulbholder out of the back of the instrument casing, then pull the bulb out of the bulbholder **(see illustrations)**.

3 To test the bulb, use jumper wires to connect one of the bulb terminal wires to the battery positive (+ve) terminal and the other

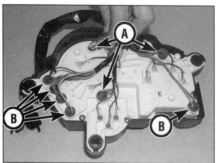

18.7a CB600FS instrument cluster light (A) and warning light (B) locations

bulb terminal wire to the battery negative (-ve) terminal. If the bulb fails to illuminate, renew the bulb.

4 Check that the contacts inside the bulbholder are clean and free from corrosion and spray with electrical contact cleaner before a new bulb is installed.

5 Carefully push the new bulb into the holder, then push the holder into the casing.

6 Installation of the instrument cluster is the reverse of removal.

CB600FS models

7 Remove the fairing (see Chapter 8). Some of the bulbs are accessible with the instrument cluster in place, but access to others requires removing the cluster from the fairing bracket **(see illustrations)** (see Section 15).

8 Follow steps 3 to 5 to test and renew the bulbs

9 Installation of the instrument cluster is the reverse of removal.

---

19 Ignition (main) switch – check, removal and installation

⚠️ **Warning: To prevent the risk of short circuits, remove the rider's seat (see Chapter 8) and disconnect the battery negative (-ve) lead before making any ignition (main) switch checks.**

18.7b Bulbholders are a push fit in the casing

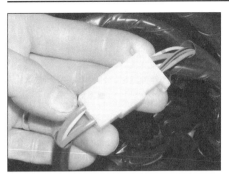

19.1 CB600F ignition switch wiring connector

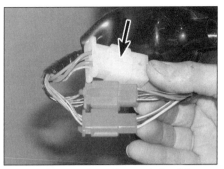

19.2 CB600FS ignition switch wiring connector (arrowed)

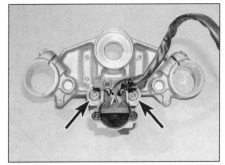

19.5 Torx bolts (arrowed) secure the ignition switch to the yoke

Check

1 On CB600F models, remove the headlight and trace the ignition (main) switch wiring back from the base of the switch and disconnect it at the white 4-pin connector inside the headlight shell **(see illustration)**.

2 On CB600FS models, remove the fairing (see Chapter 8). Trace the ignition (main) switch wiring back from the base of the switch and disconnect it at the white 4-pin connector **(see illustration)**.

3 Using an ohmmeter or a continuity tester, check the continuity of the connector terminal pairs (see the *Wiring Diagrams* at the end of this Chapter). Insert the key in the switch. Continuity should exist between the terminals connected by a solid line on the diagram when the switch is in the indicated position.

4 If the switch fails any of the tests, renew it.

Removal

5 The ignition switch is secured to the underside of the fork top yoke with two Torx bolts **(see illustration)**. To gain access to these bolts, disconnect the ignition wiring connector (see Steps 1 or 2), then remove the handlebars and top yoke (see Chapter 6).

6 Remove the bolts and withdraw the switch from the top yoke.

Installation

7 Installation is the reverse of removal. Tighten the Torx bolts to the torque setting specified at the beginning of this Chapter. Make sure the wiring is securely connected and correctly routed.

20 Oil pressure switch – check, removal and installation

Check

1 The oil pressure switch is screwed into the crankcase behind the cylinder block. If the oil pressure warning light does not come on when the ignition is turned on, pull the rubber boot off the switch and remove the screw securing the wiring connector **(see illustrations)**.

2 With the ignition switched ON, earth (ground) the wire on the crankcase and check to see if the warning light comes on. If the light comes on, the switch is defective and must be renewed.

3 If the light does not come on, check for voltage at the wire terminal and check the wire for continuity between the terminal, the instrument cluster and the fusebox (see the *Wiring Diagrams* at the end of this Chapter). Also check the warning light bulb (see Section 18) and the fuse (see Section 5).

4 If the warning light comes on whilst the engine is running, yet the oil pressure is known to be good (see Chapter 1), remove the wire from the oil pressure switch with the engine running. If the light goes out, the switch is defective and must be renewed. If the light remains illuminated, the wire between the switch and instrument cluster must be earthed (grounded) at some point (see the *Wiring Diagrams* at the end of this Chapter).

 Warning: Avoid working on a hot engine – the exhaust pipes, crankcases and engine oil can cause severe burns. Do not allow exhaust gases to build up in the work area; either perform the check outside or use an exhaust gas extraction system

Removal

5 Pull the rubber boot off the switch and remove the screw securing the wiring connector **(see illustration 20.1a and b)**.

6 Unscrew the oil pressure switch and withdraw it from the crankcase.

Installation

7 Apply a suitable sealant to the upper portion of the switch threads near the switch body, leaving the bottom 3 to 4 mm of thread clean. Install the switch in the crankcase and tighten it to the torque setting specified at the beginning of this Chapter **(see illustration)**.

8 Attach the wiring connector and secure it with the screw, then fit the rubber boot.

9 Run the engine and check that the switch operates correctly.

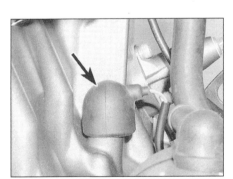

20.1a Remove the boot from the oil pressure switch . . .

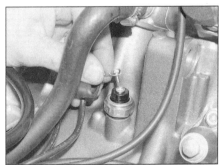

20.1b . . . and disconnect the wire

20.7 Apply sealant to the switch threads before installation

9

21.1 The neutral switch (arrowed) is located behind the water pump

21.2 Earth the wiring connector (arrowed) to test the switch

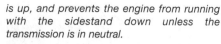

is up, and prevents the engine from running with the sidestand down unless the transmission is in neutral.

21 Neutral switch – check, removal and installation

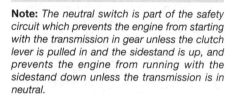

Note: *The neutral switch is part of the safety circuit which prevents the engine from starting with the transmission in gear unless the clutch lever is pulled in and the sidestand is up, and prevents the engine from running with the sidestand down unless the transmission is in neutral.*

Check

1 The neutral switch is screwed into the left-hand side of the engine behind the water pump **(see illustration)**.

2 If the neutral warning light does not come on when the ignition is turned ON with the transmission in neutral, detach the wiring connector and earth (ground) the wire on the crankcase **(see illustration)**. If the light comes on, the switch is defective and must be renewed.

3 If the light does not come on, check for voltage at the connector and check the wire for continuity between the connector, diode (see Section 24), instrument cluster and fusebox (see the *Wiring Diagrams* at the end of this Chapter). Also check the warning light bulb (see Section 18) and the fuse (see Section 5).

4 If the warning light does not extinguish when a gear is selected and the ignition is ON, detach the wiring connector. If the light goes out, the switch is defective and must be

renewed. If the light remains on, the wire between the connector and instrument cluster must be earthed (grounded) at some point.

Removal

5 On CB600F models, remove the screw retaining the speedometer cable in the speedometer gearbox and disconnect the cable **(see illustrations 16.4a and b)**. On all models, unscrew the two bolts securing the front sprocket cover to the engine unit, then remove the cover, the drive chain guide plate and, if they are loose, the two dowels **(see illustrations)**.

6 Detach the wire connector from the switch. Unscrew the switch and withdraw it from the engine casing.

Installation

7 Apply a smear of sealant to the switch threads, then install the switch and tighten it to the torque setting specified at the beginning of this Chapter.

8 Reconnect the switch wire and check the operation of the neutral light, then install the front sprocket cover.

22 Sidestand switch – check and replacement

Note: *The sidestand switch is part of the safety circuit which prevents the engine from starting with the transmission in gear unless the clutch lever is pulled in and the sidestand*

is up, and prevents the engine from running with the sidestand down unless the transmission is in neutral.

Check

1 The sidestand switch is mounted on the back of the sidestand bracket.

2 Sit astride the motorcycle and start the engine with the sidestand up and the transmission in neutral. Pull the clutch lever in and engage first gear, then lower the sidestand; the engine should stop.

3 Check the operation of the switch using a multimeter or test light and battery. Remove the left-hand side panel (see Chapter 8) and trace the wiring back from the switch to the green 3-pin connector and disconnect it. Test for continuity between the green/white and green wire terminals on the switch side of the connector. With the sidestand up there should be continuity (zero resistance), and with the stand down there should be no continuity (infinite resistance). Now test for continuity between the yellow/black and green wire terminals. With the sidestand down there should be continuity (zero resistance), and with the stand up there should be no continuity (infinite resistance).

4 If the switch fails either of these tests it is defective and must be renewed.

5 If the switch is good, check the wiring between the various components in the starter safety circuit (see the *Wiring Diagrams* at the end of this Chapter).

Replacement

6 Support the motorcycle using an auxiliary stand and disconnect the switch wiring (see Step 3), then feed the wiring down to the switch, freeing it from any retaining clips and ties, and noting its correct routing.

7 Unscrew the switch bolt and remove the switch from the stand, noting how it fits **(see illustration)**. **Note:** *Honda recommend using a new bolt when the old one is removed. This is because the bolt is pre-treated with a locking compound. It is possible, however, to clean up the old bolt and reinstall it using a suitable non-permanent thread locking compound that is commercially available.*

8 Locate the tab on the inside of the new switch in the hole in the sidestand and align

21.5a Remove the sprocket cover . . .

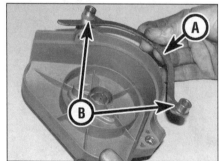

21.5b . . . with the chain guide plate (A) and dowels (B)

22.7 Sidestand switch bolt (arrowed)

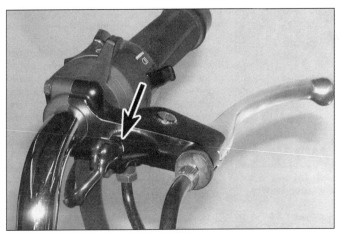

23.1 Clutch switch (arrowed) is located inside the lever bracket

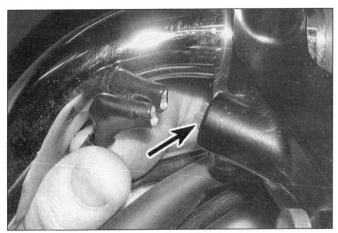

23.2 Disconnect the wiring from the switch terminals (arrowed)

the switch body with the stand spring post **(see illustration 22.7)**. Install the new bolt (or apply locking compound to the existing bolt) and tighten it to the torque setting specified at the beginning of this Chapter.

9 Make sure the wiring is correctly routed up to the connector and retained by all the necessary clips and ties.

10 Reconnect the wiring connector and check the operation of the sidestand switch (see Step 2), then install the side panel.

23 Clutch switch – check and replacement

Note: *The clutch switch is part of the safety circuit which prevents the engine from starting with the transmission in gear unless the clutch lever is pulled in and the sidestand is up, and prevents the engine from running with the sidestand down unless the transmission is in neutral.*

Check

1 The clutch switch is housed in the clutch lever bracket **(see illustration)**.

2 Check the operation of the switch using a multimeter or test light and battery. Disconnect the wiring connectors from the switch and test for continuity between the two switch terminals **(see illustration)**. With the clutch lever out there should be no continuity (infinite resistance) and with the clutch lever pulled in there should be continuity (zero resistance).

3 If the switch is good, check for voltage at one of the wiring connectors with the ignition ON – there should be voltage at one terminal and none at the other. If voltage is indicated, check the other components in the starter circuit as described in the relevant sections of this Chapter. If no voltage is indicated, check the wiring between the various components (see the *Wiring Diagrams* at the end of this Chapter).

Replacement

4 Remove the clutch lever (see Chapter 6).

5 Disconnect the wiring connectors from the clutch switch **(see illustration 23.2)**. Using a small screwdriver, push the switch from the connector end and withdraw it from inside the bracket.

6 Installation is the reverse of removal. Make sure the ridge on the top of the switch locates in the cut-out in the lever bracket, and push the switch fully home.

24 Diode – check and replacement

Note: *The diode switch is part of the safety circuit which prevents the engine from starting with the transmission in gear unless the clutch lever is pulled in and the sidestand is up, and prevents the engine from running with the sidestand down unless the transmission is in neutral.*

Check

1 Remove the left-hand side panel (see Chapter 8) and open the fusebox lid. The diode is a small block that plugs into a socket in the fuse box **(see illustration)**.

2 Check the operation of the diode using a multimeter or test light and battery. Remove the diode and test for continuity between the centre terminal and one of the outer terminals, then reverse the test probes and check for continuity again between the same two terminals.

3 The diode should only show continuity in one direction (as indicated by the symbol on the body of the diode). If the diode shows continuity, or no continuity, in both directions, it should be replaced with a new one.

4 Repeat the test between the centre terminal and the other outer terminal. Again, the diode should only show continuity in one direction. If it doesn't it should be renewed.

5 If the diode is good, check the other

components in the starter circuit as described in the relevant sections of this Chapter. If all components are good, check the wiring between the various components (see the *wiring diagrams* at the end of this Chapter).

Replacement

6 Follow Step 1 and install the new diode in the fusebox.

25 Handlebar switches – check

1 Generally speaking, the handlebar switches are reliable and trouble-free. Most problems, when they do occur, are caused by dirty or corroded contacts, but wear and breakage of internal parts is a possibility that should not be overlooked when tracing a fault. If breakage does occur, the entire switch and related wiring harness will have to be renewed as individual parts are not available.

2 The switches can be checked for continuity using a multimeter or test light and battery. Always disconnect the motorcycle battery negative (-ve) lead, which will prevent the possibility of a short circuit, before making the checks.

3 Trace the wiring from the switch in question back to its connector and disconnect it.

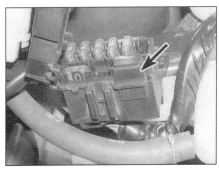

24.1 The diode plugs into the side of the fusebox

9

25.4a CB600F models brown 9-pin right-hand switch connector . . .

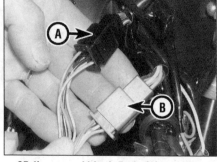

25.4b . . . and black 5-pin (A) and blue 6-pin (B) left-hand switch connectors

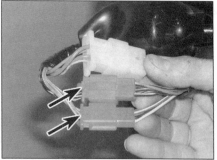

25.5a CB600FS models red 4 and 5-pin right-hand switch connectors . . .

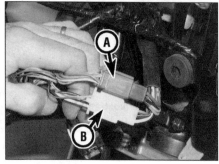

25.5b . . . and blue 6-pin (A) and white 5-pin (B) left-hand switch connectors

4 On CB600F models the connectors are inside the headlight shell (see Section 8). The right-hand switch connector is the brown 9-pin connector and the left-hand switch connectors are the black 5-pin and blue 6-pin connectors (see illustrations).

5 On CB600FS models the connectors are inside the fairing (see Chapter 8). The right-hand switch connectors are the red 4 and 5-pin connectors and the left-hand switch connectors are the blue 6-pin and white 5-pin connectors (see illustrations).

6 Check for continuity between the terminals of the switch wiring with the switch in the various positions (i.e. switch off – no continuity, switch on – continuity) referring to the Wiring Diagrams at the end of this Chapter.

7 If the checks indicate a problem exists, refer to Section 26, remove the switch and

spray the switch contacts with electrical contact cleaner. If they are accessible, the contacts can be scraped clean carefully with a knife or polished with crocus cloth. If switch components are damaged or broken, it will be obvious when the switch is disassembled.

8 Clean the inside of the switch body thoroughly and smear the contacts with suitable grease before reassembly

26 Handlebar switches – removal and installation

Removal

1 If the switch unit is to be removed from the motorcycle, rather than just displaced from

the handlebar, it will be necessary to disconnect the switch wiring from the main wiring harness.

2 Trace the wiring from the switch in question back to its connector and disconnect it (see Section 25). Note: The wiring loom for the right-hand switch includes the wiring for the front brake light switch; the wiring loom for the left-hand switch includes the wiring for the clutch switch and individual wires from the left-hand switch connect to the horn and the front turn indicators.

3 Work back along the wiring, freeing it from all the relevant clips and ties and noting its correct routing.

4 The right-hand switch housing is integral with the twistgrip housing, the left-hand switch housing incorporates the choke lever pulley. To remove the right-hand housing it is first necessary to displace the throttle cables (see Chapter 4, Section 11). To remove the left-hand housing it is first necessary to displace the choke cable (see Chapter 4, Section 12).

5 Separate the two halves of the switch housing and inspect the switch contacts (see illustrations). If a component part is worn or broken the switch unit will have to be replaced as a complete assembly.

Installation

6 Installation is the reverse of removal. Ensure the two halves of the switch housing are aligned and the screws are replaced in their correct positions (see illustration). Make sure that all the wiring is correctly connected and secured and check the operation of the switches and related components before riding the motorcycle.

27 Horn – check and replacement

Check

1 The horn is mounted to a bracket on the bottom front fork yoke.

2 Disconnect the wiring connectors from the

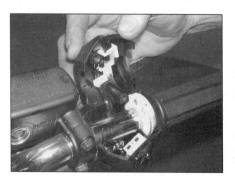

26.5a Separate the halves of the housing . . .

26.5b . . . to inspect the switch contacts

26.6 Housing screws differ in length – replace them correctly

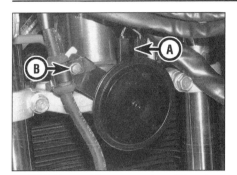

27.2 Horn wiring connectors (A) and mounting bolt (B)

28.3 Disconnect the starter motor lead (arrowed)

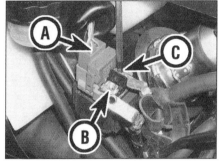

28.9 Relay wiring connector (A), starter motor lead (B) and battery lead (C)

horn and ensure that the contacts are clean and free from corrosion **(see illustration)**.

3 To test the horn, use jumper wires to connect one of the horn terminals to the battery positive (+ve) terminal and the other horn terminal to the battery negative (-ve) terminal. If the horn sounds, check the switch (see Section 25) and the wiring between the switch and the horn (see the *Wiring Diagrams* at the end of this Chapter).

4 If the horn doesn't sound, replace it with a new one.

Replacement

5 Disconnect the wiring connectors from the horn, then unscrew the bolt securing the horn to the mounting bracket and remove it from the bike **(see illustration 27.2)**.

6 Install the horn and tighten the bolt securely. Connect the wiring connectors to the horn and test the horn

28 Starter relay – check and replacement

Check

1 The starter relay is located on the right-hand side of the bike behind the right-hand side panel.

2 If the starter circuit is faulty, first check the main fuse and ignition/starter fuse (see Section 5).

3 To check the relay, lift the rubber terminal cover and unscrew the bolt securing the

starter motor lead **(see illustration)**; position the lead well away from the relay terminal. With the engine kill switch in the RUN position and the transmission in neutral, turn the ignition switch ON and press the starter switch. The relay should be heard to click.

4 If the relay doesn't click, switch the ignition OFF, disconnect the battery negative (-ve) terminal and remove the relay (see Steps 8 and 9), then test it as follows.

5 Set a multimeter to the ohms x 1 scale and connect it across the relay's starter motor and battery lead terminals **(see illustration 28.9)**. Using a fully-charged 12 volt battery and two insulated jumper wires, connect the positive (+ve) terminal of the battery to the yellow/red wire terminal of the relay, and the negative (-ve) terminal to the green/red wire terminal of the relay. At this point the relay should be heard to click and the multimeter read 0 ohms (continuity). If the relay does not click when voltage is applied and indicates no continuity (infinite resistance) across its terminals, it is faulty and must be renewed.

6 If the relay is good, check for battery voltage between the yellow/red wire and the green/red wire terminals in the connector when the starter button is pressed with the ignition switch ON, the engine kill switch in the RUN position and the transmission in neutral.

7 Check the other components in the starter circuit as described in the relevant sections of this Chapter. If all components are good, check the wiring between the various components (see the *wiring diagrams* at the end of this Chapter).

Replacement

8 Disconnect the battery negative (-ve) lead.

9 Disconnect the relay wiring connector, then unscrew the bolts securing the starter motor lead and battery positive (+ve) lead to the relay and detach the leads **(see illustration)**. Remove the relay with its rubber sleeve from its mounting lug on the frame.

10 Installation is the reverse of removal. Make sure the connector terminals, battery and starter motor leads are clean and securely tightened.

29 Starter motor – removal and installation

Removal

1 The starter motor is mounted on the crankcase behind the cylinder block. Remove the seat and disconnect the battery negative (-ve) lead.

2 Remove the air filter housing (see Chapter 4).

3 Peel back the terminal cover on the starter motor, then remove the nut securing the lead to the terminal and detach the lead **(see illustration)**.

4 Unscrew the two bolts securing the starter motor to the crankcase, noting the earth lead attached to the front bolt **(see illustration)**.

5 Slide the starter motor out from the crankcase and remove it from the machine **(see illustration)**. Discard the O-ring as a new one must be fitted on reassembly.

29.3 Disconnect the starter motor lead from its terminal (arrowed)

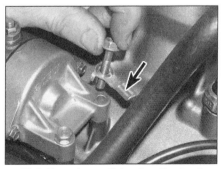

29.4 Note the earth lead on the front mounting bolt

29.5 Withdraw the starter motor and discard the O-ring

29.6 Ensure the O-ring seats in its groove (arrowed)

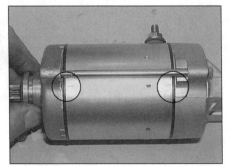

30.2 Note the alignment marks (circled) between the housing and the covers

30.4 Remove the front cover O-ring . . .

Installation

6 Install a new O-ring and ensure it is seated in its groove on the starter motor body (see illustration). Lubricate the O-ring with clean engine oil.

7 Manoeuvre the motor into place. Ensure that the motor teeth mesh correctly with those of the starter idle gear. Install the mounting bolts, not forgetting to fit the earth lead to the front bolt, and tighten them securely (see illustration 29.4).

8 Connect the starter lead to the motor terminal and secure it with the nut. Hold the lower nut on the terminal with an open ended spanner while tightening the top nut. Make sure the cover is correctly seated over the terminal.

9 Install the air filter housing (see Chapter 4).

Reconnect the battery negative lead and refit the seat.

30 Starter motor – disassembly, inspection and reassembly

Disassembly

1 Remove the starter motor (see Section 29).

2 Note the alignment marks between the motor housing and the front and rear covers, or make your own if they aren't clear (see illustration).

3 Unscrew the two long bolts and withdraw them from the starter motor.

4 Remove the front cover from the motor carefully to avoid damaging the internal oil seal. Remove the cover O-ring from the motor housing (see illustration). Remove the tabbed thrust washer from inside the front cover noting how it fits.

5 Remove the insulating washer and shim from the front end of the armature shaft, noting the order in which they are fitted (see illustration).

6 Remove the rear cover from the motor and remove the cover O-ring. Remove the shims from the rear end of the armature shaft (see illustration).

7 Note how the brushes locate against the armature commutator, then carefully withdraw the armature from the motor housing (see illustrations).

8 Displace the two brushes attached to the motor terminal from the brushplate and remove the brushplate noting how it fits (see illustrations).

9 Lift the brush springs and slide the brushes

30.5 . . . and the insulating washer (A) and shim (B)

30.6 Remove the shims from the rear end of the armature shaft

30.7a Note how the brushes locate against the commutator . . .

30.7b . . . then carefully withdraw the armature

30.8a Displace the motor terminal brushes (arrowed) . . .

30.8b . . . and remove the brushplate noting the alignment tab (arrowed)

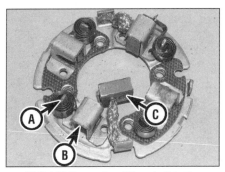

30.9 Lift the spring (A) and slide the brush (C) from its holder (B)

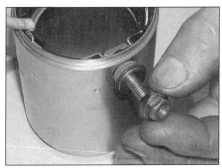

30.10a Unscrew the terminal nut and washer . . .

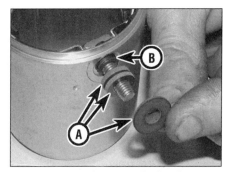

30.10b . . .and remove the insulating washers (A) and O-ring (B)

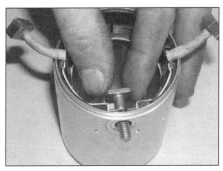

30.11a Remove the terminal . . .

30.11b . . . terminal brushes . . .

30.11c . . . and the housing insulator

out from their holders on the brushplate **(see illustration).**

10 Noting the order in which they are fitted, unscrew the terminal nut and remove it along with its washer, the insulating washers and O-ring **(see illustrations).**

11 Withdraw the terminal and terminal brushes from the motor housing, then remove the housing insulator **(see illustrations).**

Inspection

12 Check the general condition of all the starter motor components **(see illustration).** The parts that are most likely to require attention are the brushes. Measure the length of the brushes and compare the results to the brush length listed in this Chapter's Specifications **(see illustration).** If any of the brushes are worn beyond the service limit, renew them as a set.

13 Check that the brushes are firmly

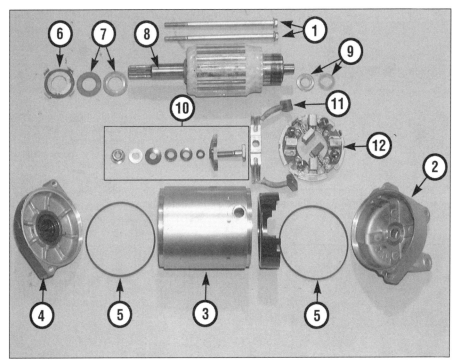

30.12a Starter motor components

1 Long bolts	6 Tabbed washer	10 Terminal bolt assembly
2 Rear cover	7 Insulating washer and	11 Terminal brush
3 Motor housing	shim	assembly
4 Front cover	8 Armature	12 Brushplate
5 O-ring	9 Rear shims	

30.12b Measuring brush length

9

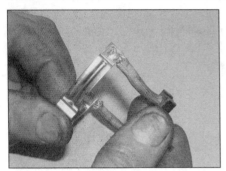

30.13 Check the brush wire connections

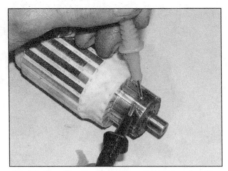

30.15 Continuity should exist between the commutator bars

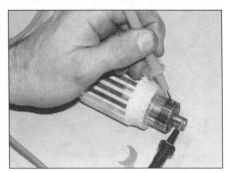

30.16 There should be no continuity between the commutator bars and the armature shaft

attached to their terminals **(see illustration)**. If the brushes are not worn excessively, cracked, chipped, or otherwise damaged, they may be re-used.

14 Inspect the commutator bars on the armature for scoring, scratches and discoloration. The commutator can be cleaned and polished with crocus cloth, but do not use sandpaper or emery paper. After cleaning, wipe away any residue with a cloth soaked in electrical system cleaner or denatured alcohol.

15 Using a multimeter or a test light and battery, check for continuity between the commutator bars **(see illustration)**. Continuity (zero resistance)

should exist between each bar and all of the others.

16 Also, check for continuity between the commutator bars and the armature shaft **(see illustration)**. There should be no continuity (infinite resistance) between the commutator and the shaft. If the checks indicate otherwise, the armature is defective. **Note:** *Apart from brush sets and O-rings, individual components are not available for the starter motor. If the armature or armature bearings are damaged or worn, or the motor housing is damaged, the motor will have to renewed as complete unit.*

17 Temporarily reassemble the housing insulator, terminal brushes, terminal and

brushplate (see Steps 21 to 23). Install the O-ring and washers and secure the assembly with the terminal nut (see Step 10).

18 Check for continuity between the terminal brushes and the terminal **(see illustration)**. There should be continuity (zero resistance). Check for continuity between the terminal brushes and the housing **(see illustration)**. There should be no continuity (infinite resistance).

19 Check for continuity between the insulated and non-insulated brush holders on the brushplate **(see illustration)**. There should be no continuity (infinite resistance).

20 Inspect the teeth on the starter motor shaft, the bearing and seal in the front cover and the bearing in the rear cover **(see illustration)**.

Reassembly

21 If not already done, install the housing insulator, terminal brushes and terminal in the motor housing **(see illustrations 30.11c, b and a)**.

22 Fit the O-ring, insulating washers and standard washer on the terminal and then fit and tighten the nut **(see illustration)**.

23 Fit the brushplate onto the motor housing, ensuring the tabs on the plate locate in the cut-outs in the housing and the terminal brush wires are not trapped by the brushplate **(see illustration 30.8b)**.

24 Install the brushes in their holders and

30.18a There should be continuity between the terminal brushes and the terminal

30.18b There should be no continuity between the terminal brushes and the housing

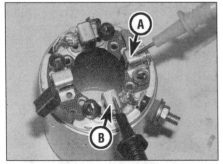

30.19 There should be no continuity between the insulated (A) and non-insulated (B) brush holders

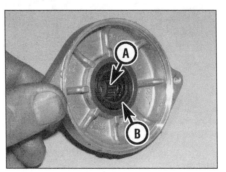

30.20 Inspect the bearing (A) and seal (B) in the front cover

30.22 Secure the terminal assembly and brushes in the housing with the terminal nut (arrowed)

30.24 Place the brush springs on the edges of the brush holders (arrowed)

30.25 Ensure the brushes press against the commutator

30.27 Install the tabbed washer in the front cover

place the ends of the brush springs onto the edges of the brush holders **(see illustration)**.

25 Carefully insert the armature into the housing until the commutator passes through the brushplate, then release the brush springs and check that each brush is securely pressed against the commutator **(see illustration)**.

26 Fit the shims onto the armature shaft and the cover O-ring onto the housing (see Step 6). Lubricate the shaft with a smear of grease then install the rear cover, aligning the marks made on removal (see Step 2).

27 Slide the shims and then the insulating washer onto the front end of the armature shaft and lubricate the shaft with a smear of grease. Apply a smear of grease to the inside of the front cover seal and fit the tabbed washer into the cover, making sure the tabs locate correctly **(see illustration)**. Fit the front cover O-ring onto the housing, then install the cover, aligning the marks made on removal (see Step 2).

28 Check the marks on the rear cover, motor housing and front cover are correctly aligned, then install the long bolts and tighten them securely.

29 Install the starter motor (see Section 29).

31 Charging system testing – general information and precautions

1 If the performance of the charging system is suspect, the system as a whole should be checked first, followed by testing of the individual components. **Note:** *Before beginning the checks, make sure the battery is fully charged and that the voltage between its terminals is greater than 13 volts, and that all system connections are clean and tight.*

2 Checking the output of the charging system and the performance of the various components within the charging system requires the use of a multimeter with voltage, current (Amps) and resistance (ohms) checking facilities. Ensure that the multimeter battery is in good condition before commencing tests.

3 When making the tests, follow the

procedures carefully to prevent incorrect connections or short circuits, as irreparable damage to electrical system components may result if short circuits occur.

4 If a multimeter is not available, the job of checking the charging system should be left to a Honda dealer or automotive electrician.

32 Charging system – leakage and output tests

1 If the charging system of the machine is thought to be faulty carry-out the following tests with a multimeter.

Leakage test

2 Ensure that the ignition switch is OFF and disconnect the lead from the battery negative (-ve) terminal (see Section 3).

3 Set the multimeter to the Amps function and connect its negative (-ve) probe to the battery negative (-ve) terminal, and positive (+ve) probe to the disconnected negative (-ve) lead. Always set the meter to a high Amps range initially and then bring it down to the mA (milli Amps) range; if there is a high current flow in the circuit it may blow the meter's fuse.

Caution: Always connect an ammeter(multimeter set to Amps) in series, never in parallel with the battery,

32.7 Checking the charging system output

otherwise it will be damaged. Do not turn the ignition ON or operate the starter motor when the ammeter is connected – a sudden surge in current will blow the meter's fuse.

4 If the current leakage indicated exceeds the amount specified at the beginning of this Chapter, there is probably a short circuit in the wiring. Disconnect the meter and reconnect the negative (-ve) lead to the battery, tightening it securely,

5 If leakage is indicated, use the wiring diagrams at the end of this book to systematically disconnect individual electrical components and repeat the test until the source is identified.

 HAYNES HiNT *If an alarm system has been fitted, note that its current draw should be taken into account when measuring current leakage.*

Output test

6 Start the engine and warm it up to normal operating temperature, then stop the engine. Remove the right-hand side panel to gain access to the battery (see Section 3).

7 Connect the multimeter set to the 0 – 20 volts DC scale (voltmeter) across the terminals of the battery, (positive (+ve) probe to battery positive (+ve) terminal, negative (-ve) probe to battery negative (-ve) terminal) **(see illustration)**. Start the engine and turn the headlight HI beam on. Slowly increase the engine speed to 5,000 rpm and note the reading obtained, then stop the engine and turn the ignition OFF; do not allow the engine to overheat. The regulated voltage output should be as specified at the beginning of this Chapter. If the voltage output is outside these limits, check the alternator and the regulator (see Sections 33 and 34).

 Warning: Do not allow exhaust gases to build up in the work area; either perform the check outside or use an exhaust gas extraction system.

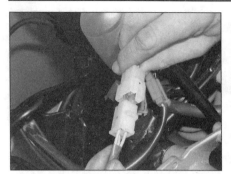

33.2 Disconnect the alternator wiring connector

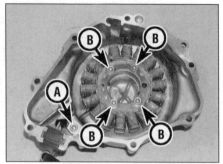

33.7 Alternator wiring clamp bolt (A) and stator bolts (B)

33.8a Hold the rotor with a strap . . .

33 Alternator – check, removal and installation

Check

1 Remove the left-hand side panel.
2 Trace the alternator wiring back from the top of the left-hand engine cover and disconnect it at the white 3-pin connector **(see illustration)**.
3 Using the multimeter set to the resistance (ohms) scale, measure the resistance between each of the yellow wire terminals on the alternator side of the connector, taking a total of three readings. If the stator coils are in good condition the three readings should be within the range shown in the Specifications at the beginning of this Chapter.

4 Check for continuity between each terminal and earth (ground); there should be no continuity (infinite resistance). If there is continuity, either the alternator stator coils are faulty or the wiring between the connector and the coils is damaged. Check the wiring carefully before condemning the stator coils.

Removal

5 Free the alternator wiring from any clips or ties and feed it through to the left-hand engine cover.
6 Remove the left-hand engine cover (see Chapter 2, Section 21).
7 To remove the alternator stator, first unscrew the bolt securing the wiring clamp to the cover and remove the bolt, clamp and the wiring grommets from the engine cover. Unscrew the bolts securing the stator to the cover and remove the stator **(see illustration)**.

8 To remove the rotor bolt from the end of the crankshaft it is necessary to stop the rotor from turning. Use the Honda service tool (Part Number 07725-0040000) or a rotor holding strap **(see illustration)**. Alternatively, if the engine is in the frame, place the transmission in gear and have an assistant apply the rear brake to stop the rotor turning, then unscrew the bolt and remove the bolt and washer **(see illustration)**.
9 To remove the rotor from the shaft it is necessary to use a rotor puller (the Honda service tool Part Number 07733-0020001 is ideal). Thread the rotor puller into the centre of the rotor and turn it until the rotor is displaced from the shaft **(see illustration)**. Remove the Woodruff key from its slot in the end of the crankshaft for safekeeping if it is loose **(see illustration)**.

Installation

10 Install the stator in the cover, aligning the wiring with the outlet hole **(see illustration 33.7)**. Apply a suitable non-permanent thread-locking compound to the stator bolt threads, then install the bolts and tighten them to the torque setting specified at the beginning of this Chapter. Apply a suitable sealant to the wiring grommets, then install them in the seats in the cover. Secure the wiring with its clamp and tighten the clamp bolt **(see illustration)**.
11 Clean the tapered end of the crankshaft and the corresponding mating surface on the inside of the rotor with a suitable solvent. If removed, fit the Woodruff key into its slot in the crankshaft **(see illustration)**. Make sure

33.8b . . . and remove the bolt and washer

33.9a Remove the rotor from the shaft with a puller . . .

33.9b . . . then remove the Woodruff key (arrowed) from the shaft

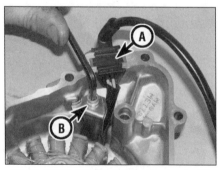

33.10 Apply sealant to the grommets (A) and tighten the clamp bolt (B) securely

33.11 Fit the Woodruff key into its slot

34.1 Location of the regulator/rectifier

that no metal objects have attached themselves to the magnet on the inside of the rotor, then install the rotor onto the shaft, aligning the slot in the rotor with the Woodruff key **(see illustration 33.9b)**.

12 Lubricate the threads of the rotor bolt with clean engine oil, then install the bolt and washer and tighten the bolt to the torque setting specified at the beginning of this Chapter. Use the method employed on removal to prevent the rotor from turning (see Step 8).

13 Install the left-hand engine cover (see Chapter 2, Section 21).

14 Feed the alternator wiring back to its connector, making sure it is correctly routed and secured, and reconnect it (see Step 2).

34 Regulator/rectifier – check and replacement

> **HAYNES HiNT** *Clues to a faulty regulator are constantly blowing bulbs, with brightness varying considerably with engine speed, and battery overheating.*

Check

1 Remove the fuel tank (see Chapter 4). The regulator/rectifier is mounted on the right-hand side of the frame **(see illustration)**.

2 Disconnect the wiring connector, and check for continuity between the green wire terminal in the wiring connector and earth (ground). There should be continuity. **Note:** *A poor earth (ground) connection will result in a higher than normal voltage output from the alternator.*

3 With the multimeter set to the 0 – 20 volts DC scale, connect the positive (+ve) probe to the red/white wire terminal in the connector and the negative (-ve) probe to earth (ground). The meter should register battery voltage.

4 Switch the multimeter to the resistance (ohms) scale. Measure the resistance between each of the yellow wire terminals in the wiring connector, taking a total of three readings. If the stator coils are in good condition (see Section 33) and the wiring between the alternator and the rectifier is good, the three readings should be within the range shown for stator coil resistance in the Specifications at the beginning of this Chapter.

5 If the above checks do not provide the specified results, check the wiring between the battery, regulator/rectifier and alternator (see the *Wiring Diagrams* at the end of this Chapter).

6 If the wiring is good, take the regulator/rectifier to a Honda dealer for confirmation of its condition before renewing it.

Replacement

7 Unscrew the two bolts securing the regulator/rectifier and remove it, noting the wire secured by the right-hand bolt **(see illustration 34.1)**.

8 To install the regulator/rectifier, ensure that the terminals in the connector are clean and connect it to the unit. Install the mounting bolts with the wire on the right-hand bolt, and tighten the bolts securely.

9 Install the fuel tank (see Chapter 4).

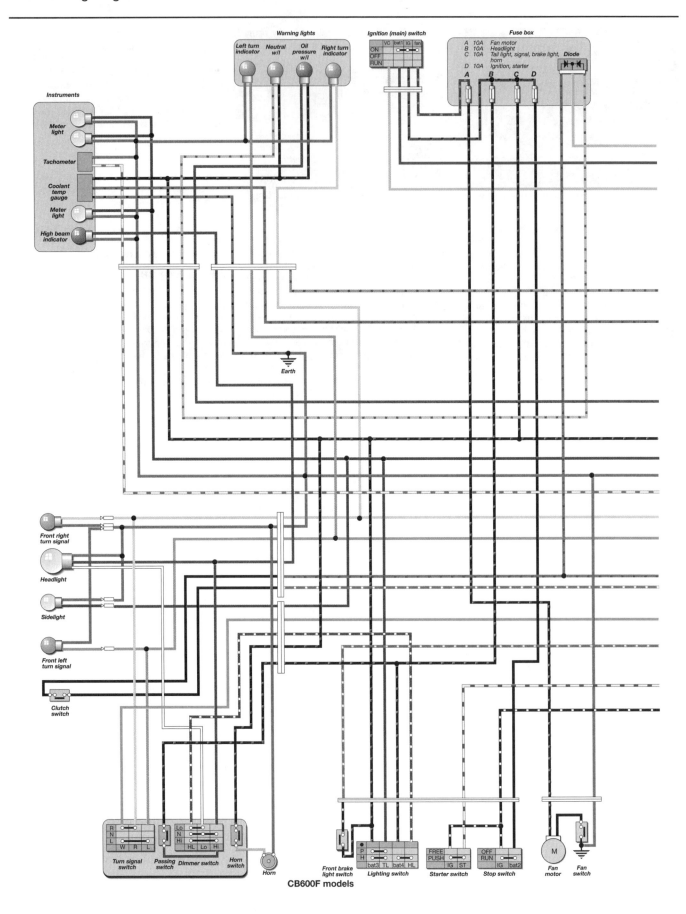

CB600F models

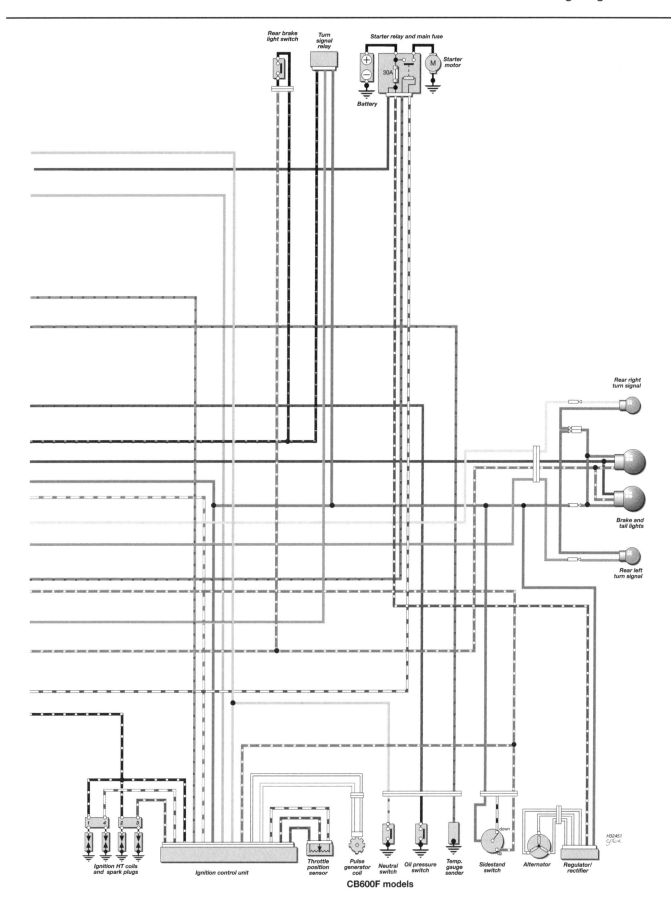

Rear brake
light switch

Turn
signal
relay

Starter relay and main fuse

30A

M

Starter
motor

Battery

Rear right
turn signal

Brake and
tail lights

Rear left
turn signal

H32451

Ignition HT coils
and spark plugs

1 4 2 3

Ignition control unit

Throttle
position
sensor

Pulse
generator
coil

Neutral
switch

Oil pressure
switch

Temp.
gauge
sender

down

up

Sidestand
switch

Alternator

Regulator/
rectifier

CB600F models

9

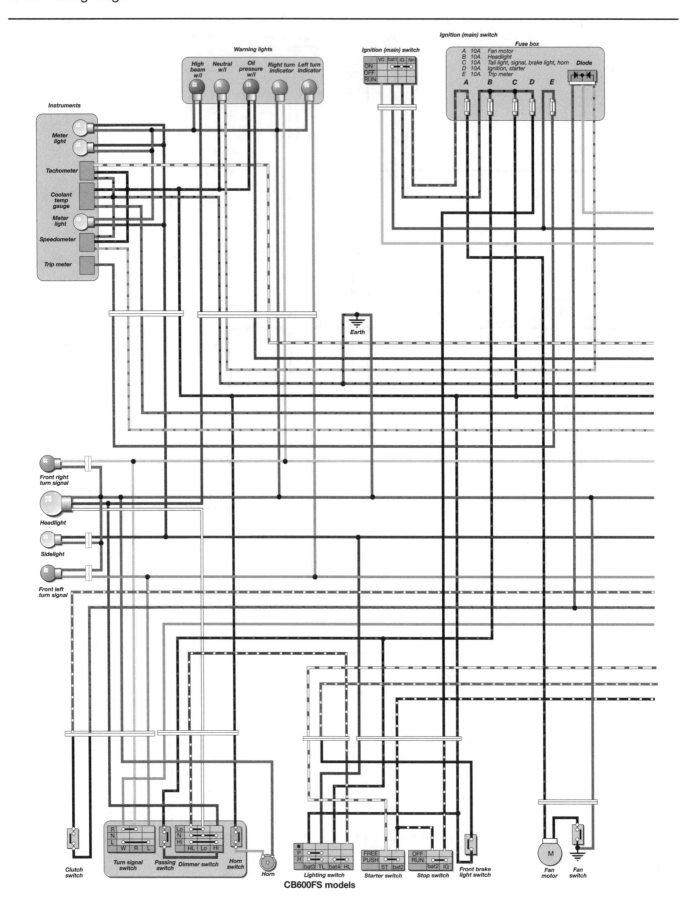

CB600FS models

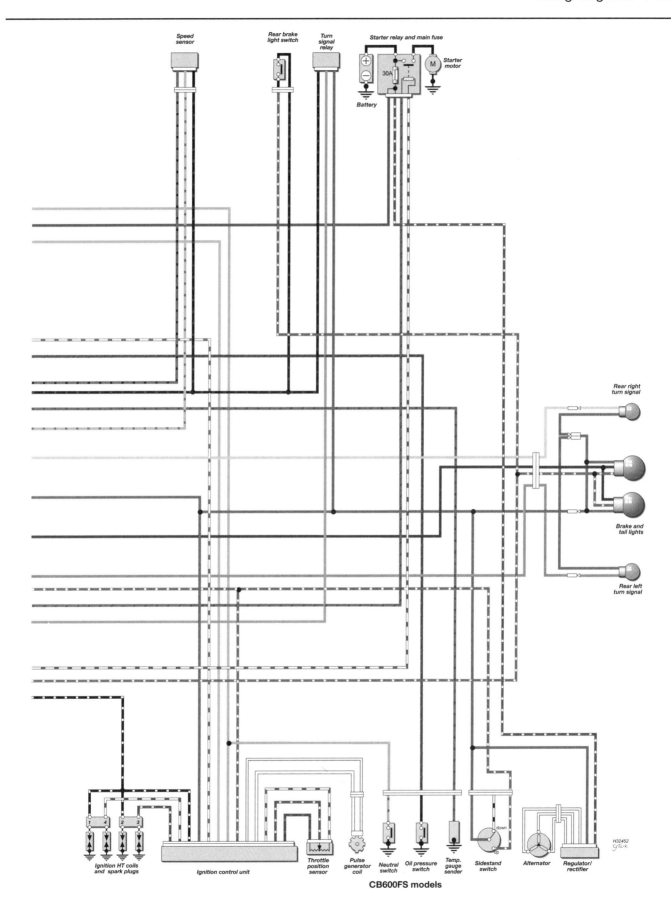

CB600FS models

Speed sensor

Rear brake light switch

Turn signal relay

Starter relay and main fuse

Starter motor

Battery

30A

M

Rear right turn signal

Brake and tail lights

Rear left turn signal

Ignition HT coils and spark plugs

Ignition control unit

Throttle position sensor

Pulse generator coil

Neutral switch

Oil pressure switch

Temp. gauge sender

Sidestand switch

Alternator

Regulator/ rectifier

down

up

H32452

9

Notes

Reference

Tools and Workshop Tips

● Building up a tool kit and equipping your workshop ● Using tools ● Understanding bearing, seal, fastener and chain sizes and markings ● Repair techniques

Security

REF•20

● Locks and chains ● U-locks ● Disc locks ● Alarms and immobilisers ● Security marking systems ● Tips on how to prevent bike theft

Lubricants and fluids

REF•23

● Engine oils ● Transmission (gear) oils ● Coolant/anti-freeze ● Fork oils and suspension fluids ● Brake/clutch fluids ● Spray lubes, degreasers and solvents

Conversion Factors

REF•26

$$34\ N_m \times 0.738$$
$$= 25\ lbf\ ft$$

● Formulae for conversion of the metric (SI) units used throughout the manual into Imperial measures

MOT Test Checks

REF•27

● A guide to the UK MOT test ● Which items are tested ● How to prepare your motorcycle for the test and perform a pre-test check

Storage

REF•32

● How to prepare your motorcycle for going into storage and protect essential systems ● How to get the motorcycle back on the road

Fault Finding

REF•35

● Common faults and their likely causes ● How to check engine cylinder compression ● How to make electrical tests and use test meters

Technical Terms Explained

REF•49

● Component names, technical terms and common abbreviations explained

Index

REF•53

Buying tools

A toolkit is a fundamental requirement for servicing and repairing a motorcycle. Although there will be an initial expense in building up enough tools for servicing, this will soon be offset by the savings made by doing the job yourself. As experience and confidence grow, additional tools can be added to enable the repair and overhaul of the motorcycle. Many of the specialist tools are expensive and not often used so it may be preferable to hire them, or for a group of friends or motorcycle club to join in the purchase.

As a rule, it is better to buy more expensive, good quality tools. Cheaper tools are likely to wear out faster and need to be renewed more often, nullifying the original saving.

> ⚠️ **Warning: To avoid the risk of a poor quality tool breaking in use, causing injury or damage to the component being worked on, always aim to purchase tools which meet the relevant national safety standards.**

The following lists of tools do not represent the manufacturer's service tools, but serve as a guide to help the owner decide which tools are needed for this level of work. In addition, items such as an electric drill, hacksaw, files, soldering iron and a workbench equipped with a vice, may be needed. Although not classed as tools, a selection of bolts, screws, nuts, washers and pieces of tubing always come in useful.

For more information about tools, refer to the Haynes *Motorcycle Workshop Practice TechBook* (Bk. No. 3470).

Manufacturer's service tools

Inevitably certain tasks require the use of a service tool. Where possible an alternative tool or method of approach is recommended, but sometimes there is no option if personal injury or damage to the component is to be avoided. Where required, service tools are referred to in the relevant procedure.

Service tools can usually only be purchased from a motorcycle dealer and are identified by a part number. Some of the commonly-used tools, such as rotor pullers, are available in aftermarket form from mail-order motorcycle tool and accessory suppliers.

Maintenance and minor repair tools

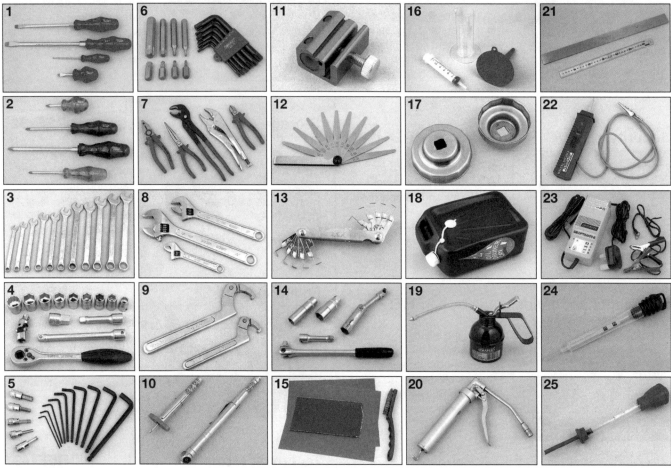

1. *Set of flat-bladed screwdrivers*
2. *Set of Phillips head screwdrivers*
3. *Combination open-end and ring spanners*
4. *Socket set (3/8 inch or 1/2 inch drive)*
5. *Set of Allen keys or bits*
6. *Set of Torx keys or bits*
7. *Pliers, cutters and self-locking grips (Mole grips)*
8. *Adjustable spanners*
9. *C-spanners*
10. *Tread depth gauge and tyre pressure gauge*
11. *Cable oiler clamp*
12. *Feeler gauges*
13. *Spark plug gap measuring tool*
14. *Spark plug spanner or deep plug sockets*
15. *Wire brush and emery paper*
16. *Calibrated syringe, measuring vessel and funnel*
17. *Oil filter adapters*
18. *Oil drainer can or tray*
19. *Pump type oil can*
20. *Grease gun*
21. *Straight-edge and steel rule*
22. *Continuity tester*
23. *Battery charger*
24. *Hydrometer (for battery specific gravity check)*
25. *Anti-freeze tester (for liquid-cooled engines)*

Repair and overhaul tools

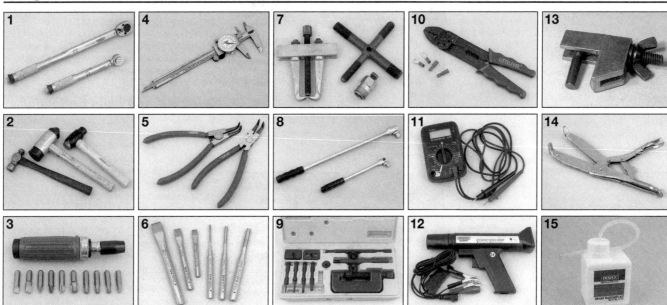

1 Torque wrench
   (small and mid-ranges)
2 Conventional, plastic or
   soft-faced hammers
3 Impact driver set
4 Vernier gauge
5 Circlip pliers (internal and
   external, or combination)
6 Set of cold chisels
   and punches
7 Selection of pullers
8 Breaker bars
9 Chain breaking/
   riveting tool set
10 Wire stripper and
    crimper tool
11 Multimeter (measures
    amps, volts and ohms)
12 Stroboscope (for
    dynamic timing checks)
13 Hose clamp
    (wingnut type shown)
14 Clutch holding tool
15 One-man brake/clutch
    bleeder kit

Specialist tools

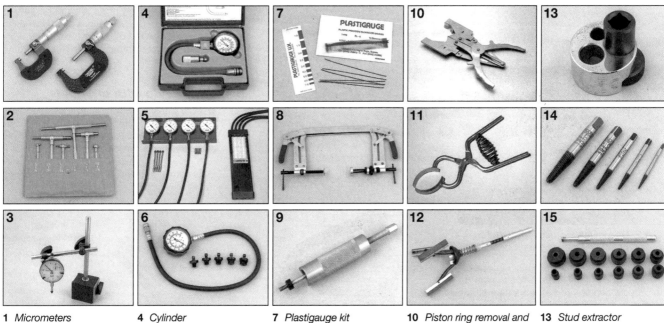

1 Micrometers
   (external type)
2 Telescoping gauges
3 Dial gauge
4 Cylinder
   compression gauge
5 Vacuum gauges (left) or
   manometer (right)
6 Oil pressure gauge
7 Plastigauge kit
8 Valve spring compressor
   (4-stroke engines)
9 Piston pin drawbolt tool
10 Piston ring removal and
    installation tool
11 Piston ring clamp
12 Cylinder bore hone
    (stone type shown)
13 Stud extractor
14 Screw extractor set
15 Bearing driver set

1 Workshop equipment and facilities

The workbench

● Work is made much easier by raising the bike up on a ramp - components are much more accessible if raised to waist level. The hydraulic or pneumatic types seen in the dealer's workshop are a sound investment if you undertake a lot of repairs or overhauls (see illustration 1.1).

1.1 Hydraulic motorcycle ramp

● If raised off ground level, the bike must be supported on the ramp to avoid it falling. Most ramps incorporate a front wheel locating clamp which can be adjusted to suit different diameter wheels. When tightening the clamp, take care not to mark the wheel rim or damage the tyre - use wood blocks on each side to prevent this.
● Secure the bike to the ramp using tie-downs (see illustration 1.2). If the bike has only a sidestand, and hence leans at a dangerous angle when raised, support the bike on an auxiliary stand.

1.2 Tie-downs are used around the passenger footrests to secure the bike

● Auxiliary (paddock) stands are widely available from mail order companies or motorcycle dealers and attach either to the wheel axle or swingarm pivot (see illustration 1.3). If the motorcycle has a centrestand, you can support it under the crankcase to prevent it toppling whilst either wheel is removed (see illustration 1.4).

1.3 This auxiliary stand attaches to the swingarm pivot

1.4 Always use a block of wood between the engine and jack head when supporting the engine in this way

Fumes and fire

● Refer to the Safety first! page at the beginning of the manual for full details. Make sure your workshop is equipped with a fire extinguisher suitable for fuel-related fires (Class B fire - flammable liquids) - it is not sufficient to have a water-filled extinguisher.
● Always ensure adequate ventilation is available. Unless an exhaust gas extraction system is available for use, ensure that the engine is run outside of the workshop.
● If working on the fuel system, make sure the workshop is ventilated to avoid a build-up of fumes. This applies equally to fume build-up when charging a battery. Do not smoke or allow anyone else to smoke in the workshop.

Fluids

● If you need to drain fuel from the tank, store it in an approved container marked as suitable for the storage of petrol (gasoline) (see illustration 1.5). Do not store fuel in glass jars or bottles.

1.5 Use an approved can only for storing petrol (gasoline)

● Use proprietary engine degreasers or solvents which have a high flash-point, such as paraffin (kerosene), for cleaning off oil, grease and dirt - never use petrol (gasoline) for cleaning. Wear rubber gloves when handling solvent and engine degreaser. The fumes from certain solvents can be dangerous - always work in a well-ventilated area.

Dust, eye and hand protection

● Protect your lungs from inhalation of dust particles by wearing a filtering mask over the nose and mouth. Many frictional materials still contain asbestos which is dangerous to your health. Protect your eyes from spouts of liquid and sprung components by wearing a pair of protective goggles (see illustration 1.6).

1.6 A fire extinguisher, goggles, mask and protective gloves should be at hand in the workshop

● Protect your hands from contact with solvents, fuel and oils by wearing rubber gloves. Alternatively apply a barrier cream to your hands before starting work. If handling hot components or fluids, wear suitable gloves to protect your hands from scalding and burns.

What to do with old fluids

● Old cleaning solvent, fuel, coolant and oils should not be poured down domestic drains or onto the ground. Package the fluid up in old oil containers, label it accordingly, and take it to a garage or disposal facility. Contact your local authority for location of such sites or ring the oil care hotline.

OIL CARE
FOLLOW THE CODE
OIL BANK LINE
0800 66 33 66
www.oilbankline.org.uk

Note: It is antisocial and illegal to dump oil down the drain. To find the location of your local oil recycling bank, call this number free.

In the USA, note that any oil supplier must accept used oil for recycling.

2 Fasteners -
screws, bolts and nuts

Fastener types and applications

Bolts and screws

● Fastener head types are either of hexagonal, Torx or splined design, with internal and external versions of each type **(see illustrations 2.1 and 2.2)**; splined head fasteners are not in common use on motorcycles. The conventional slotted or Phillips head design is used for certain screws. Bolt or screw length is always measured from the underside of the head to the end of the item **(see illustration 2.11)**.

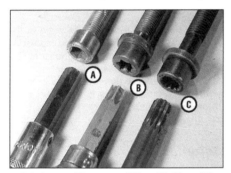

2.1 **Internal hexagon/Allen (A), Torx (B) and splined (C) fasteners, with corresponding bits**

2.2 **External Torx (A), splined (B) and hexagon (C) fasteners, with corresponding sockets**

● Certain fasteners on the motorcycle have a tensile marking on their heads, the higher the marking the stronger the fastener. High tensile fasteners generally carry a 10 or higher marking. Never replace a high tensile fastener with one of a lower tensile strength.

Washers (see illustration 2.3)

● Plain washers are used between a fastener head and a component to prevent damage to the component or to spread the load when torque is applied. Plain washers can also be used as spacers or shims in certain assemblies. Copper or aluminium plain washers are often used as sealing washers on drain plugs.

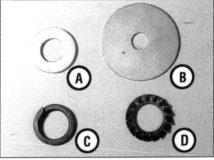

2.3 **Plain washer (A), penny washer (B), spring washer (C) and serrated washer (D)**

● The split-ring spring washer works by applying axial tension between the fastener head and component. If flattened, it is fatigued and must be renewed. If a plain (flat) washer is used on the fastener, position the spring washer between the fastener and the plain washer.
● Serrated star type washers dig into the fastener and component faces, preventing loosening. They are often used on electrical earth (ground) connections to the frame.
● Cone type washers (sometimes called Belleville) are conical and when tightened apply axial tension between the fastener head and component. They must be installed with the dished side against the component and often carry an OUTSIDE marking on their outer face. If flattened, they are fatigued and must be renewed.
● Tab washers are used to lock plain nuts or bolts on a shaft. A portion of the tab washer is bent up hard against one flat of the nut or bolt to prevent it loosening. Due to the tab washer being deformed in use, a new tab washer should be used every time it is disturbed.
● Wave washers are used to take up endfloat on a shaft. They provide light springing and prevent excessive side-to-side play of a component. Can be found on rocker arm shafts.

Nuts and split pins

● Conventional plain nuts are usually six-sided **(see illustration 2.4)**. They are sized by thread diameter and pitch. High tensile nuts carry a number on one end to denote their tensile strength.

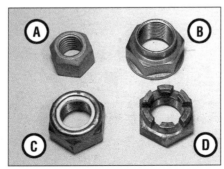

2.4 **Plain nut (A), shouldered locknut (B), nylon insert nut (C) and castellated nut (D)**

● Self-locking nuts either have a nylon insert, or two spring metal tabs, or a shoulder which is staked into a groove in the shaft - their advantage over conventional plain nuts is a resistance to loosening due to vibration. The nylon insert type can be used a number of times, but must be renewed when the friction of the nylon insert is reduced, ie when the nut spins freely on the shaft. The spring tab type can be reused unless the tabs are damaged. The shouldered type must be renewed every time it is disturbed.
● Split pins (cotter pins) are used to lock a castellated nut to a shaft or to prevent slackening of a plain nut. Common applications are wheel axles and brake torque arms. Because the split pin arms are deformed to lock around the nut a new split pin must always be used on installation - always fit the correct size split pin which will fit snugly in the shaft hole. Make sure the split pin arms are correctly located around the nut **(see illustrations 2.5 and 2.6)**.

2.5 **Bend split pin (cotter pin) arms as shown (arrows) to secure a castellated nut**

2.6 **Bend split pin (cotter pin) arms as shown to secure a plain nut**

Caution: If the castellated nut slots do not align with the shaft hole after tightening to the torque setting, tighten the nut until the next slot aligns with the hole - never slacken the nut to align its slot.

● R-pins (shaped like the letter R), or slip pins as they are sometimes called, are sprung and can be reused if they are otherwise in good condition. Always install R-pins with their closed end facing forwards **(see illustration 2.7)**.

2.7 Correct fitting of R-pin. Arrow indicates forward direction

Circlips (see illustration 2.8)

● Circlips (sometimes called snap-rings) are used to retain components on a shaft or in a housing and have corresponding external or internal ears to permit removal. Parallel-sided (machined) circlips can be installed either way round in their groove, whereas stamped circlips (which have a chamfered edge on one face) must be installed with the chamfer facing away from the direction of thrust load **(see illustration 2.9).**

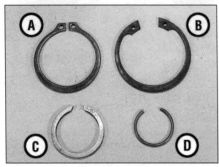

2.8 External stamped circlip (A), internal stamped circlip (B), machined circlip (C) and wire circlip (D)

● Always use circlip pliers to remove and install circlips; expand or compress them just enough to remove them. After installation, rotate the circlip in its groove to ensure it is securely seated. If installing a circlip on a splined shaft, always align its opening with a shaft channel to ensure the circlip ends are well supported and unlikely to catch **(see illustration 2.10).**

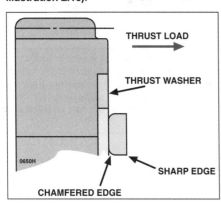

2.9 Correct fitting of a stamped circlip

THRUST LOAD

THRUST WASHER

SHARP EDGE

CHAMFERED EDGE

0650H

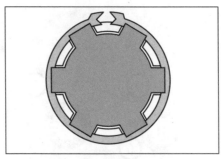

2.10 Align circlip opening with shaft channel

● Circlips can wear due to the thrust of components and become loose in their grooves, with the subsequent danger of becoming dislodged in operation. For this reason, renewal is advised every time a circlip is disturbed.

● Wire circlips are commonly used as piston pin retaining clips. If a removal tang is provided, long-nosed pliers can be used to dislodge them, otherwise careful use of a small flat-bladed screwdriver is necessary. Wire circlips should be renewed every time they are disturbed.

Thread diameter and pitch

● Diameter of a male thread (screw, bolt or stud) is the outside diameter of the threaded portion **(see illustration 2.11)**. Most motorcycle manufacturers use the ISO (International Standards Organisation) metric system expressed in millimetres, eg M6 refers to a 6 mm diameter thread. Sizing is the same for nuts, except that the thread diameter is measured across the valleys of the nut.

● Pitch is the distance between the peaks of the thread **(see illustration 2.11)**. It is expressed in millimetres, thus a common bolt size may be expressed as 6.0 x 1.0 mm (6 mm thread diameter and 1 mm pitch). Generally pitch increases in proportion to thread diameter, although there are always exceptions.

● Thread diameter and pitch are related for conventional fastener applications and the accompanying table can be used as a guide. Additionally, the AF (Across Flats), spanner or socket size dimension of the bolt or nut **(see illustration 2.11)** is linked to thread and pitch specification. Thread pitch can be measured with a thread gauge **(see illustration 2.12)**.

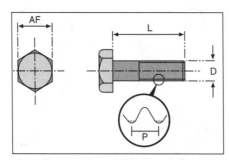

2.11 Fastener length (L), thread diameter (D), thread pitch (P) and head size (AF)

AF

L

D

P

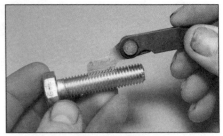

2.12 Using a thread gauge to measure pitch

AF size	Thread diameter x pitch (mm)
8 mm	M5 x 0.8
8 mm	M6 x 1.0
10 mm	M6 x 1.0
12 mm	M8 x 1.25
14 mm	M10 x 1.25
17 mm	M12 x 1.25

● The threads of most fasteners are of the right-hand type, ie they are turned clockwise to tighten and anti-clockwise to loosen. The reverse situation applies to left-hand thread fasteners, which are turned anti-clockwise to tighten and clockwise to loosen. Left-hand threads are used where rotation of a component might loosen a conventional right-hand thread fastener.

Seized fasteners

● Corrosion of external fasteners due to water or reaction between two dissimilar metals can occur over a period of time. It will build up sooner in wet conditions or in countries where salt is used on the roads during the winter. If a fastener is severely corroded it is likely that normal methods of removal will fail and result in its head being ruined. When you attempt removal, the fastener thread should be heard to crack free and unscrew easily - if it doesn't, stop there before damaging something.

● A smart tap on the head of the fastener will often succeed in breaking free corrosion which has occurred in the threads **(see illustration 2.13)**.

● An aerosol penetrating fluid (such as WD-40) applied the night beforehand may work its way down into the thread and ease removal. Depending on the location, you may be able to make up a Plasticine well around the fastener head and fill it with penetrating fluid.

2.13 A sharp tap on the head of a fastener will often break free a corroded thread

● If you are working on an engine internal component, corrosion will most likely not be a problem due to the well lubricated environment. However, components can be very tight and an impact driver is a useful tool in freeing them **(see illustration 2.14)**.

2.14 Using an impact driver to free a fastener

● Where corrosion has occurred between dissimilar metals (eg steel and aluminium alloy), the application of heat to the fastener head will create a disproportionate expansion rate between the two metals and break the seizure caused by the corrosion. Whether heat can be applied depends on the location of the fastener - any surrounding components likely to be damaged must first be removed **(see illustration 2.15)**. Heat can be applied using a paint stripper heat gun or clothes iron, or by immersing the component in boiling water - wear protective gloves to prevent scalding or burns to the hands.

2.15 Using heat to free a seized fastener

● As a last resort, it is possible to use a hammer and cold chisel to work the fastener head unscrewed **(see illustration 2.16)**. This will damage the fastener, but more importantly extreme care must be taken not to damage the surrounding component.

Caution: Remember that the component being secured is generally of more value than the bolt, nut or screw - when the fastener is freed, do not unscrew it with force, instead work the fastener back and forth when resistance is felt to prevent thread damage.

2.16 Using a hammer and chisel to free a seized fastener

Broken fasteners and damaged heads

● If the shank of a broken bolt or screw is accessible you can grip it with self-locking grips. The knurled wheel type stud extractor tool or self-gripping stud puller tool is particularly useful for removing the long studs which screw into the cylinder mouth surface of the crankcase or bolts and screws from which the head has broken off **(see illustration 2.17)**. Studs can also be removed by locking two nuts together on the threaded end of the stud and using a spanner on the lower nut **(see illustration 2.18)**.

2.17 Using a stud extractor tool to remove a broken crankcase stud

2.18 Two nuts can be locked together to unscrew a stud from a component

● A bolt or screw which has broken off below or level with the casing must be extracted using a screw extractor set. Centre punch the fastener to centralise the drill bit, then drill a hole in the fastener **(see illustration 2.19)**. Select a drill bit which is approximately half to three-quarters the

2.19 When using a screw extractor, first drill a hole in the fastener . . .

diameter of the fastener and drill to a depth which will accommodate the extractor. Use the largest size extractor possible, but avoid leaving too small a wall thickness otherwise the extractor will merely force the fastener walls outwards wedging it in the casing thread.

● If a spiral type extractor is used, thread it anti-clockwise into the fastener. As it is screwed in, it will grip the fastener and unscrew it from the casing **(see illustration 2.20)**.

2.20 . . . then thread the extractor anti-clockwise into the fastener

● If a taper type extractor is used, tap it into the fastener so that it is firmly wedged in place. Unscrew the extractor (anti-clockwise) to draw the fastener out.

⚠️ *Warning: Stud extractors are very hard and may break off in the fastener if care is not taken - ask an engineer about spark erosion if this happens.*

● Alternatively, the broken bolt/screw can be drilled out and the hole retapped for an oversize bolt/screw or a diamond-section thread insert. It is essential that the drilling is carried out squarely and to the correct depth, otherwise the casing may be ruined - if in doubt, entrust the work to an engineer.

● Bolts and nuts with rounded corners cause the correct size spanner or socket to slip when force is applied. Of the types of spanner/socket available always use a six-point type rather than an eight or twelve-point type - better grip

2.21 Comparison of surface drive ring spanner (left) with 12-point type (right)

is obtained. Surface drive spanners grip the middle of the hex flats, rather than the corners, and are thus good in cases of damaged heads **(see illustration 2.21).**

● Slotted-head or Phillips-head screws are often damaged by the use of the wrong size screwdriver. Allen-head and Torx-head screws are much less likely to sustain damage. If enough of the screw head is exposed you can use a hacksaw to cut a slot in its head and then use a conventional flat-bladed screwdriver to remove it. Alternatively use a hammer and cold chisel to tap the head of the fastener around to slacken it. Always replace damaged fasteners with new ones, preferably Torx or Allen-head type.

HAYNES HiNT

A dab of valve grinding compound between the screw head and screwdriver tip will often give a good grip.

Thread repair

● Threads (particularly those in aluminium alloy components) can be damaged by overtightening, being assembled with dirt in the threads, or from a component working loose and vibrating. Eventually the thread will fail completely, and it will be impossible to tighten the fastener.

● If a thread is damaged or clogged with old locking compound it can be renovated with a thread repair tool (thread chaser) **(see illustrations 2.22 and 2.23);** special thread

2.22 A thread repair tool being used to correct an internal thread

2.23 A thread repair tool being used to correct an external thread

chasers are available for spark plug hole threads. The tool will not cut a new thread, but clean and true the original thread. Make sure that you use the correct diameter and pitch tool. Similarly, external threads can be cleaned up with a die or a thread restorer file **(see illustration 2.24).**

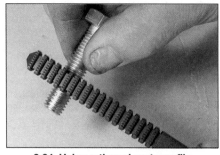

2.24 Using a thread restorer file

● It is possible to drill out the old thread and retap the component to the next thread size. This will work where there is enough surrounding material and a new bolt or screw can be obtained. Sometimes, however, this is not possible - such as where the bolt/screw passes through another component which must also be suitably modified, also in cases where a spark plug or oil drain plug cannot be obtained in a larger diameter thread size.

● The diamond-section thread insert (often known by its popular trade name of Heli-Coil) is a simple and effective method of renewing the thread and retaining the original size. A kit can be purchased which contains the tap, insert and installing tool **(see illustration 2.25).** Drill out the damaged thread with the size drill specified **(see illustration 2.26).** Carefully retap the thread **(see illustration 2.27).** Install the

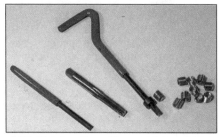

2.25 Obtain a thread insert kit to suit the thread diameter and pitch required

2.26 To install a thread insert, first drill out the original thread . . .

2.27 . . . tap a new thread . . .

2.28 . . . fit insert on the installing tool . . .

2.29 . . . and thread into the component . . .

2.30 . . . break off the tang when complete

insert on the installing tool and thread it slowly into place using a light downward pressure **(see illustrations 2.28 and 2.29).** When positioned between a 1/4 and 1/2 turn below the surface withdraw the installing tool and use the break-off tool to press down on the tang, breaking it off **(see illustration 2.30).**

● There are epoxy thread repair kits on the market which can rebuild stripped internal threads, although this repair should not be used on high load-bearing components.

Thread locking and sealing compounds

● Locking compounds are used in locations where the fastener is prone to loosening due to vibration or on important safety-related items which might cause loss of control of the motorcycle if they fail. It is also used where important fasteners cannot be secured by other means such as lockwashers or split pins.

● Before applying locking compound, make sure that the threads (internal and external) are clean and dry with all old compound removed. Select a compound to suit the component being secured - a non-permanent general locking and sealing type is suitable for most applications, but a high strength type is needed for permanent fixing of studs in castings. Apply a drop or two of the compound to the first few threads of the fastener, then thread it into place and tighten to the specified torque. Do not apply excessive thread locking compound otherwise the thread may be damaged on subsequent removal.

● Certain fasteners are impregnated with a dry film type coating of locking compound on their threads. Always renew this type of fastener if disturbed.

● Anti-seize compounds, such as copper-based greases, can be applied to protect threads from seizure due to extreme heat and corrosion. A common instance is spark plug threads and exhaust system fasteners.

3 Measuring tools and gauges

Feeler gauges

● Feeler gauges (or blades) are used for measuring small gaps and clearances (see illustration 3.1). They can also be used to measure endfloat (sideplay) of a component on a shaft where access is not possible with a dial gauge.

● Feeler gauge sets should be treated with care and not bent or damaged. They are etched with their size on one face. Keep them clean and very lightly oiled to prevent corrosion build-up.

3.1 Feeler gauges are used for measuring small gaps and clearances - thickness is marked on one face of gauge

● When measuring a clearance, select a gauge which is a light sliding fit between the two components. You may need to use two gauges together to measure the clearance accurately.

Micrometers

● A micrometer is a precision tool capable of measuring to 0.01 or 0.001 of a millimetre. It should always be stored in its case and not in the general toolbox. It must be kept clean and never dropped, otherwise its frame or measuring anvils could be distorted resulting in inaccurate readings.

● External micrometers are used for measuring outside diameters of components and have many more applications than internal micrometers. Micrometers are available in different size ranges, eg 0 to 25 mm, 25 to 50 mm, and upwards in 25 mm steps; some large micrometers have interchangeable anvils to allow a range of measurements to be taken. Generally the largest precision measurement you are likely to take on a motorcycle is the piston diameter.

● Internal micrometers (or bore micrometers) are used for measuring inside diameters, such as valve guides and cylinder bores. Telescoping gauges and small hole gauges are used in conjunction with an external micrometer, whereas the more expensive internal micrometers have their own measuring device.

External micrometer

Note: *The conventional analogue type instrument is described. Although much easier to read, digital micrometers are considerably more expensive.*

● Always check the calibration of the micrometer before use. With the anvils closed (0 to 25 mm type) or set over a test gauge (for

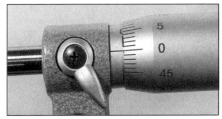

3.2 Check micrometer calibration before use

the larger types) the scale should read zero (see illustration 3.2); make sure that the anvils (and test piece) are clean first. Any discrepancy can be adjusted by referring to the instructions supplied with the tool. Remember that the micrometer is a precision measuring tool - don't force the anvils closed, use the ratchet (4) on the end of the micrometer to close it. In this way, a measured force is always applied.

● To use, first make sure that the item being measured is clean. Place the anvil of the micrometer (1) against the item and use the thimble (2) to bring the spindle (3) lightly into contact with the other side of the item (see illustration 3.3). Don't tighten the thimble down because this will damage the micrometer - instead use the ratchet (4) on the end of the micrometer. The ratchet mechanism applies a measured force preventing damage to the instrument.

● The micrometer is read by referring to the linear scale on the sleeve and the annular scale on the thimble. Read off the sleeve first to obtain the base measurement, then add the fine measurement from the thimble to obtain the overall reading. The linear scale on the sleeve represents the measuring range of the micrometer (eg 0 to 25 mm). The annular scale

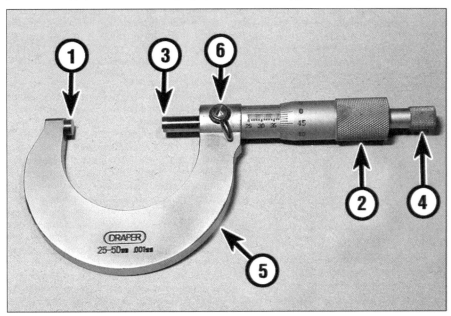

3.3 Micrometer component parts

1 Anvil	3 Spindle	5 Frame
2 Thimble	4 Ratchet	6 Locking lever

on the thimble will be in graduations of 0.01 mm (or as marked on the frame) - one full revolution of the thimble will move 0.5 mm on the linear scale. Take the reading where the datum line on the sleeve intersects the thimble's scale. Always position the eye directly above the scale otherwise an inaccurate reading will result.

In the example shown the item measures 2.95 mm **(see illustration 3.4)**:

Linear scale	2.00 mm
Linear scale	0.50 mm
Annular scale	0.45 mm
Total figure	**2.95 mm**

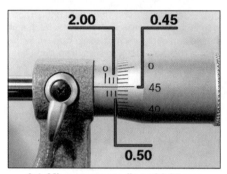

3.4 Micrometer reading of 2.95 mm

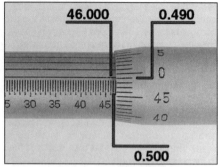

3.5 Micrometer reading of 46.99 mm on linear and annular scales . . .

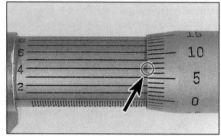

3.6 . . . and 0.004 mm on vernier scale

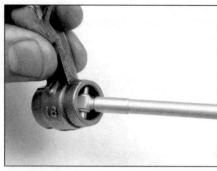

3.7 Expand the telescoping gauge in the bore, lock its position . . .

3.8 . . . then measure the gauge with a micrometer

3.9 Expand the small hole gauge in the bore, lock its position . . .

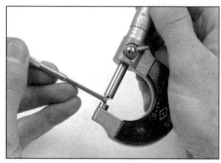

3.10 . . . then measure the gauge with a micrometer

Most micrometers have a locking lever (6) on the frame to hold the setting in place, allowing the item to be removed from the micrometer.
● Some micrometers have a vernier scale on their sleeve, providing an even finer measurement to be taken, in 0.001 increments of a millimetre. Take the sleeve and thimble measurement as described above, then check which graduation on the vernier scale aligns with that of the annular scale on the thimble **Note**: *The eye must be perpendicular to the scale when taking the vernier reading - if necessary rotate the body of the micrometer to ensure this.* Multiply the vernier scale figure by 0.001 and add it to the base and fine measurement figures.

In the example shown the item measures 46.994 mm **(see illustrations 3.5 and 3.6)**:

Linear scale (base)	46.000 mm
Linear scale (base)	00.500 mm
Annular scale (fine)	00.490 mm
Vernier scale	00.004 mm
Total figure	**46.994 mm**

Internal micrometer

● Internal micrometers are available for measuring bore diameters, but are expensive and unlikely to be available for home use. It is suggested that a set of telescoping gauges and small hole gauges, both of which must be used with an external micrometer, will suffice for taking internal measurements on a motorcycle.
● Telescoping gauges can be used to measure internal diameters of components. Select a gauge with the correct size range, make sure its ends are clean and insert it into the bore. Expand the gauge, then lock its position and withdraw it from the bore **(see illustration 3.7)**. Measure across the gauge ends with a micrometer **(see illustration 3.8)**.
● Very small diameter bores (such as valve guides) are measured with a small hole gauge. Once adjusted to a slip-fit inside the component, its position is locked and the gauge withdrawn for measurement with a micrometer **(see illustrations 3.9 and 3.10)**.

Vernier caliper

Note: *The conventional linear and dial gauge type instruments are described. Digital types are easier to read, but are far more expensive.*
● The vernier caliper does not provide the precision of a micrometer, but is versatile in being able to measure internal and external diameters. Some types also incorporate a depth gauge. It is ideal for measuring clutch plate friction material and spring free lengths.
● To use the conventional linear scale vernier, slacken off the vernier clamp screws (1) and set its jaws over (2), or inside (3), the item to be measured **(see illustration 3.11)**. Slide the jaw into contact, using the thumb-wheel (4) for fine movement of the sliding scale (5) then tighten the clamp screws (1). Read off the main scale (6) where the zero on the sliding scale (5) intersects it, taking the whole number to the left of the zero; this provides the base measurement. View along the sliding scale and select the division which lines up exactly with any of the divisions on the main scale, noting that the divisions usually represents 0.02 of a millimetre. Add this fine measurement to the base measurement to obtain the total reading.

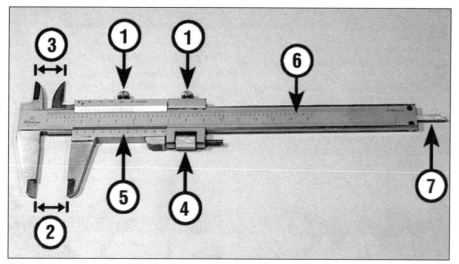

3.11 Vernier component parts (linear gauge)

1 Clamp screws
2 External jaws
3 Internal jaws
4 Thumbwheel
5 Sliding scale
6 Main scale
7 Depth gauge

In the example shown the item measures 55.92 mm **(see illustration 3.12)**:

Base measurement	55.00 mm
Fine measurement	00.92 mm
Total figure	**55.92 mm**

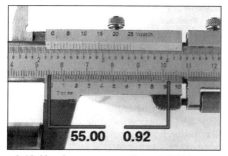

3.12 Vernier gauge reading of 55.92 mm

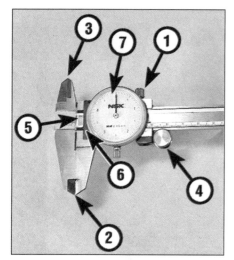

3.13 Vernier component parts (dial gauge)

1 Clamp screw
2 External jaws
3 Internal jaws
4 Thumbwheel
5 Main scale
6 Sliding scale
7 Dial gauge

● Some vernier calipers are equipped with a dial gauge for fine measurement. Before use, check that the jaws are clean, then close them fully and check that the dial gauge reads zero. If necessary adjust the gauge ring accordingly. Slacken the vernier clamp screw (1) and set its jaws over (2), or inside (3), the item to be measured **(see illustration 3.13)**. Slide the jaws into contact, using the thumbwheel (4) for fine movement. Read off the main scale (5) where the edge of the sliding scale (6) intersects it, taking the whole number to the left of the zero; this provides the base measurement. Read off the needle position on the dial gauge (7) scale to provide the fine measurement; each division represents 0.05 of a millimetre. Add this fine measurement to the base measurement to obtain the total reading.

In the example shown the item measures 55.95 mm **(see illustration 3.14)**:

Base measurement	55.00 mm
Fine measurement	00.95 mm
Total figure	**55.95 mm**

3.14 Vernier gauge reading of 55.95 mm

Plastigauge

● Plastigauge is a plastic material which can be compressed between two surfaces to measure the oil clearance between them. The width of the compressed Plastigauge is measured against a calibrated scale to determine the clearance.

● Common uses of Plastigauge are for measuring the clearance between crankshaft journal and main bearing inserts, between crankshaft journal and big-end bearing inserts, and between camshaft and bearing surfaces. The following example describes big-end oil clearance measurement.

● Handle the Plastigauge material carefully to prevent distortion. Using a sharp knife, cut a length which corresponds with the width of the bearing being measured and place it carefully across the journal so that it is parallel with the shaft **(see illustration 3.15)**. Carefully install both bearing shells and the connecting rod. Without rotating the rod on the journal tighten its bolts or nuts (as applicable) to the specified torque. The connecting rod and bearings are then disassembled and the crushed Plastigauge examined.

3.15 Plastigauge placed across shaft journal

● Using the scale provided in the Plastigauge kit, measure the width of the material to determine the oil clearance **(see illustration 3.16)**. Always remove all traces of Plastigauge after use using your fingernails.

Caution: Arriving at the correct clearance demands that the assembly is torqued correctly, according to the settings and sequence (where applicable) provided by the motorcycle manufacturer.

3.16 Measuring the width of the crushed Plastigauge

Dial gauge or DTI (Dial Test Indicator)

● A dial gauge can be used to accurately measure small amounts of movement. Typical uses are measuring shaft runout or shaft endfloat (sideplay) and setting piston position for ignition timing on two-strokes. A dial gauge set usually comes with a range of different probes and adapters and mounting equipment.

● The gauge needle must point to zero when at rest. Rotate the ring around its periphery to zero the gauge.

● Check that the gauge is capable of reading the extent of movement in the work. Most gauges have a small dial set in the face which records whole millimetres of movement as well as the fine scale around the face periphery which is calibrated in 0.01 mm divisions. Read off the small dial first to obtain the base measurement, then add the measurement from the fine scale to obtain the total reading.

In the example shown the gauge reads 1.48 mm **(see illustration 3.17)**:

Base measurement	1.00 mm
Fine measurement	0.48 mm
Total figure	**1.48 mm**

3.17 Dial gauge reading of 1.48 mm

● If measuring shaft runout, the shaft must be supported in vee-blocks and the gauge mounted on a stand perpendicular to the shaft. Rest the tip of the gauge against the centre of the shaft and rotate the shaft slowly whilst watching the gauge reading **(see illustration 3.18)**. Take several measurements along the length of the shaft and record the

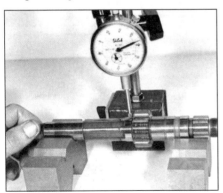

3.18 Using a dial gauge to measure shaft runout

maximum gauge reading as the amount of runout in the shaft. **Note:** *The reading obtained will be total runout at that point - some manufacturers specify that the runout figure is halved to compare with their specified runout limit.*

● Endfloat (sideplay) measurement requires that the gauge is mounted securely to the surrounding component with its probe touching the end of the shaft. Using hand pressure, push and pull on the shaft noting the maximum endfloat recorded on the gauge **(see illustration 3.19)**.

3.19 Using a dial gauge to measure shaft endfloat

● A dial gauge with suitable adapters can be used to determine piston position BTDC on two-stroke engines for the purposes of ignition timing. The gauge, adapter and suitable length probe are installed in the place of the spark plug and the gauge zeroed at TDC. If the piston position is specified as 1.14 mm BTDC, rotate the engine back to 2.00 mm BTDC, then slowly forwards to 1.14 mm BTDC.

Cylinder compression gauges

● A compression gauge is used for measuring cylinder compression. Either the rubber-cone type or the threaded adapter type can be used. The latter is preferred to ensure a perfect seal against the cylinder head. A 0 to 300 psi (0 to 20 Bar) type gauge (for petrol/gasoline engines) will be suitable for motorcycles.

● The spark plug is removed and the gauge either held hard against the cylinder head (cone type) or the gauge adapter screwed into the cylinder head (threaded type) **(see illustration 3.20)**. Cylinder compression is measured with the engine turning over, but not running - carry out the compression test as described in

3.20 Using a rubber-cone type cylinder compression gauge

Fault Finding Equipment. The gauge will hold the reading until manually released.

Oil pressure gauge

● An oil pressure gauge is used for measuring engine oil pressure. Most gauges come with a set of adapters to fit the thread of the take-off point **(see illustration 3.21)**. If the take-off point specified by the motorcycle manufacturer is an external oil pipe union, make sure that the specified replacement union is used to prevent oil starvation.

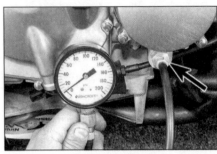

3.21 Oil pressure gauge and take-off point adapter (arrow)

● Oil pressure is measured with the engine running (at a specific rpm) and often the manufacturer will specify pressure limits for a cold and hot engine.

Straight-edge and surface plate

● If checking the gasket face of a component for warpage, place a steel rule or precision straight-edge across the gasket face and measure any gap between the straight-edge and component with feeler gauges **(see illustration 3.22)**. Check diagonally across the component and between mounting holes **(see illustration 3.23)**.

3.22 Use a straight-edge and feeler gauges to check for warpage

3.23 Check for warpage in these directions

● Checking individual components for warpage, such as clutch plain (metal) plates, requires a perfectly flat plate or piece or plate glass and feeler gauges.

4 Torque and leverage

What is torque?

● Torque describes the twisting force about a shaft. The amount of torque applied is determined by the distance from the centre of the shaft to the end of the lever and the amount of force being applied to the end of the lever; distance multiplied by force equals torque.

● The manufacturer applies a measured torque to a bolt or nut to ensure that it will not slacken in use and to hold two components securely together without movement in the joint. The actual torque setting depends on the thread size, bolt or nut material and the composition of the components being held.

● Too little torque may cause the fastener to loosen due to vibration, whereas too much torque will distort the joint faces of the component or cause the fastener to shear off. Always stick to the specified torque setting.

Using a torque wrench

● Check the calibration of the torque wrench and make sure it has a suitable range for the job. Torque wrenches are available in Nm (Newton-metres), kgf m (kilograms-force metre), lbf ft (pounds-feet), lbf in (inch-pounds). Do not confuse lbf ft with lbf in.

● Adjust the tool to the desired torque on the scale (see illustration 4.1). If your torque wrench is not calibrated in the units specified, carefully convert the figure (see Conversion Factors). A manufacturer sometimes gives a torque setting as a range (8 to 10 Nm) rather than a single figure - in this case set the tool midway between the two settings. The same torque may be expressed as 9 Nm ± 1 Nm. Some torque wrenches have a method of locking the setting so that it isn't inadvertently altered during use.

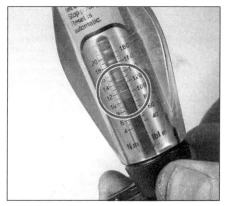

4.1 Set the torque wrench index mark to the setting required, in this case 12 Nm

● Install the bolts/nuts in their correct location and secure them lightly. Their threads must be clean and free of any old locking compound. Unless specified the threads and flange should be dry - oiled threads are necessary in certain circumstances and the manufacturer will take this into account in the specified torque figure. Similarly, the manufacturer may also specify the application of thread-locking compound.

● Tighten the fasteners in the specified sequence until the torque wrench clicks, indicating that the torque setting has been reached. Apply the torque again to double-check the setting. Where different thread diameter fasteners secure the component, as a rule tighten the larger diameter ones first.

● When the torque wrench has been finished with, release the lock (where applicable) and fully back off its setting to zero - do not leave the torque wrench tensioned. Also, do not use a torque wrench for slackening a fastener.

Angle-tightening

● Manufacturers often specify a figure in degrees for final tightening of a fastener. This usually follows tightening to a specific torque setting.

● A degree disc can be set and attached to the socket (see illustration 4.2) or a protractor can be used to mark the angle of movement on the bolt/nut head and the surrounding casting (see illustration 4.3).

4.2 Angle tightening can be accomplished with a torque-angle gauge ...

4.3 ... or by marking the angle on the surrounding component

Loosening sequences

● Where more than one bolt/nut secures a component, loosen each fastener evenly a little at a time. In this way, not all the stress of the joint is held by one fastener and the components are not likely to distort.

● If a tightening sequence is provided, work in the REVERSE of this, but if not, work from the outside in, in a criss-cross sequence (see illustration 4.4).

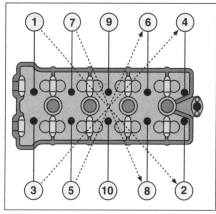

4.4 When slackening, work from the outside inwards

Tightening sequences

● If a component is held by more than one fastener it is important that the retaining bolts/nuts are tightened evenly to prevent uneven stress build-up and distortion of sealing faces. This is especially important on high-compression joints such as the cylinder head.

● A sequence is usually provided by the manufacturer, either in a diagram or actually marked in the casting. If not, always start in the centre and work outwards in a criss-cross pattern (see illustration 4.5). Start off by securing all bolts/nuts finger-tight, then set the torque wrench and tighten each fastener by a small amount in sequence until the final torque is reached. By following this practice,

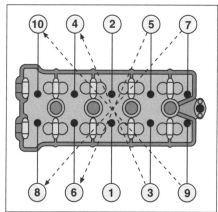

4.5 When tightening, work from the inside outwards

REF•14 **Tools and Workshop Tips**

the joint will be held evenly and will not be distorted. Important joints, such as the cylinder head and big-end fasteners often have two- or three-stage torque settings.

Applying leverage

● Use tools at the correct angle. Position a socket wrench or spanner on the bolt/nut so that you pull it towards you when loosening. If this can't be done, push the spanner without curling your fingers around it **(see illustration 4.6)** - the spanner may slip or the fastener loosen suddenly, resulting in your fingers being crushed against a component.

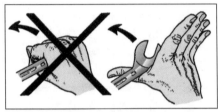

4.6 If you can't pull on the spanner to loosen a fastener, push with your hand open

● Additional leverage is gained by extending the length of the lever. The best way to do this is to use a breaker bar instead of the regular length tool, or to slip a length of tubing over the end of the spanner or socket wrench.
● If additional leverage will not work, the fastener head is either damaged or firmly corroded in place (see *Fasteners*).

5	Bearings

Bearing removal and installation

Drivers and sockets

● Before removing a bearing, always inspect the casing to see which way it must be driven out - some casings will have retaining plates or a cast step. Also check for any identifying markings on the bearing and if installed to a certain depth, measure this at this stage. Some roller bearings are sealed on one side - take note of the original fitted position.
● Bearings can be driven out of a casing using a bearing driver tool (with the correct size head) or a socket of the correct diameter. Select the driver head or socket so that it contacts the outer race of the bearing, not the balls/rollers or inner race. Always support the casing around the bearing housing with wood blocks, otherwise there is a risk of fracture. The bearing is driven out with a few blows on the driver or socket from a heavy mallet. Unless access is severely restricted (as with wheel bearings), a pin-punch is not recommended unless it is moved around the bearing to keep it square in its housing.

● The same equipment can be used to install bearings. Make sure the bearing housing is supported on wood blocks and line up the bearing in its housing. Fit the bearing as noted on removal - generally they are installed with their marked side facing outwards. Tap the bearing squarely into its housing using a driver or socket which bears only on the bearing's outer race - contact with the bearing balls/rollers or inner race will destroy it **(see illustrations 5.1 and 5.2)**.
● Check that the bearing inner race and balls/rollers rotate freely.

5.1 Using a bearing driver against the bearing's outer race

5.2 Using a large socket against the bearing's outer race

Pullers and slide-hammers

● Where a bearing is pressed on a shaft a puller will be required to extract it **(see illustration 5.3)**. Make sure that the puller clamp or legs fit securely behind the bearing and are unlikely to slip out. If pulling a bearing

5.3 This bearing puller clamps behind the bearing and pressure is applied to the shaft end to draw the bearing off

off a gear shaft for example, you may have to locate the puller behind a gear pinion if there is no access to the race and draw the gear pinion off the shaft as well **(see illustration 5.4)**.

> *Caution: Ensure that the puller's centre bolt locates securely against the end of the shaft and will not slip when pressure is applied. Also ensure that puller does not damage the shaft end.*

5.4 Where no access is available to the rear of the bearing, it is sometimes possible to draw off the adjacent component

● Operate the puller so that its centre bolt exerts pressure on the shaft end and draws the bearing off the shaft.
● When installing the bearing on the shaft, tap only on the bearing's inner race - contact with the balls/rollers or outer race with destroy the bearing. Use a socket or length of tubing as a drift which fits over the shaft end **(see illustration 5.5)**.

5.5 When installing a bearing on a shaft use a piece of tubing which bears only on the bearing's inner race

● Where a bearing locates in a blind hole in a casing, it cannot be driven or pulled out as described above. A slide-hammer with knife-edged bearing puller attachment will be required. The puller attachment passes through the bearing and when tightened expands to fit firmly behind the bearing **(see illustration 5.6)**. By operating the slide-hammer part of the tool the bearing is jarred out of its housing **(see illustration 5.7)**.
● It is possible, if the bearing is of reasonable weight, for it to drop out of its housing if the casing is heated as described opposite. If this

5.6 Expand the bearing puller so that it locks behind the bearing . . .

5.7 . . . attach the slide hammer to the bearing puller

method is attempted, first prepare a work surface which will enable the casing to be tapped face down to help dislodge the bearing - a wood surface is ideal since it will not damage the casing's gasket surface. Wearing protective gloves, tap the heated casing several times against the work surface to dislodge the bearing under its own weight **(see illustration 5.8)**.

5.8 Tapping a casing face down on wood blocks can often dislodge a bearing

● Bearings can be installed in blind holes using the driver or socket method described above.

Drawbolts

● Where a bearing or bush is set in the eye of a component, such as a suspension linkage arm or connecting rod small-end, removal by drift may damage the component. Furthermore, a rubber bushing in a shock absorber eye cannot successfully be driven out of position. If access is available to a engineering press, the task is straightforward. If not, a drawbolt can be fabricated to extract the bearing or bush.

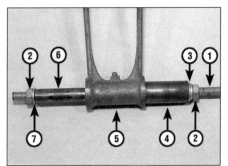

5.9 Drawbolt component parts assembled on a suspension arm

1 Bolt or length of threaded bar
2 Nuts
3 Washer (external diameter greater than tubing internal diameter)
4 Tubing (internal diameter sufficient to accommodate bearing)
5 Suspension arm with bearing
6 Tubing (external diameter slightly smaller than bearing)
7 Washer (external diameter slightly smaller than bearing)

5.10 Drawing the bearing out of the suspension arm

● To extract the bearing/bush you will need a long bolt with nut (or piece of threaded bar with two nuts), a piece of tubing which has an internal diameter larger than the bearing/bush, another piece of tubing which has an external diameter slightly smaller than the bearing/bush, and a selection of washers **(see illustrations 5.9 and 5.10)**. Note that the pieces of tubing must be of the same length, or longer, than the bearing/bush.
● The same kit (without the pieces of tubing) can be used to draw the new bearing/bush back into place **(see illustration 5.11)**.

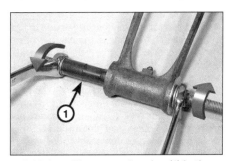

5.11 Installing a new bearing (1) in the suspension arm

Temperature change

● If the bearing's outer race is a tight fit in the casing, the aluminium casing can be heated to release its grip on the bearing. Aluminium will expand at a greater rate than the steel bearing outer race. There are several ways to do this, but avoid any localised extreme heat (such as a blow torch) - aluminium alloy has a low melting point.
● Approved methods of heating a casing are using a domestic oven (heated to 100°C) or immersing the casing in boiling water **(see illustration 5.12)**. Low temperature range localised heat sources such as a paint stripper heat gun or clothes iron can also be used **(see illustration 5.13)**. Alternatively, soak a rag in boiling water, wring it out and wrap it around the bearing housing.

> ⚠ **Warning: All of these methods require care in use to prevent scalding and burns to the hands. Wear protective gloves when handling hot components.**

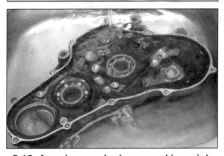

5.12 A casing can be immersed in a sink of boiling water to aid bearing removal

5.13 Using a localised heat source to aid bearing removal

● If heating the whole casing note that plastic components, such as the neutral switch, may suffer - remove them beforehand.
● After heating, remove the bearing as described above. You may find that the expansion is sufficient for the bearing to fall out of the casing under its own weight or with a light tap on the driver or socket.
● If necessary, the casing can be heated to aid bearing installation, and this is sometimes the recommended procedure if the motorcycle manufacturer has designed the housing and bearing fit with this intention.

● Installation of bearings can be eased by placing them in a freezer the night before installation. The steel bearing will contract slightly, allowing easy insertion in its housing. This is often useful when installing steering head outer races in the frame.

Bearing types and markings

● Plain shell bearings, ball bearings, needle roller bearings and tapered roller bearings will all be found on motorcycles **(see illustrations 5.14 and 5.15)**. The ball and roller types are usually caged between an inner and outer race, but uncaged variations may be found.

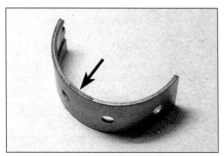

5.14 Shell bearings are either plain or grooved. They are usually identified by colour code (arrow)

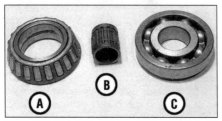

5.15 Tapered roller bearing (A), needle roller bearing (B) and ball journal bearing (C)

● Shell bearings (often called inserts) are usually found at the crankshaft main and connecting rod big-end where they are good at coping with high loads. They are made of a phosphor-bronze material and are impregnated with self-lubricating properties.

● Ball bearings and needle roller bearings consist of a steel inner and outer race with the balls or rollers between the races. They require constant lubrication by oil or grease and are good at coping with axial loads. Taper roller bearings consist of rollers set in a tapered cage set on the inner race; the outer race is separate. They are good at coping with axial loads and prevent movement along the shaft - a typical application is in the steering head.

● Bearing manufacturers produce bearings to ISO size standards and stamp one face of the bearing to indicate its internal and external diameter, load capacity and type **(see illustration 5.16)**.

● Metal bushes are usually of phosphor-bronze material. Rubber bushes are used in suspension mounting eyes. Fibre bushes have also been used in suspension pivots.

5.16 Typical bearing marking

Bearing fault finding

● If a bearing outer race has spun in its housing, the housing material will be damaged. You can use a bearing locking compound to bond the outer race in place if damage is not too severe.

● Shell bearings will fail due to damage of their working surface, as a result of lack of lubrication, corrosion or abrasive particles in the oil **(see illustration 5.17)**. Small particles of dirt in the oil may embed in the bearing material whereas larger particles will score the bearing and shaft journal. If a number of short journeys are made, insufficient heat will be generated to drive off condensation which has built up on the bearings.

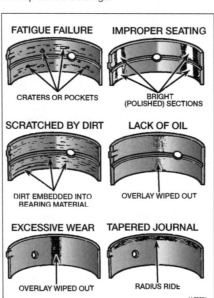

5.17 Typical bearing failures

● Ball and roller bearings will fail due to lack of lubrication or damage to the balls or rollers. Tapered-roller bearings can be damaged by overloading them. Unless the bearing is sealed on both sides, wash it in paraffin (kerosene) to remove all old grease then allow it to dry. Make a visual inspection looking to dented balls or rollers, damaged cages and worn or pitted races **(see illustration 5.18)**.

● A ball bearing can be checked for wear by listening to it when spun. Apply a film of light oil to the bearing and hold it close to the ear - hold the outer race with one hand and spin the inner

5.18 Example of ball journal bearing with damaged balls and cages

5.19 Hold outer race and listen to inner race when spun

race with the other hand **(see illustration 5.19)**. The bearing should be almost silent when spun; if it grates or rattles it is worn.

6 Oil seals

Oil seal removal and installation

● Oil seals should be renewed every time a component is dismantled. This is because the seal lips will become set to the sealing surface and will not necessarily reseal.

● Oil seals can be prised out of position using a large flat-bladed screwdriver **(see illustration 6.1)**. In the case of crankcase seals, check first that the seal is not lipped on the inside, preventing its removal with the crankcases joined.

6.1 Prise out oil seals with a large flat-bladed screwdriver

● New seals are usually installed with their marked face (containing the seal reference code) outwards and the spring side towards the fluid being retained. In certain cases, such as a two-stroke engine crankshaft seal, a double lipped seal may be used due to there being fluid or gas on each side of the joint.

● Use a bearing driver or socket which bears only on the outer hard edge of the seal to install it in the casing - tapping on the inner edge will damage the sealing lip.

Oil seal types and markings

● Oil seals are usually of the single-lipped type. Double-lipped seals are found where a liquid or gas is on both sides of the joint.
● Oil seals can harden and lose their sealing ability if the motorcycle has been in storage for a long period - renewal is the only solution.
● Oil seal manufacturers also conform to the ISO markings for seal size - these are moulded into the outer face of the seal (see illustration 6.2).

6.2 These oil seal markings indicate inside diameter, outside diameter and seal thickness

7 Gaskets and sealants

Types of gasket and sealant

● Gaskets are used to seal the mating surfaces between components and keep lubricants, fluids, vacuum or pressure contained within the assembly. Aluminium gaskets are sometimes found at the cylinder joints, but most gaskets are paper-based. If the mating surfaces of the components being joined are undamaged the gasket can be installed dry, although a dab of sealant or grease will be useful to hold it in place during assembly.
● RTV (Room Temperature Vulcanising) silicone rubber sealants cure when exposed to moisture in the atmosphere. These sealants are good at filling pits or irregular gasket faces, but will tend to be forced out of the joint under very high torque. They can be used to replace a paper gasket, but first make sure that the width of the paper gasket is not essential to the shimming of internal components. RTV sealants should not be used on components containing petrol (gasoline).
● Non-hardening, semi-hardening and hard setting liquid gasket compounds can be used with a gasket or between a metal-to-metal joint. Select the sealant to suit the application: universal non-hardening sealant can be used on virtually all joints; semi-hardening on joint faces which are rough or damaged; hard setting sealant on joints which require a permanent bond and are subjected to high temperature and pressure. **Note:** Check first if the paper gasket has a bead of sealant

impregnated in its surface before applying additional sealant.
● When choosing a sealant, make sure it is suitable for the application, particularly if being applied in a high-temperature area or in the vicinity of fuel. Certain manufacturers produce sealants in either clear, silver or black colours to match the finish of the engine. This has a particular application on motorcycles where much of the engine is exposed.
● Do not over-apply sealant. That which is squeezed out on the outside of the joint can be wiped off, whereas an excess of sealant on the inside can break off and clog oilways.

Breaking a sealed joint

● Age, heat, pressure and the use of hard setting sealant can cause two components to stick together so tightly that they are difficult to separate using finger pressure alone. Do not resort to using levers unless there is a pry point provided for this purpose (see illustration 7.1) or else the gasket surfaces will be damaged.
● Use a soft-faced hammer (see illustration 7.2) or a wood block and conventional hammer to strike the component near the mating surface. Avoid hammering against cast extremities since they may break off. If this method fails, try using a wood wedge between the two components.

Caution: If the joint will not separate, double-check that you have removed all the fasteners.

7.1 If a pry point is provided, apply gently pressure with a flat-bladed screwdriver

7.2 Tap around the joint with a soft-faced mallet if necessary - don't strike cooling fins

Removal of old gasket and sealant

● Paper gaskets will most likely come away complete, leaving only a few traces stuck on

Most components have one or two hollow locating dowels between the two gasket faces. If a dowel cannot be removed, do not resort to gripping it with pliers - it will almost certainly be distorted. Install a close-fitting socket or Phillips screwdriver into the dowel and then grip the outer edge of the dowel to free it.

the sealing faces of the components. It is imperative that all traces are removed to ensure correct sealing of the new gasket.
● Very carefully scrape all traces of gasket away making sure that the sealing surfaces are not gouged or scored by the scraper (see illustrations 7.3, 7.4 and 7.5). Stubborn deposits can be removed by spraying with an aerosol gasket remover. Final preparation of

7.3 Paper gaskets can be scraped off with a gasket scraper tool . . .

7.4 . . . a knife blade . . .

7.5 . . . or a household scraper

7.6 Fine abrasive paper is wrapped around a flat file to clean up the gasket face

7.7 A kitchen scourer can be used on stubborn deposits

the gasket surface can be made with very fine abrasive paper or a plastic kitchen scourer **(see illustrations 7.6 and 7.7)**.

● Old sealant can be scraped or peeled off components, depending on the type originally used. Note that gasket removal compounds are available to avoid scraping the components clean; make sure the gasket remover suits the type of sealant used.

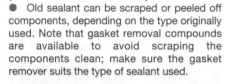

8 Chains

Breaking and joining final drive chains

● Drive chains for all but small bikes are continuous and do not have a clip-type connecting link. The chain must be broken using a chain breaker tool and the new chain securely riveted together using a new soft rivet-type link. Never use a clip-type connecting link instead of a rivet-type link, except in an emergency. Various chain breaking and riveting tools are available, either as separate tools or combined as illustrated in the accompanying photographs - read the instructions supplied with the tool carefully.

> ⚠ **Warning: The need to rivet the new link pins correctly cannot be overstressed - loss of control of the motorcycle is very likely to result if the chain breaks in use.**

● Rotate the chain and look for the soft link. The soft link pins look like they have been

8.1 Tighten the chain breaker to push the pin out of the link . . .

8.2 . . . withdraw the pin, remove the tool . . .

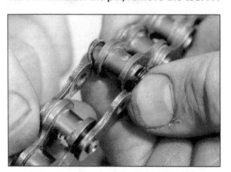

8.3 . . . and separate the chain link

deeply centre-punched instead of peened over like all the other pins **(see illustration 8.9)** and its sideplate may be a different colour. Position the soft link midway between the sprockets and assemble the chain breaker tool over one of the soft link pins **(see illustration 8.1)**. Operate the tool to push the pin out through the chain **(see illustration 8.2)**. On an O-ring chain, remove the O-rings **(see illustration 8.3)**. Carry out the same procedure on the other soft link pin.

> *Caution: Certain soft link pins (particularly on the larger chains) may require their ends to be filed or ground off before they can be pressed out using the tool.*

● Check that you have the correct size and strength (standard or heavy duty) new soft link - do not reuse the old link. Look for the size marking on the chain sideplates **(see illustration 8.10)**.

● Position the chain ends so that they are engaged over the rear sprocket. On an O-ring

8.4 Insert the new soft link, with O-rings, through the chain ends . . .

8.5 . . . install the O-rings over the pin ends . . .

8.6 . . . followed by the sideplate

chain, install a new O-ring over each pin of the link and insert the link through the two chain ends **(see illustration 8.4)**. Install a new O-ring over the end of each pin, followed by the sideplate (with the chain manufacturer's marking facing outwards) **(see illustrations 8.5 and 8.6)**. On an unsealed chain, insert the link through the two chain ends, then install the sideplate with the chain manufacturer's marking facing outwards.

● Note that it may not be possible to install the sideplate using finger pressure alone. If using a joining tool, assemble it so that the plates of the tool clamp the link and press the sideplate over the pins **(see illustration 8.7)**. Otherwise, use two small sockets placed over

8.7 Push the sideplate into position using a clamp

8.8 Assemble the chain riveting tool over one pin at a time and tighten it fully

8.9 Pin end correctly riveted (A), pin end unriveted (B)

the rivet ends and two pieces of the wood between a G-clamp. Operate the clamp to press the sideplate over the pins.

● Assemble the joining tool over one pin (following the maker's instructions) and tighten the tool down to spread the pin end securely **(see illustrations 8.8 and 8.9)**. Do the same on the other pin.

> ⚠ *Warning: Check that the pin ends are secure and that there is no danger of the sideplate coming loose. If the pin ends are cracked the soft link must be renewed.*

Final drive chain sizing

● Chains are sized using a three digit number, followed by a suffix to denote the chain type **(see illustration 8.10)**. Chain type is either standard or heavy duty (thicker sideplates), and also unsealed or O-ring/X-ring type.

● The first digit of the number relates to the pitch of the chain, ie the distance from the centre of one pin to the centre of the next pin **(see illustration 8.11)**. Pitch is expressed in eighths of an inch, as follows:

8.10 Typical chain size and type marking

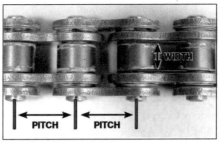

8.11 Chain dimensions

Sizes commencing with a 4 (eg 428) have a pitch of 1/2 inch (12.7 mm)
Sizes commencing with a 5 (eg 520) have a pitch of 5/8 inch (15.9 mm)
Sizes commencing with a 6 (eg 630) have a pitch of 3/4 inch (19.1 mm)

● The second and third digits of the chain size relate to the width of the rollers, again in imperial units, eg the 525 shown has 5/16 inch (7.94 mm) rollers **(see illustration 8.11)**.

9 Hoses

Clamping to prevent flow

● Small-bore flexible hoses can be clamped to prevent fluid flow whilst a component is worked on. Whichever method is used, ensure that the hose material is not permanently distorted or damaged by the clamp.

a) A brake hose clamp available from auto accessory shops **(see illustration 9.1)**.
b) A wingnut type hose clamp **(see illustration 9.2)**.

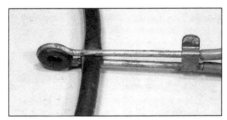

9.1 Hoses can be clamped with an automotive brake hose clamp . . .

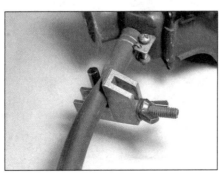

9.2 . . . a wingnut type hose clamp . . .

c) Two sockets placed each side of the hose and held with straight-jawed self-locking grips **(see illustration 9.3)**.
d) Thick card each side of the hose held between straight-jawed self-locking grips **(see illustration 9.4)**.

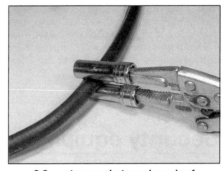

9.3 . . . two sockets and a pair of self-locking grips . . .

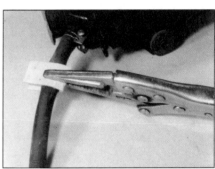

9.4 . . . or thick card and self-locking grips

Freeing and fitting hoses

● Always make sure the hose clamp is moved well clear of the hose end. Grip the hose with your hand and rotate it whilst pulling it off the union. If the hose has hardened due to age and will not move, slit it with a sharp knife and peel its ends off the union **(see illustration 9.5)**.

● Resist the temptation to use grease or soap on the unions to aid installation; although it helps the hose slip over the union it will equally aid the escape of fluid from the joint. It is preferable to soften the hose ends in hot water and wet the inside surface of the hose with water or a fluid which will evaporate.

9.5 Cutting a coolant hose free with a sharp knife

Introduction

In less time than it takes to read this introduction, a thief could steal your motorcycle. Returning only to find your bike has gone is one of the worst feelings in the world. Even if the motorcycle is insured against theft, once you've got over the initial shock, you will have the inconvenience of dealing with the police and your insurance company.

The motorcycle is an easy target for the professional thief and the joyrider alike and the official figures on motorcycle theft make for depressing reading; on average a motorcycle is stolen every 16 minutes in the UK!

Motorcycle thefts fall into two categories, those stolen 'to order' and those taken by opportunists. The thief stealing to order will be on the look out for a specific make and model and will go to extraordinary lengths to obtain that motorcycle. The opportunist thief on the other hand will look for easy targets which can be stolen with the minimum of effort and risk.

Whilst it is never going to be possible to make your machine 100% secure, it is estimated that around half of all stolen motorcycles are taken by opportunist thieves. Remember that the opportunist thief is always on the look out for the easy option: if there are two similar motorcycles parked side-by-side, they will target the one with the lowest level of security. By taking a few precautions, you can reduce the chances of your motorcycle being stolen.

Security equipment

There are many specialised motorcycle security devices available and the following text summarises their applications and their good and bad points.

Once you have decided on the type of security equipment which best suits your needs, we recommended that you read one of the many equipment tests regularly carried

Ensure the lock and chain you buy is of good quality and long enough to shackle your bike to a solid object

out by the motorcycle press. These tests compare the products from all the major manufacturers and give impartial ratings on their effectiveness, value-for-money and ease of use.

No one item of security equipment can provide complete protection. It is highly recommended that two or more of the items described below are combined to increase the security of your motorcycle (a lock and chain plus an alarm system is just about ideal). The more security measures fitted to the bike, the less likely it is to be stolen.

Lock and chain

Pros: *Very flexible to use; can be used to secure the motorcycle to almost any immovable object. On some locks and chains, the lock can be used on its own as a disc lock (see below).*

Cons: *Can be very heavy and awkward to carry on the motorcycle, although some types*

will be supplied with a carry bag which can be strapped to the pillion seat.

● Heavy-duty chains and locks are an excellent security measure **(see illustration 1)**. Whenever the motorcycle is parked, use the lock and chain to secure the machine to a solid, immovable object such as a post or railings. This will prevent the machine from being ridden away or being lifted into the back of a van.

● When fitting the chain, always ensure the chain is routed around the motorcycle frame or swingarm **(see illustrations 2 and 3)**. Never merely pass the chain around one of the wheel rims; a thief may unbolt the wheel and lift the rest of the machine into a van, leaving you with just the wheel! Try to avoid having excess chain free, thus making it difficult to use cutting tools, and keep the chain and lock off the ground to prevent thieves attacking it with a cold chisel. Position the lock so that its lock barrel is facing downwards; this will make it harder for the thief to attack the lock mechanism.

Pass the chain through the bike's frame, rather than just through a wheel . . .

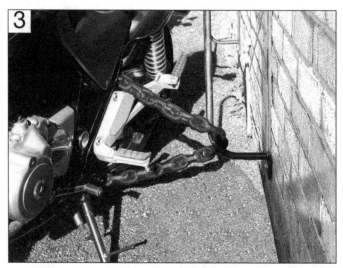

. . . and loop it around a solid object

U-locks

Pros: *Highly effective deterrent which can be used to secure the bike to a post or railings. Most U-locks come with a carrier which allows the lock to be easily carried on the bike.*

Cons: *Not as flexible to use as a lock and chain.*

● These are solid locks which are similar in use to a lock and chain. U-locks are lighter than a lock and chain but not so flexible to use. The length and shape of the lock shackle limit the objects to which the bike can be secured **(see illustration 4)**.

Disc locks

Pros: *Small, light and very easy to carry; most can be stored underneath the seat.*

Cons: *Does not prevent the motorcycle being lifted into a van. Can be very embarrassing if you*

U-locks can be used to secure the bike to a solid object – ensure you purchase one which is long enough

forget to remove the lock before attempting to ride off!

● Disc locks are designed to be attached to the front brake disc. The lock passes through one of the holes in the disc and prevents the wheel rotating by jamming against the fork/brake caliper **(see illustration 5)**. Some are equipped with an alarm siren which sounds if the disc lock is moved; this not only acts as a theft deterrent but also as a handy reminder if you try to move the bike with the lock still fitted.

● Combining the disc lock with a length of cable which can be looped around a post or railings provides an additional measure of security **(see illustration 6)**.

Alarms and immobilisers

Pros: *Once installed it is completely hassle-free to use. If the system is 'Thatcham' or 'Sold Secure-approved', insurance companies may give you a discount.*

Cons: *Can be expensive to buy and complex to install. No system will prevent the motorcycle from being lifted into a van and taken away.*

● Electronic alarms and immobilisers are available to suit a variety of budgets. There are three different types of system available: pure alarms, pure immobilisers, and the more expensive systems which are combined alarm/immobilisers **(see illustration 7)**.
● An alarm system is designed to emit an audible warning if the motorcycle is being tampered with.
● An immobiliser prevents the motorcycle being started and ridden away by disabling its electrical systems.
● When purchasing an alarm/immobiliser system, check the cost of installing the system unless you are able to do it yourself. If the motorcycle is not used regularly, another consideration is the current drain of the system. All alarm/immobiliser systems are powered by the motorcycle's battery; purchasing a system with a very low current drain could prevent the battery losing its charge whilst the motorcycle is not being used.

A typical disc lock attached through one of the holes in the disc

A disc lock combined with a security cable provides additional protection

A typical alarm/immobiliser system

Indelible markings can be applied to most areas of the bike – always apply the manufacturer's sticker to warn off thieves

Chemically-etched code numbers can be applied to main body panels . . .

. . . again, always ensure that the kit manufacturer's sticker is applied in a prominent position

Security marking kits

Pros: *Very cheap and effective deterrent. Many insurance companies will give you a discount on your insurance premium if a recognised security marking kit is used on your motorcycle.*

Cons: *Does not prevent the motorcycle being stolen by joyriders.*

● There are many different types of security marking kits available. The idea is to mark as many parts of the motorcycle as possible with a unique security number **(see illustrations 8, 9 and 10)**. A form will be included with the kit to register your personal details and those of the motorcycle with the kit manufacturer. This register is made available to the police to help them trace the rightful owner of any motorcycle or components which they recover should all other forms of identification have been removed. Always apply the warning stickers provided with the kit to deter thieves.

Ground anchors, wheel clamps and security posts

Pros: *An excellent form of security which will deter all but the most determined of thieves.*

Cons: *Awkward to install and can be expensive.*

● Whilst the motorcycle is at home, it is a good idea to attach it securely to the floor or a solid wall, even if it is kept in a securely locked garage. Various types of ground anchors, security posts and wheel clamps are available for this purpose **(see illustration 11)**. These security devices are either bolted to a solid concrete or brick structure or can be cemented into the ground.

Permanent ground anchors provide an excellent level of security when the bike is at home

Security at home

A high percentage of motorcycle thefts are from the owner's home. Here are some things to consider whenever your motorcycle is at home:
✔ Where possible, always keep the motorcycle in a securely locked garage. Never rely solely on the standard lock on the garage door, these are usual hopelessly inadequate. Fit an additional locking mechanism to the door and consider having the garage alarmed. A security light, activated by a movement sensor, is also a good investment.

✔ Always secure the motorcycle to the ground or a wall, even if it is inside a securely locked garage.
✔ Do not regularly leave the motorcycle outside your home, try to keep it out of sight wherever possible. If a garage is not available, fit a motorcycle cover over the bike to disguise its true identity.
✔ It is not uncommon for thieves to follow a motorcyclist home to find out where the bike is kept. They will then return at a later date. Be aware of this whenever you are returning

home on your motorcycle. If you suspect you are being followed, do not return home, instead ride to a garage or shop and stop as a precaution.
✔ When selling a motorcycle, do not provide your home address or the location where the bike is normally kept. Arrange to meet the buyer at a location away from your home. Thieves have been known to pose as potential buyers to find out where motorcycles are kept and then return later to steal them.

Security away from the home

As well as fitting security equipment to your motorcycle here are a few general rules to follow whenever you park your motorcycle.
✔ Park in a busy, public place.
✔ Use car parks which incorporate security features, such as CCTV.

✔ At night, park in a well-lit area, preferably directly underneath a street light.
✔ Engage the steering lock.
✔ Secure the motorcycle to a solid, immovable object such as a post or railings with an additional lock. If this is not possible,

secure the bike to a friend's motorcycle. Some public parking places provide security loops for motorcycles.
✔ Never leave your helmet or luggage attached to the motorcycle. Take them with you at all times.

Lubricants and fluids

A wide range of lubricants, fluids and cleaning agents is available for motor-cycles. This is a guide as to what is available, its applications and properties.

Four-stroke engine oil

● Engine oil is without doubt the most important component of any four-stroke engine. Modern motorcycle engines place a lot of demands on their oil and choosing the right type is essential. Using an unsuitable oil will lead to an increased rate of engine wear and could result in serious engine damage. Before purchasing oil, always check the recommended oil specification given by the manufacturer. The manufacturer will state a recommended 'type or classification' and also a specific 'viscosity' range for engine oil.

● The oil 'type or classification' is identified by its API (American Petroleum Institute) rating. The API rating will be in the form of two letters, e.g. SG. The S identifies the oil as being suitable for use in a petrol (gasoline) engine (S stands for spark ignition) and the second letter, ranging from A to J, identifies the oil's performance rating. The later this letter, the higher the specification of the oil; for example API SG oil exceeds the requirements of API SF oil. **Note:** *On some oils there may also be a second rating consisting of another two letters, the first letter being C, e.g. API SF/CD. This rating indicates the oil is also suitable for use in a diesel engines (the C stands for compression ignition) and is thus of no relevance for motorcycle use.*

● The 'viscosity' of the oil is identified by its SAE (Society of Automotive Engineers) rating. All modern engines require multigrade oils and the SAE rating will consist of two numbers, the first followed by a W, e.g.

10W/40. The first number indicates the viscosity rating of the oil at low temperatures (W stands for winter – tested at –20°C) and the second number represents the viscosity of the oil at high temperatures (tested at 100°C). The lower the number, the thinner the oil. For example an oil with an SAE 10W/40 rating will give better cold starting and running than an SAE 15W/40 oil.

● As well as ensuring the 'type' and 'viscosity' of the oil match the recommendations, another consideration to make when buying engine oil is whether to purchase a standard mineral-based oil, a semi-synthetic oil (also known as a synthetic blend or synthetic-based oil) or a fully-synthetic oil. Although all oils will have a similar rating and viscosity, their cost will vary considerably; mineral-based oils are the cheapest, the fully-synthetic oils the most expensive with the semi-synthetic oils falling somewhere in-between. This decision is very much up to the owner, but it should be noted that modern synthetic oils have far better lubricating and cleaning qualities than traditional mineral-based oils and tend to retain these properties for far longer. Bearing in mind the operating conditions inside a modern, high-revving motorcycle engine it is highly recommended that a fully synthetic oil is used. The extra expense at each service could save you money in the long term by preventing premature engine wear.

● As a final note always ensure that the oil is specifically designed for use in motorcycle engines. Engine oils designed primarily for use in car engines sometimes contain additives or friction modifiers which could cause clutch slip on a motorcycle fitted with a wet-clutch.

Two-stroke engine oil

● Modern two-stroke engines, with their high power outputs, place high demands on their oil. If engine seizure is to be avoided it is essential that a high-quality oil is used. Two-stroke oils differ hugely from four-stroke oils. The oil lubricates only the crankshaft and piston(s) (the transmission has its own lubricating oil) and is used on a total-loss basis where it is burnt completely during the combustion process.

● The Japanese have recently introduced a classification system for two-stroke oils, the JASO rating. This rating is in the form of two letters, either FA, FB or FC – FA is the lowest classification and FC the highest. Ensure the oil being used meets or exceeds the recommended rating specified by the manufacturer.

● As well as ensuring the oil rating matches the recommendation, another consideration to make when buying engine oil is whether to purchase a standard mineral-based oil, a semi-synthetic oil (also known as a synthetic blend or synthetic-based oil) or a fully-synthetic oil. The cost of each type of oil varies considerably; mineral-based oils are the cheapest, the fully-synthetic oils the most expensive with the semi-synthetic oils falling somewhere in-between. This decision is very much up to the owner, but it should be noted that modern synthetic oils have far better lubricating properties and burn cleaner than traditional mineral-based oils. It is therefore recommended that a fully synthetic oil is used. The extra expense could save you money in the long term by preventing premature engine wear, engine performance will be improved, carbon deposits and exhaust smoke will be reduced.

● Always ensure that the oil is specifically designed for use in an injector system. Many high quality two-stroke oils are designed for competition use and need to be pre-mixed with fuel. These oils are of a much higher viscosity and are not designed to flow through the injector pumps used on road-going two-stroke motorcycles.

Transmission (gear) oil

● On a two-stroke engine, the transmission and clutch are lubricated by their own separate oil bath which must be changed in accordance with the Maintenance Schedule.
● Although the engine and transmission units of most four-strokes use a common lubrication supply, there are some exceptions where the engine and gearbox have separate oil reservoirs and a dry clutch is used.
● Motorcycle manufacturers will either recommend a monograde transmission oil or a four-stroke multigrade engine oil to lubricate the transmission.
● Transmission oils, or gear oils as they are often called, are designed specifically for use in transmission systems. The viscosity of these oils is represented by an SAE number, but the scale of measurement applied is different to that used to grade engine oils. As a rough guide a SAE90 gear oil will be of the same viscosity as an SAE50 engine oil.

Shaft drive oil

● On models equipped with shaft final drive, the shaft drive gears are will have their own oil supply. The manufacturer will state a recommended 'type or classification' and also a specific 'viscosity' range in the same manner as for four-stroke engine oil.
● Gear oil classification is given by the number which follows the API GL (GL standing for gear lubricant) rating, the higher the number, the higher the specification of the oil, e.g. API GL5 oil is a higher specification than API GL4 oil. Ensure the oil meets or

exceeds the classification specified and is of the correct viscosity. The viscosity of gear oils is also represented by an SAE number but the scale of measurement used is different to that used to grade engine oils. As a rough guide an SAE90 gear oil will be of the same viscosity as an SAE50 engine oil.
● If the use of an EP (Extreme Pressure) gear oil is specified, ensure the oil purchased is suitable.

Fork oil and suspension fluid

● Conventional telescopic front forks are hydraulic and require fork oil to work. To ensure the forks function correctly, the fork oil must be changed in accordance with the Maintenance Schedule.
● Fork oil is available in a variety of viscosities, identified by their SAE rating; fork oil ratings vary from light (SAE 5) to heavy (SAE 30). When purchasing fork oil, ensure the viscosity rating matches that specified by the manufacturer.
● Some lubricant manufacturers also produce a range of high-quality suspension fluids which are very similar to fork oil but are designed mainly for competition use. These fluids may have a different viscosity rating system which is not to be confused with the SAE rating of normal fork oil. Refer to the manufacturer's instructions if in any doubt.

Brake and clutch fluid

● All disc brake systems and some clutch systems are hydraulically operated. To ensure correct operation, the hydraulic fluid must be changed in accordance with the Maintenance Schedule.
● Brake and clutch fluid is classified by its DOT rating with most motorcycle manufacturers specifying DOT 3 or 4 fluid. Both fluid types are glycol-based and can be mixed together without adverse effect; DOT 4 fluid exceeds the requirements of DOT 3

fluid. Although it is safe to use DOT 4 fluid in a system designed for use with DOT 3 fluid, never use DOT 3 fluid in a system which specifies the use of DOT 4 as this will adversely affect the system's performance. The type required for the system will be marked on the fluid reservoir cap.
● Some manufacturers also produce a DOT 5 hydraulic fluid. DOT 5 hydraulic fluid is silicone-based and is not compatible with the glycol-based DOT 3 and 4 fluids. Never mix DOT 5 fluid with DOT 3 or 4 fluid as this will seriously affect the performance of the hydraulic system.

Coolant/antifreeze

● When purchasing coolant/antifreeze, always ensure it is suitable for use in an aluminium engine and contains corrosion inhibitors to prevent possible blockages of the internal coolant passages of the system. As a general rule, most coolants are designed to be used neat and should not be diluted whereas antifreeze can be mixed with distilled water to  provide a coolant solution of the required strength. Refer to the manufacturer's instructions on the bottle.
● Ensure the coolant is changed in accordance with the Maintenance Schedule.

Chain lube

● Chain lube is an aerosol-type spray lubricant specifically designed for use on motorcycle final drive chains. Chain lube has two functions, to minimise friction between the final drive chain and sprockets and to prevent corrosion of the chain. Regular use of a good-quality chain lube will extend the life of the drive chain and sprockets and thus maximise the power being transmitted from the transmission to the rear wheel.
● When using chain lube, always allow some time for the solvents in the lube to evaporate before riding the motorcycle. This will minimise the amount of lube which will

'fling' off from the chain when the motorcycle is used. If the motorcycle is equipped with an 'O-ring' chain, ensure the chain lube is labelled as being suitable for use on 'O-ring' chains.

Degreasers and solvents

● There are many different types of solvents and degreasers available to remove the grime and grease which accumulate around the motorcycle during normal use. Degreasers and solvents are usually available as an aerosol-type spray or as a liquid which you apply with a brush. Always closely follow the manufacturer's instructions and wear eye protection during use. Be aware that many solvents are flammable and may give off noxious fumes; take adequate precautions when using them (see Safety First!).
● For general cleaning, use one of the many solvents or degreasers available from most motorcycle accessory shops. These solvents are usually applied then left for a certain time before being washed off with water.

Brake cleaner is a solvent specifically designed to remove all traces of oil, grease and dust from braking system components. Brake cleaner is designed to evaporate quickly and leaves behind no residue.

Carburettor cleaner is an aerosol-type solvent specifically designed to clear carburettor blockages and break down the hard deposits and gum often found inside carburettors during overhaul.

Contact cleaner is an aerosol-type solvent designed for cleaning electrical components. The cleaner will remove all traces of oil and dirt from components such as switch contacts or fouled spark plugs and then dry, leaving behind no residue.

Gasket remover is an aerosol-type solvent designed for removing stubborn gaskets from engine components during overhaul. Gasket remover will minimise the amount of scraping required to remove the gasket and therefore reduce the risk of damage to the mating surface.

Spray lubricants

● Aerosol-based spray lubricants are widely available and are excellent for lubricating lever pivots and exposed cables and switches. Try to use a lubricant which is of the dry-film type as the fluid evaporates, leaving behind a dry-film of lubricant. Lubricants which leave behind an oily residue will attract dust and dirt which will increase the rate of wear of the cable/lever.

● Most lubricants also act as a moisture dispersant and a penetrating fluid. This means they can also be used to 'dry out' electrical components such as wiring connectors or switches as well as helping to free seized fasteners.

Greases

● Grease is used to lubricate many of the pivot-points. A good-quality multi-purpose grease is suitable for most applications but some manufacturers will specify the use of specialist greases for use on components such as swingarm and suspension linkage bushes. These specialist greases can be purchased from most motorcycle (or car) accessory shops; commonly specified types include molybdenum disulphide grease, lithium-based grease, graphite-based grease, silicone-based grease and high-temperature copper-based grease.

Gasket sealing compounds

● Gasket sealing compounds can be used in conjunction with gaskets, to improve their sealing capabilities, or on their own to seal metal-to-metal joints. Depending on their type, sealing compounds either set hard or stay relatively soft and pliable.

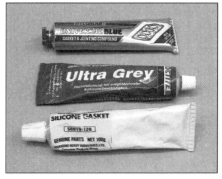

● When purchasing a gasket sealing compound, ensure that it is designed specifically for use on an internal combustion engine. General multi-purpose sealants available from DIY stores may appear visibly similar but they are not designed to withstand the extreme heat or contact with fuel and oil encountered when used on an engine (see 'Tools and Workshop Tips' for further information).

Thread locking compound

● Thread locking compounds are used to secure certain threaded fasteners in position to prevent them from loosening due to vibration. Thread locking compounds can be purchased from most motorcycle (and car) accessory shops. Ensure the threads of the both components are completely clean and dry before sparingly applying the locking compound (see 'Tools and Workshop Tips' for further information).

Fuel additives

● Fuel additives which protect and clean the fuel system components are widely available. These additives are designed to remove all traces of deposits that build up on the carburettors/injectors and prevent wear, helping the fuel system to operate more efficiently. If a fuel additive is being used, check that it is suitable for use with your motorcycle, especially if your motorcycle is equipped with a catalytic converter.

● Octane boosters are also available. These additives are designed to improve the performance of highly-tuned engines being run on normal pump-fuel and are of no real use on standard motorcycles.

Conversion Factors

Length (distance)

Inches (in)	x 25.4	= Millimetres (mm)	x 0.0394	=	Inches (in)
Feet (ft)	x 0.305	= Metres (m)	x 3.281	=	Feet (ft)
Miles	x 1.609	= Kilometres (km)	x 0.621	=	Miles

Volume (capacity)

Cubic inches (cu in; in³)	x 16.387	= Cubic centimetres (cc; cm³)	x 0.061	=	Cubic inches (cu in; in³)
Imperial pints (Imp pt)	x 0.568	= Litres (l)	x 1.76	=	Imperial pints (Imp pt)
Imperial quarts (Imp qt)	x 1.137	= Litres (l)	x 0.88	=	Imperial quarts (Imp qt)
Imperial quarts (Imp qt)	x 1.201	= US quarts (US qt)	x 0.833	=	Imperial quarts (Imp qt)
US quarts (US qt)	x 0.946	= Litres (l)	x 1.057	=	US quarts (US qt)
Imperial gallons (Imp gal)	x 4.546	= Litres (l)	x 0.22	=	Imperial gallons (Imp gal)
Imperial gallons (Imp gal)	x 1.201	= US gallons (US gal)	x 0.833	=	Imperial gallons (Imp gal)
US gallons (US gal)	x 3.785	= Litres (l)	x 0.264	=	US gallons (US gal)

Mass (weight)

Ounces (oz)	x 28.35	= Grams (g)	x 0.035	=	Ounces (oz)
Pounds (lb)	x 0.454	= Kilograms (kg)	x 2.205	=	Pounds (lb)

Force

Ounces-force (ozf; oz)	x 0.278	= Newtons (N)	x 3.6	=	Ounces-force (ozf; oz)
Pounds-force (lbf; lb)	x 4.448	= Newtons (N)	x 0.225	=	Pounds-force (lbf; lb)
Newtons (N)	x 0.1	= Kilograms-force (kgf; kg)	x 9.81	=	Newtons (N)

Pressure

Pounds-force per square inch (psi; lbf/in²; lb/in²)	x 0.070	= Kilograms-force per square centimetre (kgf/cm²; kg/cm²)	x 14.223	=	Pounds-force per square inch (psi; lbf/in²; lb/in²)
Pounds-force per square inch (psi; lbf/in²; lb/in²)	x 0.068	= Atmospheres (atm)	x 14.696	=	Pounds-force per square inch (psi; lbf/in²; lb/in²)
Pounds-force per square inch (psi; lbf/in²; lb/in²)	x 0.069	= Bars	x 14.5	=	Pounds-force per square inch (psi; lbf/in²; lb/in²)
Pounds-force per square inch (psi; lbf/in²; lb/in²)	x 6.895	= Kilopascals (kPa)	x 0.145	=	Pounds-force per square inch (psi; lbf/in²; lb/in²)
Kilopascals (kPa)	x 0.01	= Kilograms-force per square centimetre (kgf/cm²; kg/cm²)	x 98.1	=	Kilopascals (kPa)
Millibar (mbar)	x 100	= Pascals (Pa)	x 0.01	=	Millibar (mbar)
Millibar (mbar)	x 0.0145	= Pounds-force per square inch (psi; lbf/in²; lb/in²)	x 68.947	=	Millibar (mbar)
Millibar (mbar)	x 0.75	= Millimetres of mercury (mmHg)	x 1.333	=	Millibar (mbar)
Millibar (mbar)	x 0.401	= Inches of water (inH₂O)	x 2.491	=	Millibar (mbar)
Millimetres of mercury (mmHg)	x 0.535	= Inches of water (inH₂O)	x 1.868	=	Millimetres of mercury (mmHg)
Inches of water (inH₂O)	x 0.036	= Pounds-force per square inch (psi; lbf/in²; lb/in²)	x 27.68	=	Inches of water (inH₂O)

Torque (moment of force)

Pounds-force inches (lbf in; lb in)	x 1.152	= Kilograms-force centimetre (kgf cm; kg cm)	x 0.868	=	Pounds-force inches (lbf in; lb in)
Pounds-force inches (lbf in; lb in)	x 0.113	= Newton metres (Nm)	x 8.85	=	Pounds-force inches (lbf in; lb in)
Pounds-force inches (lbf in; lb in)	x 0.083	= Pounds-force feet (lbf ft; lb ft)	x 12	=	Pounds-force inches (lbf in; lb in)
Pounds-force feet (lbf ft; lb ft)	x 0.138	= Kilograms-force metres (kgf m; kg m)	x 7.233	=	Pounds-force feet (lbf ft; lb ft)
Pounds-force feet (lbf ft; lb ft)	x 1.356	= Newton metres (Nm)	x 0.738	=	Pounds-force feet (lbf ft; lb ft)
Newton metres (Nm)	x 0.102	= Kilograms-force metres (kgf m; kg m)	x 9.804	=	Newton metres (Nm)

Power

Horsepower (hp)	x 745.7	= Watts (W)	x 0.0013	=	Horsepower (hp)

Velocity (speed)

Miles per hour (miles/hr; mph)	x 1.609	= Kilometres per hour (km/hr; kph)	x 0.621	=	Miles per hour (miles/hr; mph)

Fuel consumption*

Miles per gallon (mpg)	x 0.354	= Kilometres per litre (km/l)	x 2.825	=	Miles per gallon (mpg)

Temperature

Degrees Fahrenheit = (°C x 1.8) + 32   Degrees Celsius (Degrees Centigrade; °C) = (°F - 32) x 0.56

It is common practice to convert from miles per gallon (mpg) to litres/100 kilometres (l/100km), where mpg x l/100 km = 282

About the MOT Test

In the UK, all vehicles more than three years old are subject to an annual test to ensure that they meet minimum safety requirements. A current test certificate must be issued before a machine can be used on public roads, and is required before a road fund licence can be issued. Riding without a current test certificate will also invalidate your insurance.

For most owners, the MOT test is an annual cause for anxiety, and this is largely due to owners not being sure what needs to be checked prior to submitting the motorcycle for testing. The simple answer is that a fully roadworthy motorcycle will have no difficulty in passing the test.

This is a guide to getting your motorcycle through the MOT test. Obviously it will not be possible to examine the motorcycle to the same standard as the professional MOT tester, particularly in view of the equipment required for some of the checks. However, working through the following procedures will enable you to identify any problem areas before submitting the motorcycle for the test.

It has only been possible to summarise the test requirements here, based on the regulations in force at the time of printing. Test standards are becoming increasingly stringent, although there are some exemptions for older vehicles. More information about the MOT test can be obtained from the TSO publications, *How Safe is your Motorcycle* and *The MOT Inspection Manual for Motorcycle Testing*.

Many of the checks require that one of the wheels is raised off the ground. If the motorcycle doesn't have a centre stand, note that an auxiliary stand will be required. Additionally, the help of an assistant may prove useful.

Certain exceptions apply to machines under 50 cc, machines without a lighting system, and Classic bikes - if in doubt about any of the requirements listed below seek confirmation from an MOT tester prior to submitting the motorcycle for the test.

Check that the frame number is clearly visible.

> **HAYNES HiNT**
> *If a component is in borderline condition, the tester has discretion in deciding whether to pass or fail it. If the motorcycle presented is clean and evidently well cared for, the tester may be more inclined to pass a borderline component than if the motorcycle is scruffy and apparently neglected.*

Electrical System

Lights, turn signals, horn and reflector

✔ With the ignition on, check the operation of the following electrical components. **Note:** *The electrical components on certain small-capacity machines are powered by the generator, requiring that the engine is run for this check.*

a) *Headlight and tail light. Check that both illuminate in the low and high beam switch positions.*

b) *Position lights. Check that the front position (or sidelight) and tail light illuminate in this switch position.*

c) *Turn signals. Check that all flash at the correct rate, and that the warning light(s) function correctly. Check that the turn signal switch works correctly.*

d) *Hazard warning system (where fitted). Check that all four turn signals flash in this switch position.*

e) *Brake stop light. Check that the light comes on when the front and rear brakes are independently applied. Models first used on or after 1st April 1986 must have a brake light switch on each brake.*

f) *Horn. Check that the sound is continuous and of reasonable volume.*

✔ Check that there is a red reflector on the rear of the machine, either mounted separately or as part of the tail light lens.

✔ Check the condition of the headlight, tail light and turn signal lenses.

Headlight beam height

✔ The MOT tester will perform a headlight beam height check using specialised beam setting equipment **(see illustration 1)**. This equipment will not be available to the home mechanic, but if you suspect that the headlight is incorrectly set or may have been maladjusted in the past, you can perform a rough test as follows.

✔ Position the bike in a straight line facing a brick wall. The bike must be off its stand, upright and with a rider seated. Measure the height from the ground to the centre of the headlight and mark a horizontal line on the wall at this height. Position the motorcycle 3.8 metres from the wall and draw a vertical

Headlight beam height checking equipment

line up the wall central to the centreline of the motorcycle. Switch to dipped beam and check that the beam pattern falls slightly lower than the horizontal line and to the left of the vertical line **(see illustration 2)**.

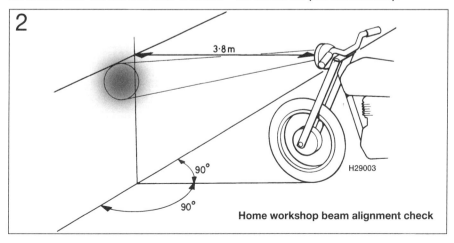

Home workshop beam alignment check

Exhaust System and Final Drive

Exhaust

✔ Check that the exhaust mountings are secure and that the system does not foul any of the rear suspension components.

✔ Start the motorcycle. When the revs are increased, check that the exhaust is neither holed nor leaking from any of its joints. On a linked system, check that the collector box is not leaking due to corrosion.

✔ Note that the exhaust decibel level ("loudness" of the exhaust) is assessed at the discretion of the tester. If the motorcycle was first used on or after 1st January 1985 the silencer must carry the BSAU 193 stamp, or a marking relating to its make and model, or be of OE (original equipment) manufacture. If the silencer is marked NOT FOR ROAD USE, RACING USE ONLY or similar, it will fail the MOT.

Final drive

✔ On chain or belt drive machines, check that the chain/belt is in good condition and does not have excessive slack. Also check that the sprocket is securely mounted on the rear wheel hub. Check that the chain/belt guard is in place.

✔ On shaft drive bikes, check for oil leaking from the drive unit and fouling the rear tyre.

Steering and Suspension

Steering

✔ With the front wheel raised off the ground, rotate the steering from lock to lock. The handlebar or switches must not contact the fuel tank or be close enough to trap the rider's hand. Problems can be caused by damaged lock stops on the lower yoke and frame, or by the fitting of non-standard handlebars.

✔ When performing the lock to lock check, also ensure that the steering moves freely without drag or notchiness. Steering movement can be impaired by poorly routed cables, or by overtight head bearings or worn bearings. The tester will perform a check of the steering head bearing lower race by mounting the front wheel on a surface plate, then performing a lock to

lock check with the weight of the machine on the lower bearing (see illustration 3).

✔ Grasp the fork sliders (lower legs) and attempt to push and pull on the forks (see

Front wheel mounted on a surface plate for steering head bearing lower race check

illustration 4). Any play in the steering head bearings will be felt. Note that in extreme cases, wear of the front fork bushes can be misinterpreted for head bearing play.

✔ Check that the handlebars are securely mounted.

✔ Check that the handlebar grip rubbers are secure. They should by bonded to the bar left end and to the throttle cable pulley on the right end.

Front suspension

✔ With the motorcycle off the stand, hold the front brake on and pump the front forks up and down (see illustration 5). Check that they are adequately damped.

Checking the steering head bearings for freeplay

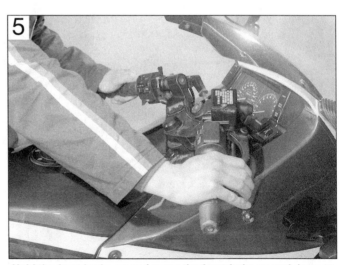

Hold the front brake on and pump the front forks up and down to check operation

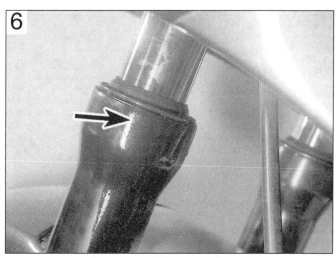

Inspect the area around the fork dust seal for oil leakage (arrow)

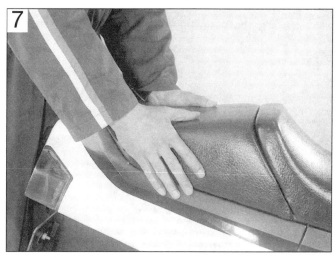

Bounce the rear of the motorcycle to check rear suspension operation

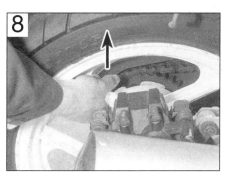

Checking for rear suspension linkage play

✔ Inspect the area above and around the front fork oil seals **(see illustration 6)**. There should be no sign of oil on the fork tube (stanchion) nor leaking down the slider (lower leg). On models so equipped, check that there is no oil leaking from the anti-dive units.

✔ On models with swingarm front suspension, check that there is no freeplay in the linkage when moved from side to side.

Rear suspension

✔ With the motorcycle off the stand and an assistant supporting the motorcycle by its handlebars, bounce the rear suspension **(see illustration 7)**. Check that the suspension components do not foul on any of the cycle parts and check that the shock absorber(s) provide adequate damping.

✔ Visually inspect the shock absorber(s) and check that there is no sign of oil leakage from its damper. This is somewhat restricted on certain single shock models due to the location of the shock absorber.

✔ With the rear wheel raised off the ground, grasp the wheel at the highest point and attempt to pull it up **(see illustration 8)**. Any play in the swingarm pivot or suspension linkage bearings will be felt as movement. **Note:** *Do not confuse play with actual suspension movement.* Failure to lubricate suspension linkage bearings can lead to bearing failure **(see illustration 9)**.

✔ With the rear wheel raised off the ground, grasp the swingarm ends and attempt to move the swingarm from side to side and forwards and backwards - any play indicates wear of the swingarm pivot bearings **(see illustration 10)**.

Worn suspension linkage pivots (arrows) are usually the cause of play in the rear suspension

Grasp the swingarm at the ends to check for play in its pivot bearings

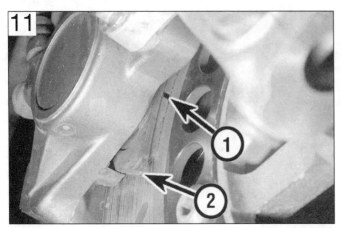

Brake pad wear can usually be viewed without removing the caliper. Most pads have wear indicator grooves (1) and some also have indicator tangs (2)

On drum brakes, check the angle of the operating lever with the brake fully applied. Most drum brakes have a wear indicator pointer and scale.

Brakes, Wheels and Tyres

Brakes

✔ With the wheel raised off the ground, apply the brake then free it off, and check that the wheel is about to revolve freely without brake drag.

✔ On disc brakes, examine the disc itself. Check that it is securely mounted and not cracked.

✔ On disc brakes, view the pad material through the caliper mouth and check that the pads are not worn down beyond the limit **(see illustration 11)**.

✔ On drum brakes, check that when the brake is applied the angle between the operating lever and cable or rod is not too great **(see illustration 12)**. Check also that the operating lever doesn't foul any other components.

✔ On disc brakes, examine the flexible hoses from top to bottom. Have an assistant hold the brake on so that the fluid in the hose is under pressure, and check that there is no sign of fluid leakage, bulges or cracking. If there are any metal brake pipes or unions, check that these are free from corrosion and damage. Where a brake-linked anti-dive system is fitted, check the hoses to the anti-dive in a similar manner.

✔ Check that the rear brake torque arm is secure and that its fasteners are secured by self-locking nuts or castellated nuts with split-pins or R-pins **(see illustration 13)**.

✔ On models with ABS, check that the self-check warning light in the instrument panel works.

✔ The MOT tester will perform a test of the motorcycle's braking efficiency based on a calculation of rider and motorcycle weight. Although this cannot be carried out at home, you can at least ensure that the braking systems are properly maintained. For hydraulic disc brakes, check the fluid level, lever/pedal feel (bleed of air if its spongy) and pad material. For drum brakes, check adjustment, cable or rod operation and shoe lining thickness.

Wheels and tyres

✔ Check the wheel condition. Cast wheels should be free from cracks and if of the built-up design, all fasteners should be secure. Spoked wheels should be checked for broken, corroded, loose or bent spokes.

✔ With the wheel raised off the ground, spin the wheel and visually check that the tyre and wheel run true. Check that the tyre does not foul the suspension or mudguards.

✔ With the wheel raised off the ground, grasp the wheel and attempt to move it about the axle (spindle) **(see illustration 14)**. Any play felt here indicates wheel bearing failure.

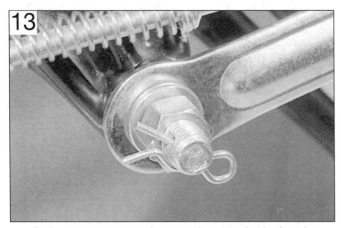

Brake torque arm must be properly secured at both ends

Check for wheel bearing play by trying to move the wheel about the axle (spindle)

Checking the tyre tread depth

Tyre direction of rotation arrow can be found on tyre sidewall

Castellated type wheel axle (spindle) nut must be secured by a split pin or R-pin

Two straightedges are used to check wheel alignment

✔ Check the tyre tread depth, tread condition and sidewall condition (see illustration 15).
✔ Check the tyre type. Front and rear tyre types must be compatible and be suitable for road use. Tyres marked NOT FOR ROAD USE, COMPETITION USE ONLY or similar, will fail the MOT.

✔ If the tyre sidewall carries a direction of rotation arrow, this must be pointing in the direction of normal wheel rotation (see illustration 16).
✔ Check that the wheel axle (spindle) nuts (where applicable) are properly secured. A self-locking nut or castellated nut with a split-pin or R-pin can be used (see illustration 17).
✔ Wheel alignment is checked with the motorcycle off the stand and a rider seated. With the front wheel pointing straight ahead, two perfectly straight lengths of metal or wood and placed against the sidewalls of both tyres (see illustration 18). The gap each side of the front tyre must be equidistant on both sides. Incorrect wheel alignment may be due to a cocked rear wheel (often as the result of poor chain adjustment) or in extreme cases, a bent frame.

General checks and condition

✔ Check the security of all major fasteners, bodypanels, seat, fairings (where fitted) and mudguards.

✔ Check that the rider and pillion footrests, handlebar levers and brake pedal are securely mounted.

✔ Check for corrosion on the frame or any load-bearing components. If severe, this may affect the structure, particularly under stress.

Sidecars

A motorcycle fitted with a sidecar requires additional checks relating to the stability of the machine and security of attachment and swivel joints, plus specific wheel alignment (toe-in) requirements. Additionally, tyre and lighting requirements differ from conventional motorcycle use. Owners are advised to check MOT test requirements with an official test centre.

Preparing for storage

Before you start

If repairs or an overhaul is needed, see that this is carried out now rather than left until you want to ride the bike again.

Give the bike a good wash and scrub all dirt from its underside. Make sure the bike dries completely before preparing for storage.

Engine

● Remove the spark plug(s) and lubricate the cylinder bores with approximately a teaspoon of motor oil using a spout-type oil can (see illustration 1). Reinstall the spark plug(s). Crank the engine over a couple of times to coat the piston rings and bores with oil. If the bike has a kickstart, use this to turn the engine over. If not, flick the kill switch to the OFF position and crank the engine over on the starter (see illustration 2). If the nature on the ignition system prevents the starter operating with the kill switch in the OFF position,

remove the spark plugs and fit them back in their caps; ensure that the plugs are earthed (grounded) against the cylinder head when the starter is operated (see illustration 3).

⚠ *Warning: It is important that the plugs are earthed (grounded) away from the spark plug holes otherwise there is a risk of atomised fuel from the cylinders igniting.*

HAYNES HiNT *On a single cylinder four-stroke engine, you can seal the combustion chamber completely by positioning the piston at TDC on the compression stroke.*

● Drain the carburettor(s) otherwise there is a risk of jets becoming blocked by gum deposits from the fuel (see illustration 4).

● If the bike is going into long-term storage, consider adding a fuel stabiliser to the fuel in the tank. If the tank is drained completely, corrosion of its internal surfaces may occur if left unprotected for a long period. The tank can be treated with a rust preventative especially for this purpose. Alternatively, remove the tank and pour half a litre of motor oil into it, install the filler cap and shake the tank to coat its internals with oil before draining off the excess. The same effect can also be achieved by spraying WD40 or a similar water-dispersant around the inside of the tank via its flexible nozzle.

● Make sure the cooling system contains the correct mix of antifreeze. Antifreeze also contains important corrosion inhibitors.

● The air intakes and exhaust can be sealed off by covering or plugging the openings. Ensure that you do not seal in any condensation; run the engine until it is hot,

Squirt a drop of motor oil into each cylinder

Flick the kill switch to OFF . . .

. . . and ensure that the metal bodies of the plugs (arrows) are earthed against the cylinder head

Connect a hose to the carburettor float chamber drain stub (arrow) and unscrew the drain screw

Exhausts can be sealed off with a plastic bag

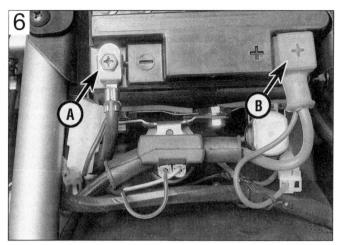

Disconnect the negative lead (A) first, followed by the positive lead (B)

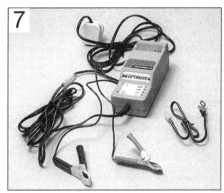

Use a suitable battery charger - this kit also assess battery condition

then switch off and allow to cool. Tape a piece of thick plastic over the silencer end(s) **(see illustration 5)**. Note that some advocate pouring a tablespoon of motor oil into the silencer(s) before sealing them off.

Battery

● Remove it from the bike - in extreme cases of cold the battery may freeze and crack its case **(see illustration 6)**.

● Check the electrolyte level and top up if necessary (conventional refillable batteries). Clean the terminals.
● Store the battery off the motorcycle and away from any sources of fire. Position a wooden block under the battery if it is to sit on the ground.
● Give the battery a trickle charge for a few hours every month **(see illustration 7)**.

Tyres

● Place the bike on its centrestand or an auxiliary stand which will support the motorcycle in an upright position. Position wood blocks under the tyres to keep them off the ground and to provide insulation from damp. If the bike is being put into long-term storage, ideally both tyres should be off the ground; not only will this protect the tyres, but will also ensure that no load is placed on the steering head or wheel bearings.
● Deflate each tyre by 5 to 10 psi, no more or the beads may unseat from the rim, making subsequent inflation difficult on tubeless tyres.

Pivots and controls

● Lubricate all lever, pedal, stand and

footrest pivot points. If grease nipples are fitted to the rear suspension components, apply lubricant to the pivots.
● Lubricate all control cables.

Cycle components

● Apply a wax protectant to all painted and plastic components. Wipe off any excess, but don't polish to a shine. Where fitted, clean the screen with soap and water.
● Coat metal parts with Vaseline (petroleum jelly). When applying this to the fork tubes, do not compress the forks otherwise the seals will rot from contact with the Vaseline.
● Apply a vinyl cleaner to the seat.

Storage conditions

● Aim to store the bike in a shed or garage which does not leak and is free from damp.
● Drape an old blanket or bedspread over the bike to protect it from dust and direct contact with sunlight (which will fade paint). This also hides the bike from prying eyes. Beware of tight-fitting plastic covers which may allow condensation to form and settle on the bike.

Getting back on the road

Engine and transmission

● Change the oil and replace the oil filter. If this was done prior to storage, check that the oil hasn't emulsified - a thick whitish substance which occurs through condensation.
● Remove the spark plugs. Using a spout-type oil can, squirt a few drops of oil into the cylinder(s). This will provide initial lubrication as the piston rings and bores comes back into contact. Service the spark plugs, or fit new ones, and install them in the engine.

● Check that the clutch isn't stuck on. The plates can stick together if left standing for some time, preventing clutch operation. Engage a gear and try rocking the bike back and forth with the clutch lever held against the handlebar. If this doesn't work on cable-operated clutches, hold the clutch lever back against the handlebar with a strong elastic band or cable tie for a couple of hours **(see illustration 8)**.
● If the air intakes or silencer end(s) were blocked off, remove the bung or cover used.
● If the fuel tank was coated with a rust

Hold clutch lever back against the handlebar with elastic bands or a cable tie

preventative, oil or a stabiliser added to the fuel, drain and flush the tank and dispose of the fuel sensibly. If no action was taken with the fuel tank prior to storage, it is advised that the old fuel is disposed of since it will go off over a period of time. Refill the fuel tank with fresh fuel.

Frame and running gear

● Oil all pivot points and cables.
● Check the tyre pressures. They will definitely need inflating if pressures were reduced for storage.
● Lubricate the final drive chain (where applicable).
● Remove any protective coating applied to the fork tubes (stanchions) since this may well destroy the fork seals. If the fork tubes weren't protected and have picked up rust spots, remove them with very fine abrasive paper and refinish with metal polish.
● Check that both brakes operate correctly. Apply each brake hard and check that it's not possible to move the motorcycle forwards, then check that the brake frees off again once released. Brake caliper pistons can stick due to corrosion around the piston head, or on the sliding caliper types, due to corrosion of the slider pins. If the brake doesn't free after repeated operation, take the caliper off for examination. Similarly drum brakes can stick due to a seized operating cam, cable or rod linkage.
● If the motorcycle has been in long-term storage, renew the brake fluid and clutch fluid (where applicable).
● Depending on where the bike has been stored, the wiring, cables and hoses may have been nibbled by rodents. Make a visual check and investigate disturbed wiring loom tape.

Battery

● If the battery has been previously removal and given top up charges it can simply be reconnected. Remember to connect the positive cable first and the negative cable last.
● On conventional refillable batteries, if the battery has not received any attention, remove it from the motorcycle and check its electrolyte level. Top up if necessary then charge the battery. If the battery fails to hold a charge and a visual checks show heavy white sulphation of the plates, the battery is probably defective and must be renewed. This is particularly likely if the battery is old. Confirm battery condition with a specific gravity check.
● On sealed (MF) batteries, if the battery has not received any attention, remove it from the motorcycle and charge it according to the information on the battery case - if the battery fails to hold a charge it must be renewed.

Starting procedure

● If a kickstart is fitted, turn the engine over a couple of times with the ignition OFF to distribute oil around the engine. If no kickstart is fitted, flick the engine kill switch OFF and the ignition ON and crank the engine over a couple of times to work oil around the upper cylinder components. If the nature of the ignition system is such that the starter won't work with the kill switch OFF, remove the spark plugs, fit them back into their caps and earth (ground) their bodies on the cylinder head. Reinstall the spark plugs afterwards.
● Switch the kill switch to RUN, operate the choke and start the engine. If the engine won't start don't continue cranking the engine - not only will this flatten the battery, but the starter motor will overheat. Switch the ignition off and try again later. If the engine refuses to start, go through the fault finding procedures in this manual. **Note:** *If the bike has been in storage for a long time, old fuel or a carburettor blockage may be the problem. Gum deposits in carburettors can block jets - if a carburettor cleaner doesn't prove successful the carburettors must be dismantled for cleaning.*
● Once the engine has started, check that the lights, turn signals and horn work properly.
● Treat the bike gently for the first ride and check all fluid levels on completion. Settle bike back into the maintenance schedule.

This Section provides an easy reference-guide to the more common faults that are likely to afflict your machine. Obviously, the opportunities are almost limitless for faults to occur as a result of obscure failures, and to try and cover all eventualities would require a book. Indeed, a number have been written on the subject.

Successful troubleshooting is not a mysterious 'black art' but the application of a bit of knowledge combined with a systematic and logical approach to the problem. Approach any troubleshooting by first accurately identifying the symptom and then checking through the list of possible causes, starting with the simplest or most obvious and progressing in stages to the most complex.

Take nothing for granted, but above all apply liberal quantities of common sense.

The main symptom of a fault is given in the text as a major heading below which are listed the various systems or areas which may contain the fault. Details of each possible cause for a fault and the remedial action to be taken are given, in brief, in the paragraphs below each heading. Further information should be sought in the relevant Chapter.

1 Engine doesn't start or is difficult to start

- [ ] Starter motor doesn't rotate
- [ ] Starter motor rotates but engine does not turn over
- [ ] Starter works but engine won't turn over (seized)
- [ ] No fuel flow
- [ ] Engine flooded
- [ ] No spark or weak spark
- [ ] Compression low
- [ ] Stalls after starting
- [ ] Rough idle

2 Poor running at low speed

- [ ] Spark weak
- [ ] Fuel/air mixture incorrect
- [ ] Compression low
- [ ] Poor acceleration

3 Poor running or no power at high speed

- [ ] Firing incorrect
- [ ] Fuel/air mixture incorrect
- [ ] Compression low
- [ ] Knocking or pinking
- [ ] Miscellaneous causes

4 Overheating

- [ ] Engine overheats
- [ ] Firing incorrect
- [ ] Fuel/air mixture incorrect
- [ ] Compression too high
- [ ] Engine load excessive
- [ ] Lubrication inadequate
- [ ] Miscellaneous causes

5 Clutch problems

- [ ] Clutch slipping
- [ ] Clutch not disengaging completely

6 Gearchange problems

- [ ] Doesn't go into gear, or lever doesn't return
- [ ] Jumps out of gear
- [ ] Overselects

7 Abnormal engine noise

- [ ] Knocking or pinking
- [ ] Piston slap or rattling
- [ ] Valve noise
- [ ] Other noise

8 Abnormal driveline noise

- [ ] Clutch noise
- [ ] Transmission noise
- [ ] Final drive noise

9 Abnormal frame and suspension noise

- [ ] Front end noise
- [ ] Rear suspension noise
- [ ] Brake noise

10 Oil pressure warning light comes on

- [ ] Engine lubrication system
- [ ] Electrical system

11 Excessive exhaust smoke

- [ ] White smoke
- [ ] Black smoke
- [ ] Brown smoke

12 Poor handling or stability

- [ ] Handlebar hard to turn
- [ ] Handlebar shakes or vibrates excessively
- [ ] Handlebar pulls to one side
- [ ] Poor shock absorbing qualities

13 Braking problems

- [ ] Brakes are spongy, don't hold
- [ ] Brake lever or pedal pulsates
- [ ] Brakes drag

14 Electrical problems

- [ ] Battery dead or weak
- [ ] Battery overcharged

1 Engine doesn't start or is difficult to start

Starter motor doesn't rotate

- [ ] Engine kill switch OFF.
- [ ] Fuse blown. Check main fuse and ignition/starter circuit fuse (Chapter 9).
- [ ] Battery voltage low. Check and recharge battery (Chapter 9).
- [ ] Starter motor defective. Make sure the wiring to the starter is secure. Make sure the starter relay clicks when the start button is pushed. If the relay clicks, then the fault is in the wiring or motor.
- [ ] Starter relay faulty. Check it according to the procedure in Chapter 9.
- [ ] Starter switch not contacting. The contacts could be wet, corroded or dirty. Disassemble and clean the switch (Chapter 9).
- [ ] Wiring open or shorted. Check all wiring connections and harnesses to make sure that they are dry, tight and not corroded. Also check for broken or frayed wires that can cause a short to ground (earth) (see wiring diagram, Chapter 9).
- [ ] Ignition (main) switch defective. Check the switch according to the procedure in Chapter 9. Replace the switch with a new one if it is defective.
- [ ] Engine kill switch defective. Check for wet, dirty or corroded contacts. Clean or replace the switch as necessary (Chapter 9).
- [ ] Faulty neutral, side stand or clutch switch. Check the wiring to each switch and the switch itself according to the procedures in Chapter 9.

Starter motor rotates but engine does not turn over

- [ ] Starter clutch defective. Inspect and repair or replace (Chapter 2).
- [ ] Damaged idle/reduction or starter gears. Inspect and renew the damaged parts (Chapter 2).

Starter works but engine won't turn over (seized)

- [ ] Seized engine caused by one or more internally damaged components. Failure due to wear, abuse or lack of lubrication. Damage can include seized valves, followers, camshafts, pistons, crankshaft, connecting rod bearings, or transmission gears or bearings. Refer to Chapter 2 for engine disassembly.

No fuel flow

- [ ] No fuel in tank.
- [ ] Fuel tank breather hose obstructed.
- [ ] Fuel tap filter clogged. Remove the tap or pump and clean or renew the filter (Chapter 1 and 4).
- [ ] Fuel line clogged. Pull the fuel line loose and carefully blow through it.
- [ ] Float needle valve clogged. For all of the valves to be clogged, either a very bad batch of fuel with an unusual additive has been used, or some other foreign material has entered the tank. Many times after a machine has been stored for many months without running, the fuel turns to a varnish-like liquid and forms deposits on the inlet needle valves and jets. The carburettors should be removed and overhauled if draining the float chambers doesn't solve the problem.

Engine flooded

- [ ] Float height too high. Check as described in Chapter 4.
- [ ] Float needle valve worn or stuck open. A piece of dirt, rust or other debris can cause the valve to seat improperly, causing excess fuel to be admitted to the float chamber. In this case, the float chamber should be cleaned and the needle valve and seat inspected. If the needle and seat are worn, then the leaking will persist and the parts should be replaced with new ones (Chapter 4).
- [ ] Starting technique incorrect. Under normal circumstances (i.e., if all the carburettor functions are sound) the machine should start with little or no throttle. When the engine is cold, the choke should be operated and the engine started without opening the throttle. When the engine is at operating temperature, only a very slight amount of throttle should be necessary. If the engine is flooded, move the choke lever to the OFF position, hold the throttle fully open and crank the engine for five seconds; this will allow additional air to reach the cylinders. Quickly close the throttle if the engine starts. If the engine doesn't start, turn the ignition OFF and wait 10 seconds before starting the engine normally.

No spark or weak spark

- [ ] Engine kill switch turned to the OFF position.
- [ ] Battery voltage low. Check and recharge the battery as necessary (Chapter 9).
- [ ] Spark plugs dirty, defective or worn out. Locate reason for fouled plugs using spark plug condition chart and follow the plug maintenance procedures (Chapter 1).
- [ ] Spark plug caps faulty or not making good contact over the spark plugs. Check condition. Replace if cracks or deterioration are evident (Chapter 5).
- [ ] HT coils or leads faulty. Check condition (Chapter 5).
- [ ] Ignition control unit defective. Check the unit, referring to Chapter 5 for details.
- [ ] Pulse generator defective. Check the unit, referring to Chapter 5 for details.
- [ ] Ignition or kill switch shorted. This is usually caused by water, corrosion, damage or excessive wear. The switches can be disassembled and cleaned with electrical contact cleaner. If cleaning does not help, renew the switches (Chapter 9).
- [ ] Wiring shorted or broken between:
    - a) Ignition (main) switch and engine kill switch (or blown fuse)
    - b) Ignition control unit and engine kill switch
    - c) Ignition control unit and ignition HT coils
    - d) Ignition control unit and pulse generator
- [ ] Make sure that all wiring connections are clean, dry and tight. Look for chafed and broken wires (Chapters 5 and 9).

Compression low

- [ ] Spark plugs loose. Remove the plugs and inspect their threads. Reinstall and tighten to the specified torque (Chapter 1).
- [ ] Cylinder head not sufficiently tightened down. If a cylinder head is suspected of being loose, then there's a chance that the gasket or head is damaged if the problem has persisted for any length of time. The head bolts should be tightened to the proper torque in the correct sequence (Chapter 2).
- [ ] Incorrect valve clearance. This means that the valve is not closing completely and compression pressure is leaking past the valve. Check and adjust the valve clearances (Chapter 1).
- [ ] Cylinder bores and/or piston worn. Excessive wear will cause compression pressure to leak past the rings. This is usually accompanied by worn rings as well.
- [ ] Piston rings worn, weak, broken, or sticking. Broken or sticking piston rings usually indicate a lubrication or carburation problem that causes excess carbon deposits or seizures to form on the pistons and rings.
- [ ] Piston ring-to-groove clearance excessive. This is caused by excessive wear of the piston ring lands. Piston replacement is necessary (Chapter 2).
- [ ] Cylinder head gasket damaged. If a head is allowed to become loose, or if excessive carbon build-up on the piston crown and combustion chamber causes extremely high compression, the head gasket may leak. Retorquing the head is not always sufficient to restore the seal, so gasket renewal is necessary (Chapter 2).

1 Engine doesn't start or is difficult to start (continued)

- [ ] Cylinder head warped. This is caused by overheating or improperly tightened head bolts. Machine shop resurfacing or head replacement is necessary (Chapter 2).
- [ ] Valve spring broken or weak. Caused by component failure or wear; the springs must be renewed (Chapter 2).
- [ ] Valve not seating properly. This is caused by a bent valve (from over-revving or improper valve adjustment), burned valve or seat (improper carburation) or an accumulation of carbon deposits on the seat (from carburation or lubrication problems). The valves must be cleaned and/or renewed and the seats serviced if possible (Chapter 2).

Stalls after starting

- [ ] Improper choke action. Make sure the choke linkage shaft is getting a full stroke and staying in the out position (Chapter 4).
- [ ] Ignition malfunction. See Chapter 5.
- [ ] Carburettor malfunction. See Chapter 4.
- [ ] Fuel contaminated. The fuel can be contaminated with either dirt or water, or can change chemically if the machine is allowed to sit for several months or more. Drain the tank and float chambers (Chapter 4). Also check that the fuel flows freely and is not being restricted.

- [ ] Intake air leak. Check for loose carburettor-to-intake manifold connections, loose or missing vacuum gauge adapter plugs/caps, or loose carburettor tops (Chapter 4).
- [ ] Engine idle speed incorrect. Turn idle adjusting screw until the engine idles at the specified rpm (Chapter 1).

Rough idle

- [ ] Ignition malfunction. See Chapter 5.
- [ ] Idle speed incorrect. See Chapter 1.
- [ ] Carburettors not synchronised. Adjust with vacuum gauge or manometer set as described in Chapter 1.
- [ ] Carburettor malfunction. See Chapter 4.
- [ ] Fuel contaminated. The fuel can be contaminated with either dirt or water, or can change chemically if the machine is allowed to sit for several months or more. Drain the tank and float chambers (Chapter 4).
- [ ] Intake air leak. Check for loose carburettor or throttle body-to-intake manifold connections, loose or missing vacuum gauge adapter plugs/caps, or loose carburettor tops (Chapter 4).
- [ ] Air filter clogged. Clean or renew the air filter element (Chapter 1).

2 Poor running at low speeds

Spark weak

- [ ] Battery voltage low. Check and recharge battery (Chapter 9).
- [ ] Spark plugs fouled, defective or worn out. Refer to Chapter 1 for spark plug maintenance.
- [ ] Incorrect spark plugs. Wrong type, heat range or cap configuration. Check and install correct plugs listed in Chapter 1.
- [ ] Ignition control unit defective. Check the unit, referring to Chapter 5.
- [ ] Pulse generator defective. See Chapter 5.
- [ ] Spark plug caps defective or not making good contact with spark plugs. See Chapter 1.

Fuel/air mixture incorrect

- [ ] Pilot screws out of adjustment (Chapter 4).
- [ ] Pilot jet or air passage clogged. Remove and overhaul the carburettors (Chapter 4).
- [ ] Air bleed holes clogged. Remove carburettor and blow out all passages (Chapter 4).
- [ ] Fuel level too high or too low. Check the float height (Chapter 4).
- [ ] Carburettor intake manifolds loose. Check for cracks, breaks, tears or loose clamps. Renew the rubber intake manifold joints if split or perished.
- [ ] Air filter clogged, poorly sealed or missing (Chapter 1).
- [ ] Air filter housing poorly sealed. Look for cracks, holes or loose clamps and renew or repair defective parts.
- [ ] Fuel tank breather hose obstructed.

Compression low

- [ ] Spark plugs loose. Remove the plugs and inspect their threads. Reinstall and tighten to the specified torque (Chapter 1).
- [ ] Cylinder head not sufficiently tightened down. If the cylinder head is suspected of being loose, then there's a chance that the gasket and head are damaged if the problem has persisted for any length of time. The head bolts should be tightened to the proper torque in the correct sequence (Chapter 2).
- [ ] Incorrect valve clearance. This means that the valve is not closing completely and compression pressure is leaking past the valve. Check and adjust the valve clearances (Chapter 1).

- [ ] Cylinder bores and/or pistons worn. Excessive wear will cause compression pressure to leak past the rings. This is usually accompanied by worn rings as well.
- [ ] Piston rings worn, weak, broken, or sticking. Broken or sticking piston rings usually indicate a lubrication or carburation problem that causes excess carbon deposits or seizures to form on the pistons and rings.
- [ ] Piston ring-to-groove clearance excessive. This is caused by excessive wear of the piston ring lands. Piston renewal is necessary (Chapter 2).
- [ ] Cylinder head gasket damaged. If a head is allowed to become loose, or if excessive carbon build-up on the piston crown and combustion chamber causes extremely high compression, the head gasket may leak. Retorquing the head is not always sufficient to restore the seal, so gasket renewal is necessary (Chapter 2).
- [ ] Cylinder head warped. This is caused by overheating or improperly tightened head bolts. Machine shop resurfacing or head renewal is necessary (Chapter 2).
- [ ] Valve spring broken or weak. Caused by component failure or wear; the springs must be renewed (Chapter 2).
- [ ] Valve not seating properly. This is caused by a bent valve (from over-revving or improper valve adjustment), burned valve or seat (improper carburation) or an accumulation of carbon deposits on the seat (from carburation, lubrication problems). The valves must be cleaned and/or renewed and the seats serviced if possible (Chapter 2).

Poor acceleration

- [ ] Carburettors leaking or dirty. Overhaul them (Chapter 4).
- [ ] Timing not advancing. The ignition control unit may be defective (see Chapter 5).
- [ ] Carburettors not synchronised. Adjust them with a vacuum gauge set or manometer as described in Chapter 1.
- [ ] Engine oil viscosity too high. Using a heavier oil than that recommended in Chapter 1 can damage the oil pump or lubrication system and cause drag on the engine.
- [ ] Brakes dragging. Usually caused by debris which has entered the brake piston seals, or from a warped disc or bent axle. Repair as necessary (Chapter 7).

3 Poor running or no power at high speed

Firing incorrect

☐ Air filter restricted. Clean or renew filter (Chapter 1).
☐ Spark plugs fouled, defective or worn out. See Chapter 1 for spark plug maintenance.
☐ Incorrect spark plugs. Wrong type, heat range or cap configuration. Check and install correct plugs listed in Chapter 1.
☐ Ignition control unit defective. See Chapter 5.
☐ Spark plug caps defective or not making good contact with spark plugs. See Chapter 1.

Fuel/air mixture incorrect

☐ Main jet clogged. Dirt, water or other contaminants can clog the main jets. Clean the fuel tap filter, the float chamber area, and the jets and carburettor orifices (Chapter 4).
☐ Main jet wrong size. The standard jetting is for sea level atmospheric pressure and oxygen content.
☐ Throttle shaft-to-carburettor body clearance excessive.
☐ Air bleed holes clogged. Remove carburettor and blow out all passages (Chapter 4).
☐ Fuel level too high or too low. Check the float height (Chapter 4).
☐ Carburettor intake manifolds loose. Check for cracks, breaks, tears or loose clamps. Renew the rubber intake manifold joints if split or perished.
☐ Air filter clogged, poorly sealed or missing (Chapter 1).
☐ Air filter housing poorly sealed. Look for cracks, holes or loose clamps and renew or repair defective parts.
☐ Fuel tank breather hose obstructed.

Compression low

☐ Spark plugs loose. Remove the plugs and inspect their threads. Reinstall and tighten to the specified torque (Chapter 1).
☐ Cylinder head not sufficiently tightened down. If the cylinder head is suspected of being loose, then there's a chance that the gasket and head are damaged if the problem has persisted for any length of time. The head bolts should be tightened to the proper torque in the correct sequence (Chapter 2).
☐ Incorrect valve clearance. This means that the valve is not closing completely and compression pressure is leaking past the valve. Check and adjust the valve clearances (Chapter 1).
☐ Cylinder bores and/or pistons worn. Excessive wear will cause compression pressure to leak past the rings. This is usually accompanied by worn rings as well.
☐ Piston rings worn, weak, broken, or sticking. Broken or sticking piston rings usually indicate a lubrication problem that causes excess carbon deposits or seizures to form on the pistons and rings.
☐ Piston ring-to-groove clearance excessive. This is caused by excessive wear of the piston ring lands. Piston renewal is necessary (Chapter 2).

☐ Cylinder head gasket damaged. If a head is allowed to become loose, or if excessive carbon build-up on the piston crown and combustion chamber causes extremely high compression, the head gasket may leak. Retorquing the head is not always sufficient to restore the seal, so gasket renewal is necessary (Chapter 2).
☐ Cylinder head warped. This is caused by overheating or improperly tightened head bolts. Machine shop resurfacing or head renewal is necessary (Chapter 2).
☐ Valve spring broken or weak. Caused by component failure or wear; the springs must be renewed (Chapter 2).
☐ Valve not seating properly. This is caused by a bent valve (from over-revving or improper valve adjustment), burned valve or seat (improper carburation) or an accumulation of carbon deposits on the seat (from fuelling or lubrication problems). The valves must be cleaned and/or renewed and the seats serviced if possible (Chapter 2).

Knocking or pinking

☐ Carbon build-up in combustion chamber. Use of a fuel additive that will dissolve the adhesive bonding the carbon particles to the crown and chamber is the easiest way to remove the build-up. Otherwise, the cylinder head will have to be removed and decarbonised (Chapter 2).
☐ Incorrect or poor quality fuel. Old or improper grades of fuel can cause detonation. This causes the piston to rattle, thus the knocking or pinking sound. Drain old fuel and always use the recommended fuel grade.
☐ Spark plug heat range incorrect. Uncontrolled detonation indicates the plug heat range is too hot. The plug in effect becomes a glow plug, raising cylinder temperatures. Install the proper heat range plug (Chapter 1).
☐ Improper air/fuel mixture. This will cause the cylinders to run hot, which leads to detonation. Clogged jets or an air leak can cause this imbalance. See Chapter 4.

Miscellaneous causes

☐ Throttle valve doesn't open fully. Adjust the throttle grip freeplay (Chapter 1).
☐ Clutch slipping. May be caused by loose or worn clutch components. Refer to Chapter 2 for clutch overhaul procedures.
☐ Timing not advancing – faulty ignition control unit.
☐ Engine oil viscosity too high. Using a heavier oil than the one recommended in Chapter 1 can damage the oil pump or lubrication system and cause drag on the engine.
☐ Brakes dragging. Usually caused by debris which has entered the brake piston seals, or from a warped disc or bent axle. Repair as necessary.

4 Overheating

Engine overheats

☐ Coolant level low. Check and add coolant (Chapter 1).
☐ Leak in cooling system. Check cooling system hoses and radiator for leaks and other damage. Repair or renew parts as necessary (Chapter 3).
☐ Thermostat sticking open or closed. Test as described in Chapter 3.
☐ Faulty radiator cap. Remove the cap and have it pressure tested by a dealer.
☐ Coolant passages clogged. Have the entire system drained and flushed, then refill with fresh coolant.
☐ Water pump defective. Remove the pump and check the components (Chapter 3).
☐ Clogged radiator fins. Clean them by blowing compressed air through the fins from the rear side of the radiator.
☐ Cooling fan or fan switch fault (Chapter 3).

Firing incorrect

☐ Spark plugs fouled, defective or worn out. See Chapter 1 for spark plug maintenance.
☐ Incorrect spark plugs.
☐ Ignition control unit defective (Chapter 5).
☐ Pulse generator faulty (Chapter 5).
☐ Faulty HT ignition coils (Chapter 5).

Fuel/air mixture incorrect

☐ Main jet clogged. Dirt, water or other contaminants can clog the main jets. Clean the fuel tap filter, the float chamber area, and the jets and carburettor orifices (Chapter 4).
☐ Main jet wrong size. The standard jetting is for sea level atmospheric pressure and oxygen content.
☐ Throttle shaft-to-carburettor body clearance excessive.
☐ Air bleed holes clogged. Remove carburettor and blow out all passages (Chapter 4).
☐ Fuel level too high or too low. Check the float height (Chapter 4).
☐ Carburettor intake manifolds loose. Check for cracks, breaks, tears or loose clamps. Renew the rubber intake manifold joints if split or perished.
☐ Air filter clogged, poorly sealed or missing (Chapter 1).

☐ Air filter housing poorly sealed. Look for cracks, holes or loose clamps and renew or repair defective parts.
☐ Fuel tank breather hose obstructed.

Compression too high

☐ Carbon build-up in combustion chamber. Use of a fuel additive that will dissolve the adhesive bonding the carbon particles to the piston crown and chamber is the easiest way to remove the build-up. Otherwise, the cylinder head will have to be removed and decarbonised (Chapter 2).

Engine load excessive

☐ Clutch slipping. Can be caused by damaged, loose or worn clutch components. Refer to Chapter 2 for overhaul procedures.
☐ Engine oil level too high. The addition of too much oil will cause pressurisation of the crankcase and inefficient engine operation. Check Specifications and drain to proper level (Chapter 1 and Daily (pre-ride) checks).
☐ Engine oil viscosity too high. Using a heavier oil than the one recommended in Chapter 1 can damage the oil pump or lubrication system as well as cause drag on the engine.
☐ Brakes dragging. Usually caused by debris which has entered the brake piston seals, or from a warped disc or bent axle. Repair as necessary.

Lubrication inadequate

☐ Engine oil level too low. Friction caused by intermittent lack of lubrication or from oil that is overworked can cause overheating. The oil provides a definite cooling function in the engine. Check the oil level (Daily (pre-ride) checks).
☐ Poor quality engine oil or incorrect viscosity or type. Oil is rated not only according to viscosity but also according to type. Some oils are not rated high enough for use in this engine. Check the Specifications section and change to the correct oil (Daily (pre-ride) checks).

Miscellaneous causes

☐ Modification to exhaust system. Most aftermarket exhaust systems cause the engine to run leaner, which make them run hotter.

5 Clutch problems

Clutch slipping

☐ Clutch cable incorrectly adjusted. Check and adjust (see Chapter 1).
☐ Friction plates worn or warped. Overhaul the clutch assembly (Chapter 2).
☐ Plain plates warped (Chapter 2).
☐ Clutch springs broken or weak. Old or heat-damaged (from slipping clutch) springs should be replaced with new ones (Chapter 2).
☐ Clutch release mechanism defective. Replace any defective parts (Chapter 2).
☐ Clutch centre or housing unevenly worn. This causes improper engagement of the plates. Renew the damaged or worn parts (Chapter 2).

Clutch not disengaging completely

☐ Clutch cable incorrectly adjusted. Check and adjust (see Chapter 1).
☐ Clutch plates warped or damaged. This will cause clutch drag,

which in turn will cause the machine to creep. Overhaul the clutch assembly (Chapter 2).
☐ Clutch spring tension uneven. Usually caused by a sagged or broken spring. Check and renew the springs as a set (Chapter 2).
☐ Engine oil deteriorated. Old, thin, worn out oil will not provide proper lubrication for the plates, causing the clutch to drag. Renew the oil and filter (Chapter 1).
☐ Engine oil viscosity too high. Using a heavier oil than recommended in Chapter 1 can cause the plates to stick together, putting a drag on the engine. Change to the correct weight oil (Chapter 1).
☐ Clutch housing bush seized on gearbox input shaft. Lack of lubrication, severe wear or damage can cause the bush to seize on the shaft. Overhaul of the clutch, and perhaps transmission, may be necessary to repair the damage (Chapter 2).
☐ Clutch release mechanism defective.
☐ Loose clutch centre nut. Causes housing and centre misalignment putting a drag on the engine. Engagement adjustment continually varies. Overhaul the clutch assembly (Chapter 2).

6 Gearchange problems

Doesn't go into gear or lever doesn't return

☐ Clutch not disengaging. See above.
☐ Selector fork(s) bent or seized. Overhaul the transmission (Chapter 2).
☐ Gear(s) stuck on shaft. Most often caused by a lack of lubrication or excessive wear in transmission bearings and bushes. Overhaul the transmission (Chapter 2).
☐ Selector drum binding. Caused by lubrication failure or excessive wear. Renew the drum and bearing (Chapter 2).
☐ Gearchange lever return spring weak or broken (Chapter 2).
☐ Gearchange lever broken. Splines stripped out of lever or shaft, caused by allowing the lever to get loose. Renew necessary parts (Chapter 2).
☐ Gearchange mechanism stopper arm broken or worn. Full engagement and rotary movement of selector drum results. Renew the arm (Chapter 2).
☐ Stopper arm spring broken. Allows arm to float, causing sporadic gearchange operation. Renew the spring (Chapter 2).

Jumps out of gear

☐ Selector fork(s) worn. Overhaul the transmission (Chapter 2).
☐ Gear groove(s) worn. Overhaul the transmission (Chapter 2).
☐ Gear dogs or dog slots worn or damaged. The gears should be inspected and renewed if necessary.

Overselects

☐ Stopper arm spring weak or broken (Chapter 2).
☐ Gearchange shaft return spring post broken or distorted (Chapter 2).

7 Abnormal engine noise

Knocking or pinking

☐ Carbon build-up in combustion chamber. Use of a fuel additive that will dissolve the adhesive bonding the carbon particles to the piston crown and chamber is the easiest way to remove the build-up. Otherwise, the cylinder head will have to be removed and decarbonised (Chapter 2).
☐ Incorrect or poor quality fuel. Old or improper fuel can cause detonation. This causes the pistons to rattle, thus the knocking or pinking sound. Drain the old fuel and always use the recommended grade fuel (Chapter 4).
☐ Spark plug heat range incorrect. Uncontrolled detonation indicates that the plug heat range is too hot. The plug in effect becomes a glow plug, raising cylinder temperatures. Install the proper heat range plug (Chapter 1).
☐ Improper fuel/air mixture. This will cause the cylinders to run hot and lead to detonation. Clogged jets or an air leak can cause this imbalance. See Chapter 4.

Piston slap or rattling

☐ Cylinder-to-piston clearance excessive. Check as described in Chapter 2.
☐ Connecting rod bent. Caused by over-revving, trying to start a badly flooded engine or from ingesting a foreign object into the combustion chamber. Renew the damaged parts (Chapter 2).
☐ Piston pin or piston pin bore worn or seized from wear or lack of lubrication. Renew damaged parts (Chapter 2).
☐ Piston ring(s) worn, broken or sticking. Overhaul the top-end (Chapter 2).
☐ Piston seizure damage. Usually from lack of lubrication or overheating. Renew the pistons and rebore the cylinders, as necessary (Chapter 2).
☐ Connecting rod upper or lower end clearance excessive. Caused by excessive wear or lack of lubrication. Renew worn parts.

Valve noise

☐ Incorrect valve clearances. Adjust the clearances by referring to Chapter 1.
☐ Valve spring broken or weak. Check and renew weak valve springs (Chapter 2).
☐ Camshaft or cylinder head worn or damaged. Lack of lubrication at high rpm is usually the cause of damage. Insufficient oil or failure to change the oil at the recommended intervals are the chief causes. Since there are no replaceable bearings in the head, the head and camshaft holder will have to be renewed if there is excessive wear or damage (Chapter 2).

Other noise

☐ Cylinder head gasket leaking.
☐ Exhaust pipe leaking at cylinder head connection. Caused by improper fit of pipe(s) or loose exhaust flange. All exhaust fasteners should be tightened evenly and carefully. Failure to do this will lead to a leak.
☐ Crankshaft runout excessive. Caused by a bent crankshaft (from over-revving) or damage from an upper cylinder component failure.
☐ Engine mounting bolts loose. Tighten all engine mount bolts (Chapter 2).
☐ Crankshaft bearings worn (Chapter 2).
☐ Cam chain tensioner defective, cam chain or guide blades worn. Renew according to the procedure in Chapter 2.

8 Abnormal driveline noise

Clutch noise

☐ Clutch outer drum/friction plate clearance excessive (Chapter 2).
☐ Loose or damaged clutch pressure plate and/or bolts (Chapter 2).

Transmission noise

☐ Bearings worn. Also includes the possibility that the shafts are worn. Overhaul the transmission (Chapter 2).
☐ Gears worn or chipped (Chapter 2).
☐ Metal chips jammed in gear teeth. Probably pieces from a broken clutch, gear or selector mechanism that were picked up by the gears. This will cause early bearing failure (Chapter 2).

☐ Engine oil level too low. Causes a howl from transmission. Also affects engine power and clutch operation (Chapter 1).

Final drive noise

☐ Chain not adjusted properly (Chapter 1).
☐ Front or rear sprocket loose. Tighten fasteners (Chapter 6).
☐ Sprockets worn. Renew sprockets (Chapter 6).
☐ Rear sprocket warped. Renew sprockets (Chapter 6).
☐ Rubber dampers in rear wheel hub worn. Check and renew (Chapter 7).

9 Abnormal frame and suspension noise

Front end noise

☐ Low fluid level or improper viscosity oil in forks. This can sound like spurting and is usually accompanied by irregular fork action (Chapter 6).
☐ Spring weak or broken. Makes a clicking or scraping sound. Fork oil, when drained, will have a lot of metal particles in it (Chapter 6).
☐ Steering head bearings loose or damaged. Clicks when braking. Check and adjust or replace as necessary (Chapters 1 and 6).
☐ Fork yokes loose. Make sure all clamp pinch bolts are tightened to the specified torque (Chapter 6).
☐ Fork tube bent. Good possibility if machine has been dropped. Replace tube with a new one (Chapter 6).
☐ Front axle bolt or axle clamp bolts loose. Tighten them to the specified torque (Chapter 7).
☐ Loose or worn wheel bearings. Check and renew as necessary (Chapter 7).

Rear suspension noise

☐ Fluid level incorrect. Indicates a leak caused by defective seal. Shock will be covered with oil. Renew shock or seek advice on repair from a Honda dealer or suspension specialist (Chapter 6).

☐ Defective shock absorber with internal damage. This is in the body of the shock and can't be remedied. The shock must be replaced with a new one (Chapter 6).
☐ Bent or damaged shock body. Replace the shock with a new one (Chapter 6).
☐ Loose or worn swingarm pivot components. Check and renew as necessary (Chapter 6).

Brake noise

☐ Squeal caused by pad shim not installed or positioned correctly (where fitted) (Chapter 7).
☐ Squeal caused by dust on brake pads. Usually found in combination with glazed pads. Clean using brake cleaning solvent (Chapter 7).
☐ Contamination of brake pads. Oil, brake fluid or dirt causing brake to chatter or squeal. Renew pads (Chapter 7).
☐ Pads glazed. Renew the pads (Chaper 7).
☐ Disc warped. Can cause a chattering, clicking or intermittent squeal. Usually accompanied by a pulsating lever and uneven braking. Renew the disc (Chapter 7).
☐ Loose or worn wheel bearings. Check (Chapter 1) and renew (Chapter 7) as necessary.

10 Oil pressure warning light comes on

Engine lubrication system

☐ Engine oil pump defective, blocked oil strainer gauze or failed relief valve. Carry out an oil pressure check (Chapter 1).

☐ Engine oil level low. Inspect for leak or other problem causing low oil level and add recommended oil (*Daily (pre-ride) checks*).

☐ Engine oil viscosity too low. Very old, thin oil or an improper weight of oil used in the engine. Change to correct oil (*Daily (pre-ride) checks*).

☐ Camshaft or journals worn. Excessive wear causing drop in oil pressure. Measure oil clearance (Chapter 2). Abnormal wear could be caused by oil starvation at high rpm from low oil level or improper weight or type of oil (Chapter 1).

☐ Crankshaft and/or bearings worn. Same problems as above. Measure oil connecting rod and main bearing oil clearance (Chapter 2).

Electrical system

☐ Oil pressure switch defective. Check the switch according to the procedure in Chapter 9. Replace it if it is defective.

☐ Oil pressure warning light circuit defective. Check for pinched, shorted, disconnected or damaged wiring (Chapter 9).

11 Excessive exhaust smoke

White smoke

☐ Piston oil ring worn. The ring may be broken or damaged, causing oil from the crankcase to be pulled past the piston into the combustion chamber. Replace the rings with new ones (Chapter 2).

☐ Cylinder bores worn, cracked, or scored. Caused by overheating or oil starvation. The cylinders will have to be rebored and new pistons installed.

☐ Valve oil seal damaged or worn. Replace oil seals with new ones (Chapter 2).

☐ Valve guide worn. Perform a complete valve job (Chapter 2).

☐ Engine oil level too high, which causes the oil to be forced past the rings. Drain oil to the proper level (Chapter 1 and *Daily (pre-ride) checks*).

☐ Head gasket broken between oil return and cylinder. Causes oil to be pulled into the combustion chamber. Renew the head gasket and check the head for warpage (Chapter 2).

☐ Abnormal crankcase pressurisation, which forces oil past the rings. Clogged breather is usually the cause.

Black smoke

☐ Main jet too large or loose. Compare the jet size to the Specifications (Chapter 4).

☐ Choke cable or linkage shaft stuck, causing fuel to be pulled through choke circuit (Chapter 4).

☐ Fuel level too high. Check and adjust the float height(s) as necessary (Chapter 4).

☐ Float needle valve held off needle seat. Clean the float chambers and fuel line and renew the needles and seats if necessary (Chapter 4).

☐ Air filter clogged (Chapter 1).

Brown smoke

☐ Main jet too small or clogged. Lean condition caused by wrong size main jet or by a restricted orifice. Clean float chambers and jets and compare jet size to Specifications (Chapter 4).

☐ Fuel flow insufficient. Float needle valve stuck closed due to chemical reaction with old fuel. Float height incorrect. Restricted fuel line. Clean line and float chamber and adjust floats if necessary.

☐ Carburettor intake manifold clamps loose (Chapter 4).

☐ Air filter poorly sealed or not installed (Chapter 1).

12 Poor handling or stability

Handlebars hard to turn

☐ Steering head bearing adjuster nut too tight. Check adjustment as described in Chapter 1.

☐ Bearings damaged. Roughness can be felt as the bars are turned from side-to-side. Renew bearings and races (Chapter 6).

☐ Races dented or worn. Denting results from wear in only one position (e.g., straight ahead), from a collision or hitting a pothole or from dropping the machine. Renew bearings (Chapter 6

☐ Steering stem lubrication inadequate. Causes are grease getting hard from age or being washed out by high pressure car washes. Disassemble steering head and repack bearings with fresh grease (Chapter 6).

☐ Steering stem bent. Caused by a collision, hitting a pothole or by dropping the machine. Renew damaged part. Don't try to straighten the steering stem (Chapter 6).

☐ Front tyre air pressure too low (Chapter 1).

Handlebar shakes or vibrates excessively

☐ Tyres worn or out of balance (Chapter 7).

☐ Swingarm bearings worn. Renew worn bearings (Chapter 6).

☐ Wheel rim(s) warped or damaged. Inspect wheels for runout (Chapter 7).

☐ Wheel bearings worn. Worn front or rear wheel bearings can cause poor tracking. Worn front bearings will cause wobble (Chapter 7).

☐ Handlebar clamp bolts loose (Chapter 6).

☐ Fork yoke bolts loose. Tighten them to the specified torque (Chapter 6).

☐ Engine mounting bolts loose. Will cause excessive vibration with increased engine rpm (Chapter 2).

Handlebar pulls to one side

☐ Frame bent. Definitely suspect this if the machine has been dropped. May or may not be accompanied by cracking near the bend. Renew the frame (Chapter 6).

☐ Wheels out of alignment. Caused by improper location of axle spacers or from bent steering stem or frame (Chapter 6).

☐ Swingarm bent or twisted from accident damage. Renew the swingarm (Chapter 6).

☐ Steering stem bent. Caused by impact damage or by dropping the motorcycle. Renew the steering stem (Chapter 6).

☐ Fork tube bent. Disassemble the forks and renew the damaged parts (Chapter 6).

☐ Fork oil level uneven. Check and add or drain as necessary (Chapter 6).

Poor shock absorbing qualities

☐ Too hard:
   a) Front fork oil level excessive (Chapter 6).
   b) Front fork oil viscosity too high. Use a lighter oil (see the Specifications in Chapter 6).
   c) Front fork tube bent. Causes a harsh, sticking feeling (Chapter 6).
   d) Front fork internal damage (Chapter 6).
   e) Rear shock shaft or body bent or damaged (Chapter 6).
   f) Rear shock internal damage.
   g) Rear shock pre-load setting incorrect (Chapter 6).
   h) Tyre pressures too high (Daily (pre-ride) checks).

Too soft:
   a) Front fork damaged or leaking damping oil (Chapter 6).
   b) Front fork oil level too low or too light (Chapter 6).
   c) Fork springs weak or broken (Chapter 6).
   d) Rear shock internal damage or leakage (Chapter 6).
   e) Rear shock adjustment pre-load setting incorrect (Chapter 6).

13 Braking problems

Brakes are spongy, or lack power

☐ Air in brake line. Caused by inattention to master cylinder fluid level or by leakage. Locate problem and bleed brakes (Chapter 7).

☐ Pad or disc worn (Chapters 1 and 7).

☐ Brake fluid leak. See paragraph 1.

☐ Contaminated pads. Caused by contamination with oil, grease, brake fluid, etc. Renew pads (Chapter 7). Clean disc thoroughly with brake cleaner (Chapter 7).

☐ Brake fluid deteriorated. Fluid is old or contaminated. Drain system, replenish with new fluid and bleed the system (Chapter 7).

☐ Master cylinder internal parts worn or damaged causing fluid to bypass (Chapter 7).

☐ Master cylinder bore scratched by foreign material or broken spring. Repair or renew master cylinder (Chapter 7).

Brake lever or pedal pulsates

☐ Disc warped. Renew disc (Chapter 7).

☐ Wheel axle bent. Renew axle (Chapter 7).

☐ Brake caliper bolts loose (Chapter 7).

☐ Brake caliper slider pins sticking, causing caliper to bind. Lubricate the slider pins and renew their dust boots if cracked (Chapter 7).

☐ Wheel warped or otherwise damaged (Chapter 7).

☐ Wheel bearings damaged or worn (Chapters 1 and 7).

Brakes drag

☐ Master cylinder piston seized. Caused by wear or damage to piston or cylinder bore (Chapter 7).

☐ Lever balky or stuck. Check pivot and lubricate (Chapter 7).

☐ Brake caliper slider pins sticking or seized, causing caliper to bind. Lubricate the slider pins and renew their dust boots if cracked (Chapter 7).

☐ Brake caliper piston(s) seized in bore. Caused by wear or ingestion of dirt past deteriorated seal(s) (Chapter 7).

☐ Brake pad damaged. Renew pads (Chapter 7).

☐ Pads improperly installed (Chapter 7).

14 Electrical problems

Battery dead or weak

- [ ] Battery faulty. Caused by sulphated plates which are shorted through sedimentation. Also, broken battery terminal making only occasional contact (Chapter 9).
- [ ] Battery cables making poor contact (Chapter 9).
- [ ] Load excessive. Caused by addition of high wattage lights or other electrical accessories.
- [ ] Ignition (main) switch defective. Switch either grounds (earths) internally or fails to shut off system. Renew the switch (Chapter 9).
- [ ] Regulator/rectifier defective (Chapter 9).
- [ ] Alternator stator coil open or shorted (Chapter 9).
- [ ] Wiring faulty. Wiring grounded (earthed) or connections loose in ignition, charging or lighting circuits (Chapter 9).

Battery overcharged

- [ ] Regulator/rectifier defective. Overcharging is noticed when battery gets excessively warm (Chapter 9).
- [ ] Battery defective. Replace battery with a new one (Chapter 9).
- [ ] Battery amperage too low, wrong type or size. Install manufacturer's specified amp-hour battery to handle charging load (Chapter 9).

Checking engine compression

● Low compression will result in exhaust smoke, heavy oil consumption, poor starting and poor performance. A compression test will provide useful information about an engine's condition and if performed regularly, can give warning of trouble before any other symptoms become apparent.
● A compression gauge will be required, along with an adapter to suit the spark plug hole thread size. Note that the screw-in type gauge/adapter set up is preferable to the rubber cone type.
● Before carrying out the test, first check the valve clearances as described in Chapter 1.
1 Run the engine until it reaches normal operating temperature, then stop it and remove the spark plug(s), taking care not to scald your hands on the hot components.
2 Install the gauge adapter and compression gauge in No. 1 cylinder spark plug hole **(see illustration 1)**.

Screw the compression gauge adapter into the spark plug hole, then screw the gauge into the adapter

3 On kickstart-equipped motorcycles, make sure the ignition switch is OFF, then open the throttle fully and kick the engine over a couple of times until the gauge reading stabilises.
4 On motorcycles with electric start only, the procedure will differ depending on the nature of the ignition system. Flick the engine kill switch (engine stop switch) to OFF and turn the ignition switch ON; open the throttle fully and crank the engine over on the starter motor for a couple of revolutions until the gauge reading stabilises. If the starter will not operate with the kill switch OFF, turn the ignition switch OFF and refer to the next paragraph.
5 Install the plugs back in their caps and arrange the plug electrodes so that their metal bodies are earthed (grounded) against the cylinder head; this is essential to prevent damage to the ignition system **(see illustration 2)**. Position the plugs well away from the plug holes otherwise there

All spark plugs must be earthed (grounded) against the cylinder head

is a risk of atomised fuel escaping from the plug holes and igniting. As a safety precaution, cover the cylinder head cover with rag. Turn the ignition switch and kill switch ON, open the throttle fully and crank the engine over on the starter motor for a couple of revolutions until the gauge reading stabilises.
6 After one or two revolutions the pressure should build up to a maximum figure and then stabilise. Take a note of this reading and on multi-cylinder engines repeat the test on the remaining cylinders.
7 The correct pressures are given in Chapter 1 Specifications. If the results fall within the specified range and on multi-cylinder engines all are relatively equal, the engine is in good condition. If there is a marked difference between the readings, or if the readings are lower than specified,

inspection of the top-end components will be required.
8 Low compression pressure may be due to worn cylinder bores, pistons or rings, failure of the cylinder head gasket, worn valve seals, or poor valve seating.
9 To distinguish between cylinder/piston wear and valve leakage, pour a small quantity of oil into the bore to temporarily seal the piston rings, then repeat the compression tests **(see illustration 3)**. If the readings show

Bores can be temporarily sealed with a squirt of motor oil

a noticeable increase in pressure this confirms that the cylinder bore, piston, or rings are worn. If, however, no change is indicated, the cylinder head gasket or valves should be examined.
10 High compression pressure indicates excessive carbon build-up in the combustion chamber and on the piston crown. If this is the case the cylinder head should be removed and the deposits removed. Note that excessive carbon build-up is less likely with the used on modern fuels.

Checking battery open-circuit voltage

 Warning: The gases produced by the battery are explosive - never smoke or create any sparks in the vicinity of the battery. Never allow the electrolyte to contact your skin or clothing - if it does, wash it off and seek immediate medical attention.

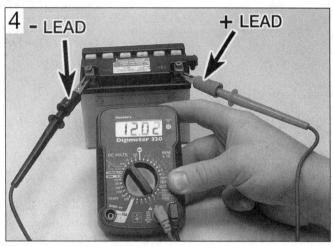

Measuring open-circuit battery voltage

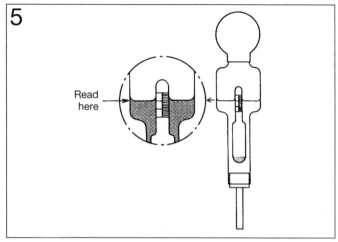

Float-type hydrometer for measuring battery specific gravity

● Before any electrical fault is investigated the battery should be checked.

● You'll need a dc voltmeter or multimeter to check battery voltage. Check that the leads are inserted in the correct terminals on the meter, red lead to positive (+ve), black lead to negative (-ve). Incorrect connections can damage the meter.

● A sound fully-charged 12 volt battery should produce between 12.3 and 12.6 volts across its terminals (12.8 volts for a maintenance-free battery). On machines with a 6 volt battery, voltage should be between 6.1 and 6.3 volts.

1 Set a multimeter to the 0 to 20 volts dc range and connect its probes across the battery terminals. Connect the meter's positive (+ve) probe, usually red, to the battery positive (+ve) terminal, followed by the meter's negative (-ve) probe, usually black, to the battery negative terminal (-ve) (see illustration 4).

2 If battery voltage is low (below 10 volts on a 12 volt battery or below 4 volts on a six volt battery), charge the battery and test the voltage again. If the battery repeatedly goes flat, investigate the motorcycle's charging system.

Checking battery specific gravity (SG)

⚠ Warning: The gases produced by the battery are explosive - never smoke or create any sparks in the vicinity of the battery. Never allow the electrolyte to contact your skin or clothing - if it does, wash it off and seek immediate medical attention.

● The specific gravity check gives an indication of a battery's state of charge.

● A hydrometer is used for measuring specific gravity. Make sure you purchase one

which has a small enough hose to insert in the aperture of a motorcycle battery.

● Specific gravity is simply a measure of the electrolyte's density compared with that of water. Water has an SG of 1.000 and fully-charged battery electrolyte is about 26% heavier, at 1.260.

● Specific gravity checks are not possible on maintenance-free batteries. Testing the open-circuit voltage is the only means of determining their state of charge.

1 To measure SG, remove the battery from the motorcycle and remove the first cell cap. Draw

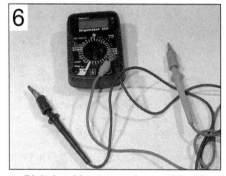

Digital multimeter can be used for all electrical tests

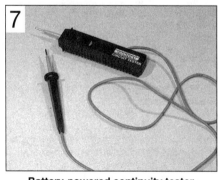

Battery-powered continuity tester

some electrolyte into the hydrometer and note the reading (see illustration 5). Return the electrolyte to the cell and install the cap.

2 The reading should be in the region of 1.260 to 1.280. If SG is below 1.200 the battery needs charging. Note that SG will vary with temperature; it should be measured at 20°C (68°F). Add 0.007 to the reading for every 10°C above 20°C, and subtract 0.007 from the reading for every 10°C below 20°C. Add 0.004 to the reading for every 10°F above 68°F, and subtract 0.004 from the reading for every 10°F below 68°F.

3 When the check is complete, rinse the hydrometer thoroughly with clean water.

Checking for continuity

● The term continuity describes the uninterrupted flow of electricity through an electrical circuit. A continuity check will determine whether an open-circuit situation exists.

● Continuity can be checked with an ohmmeter, multimeter, continuity tester or battery and bulb test circuit (see illustrations 6, 7 and 8).

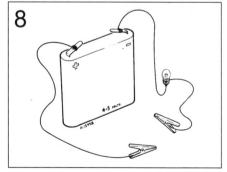

Battery and bulb test circuit

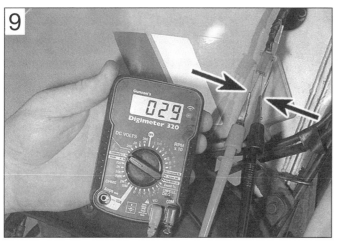

Continuity check of front brake light switch using a meter - note split pins used to access connector terminals

Continuity check of rear brake light switch using a continuity tester

● All of these instruments are self-powered by a battery, therefore the checks are made with the ignition OFF.

● As a safety precaution, always disconnect the battery negative (-ve) lead before making checks, particularly if ignition switch checks are being made.

● If using a meter, select the appropriate ohms scale and check that the meter reads infinity (∞). Touch the meter probes together and check that meter reads zero; where necessary adjust the meter so that it reads zero.

● After using a meter, always switch it OFF to conserve its battery.

Switch checks

1 If a switch is at fault, trace its wiring up to the wiring connectors. Separate the wire connectors and inspect them for security and condition. A build-up of dirt or corrosion here will most likely be the cause of the problem - clean up and apply a water dispersant such as WD40.

2 If using a test meter, set the meter to the ohms x 10 scale and connect its probes across the wires from the switch **(see illustration 9)**. Simple ON/OFF type switches, such as brake light switches, only have two wires whereas combination switches, like the ignition switch, have many internal links. Study the wiring diagram to ensure that you are connecting across the correct pair of wires. Continuity (low or no measurable resistance - 0 ohms) should be indicated with the switch ON and no continuity (high resistance) with it OFF.

3 Note that the polarity of the test probes doesn't matter for continuity checks, although care should be taken to follow specific test procedures if a diode or solid-state component is being checked.

4 A continuity tester or battery and bulb circuit can be used in the same way. Connect its probes as described above **(see illustration 10)**. The light should come on to indicate continuity in the ON switch position, but should extinguish in the OFF position.

Wiring checks

● Many electrical faults are caused by damaged wiring, often due to incorrect routing or chaffing on frame components.

● Loose, wet or corroded wire connectors can also be the cause of electrical problems, especially in exposed locations.

1 A continuity check can be made on a single length of wire by disconnecting it at each end and connecting a meter or continuity tester across both ends of the wire **(see illustration 11)**.

2 Continuity (low or no resistance - 0 ohms) should be indicated if the wire is good. If no continuity (high resistance) is shown, suspect a broken wire.

Checking for voltage

● A voltage check can determine whether current is reaching a component.

● Voltage can be checked with a dc voltmeter, multimeter set on the dc volts scale, test light or buzzer **(see illustrations 12 and 13)**. A meter has the advantage of being able to measure actual voltage.

● When using a meter, check that its leads are inserted in the correct terminals on the meter, red to positive (+ve), black to negative (-ve). Incorrect connections can damage the meter.

● A voltmeter (or multimeter set to the dc volts scale) should always be connected in parallel (across the load). Connecting it in series will destroy the meter.

● Voltage checks are made with the ignition ON.

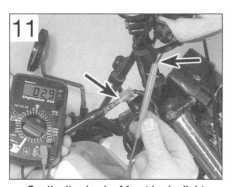

Continuity check of front brake light switch sub-harness

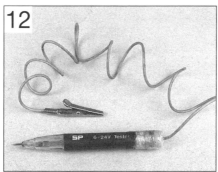

A simple test light can be used for voltage checks

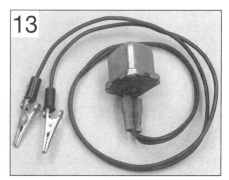

A buzzer is useful for voltage checks

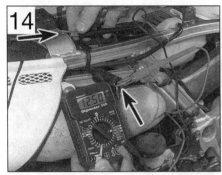

Checking for voltage at the rear brake light power supply wire using a meter . . .

1 First identify the relevant wiring circuit by referring to the wiring diagram at the end of this manual. If other electrical components share the same power supply (ie are fed from the same fuse), take note whether they are working correctly - this is useful information in deciding where to start checking the circuit.

2 If using a meter, check first that the meter leads are plugged into the correct terminals on the meter (see above). Set the meter to the dc volts function, at a range suitable for the battery voltage. Connect the meter red probe (+ve) to the power supply wire and the black probe to a good metal earth (ground) on the motorcycle's frame or directly to the battery negative (-ve) terminal **(see illustration 14)**. Battery voltage should be shown on the meter

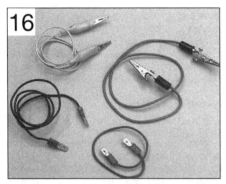

A selection of jumper wires for making earth (ground) checks

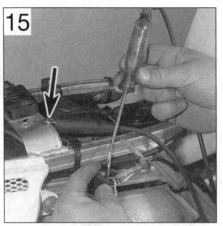

. . . or a test light - note the earth connection to the frame (arrow)

with the ignition switched ON.

3 If using a test light or buzzer, connect its positive (+ve) probe to the power supply terminal and its negative (-ve) probe to a good earth (ground) on the motorcycle's frame or directly to the battery negative (-ve) terminal **(see illustration 15)**. With the ignition ON, the test light should illuminate or the buzzer sound.

4 If no voltage is indicated, work back towards the fuse continuing to check for voltage. When you reach a point where there is voltage, you know the problem lies between that point and your last check point.

Checking the earth (ground)

● Earth connections are made either directly to the engine or frame (such as sensors, neutral switch etc. which only have a positive feed) or by a separate wire into the earth circuit of the wiring harness. Alternatively a short earth wire is sometimes run directly from the component to the motorcycle's frame.

● Corrosion is often the cause of a poor earth connection.

● If total failure is experienced, check the security of the main earth lead from the

negative (-ve) terminal of the battery and also the main earth (ground) point on the wiring harness. If corroded, dismantle the connection and clean all surfaces back to bare metal.

1 To check the earth on a component, use an insulated jumper wire to temporarily bypass its earth connection **(see illustration 16)**. Connect one end of the jumper wire between the earth terminal or metal body of the component and the other end to the motorcycle's frame.

2 If the circuit works with the jumper wire installed, the original earth circuit is faulty. Check the wiring for open-circuits or poor connections. Clean up direct earth connections, removing all traces of corrosion and remake the joint. Apply petroleum jelly to the joint to prevent future corrosion.

Tracing a short-circuit

● A short-circuit occurs where current shorts to earth (ground) bypassing the circuit components. This usually results in a blown fuse.

● A short-circuit is most likely to occur where the insulation has worn through due to wiring chafing on a component, allowing a direct path to earth (ground) on the frame.

1 Remove any bodypanels necessary to access the circuit wiring.

2 Check that all electrical switches in the circuit are OFF, then remove the circuit fuse and connect a test light, buzzer or voltmeter (set to the dc scale) across the fuse terminals. No voltage should be shown.

3 Move the wiring from side to side whilst observing the test light or meter. When the test light comes on, buzzer sounds or meter shows voltage, you have found the cause of the short. It will usually shown up as damaged or burned insulation.

4 Note that the same test can be performed on each component in the circuit, even the switch.

A

ABS (Anti-lock braking system) A system, usually electronically controlled, that senses incipient wheel lockup during braking and relieves hydraulic pressure at wheel which is about to skid.

Aftermarket Components suitable for the motorcycle, but not produced by the motorcycle manufacturer.

Allen key A hexagonal wrench which fits into a recessed hexagonal hole.

Alternating current (ac) Current produced by an alternator. Requires converting to direct current by a rectifier for charging purposes.

Alternator Converts mechanical energy from the engine into electrical energy to charge the battery and power the electrical system.

Ampere (amp) A unit of measurement for the flow of electrical current. Current = Volts ÷ Ohms.

Ampere-hour (Ah) Measure of battery capacity.

Angle-tightening A torque expressed in degrees. Often follows a conventional tightening torque for cylinder head or main bearing fasteners **(see illustration)**.

Angle-tightening cylinder head bolts

Antifreeze A substance (usually ethylene glycol) mixed with water, and added to the cooling system, to prevent freezing of the coolant in winter. Antifreeze also contains chemicals to inhibit corrosion and the formation of rust and other deposits that would tend to clog the radiator and coolant passages and reduce cooling efficiency.

Anti-dive System attached to the fork lower leg (slider) to prevent fork dive when braking hard.

Anti-seize compound A coating that reduces the risk of seizing on fasteners that are subjected to high temperatures, such as exhaust clamp bolts and nuts.

API American Petroleum Institute. A quality standard for 4-stroke motor oils.

Asbestos A natural fibrous mineral with great heat resistance, commonly used in the composition of brake friction materials. Asbestos is a health hazard and the dust created by brake systems should never be inhaled or ingested.

ATF Automatic Transmission Fluid. Often used in front forks.

ATU Automatic Timing Unit. Mechanical device for advancing the ignition timing on early engines.

ATV All Terrain Vehicle. Often called a Quad.

Axial play Side-to-side movement.

Axle A shaft on which a wheel revolves. Also known as a spindle.

B

Backlash The amount of movement between meshed components when one component is held still. Usually applies to gear teeth.

Ball bearing A bearing consisting of a hardened inner and outer race with hardened steel balls between the two races.

Bearings Used between two working surfaces to prevent wear of the components and a build-up of heat. Four types of bearing are commonly used on motorcycles: plain shell bearings, ball bearings, tapered roller bearings and needle roller bearings.

Bevel gears Used to turn the drive through 90°. Typical applications are shaft final drive and camshaft drive **(see illustration)**.

Bevel gears are used to turn the drive through 90°

BHP Brake Horsepower. The British measurement for engine power output. Power output is now usually expressed in kilowatts (kW).

Bias-belted tyre Similar construction to radial tyre, but with outer belt running at an angle to the wheel rim.

Big-end bearing The bearing in the end of the connecting rod that's attached to the crankshaft.

Bleeding The process of removing air from an hydraulic system via a bleed nipple or bleed screw.

Bottom-end A description of an engine's crankcase components and all components contained there-in.

BTDC Before Top Dead Centre in terms of piston position. Ignition timing is often expressed in terms of degrees or millimetres BTDC.

Bush A cylindrical metal or rubber component used between two moving parts.

Burr Rough edge left on a component after machining or as a result of excessive wear.

C

Cam chain The chain which takes drive from the crankshaft to the camshaft(s).

Canister The main component in an evaporative emission control system (California market only); contains activated charcoal granules to trap vapours from the fuel system rather than allowing them to vent to the atmosphere.

Castellated Resembling the parapets along the top of a castle wall. For example, a castellated wheel axle or spindle nut.

Catalytic converter A device in the exhaust system of some machines which converts certain pollutants in the exhaust gases into less harmful substances.

Charging system Description of the components which charge the battery, ie the alternator, rectifer and regulator.

Circlip A ring-shaped clip used to prevent endwise movement of cylindrical parts and shafts. An internal circlip is installed in a groove in a housing; an external circlip fits into a groove on the outside of a cylindrical piece such as a shaft. Also known as a snap-ring.

Clearance The amount of space between two parts. For example, between a piston and a cylinder, between a bearing and a journal, etc.

Coil spring A spiral of elastic steel found in various sizes throughout a vehicle, for example as a springing medium in the suspension and in the valve train.

Compression Reduction in volume, and increase in pressure and temperature, of a gas, caused by squeezing it into a smaller space.

Compression damping Controls the speed the suspension compresses when hitting a bump.

Compression ratio The relationship between cylinder volume when the piston is at top dead centre and cylinder volume when the piston is at bottom dead centre.

Continuity The uninterrupted path in the flow of electricity. Little or no measurable resistance.

Continuity tester Self-powered bleeper or test light which indicates continuity.

Cp Candlepower. Bulb rating commonly found on US motorcycles.

Crossply tyre Tyre plies arranged in a criss-cross pattern. Usually four or six plies used, hence 4PR or 6PR in tyre size codes.

Cush drive Rubber damper segments fitted between the rear wheel and final drive sprocket to absorb transmission shocks **(see illustration)**.

Cush drive rubbers dampen out transmission shocks

D

Degree disc Calibrated disc for measuring piston position. Expressed in degrees.

Dial gauge Clock-type gauge with adapters for measuring runout and piston position. Expressed in mm or inches.

Diaphragm The rubber membrane in a master cylinder or carburettor which seals the upper chamber.

Diaphragm spring A single sprung plate often used in clutches.

Direct current (dc) Current produced by a dc generator.

Decarbonisation The process of removing carbon deposits - typically from the combustion chamber, valves and exhaust port/system.

Detonation Destructive and damaging explosion of fuel/air mixture in combustion chamber instead of controlled burning.

Diode An electrical valve which only allows current to flow in one direction. Commonly used in rectifiers and starter interlock systems.

Disc valve (or rotary valve) A induction system used on some two-stroke engines.

Double-overhead camshaft (DOHC) An engine that uses two overhead camshafts, one for the intake valves and one for the exhaust valves.

Drivebelt A toothed belt used to transmit drive to the rear wheel on some motorcycles. A drivebelt has also been used to drive the camshafts. Drivebelts are usually made of Kevlar.

Driveshaft Any shaft used to transmit motion. Commonly used when referring to the final driveshaft on shaft drive motorcycles.

E

Earth return The return path of an electrical circuit, utilising the motorcycle's frame.

ECU (Electronic Control Unit) A computer which controls (for instance) an ignition system, or an anti-lock braking system.

EGO Exhaust Gas Oxygen sensor. Sometimes called a Lambda sensor.

Electrolyte The fluid in a lead-acid battery.

EMS (Engine Management System) A computer controlled system which manages the fuel injection and the ignition systems in an integrated fashion.

Endfloat The amount of lengthways movement between two parts. As applied to a crankshaft, the distance that the crankshaft can move side-to-side in the crankcase.

Endless chain A chain having no joining link. Common use for cam chains and final drive chains.

EP (Extreme Pressure) Oil type used in locations where high loads are applied, such as between gear teeth.

Evaporative emission control system Describes a charcoal filled canister which stores fuel vapours from the tank rather than allowing them to vent to the atmosphere. Usually only fitted to California models and referred to as an EVAP system.

Expansion chamber Section of two-stroke engine exhaust system so designed to improve engine efficiency and boost power.

F

Feeler blade or gauge A thin strip or blade of hardened steel, ground to an exact thickness, used to check or measure clearances between parts.

Final drive Description of the drive from the transmission to the rear wheel. Usually by chain or shaft, but sometimes by belt.

Firing order The order in which the engine cylinders fire, or deliver their power strokes, beginning with the number one cylinder.

Flooding Term used to describe a high fuel level in the carburettor float chambers, leading to fuel overflow. Also refers to excess fuel in the combustion chamber due to incorrect starting technique.

Free length The no-load state of a component when measured. Clutch, valve and fork spring lengths are measured at rest, without any preload.

Freeplay The amount of travel before any action takes place. The looseness in a linkage, or an assembly of parts, between the initial application of force and actual movement. For example, the distance the rear brake pedal moves before the rear brake is actuated.

Fuel injection The fuel/air mixture is metered electronically and directed into the engine intake ports (indirect injection) or into the cylinders (direct injection). Sensors supply information on engine speed and conditions.

Fuel/air mixture The charge of fuel and air going into the engine. See **Stoichiometric ratio**.

Fuse An electrical device which protects a circuit against accidental overload. The typical fuse contains a soft piece of metal which is calibrated to melt at a predetermined current flow (expressed as amps) and break the circuit.

G

Gap The distance the spark must travel in jumping from the centre electrode to the side electrode in a spark plug. Also refers to the distance between the ignition rotor and the pickup coil in an electronic ignition system.

Gasket Any thin, soft material - usually cork, cardboard, asbestos or soft metal - installed between two metal surfaces to ensure a good seal. For instance, the cylinder head gasket seals the joint between the block and the cylinder head.

Gauge An instrument panel display used to monitor engine conditions. A gauge with a movable pointer on a dial or a fixed scale is an analogue gauge. A gauge with a numerical readout is called a digital gauge.

Gear ratios The drive ratio of a pair of gears in a gearbox, calculated on their number of teeth.

Glaze-busting see **Honing**

Grinding Process for renovating the valve face and valve seat contact area in the cylinder head.

Gudgeon pin The shaft which connects the connecting rod small-end with the piston. Often called a piston pin or wrist pin.

H

Helical gears Gear teeth are slightly curved and produce less gear noise that straight-cut gears. Often used for primary drives.

Installing a Helicoil thread insert in a cylinder head

Helicoil A thread insert repair system. Commonly used as a repair for stripped spark plug threads **(see illustration)**.

Honing A process used to break down the glaze on a cylinder bore (also called glaze-busting). Can also be carried out to roughen a rebored cylinder to aid ring bedding-in.

HT (High Tension) Description of the electrical circuit from the secondary winding of the ignition coil to the spark plug.

Hydraulic A liquid filled system used to transmit pressure from one component to another. Common uses on motorcycles are brakes and clutches.

Hydrometer An instrument for measuring the specific gravity of a lead-acid battery.

Hygroscopic Water absorbing. In motorcycle applications, braking efficiency will be reduced if DOT 3 or 4 hydraulic fluid absorbs water from the air - care must be taken to keep new brake fluid in tightly sealed containers.

I

Ibf ft Pounds-force feet. An imperial unit of torque. Sometimes written as ft-lbs.

Ibf in Pound-force inch. An imperial unit of torque, applied to components where a very low torque is required. Sometimes written as in-lbs.

IC Abbreviation for Integrated Circuit.

Ignition advance Means of increasing the timing of the spark at higher engine speeds. Done by mechanical means (ATU) on early engines or electronically by the ignition control unit on later engines.

Ignition timing The moment at which the spark plug fires, expressed in the number of crankshaft degrees before the piston reaches the top of its stroke, or in the number of millimetres before the piston reaches the top of its stroke.

Infinity (∞) Description of an open-circuit electrical state, where no continuity exists.

Inverted forks (upside down forks) The sliders or lower legs are held in the yokes and the fork tubes or stanchions are connected to the wheel axle (spindle). Less unsprung weight and stiffer construction than conventional forks.

J

JASO Quality standard for 2-stroke oils.

Joule The unit of electrical energy.

Journal The bearing surface of a shaft.

K

Kickstart Mechanical means of turning the engine over for starting purposes. Only usually fitted to mopeds, small capacity motorcycles and off-road motorcycles.

Kill switch Handebar-mounted switch for emergency ignition cut-out. Cuts the ignition circuit on all models, and additionally prevent starter motor operation on others.

km Symbol for kilometre.

kmh Abbreviation for kilometres per hour.

L

Lambda (λ) sensor A sensor fitted in the exhaust system to measure the exhaust gas oxygen content (excess air factor).

Lapping see **Grinding**.
LCD Abbreviation for Liquid Crystal Display.
LED Abbreviation for Light Emitting Diode.
Liner A steel cylinder liner inserted in a aluminium alloy cylinder block.
Locknut A nut used to lock an adjustment nut, or other threaded component, in place.
Lockstops The lugs on the lower triple clamp (yoke) which abut those on the frame, preventing handlebar-to-fuel tank contact.
Lockwasher A form of washer designed to prevent an attaching nut from working loose.
LT Low Tension Description of the electrical circuit from the power supply to the primary winding of the ignition coil.

M

Main bearings The bearings between the crankshaft and crankcase.
Maintenance-free (MF) battery A sealed battery which cannot be topped up.
Manometer Mercury-filled calibrated tubes used to measure intake tract vacuum. Used to synchronise carburettors on multi-cylinder engines.
Micrometer A precision measuring instrument that measures component outside diameters **(see illustration)**.

Tappet shims are measured with a micrometer

MON (Motor Octane Number) A measure of a fuel's resistance to knock.
Monograde oil An oil with a single viscosity, eg SAE80W.
Monoshock A single suspension unit linking the swingarm or suspension linkage to the frame.
mph Abbreviation for miles per hour.
Multigrade oil Having a wide viscosity range (eg 10W40). The W stands for Winter, thus the viscosity ranges from SAE10 when cold to SAE40 when hot.
Multimeter An electrical test instrument with the capability to measure voltage, current and resistance. Some meters also incorporate a continuity tester and buzzer.

N

Needle roller bearing Inner race of caged needle rollers and hardened outer race. Examples of uncaged needle rollers can be found on some engines. Commonly used in rear suspension applications and in two-stroke engines.
Nm Newton metres.
NOx Oxides of Nitrogen. A common toxic pollutant emitted by petrol engines at higher temperatures.

O

Octane The measure of a fuel's resistance to knock.
OE (Original Equipment) Relates to components fitted to a motorcycle as standard or replacement parts supplied by the motorcycle manufacturer.
Ohm The unit of electrical resistance. Ohms = Volts ÷ Current.
Ohmmeter An instrument for measuring electrical resistance.
Oil cooler System for diverting engine oil outside of the engine to a radiator for cooling purposes.
Oil injection A system of two-stroke engine lubrication where oil is pump-fed to the engine in accordance with throttle position.
Open-circuit An electrical condition where there is a break in the flow of electricity - no continuity (high resistance).
O-ring A type of sealing ring made of a special rubber-like material; in use, the O-ring is compressed into a groove to provide the sealing action.
Oversize (OS) Term used for piston and ring size options fitted to a rebored cylinder.
Overhead cam (sohc) engine An engine with single camshaft located on top of the cylinder head.
Overhead valve (ohv) engine An engine with the valves located in the cylinder head, but with the camshaft located in the engine block or crankcase.
Oxygen sensor A device installed in the exhaust system which senses the oxygen content in the exhaust and converts this information into an electric current. Also called a Lambda sensor.

P

Plastigauge A thin strip of plastic thread, available in different sizes, used for measuring clearances. For example, a strip of Plastigauge is laid across a bearing journal. The parts are assembled and dismantled; the width of the crushed strip indicates the clearance between journal and bearing.
Polarity Either negative or positive earth (ground), determined by which battery lead is connected to the frame (earth return). Modern motorcycles are usually negative earth.
Pre-ignition A situation where the fuel/air mixture ignites before the spark plug fires. Often due to a hot spot in the combustion chamber caused by carbon build-up. Engine has a tendency to 'run-on'.
Pre-load (suspension) The amount a spring is compressed when in the unloaded state. Preload can be applied by gas, spacer or mechanical adjuster.
Premix The method of engine lubrication on older two-stroke engines. Engine oil is mixed with the petrol in the fuel tank in a specific ratio. The fuel/oil mix is sometimes referred to as "petroil".
Primary drive Description of the drive from the crankshaft to the clutch. Usually by gear or chain.
PS Pfedestärke - a German interpretation of BHP.
PSI Pounds-force per square inch. Imperial measurement of tyre pressure and cylinder pressure measurement.
PTFE Polytetrafluoroethylene. A low friction substance.

Pulse secondary air injection system A process of promoting the burning of excess fuel present in the exhaust gases by routing fresh air into the exhaust ports.

Q

Quartz halogen bulb Tungsten filament surrounded by a halogen gas. Typically used for the headlight **(see illustration)**.

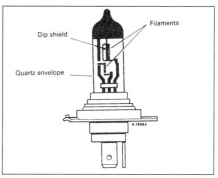

Quartz halogen headlight bulb construction

R

Rack-and-pinion A pinion gear on the end of a shaft that mates with a rack (think of a geared wheel opened up and laid flat). Sometimes used in clutch operating systems.
Radial play Up and down movement about a shaft.
Radial ply tyres Tyre plies run across the tyre (from bead to bead) and around the circumference of the tyre. Less resistant to tread distortion than other tyre types.
Radiator A liquid-to-air heat transfer device designed to reduce the temperature of the coolant in a liquid cooled engine.
Rake A feature of steering geometry - the angle of the steering head in relation to the vertical **(see illustration)**.

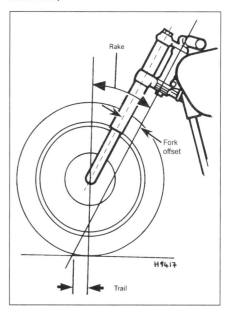

Steering geometry

Rebore Providing a new working surface to the cylinder bore by boring out the old surface. Necessitates the use of oversize piston and rings.

Rebound damping A means of controlling the oscillation of a suspension unit spring after it has been compressed. Resists the spring's natural tendency to bounce back after being compressed.

Rectifier Device for converting the ac output of an alternator into dc for battery charging.

Reed valve An induction system commonly used on two-stroke engines.

Regulator Device for maintaining the charging voltage from the generator or alternator within a specified range.

Relay A electrical device used to switch heavy current on and off by using a low current auxiliary circuit.

Resistance Measured in ohms. An electrical component's ability to pass electrical current.

RON (Research Octane Number) A measure of a fuel's resistance to knock.

rpm revolutions per minute.

Runout The amount of wobble (in-and-out movement) of a wheel or shaft as it's rotated. The amount a shaft rotates 'out-of-true'. The out-of-round condition of a rotating part.

S

SAE (Society of Automotive Engineers) A standard for the viscosity of a fluid.

Sealant A liquid or paste used to prevent leakage at a joint. Sometimes used in conjunction with a gasket.

Service limit Term for the point where a component is no longer useable and must be renewed.

Shaft drive A method of transmitting drive from the transmission to the rear wheel.

Shell bearings Plain bearings consisting of two shell halves. Most often used as big-end and main bearings in a four-stroke engine. Often called bearing inserts.

Shim Thin spacer, commonly used to adjust the clearance or relative positions between two parts. For example, shims inserted into or under tappets or followers to control valve clearances. Clearance is adjusted by changing the thickness of the shim.

Short-circuit An electrical condition where current shorts to earth (ground) bypassing the circuit components.

Skimming Process to correct warpage or repair a damaged surface, eg on brake discs or drums.

Slide-hammer A special puller that screws into or hooks onto a component such as a shaft or bearing; a heavy sliding handle on the shaft bottoms against the end of the shaft to knock the component free.

Small-end bearing The bearing in the upper end of the connecting rod at its joint with the gudgeon pin.

Spalling Damage to camshaft lobes or bearing journals shown as pitting of the working surface.

Specific gravity (SG) The state of charge of the electrolyte in a lead-acid battery. A measure of the electrolyte's density compared with water.

Straight-cut gears Common type gear used on gearbox shafts and for oil pump and water pump drives.

Stanchion The inner sliding part of the front forks, held by the yokes. Often called a fork tube.

Stoichiometric ratio The optimum chemical air/fuel ratio for a petrol engine, said to be 14.7 parts of air to 1 part of fuel.

Sulphuric acid The liquid (electrolyte) used in a lead-acid battery. Poisonous and extremely corrosive.

Surface grinding (lapping) Process to correct a warped gasket face, commonly used on cylinder heads.

T

Tapered-roller bearing Tapered inner race of caged needle rollers and separate tapered outer race. Examples of taper roller bearings can be found on steering heads.

Tappet A cylindrical component which transmits motion from the cam to the valve stem, either directly or via a pushrod and rocker arm. Also called a cam follower.

TCS Traction Control System. An electronically-controlled system which senses wheel spin and reduces engine speed accordingly.

TDC Top Dead Centre denotes that the piston is at its highest point in the cylinder.

Thread-locking compound Solution applied to fastener threads to prevent slackening. Select type to suit application.

Thrust washer A washer positioned between two moving components on a shaft. For example, between gear pinions on gearshaft.

Timing chain See **Cam Chain.**

Timing light Stroboscopic lamp for carrying out ignition timing checks with the engine running.

Top-end A description of an engine's cylinder block, head and valve gear components.

Torque Turning or twisting force about a shaft.

Torque setting A prescribed tightness specified by the motorcycle manufacturer to ensure that the bolt or nut is secured correctly. Undertightening can result in the bolt or nut coming loose or a surface not being sealed. Overtightening can result in stripped threads, distortion or damage to the component being retained.

Torx key A six-point wrench.

Tracer A stripe of a second colour applied to a wire insulator to distinguish that wire from another one with the same colour insulator. For example, Br/W is often used to denote a brown insulator with a white tracer.

Trail A feature of steering geometry. Distance from the steering head axis to the tyre's central contact point.

Triple clamps The cast components which extend from the steering head and support the fork stanchions or tubes. Often called fork yokes.

Turbocharger A centrifugal device, driven by exhaust gases, that pressurises the intake air. Normally used to increase the power output from a given engine displacement.

TWI Abbreviation for Tyre Wear Indicator. Indicates the location of the tread depth indicator bars on tyres.

U

Universal joint or U-joint (UJ) A double-pivoted connection for transmitting power from a driving to a driven shaft through an angle. Typically found in shaft drive systems.

Unsprung weight Anything not supported by the bike's suspension (ie the wheel, tyres, brakes, final drive and bottom (moving) part of the suspension).

V

Vacuum gauges Clock-type gauges for measuring intake tract vacuum. Used for carburettor synchronisation on multi-cylinder engines.

Valve A device through which the flow of liquid, gas or vacuum may be stopped, started or regulated by a moveable part that opens, shuts or partially obstructs one or more ports or passageways. The intake and exhaust valves in the cylinder head are of the poppet type.

Valve clearance The clearance between the valve tip (the end of the valve stem) and the rocker arm or tappet/follower. The valve clearance is measured when the valve is closed. The correct clearance is important - if too small the valve won't close fully and will burn out, whereas if too large noisy operation will result.

Valve lift The amount a valve is lifted off its seat by the camshaft lobe.

Valve timing The exact setting for the opening and closing of the valves in relation to piston position.

Vernier caliper A precision measuring instrument that measures inside and outside dimensions. Not quite as accurate as a micrometer, but more convenient.

VIN Vehicle Identification Number. Term for the bike's engine and frame numbers.

Viscosity The thickness of a liquid or its resistance to flow.

Volt A unit for expressing electrical "pressure" in a circuit. Volts = current x ohms.

W

Water pump A mechanically-driven device for moving coolant around the engine.

Watt A unit for expressing electrical power. Watts = volts x current.

Wear limit see **Service limit**

Wet liner A liquid-cooled engine design where the pistons run in liners which are directly surrounded by coolant **(see illustration).**

Wet liner arrangement

Wheelbase Distance from the centre of the front wheel to the centre of the rear wheel.

Wiring harness or loom Describes the electrical wires running the length of the motorcycle and enclosed in tape or plastic sheathing. Wiring coming off the main harness is usually referred to as a sub harness.

Woodruff key A key of semi-circular or square section used to locate a gear to a shaft. Often used to locate the alternator rotor on the crankshaft.

Wrist pin Another name for gudgeon or piston pin.

Haynes Motorcycle Manuals – The Complete List

Title	Book No
BMW	
BMW 2-valve Twins (70 - 96)	0249
BMW K100 & 75 2-valve Models (83 - 96)	1373
BMW R850 & R1100 4-valve Twins (93 - 97)	3466
BSA	
BSA Bantam (48 - 71)	0117
BSA Unit Singles (58 - 72)	0127
BSA Pre-unit Singles (54 - 61)	0326
BSA A7 & A10 Twins (47 - 62)	0121
BSA A50 & A65 Twins (62 - 73)	0155
DUCATI	
Ducati MK III & Desmo Singles (69 - 76)	0445
Ducati 600, 750 & 900 2-valve V-Twins (91 - 96)	3290
Ducati 748, 916 & 996 4-valve V-Twins (94 - 01)	3756
HARLEY-DAVIDSON	
Harley-Davidson Sportsters (70 - 01)	0702
Harley-Davidson Big Twins (70 - 99)	0703
Harley-Davidson Twin Cam 88 (99 - 03)	2478
HONDA	
Honda NB, ND, NP & NS50 Melody (81 - 85)	◊ 0622
Honda NE/NB50 Vision & SA50 Vision Met-in (85 - 95)	◊ 1278
Honda MB, MBX, MT & MTX50 (80 - 93)	0731
Honda C50, C70 & C90 (67 - 99)	0324
Honda XR80R & XR100R (85 - 96)	2218
Honda XL/XR 80, 100, 125, 185 & 200 2-valve Models (78 - 87)	0566
Honda H100 & H100S Singles (80 - 92)	◊ 0734
Honda CB/CD125T & CM125C Twins (77 - 88)	◊ 0571
Honda CG125 (76 - 00)	◊ 0433
Honda NS125 (86 - 93)	◊ 3056
Honda MBX/MTX125 & MTX200 (83 - 93)	◊ 1132
Honda CD/CM185 200T & CM250C 2-valve Twins (77 - 85)	0572
Honda XL/XR 250 & 500 (78 - 84)	0567
Honda XR250L, XR250R & XR400R (86 - 03)	2219
Honda CB250 & CB400N Super Dreams (78 - 84)	◊ 0540
Honda CR Motocross Bikes (86 - 01)	2222
Honda CBR400RR Fours (88 - 99)	3552
Honda VFR400 (NC30) & RVF400 (NC35) V-Fours (89 - 98)	3496
Honda CB500 (93 - 01)	3753
Honda CB400 & CB550 Fours (73 - 77)	0262
Honda CX/GL500 & 650 V-Twins (78 - 86)	0442
Honda CBX550 Four (82 - 86)	◊ 0940
Honda XL600R & XR600R (83 - 00)	2183
Honda XL600/650V Transalp & XRV750 Africa Twin (87 - 02)	3919
Honda CBR600F1 & 1000F Fours (87 - 96)	1730
Honda CBR600F2 & F3 Fours (91 - 98)	2070
Honda CBR600F4 (99 - 02)	3911
Honda CB600F Hornet (98 - 02)	3915
Honda CB650 sohc Fours (78 - 84)	0665
Honda NTV600 Revere, NTV650 & NT650V Deauville (88 - 01)	3243
Honda Shadow VT600 & 750 (USA) (88 - 00)	2312
Honda CB750 sohc Four (69 - 79)	0131
Honda V45/65 Sabre & Magna (82 - 88)	0820
Honda VFR750 & 700 V-Fours (86 - 97)	2101
Honda VFR800 V-Fours (97 - 01)	3703
Honda VTR1000 (FireStorm, Super Hawk) & XL1000V (Varadero) (97 - 00)	3744
Honda CB750 & CB900 dohc Fours (78 - 84)	0535
Honda CBR900RR FireBlade (92 - 99)	2161
Honda CBR900RR FireBlade (00 - 03)	4060
Honda CBR1100XX Super Blackbird (97 - 02)	3901
Honda ST1100 Pan European V-Fours (90 - 01)	3384
Honda Shadow VT1100 (USA) (85 - 98)	2313
Honda GL1000 Gold Wing (75 - 79)	0309
Honda GL1100 Gold Wing (79 - 81)	0669
Honda Gold Wing 1200 (USA) (84 - 87)	2199
Honda Gold Wing 1500 (USA) (88 - 00)	2225

Title	Book No
KAWASAKI	
Kawasaki AE/AR 50 & 80 (81 - 95)	1007
Kawasaki KC, KE & KH100 (75 - 99)	1371
Kawasaki KMX125 & 200 (86 - 02)	◊ 3046
Kawasaki 250, 350 & 400 Triples (72 - 79)	0134
Kawasaki 400 & 440 Twins (74 - 81)	0281
Kawasaki 400, 500 & 550 Fours (79 - 91)	0910
Kawasaki EN450 & 500 Twins (Ltd/Vulcan) (85 - 93)	2053
Kawasaki EX & ER500 (GPZ500S & ER-5) Twins (87 - 99)	2052
Kawasaki ZX600 (Ninja ZX-6, ZZ-R600) Fours (90 - 00)	2146
Kawasaki ZX-6R Ninja Fours (95 - 02)	3541
Kawasaki ZX600 (GPZ600R, GPX600R, Ninja 600R & RX) & ZX750 (GPX750R, Ninja 750R) Fours (85 - 97)	1780
Kawasaki 650 Four (76 - 78)	0373
Kawasaki Vulcan 700/750 & 800 (85 - 01)	2457
Kawasaki 750 Air-cooled Fours (80 - 91)	0574
Kawasaki ZR550 & 750 Zephyr Fours (90 - 97)	3382
Kawasaki ZX750 (Ninja ZX-7 & ZXR750) Fours (89 - 96)	2054
Kawasaki Ninja ZX-7R & ZX-9R (ZX750P, ZX900B/C/D/E) (94 - 00)	3721
Kawasaki 900 & 1000 Fours (73 - 77)	0222
Kawasaki ZX900, 1000 & 1100 Liquid-cooled Fours (83 - 97)	1681
MOTO GUZZI	
Moto Guzzi 750, 850 & 1000 V-Twins (74 - 78)	0339
MZ	
MZ ETZ Models (81 - 95)	◊ 1680
NORTON	
Norton 500, 600, 650 & 750 Twins (57 - 70)	0187
Norton Commando (68 - 77)	0125
PEUGEOT	
Peugeot Speedfight, Trekker & Vivacity Scooters (96 - 02)	3920
PIAGGIO	
Piaggio (Vespa) Scooters (91 - 98)	3492
SUZUKI	
Suzuki GT, ZR & TS50 (77 - 90)	◊ 0799
Suzuki TS50X (84 - 00)	◊ 1599
Suzuki 100, 125, 185 & 250 Air-cooled Trail bikes (79 - 89)	0797
Suzuki GP100 & 125 Singles (78 - 93)	◊ 0576
Suzuki GS, GN, GZ & DR125 Singles (82 - 99)	◊ 0888
Suzuki 250 & 350 Twins (68 - 78)	0120
Suzuki GT250X7, GT200X5 & SB200 Twins (78 - 83)	◊ 0469
Suzuki GS/GSX250, 400 & 450 Twins (79 - 85)	0736
Suzuki GS500 Twin (89 - 02)	3238
Suzuki GS550 (77 - 82) & GS750 Fours (76 - 79)	0363
Suzuki GS/GSX550 4-valve Fours (83 - 88)	1133
Suzuki SV650 (99 - 02)	3912
Suzuki GSX-R600 & 750 (96 - 00)	3553
Suzuki GSX-R600 (01 - 02), GSX-R750 (00 - 02) & GSX-R1000 (01 - 02)	3986
Suzuki GSF600 & 1200 Bandit Fours (95 - 01)	3367
Suzuki GS850 Fours (78 - 88)	0536
Suzuki GS1000 Four (77 - 79)	0484
Suzuki GSX-R750, GSX-R1100 (85 - 92), GSX600F, GSX750F, GSX1100F (Katana) Fours (88 - 96)	2055
Suzuki GSX600/750F & GSX750 (98 - 02)	3987
Suzuki GS/GSX1000, 1100 & 1150 4-valve Fours (79 - 88)	0737
Suzuki TL1000S/R & DL1000	4083
TRIUMPH	
Triumph Tiger Cub & Terrier (52 - 68)	0414
Triumph 350 & 500 Unit Twins (58 - 73)	0137
Triumph Pre-Unit Twins (47 - 62)	0251
Triumph 650 & 750 2-valve Unit Twins (63 - 83)	0122
Triumph Trident & BSA Rocket 3 (69 - 75)	0136
Triumph Fuel Injected Triples (97 - 00)	3755
Triumph Triples & Fours (carburettor engines) (91 - 99)	2162
VESPA	
Vespa P/PX125, 150 & 200 Scooters (78 - 95)	0707
Vespa Scooters (59 - 78)	0126

Title	Book No
YAMAHA	
Yamaha DT50 & 80 Trail Bikes (78 - 95)	◊ 0800
Yamaha T50 & 80 Townmate (83 - 95)	◊ 1247
Yamaha YB100 Singles (73 - 91)	◊ 0474
Yamaha RS/RXS100 & 125 Singles (74 - 95)	0331
Yamaha RD & DT125LC (82 - 87)	0887
Yamaha TZR125 (87 - 93) & DT125R (88 - 02)	1655
Yamaha TY50, 80, 125 & 175 (74 - 84)	0464
Yamaha XT & SR125 (82 - 02)	1021
Yamaha Trail Bikes (81 - 00)	2350
Yamaha 250 & 350 Twins (70 - 79)	0040
Yamaha XS250, 360 & 400 sohc Twins (75 - 84)	0378
Yamaha RD250 & 350LC Twins (80 - 82)	0803
Yamaha RD350 YPVS Twins (83 - 95)	1158
Yamaha RD400 Twin (75 - 79)	0333
Yamaha XT, TT & SR500 Singles (75 - 83)	0342
Yamaha XZ550 Vision V-Twins (82 - 85)	0821
Yamaha FJ, FZ, XJ & YX600 Radian (84 - 92)	2100
Yamaha XJ600S (Diversion, Seca II) & XJ600N Fours (92 - 99)	2145
Yamaha YZF600R Thundercat & FZS600 Fazer (96 - 01)	3702
Yamaha YZF-R6 (98 - 02)	3900
Yamaha 650 Twins (70 - 83)	0341
Yamaha XJ650 & 750 Fours (80 - 84)	0738
Yamaha XS750 & 850 Triples (76 - 85)	0340
Yamaha TDM850, TRX850 & XTZ750 (89 - 99)	3540
Yamaha YZF750R & YZF1000R Thunderace (93 - 00)	3720
Yamaha FZR600, 750 & 1000 Fours (87 - 96)	2056
Yamaha XV (Virago) V-Twins (81 - 03)	0802
Yamaha XJ900F Fours (83 - 94)	3239
Yamaha XJ900S Diversion (94 - 01)	3739
Yamaha YZF-R1 (98 - 01)	3754
Yamaha FJ1100 & 1200 Fours (84 - 96)	2057
Yamaha XJR1200 & 1300 (95 - 03)	3981
Yamaha V-Max (85 - 03)	4072
ATVs	
Honda ATC70, 90, 110, 185 & 200 (71 - 85)	0565
Honda TRX300 Shaft Drive ATVs (88 - 00)	2125
Honda TRX300EX & TRX400EX ATVs (93 - 99)	2318
Honda Foreman 400 and 450 ATVs (95 - 02)	2465
Kawasaki Bayou 220/300 & Prairie 300 ATVs (86 - 01)	2351
Polaris ATVs (85 to 97)	2302
Yamaha YFS200 Blaster ATV (88 - 98)	2317
Yamaha YFB250 Timberwolf ATV (92 - 96)	2217
Yamaha YFM350 (ER and Big Bear) ATVs (87 - 99)	2126
Yamaha Warrior and Banshee ATVs (87 - 99)	2314
ATV Basics	10450
MOTORCYCLE TECHBOOKS	
Twist and Go (automatic transmission) Scooters	4082
Motorcycle Basics TechBook (2nd Edition)	3515
Motorcycle Electrical TechBook (3rd Edition)	3471
Motorcycle Fuel Systems TechBook	3514
Motorcycle Workshop Practice TechBook (2nd Edition)	3470

◊ = not available in the USA   **Bold type** = Superbike

The manuals on this page are available through good motorcycle dealers and accessory shops.
In case of difficulty, contact: **Haynes Publishing**
(UK) +44 1963 442030   (USA) +1 805 498 6703
(FR) +33 1 47 17 66 29   (SV) +46 18 124016
(Australia/New Zealand) +61 3 9763 8100

Preserving Our Motoring Heritage

< The Model J Duesenberg Derham Tourster. Only eight of these magnificent cars were ever built – this is the only example to be found outside the United States of America

Almost every car you've ever loved, loathed or desired is gathered under one roof at the Haynes Motor Museum. Over 300 immaculately presented cars and motorbikes represent every aspect of our motoring heritage, from elegant reminders of bygone days, such as the superb Model J Duesenberg to curiosities like the bug-eyed BMW Isetta. There are also many old friends and flames. Perhaps you remember the 1959 Ford Popular that you did your courting in? The magnificent 'Red Collection' is a spectacle of classic sports cars including AC, Alfa Romeo, Austin Healey, Ferrari, Lamborghini, Maserati, MG, Riley, Porsche and Triumph.

A Perfect Day Out

Each and every vehicle at the Haynes Motor Museum has played its part in the history and culture of Motoring. Today, they make a wonderful spectacle and a great day out for all the family. Bring the kids, bring Mum and Dad, but above all bring your camera to capture those golden memories for ever. You will also find an impressive array of motoring memorabilia, a comfortable 70 seat video cinema and one of the most extensive transport book shops in Britain. The Pit Stop Cafe serves everything from a cup of tea to wholesome, home-made meals or, if you prefer, you can enjoy the large picnic area nestled in the beautiful rural surroundings of Somerset.

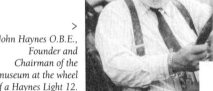

> John Haynes O.B.E., Founder and Chairman of the museum at the wheel of a Haynes Light 12.

< The 1936 490cc sohc-engined International Norton – well known for its racing success

The Museum is situated on the A359 Yeovil to Frome road at Sparkford, just off the A303 in Somerset. It is about 40 miles south of Bristol, and 25 minutes drive from the M5 intersection at Taunton.
Open 9.30am - 5.30pm (10.00am - 4.00pm Winter) 7 days a week, *except Christmas Day, Boxing Day and New Years Day*
Special rates available for schools, coach parties and outings Charitable Trust No. 292048